DIAKONIA

DIAKONIA

Studies in Honor of
ROBERT T. MEYER

edited by Thomas Halton
and Joseph P. Williman

The Catholic University of America Press
Washington, D.C.

LIBRARY OF CONGRESS CATALOGING-IN-PUBLICATION DATA

Main entry under title:
Diakonia : Studies in honor of Robert T. Meyer.

Includes indexes.
1. Fathers of the church—Addresses, essays,
lectures.   2. Hagiography—Addresses, essays,
lectures.   3. Christianity in literature—Addresses,
essays, lectures.   4. Meyer, Robert T., 1911–
I. Meyer, Robert T., 1911–   .   II. Halton, Thomas,
1925– .   III. Williman, Joseph P., 1925– .
BR67.D44   1986   270   85-21254
ISBN 0-8132-0596-4

Contents

HUMANISTICA

Contents

HAGIOGRAPHICA

Preface

Robert T. Meyer was born in Cleveland, Ohio, on August 6, 1911, and took his B.A. degree at John Carroll University in 1931, and his M.A. a year later. He went to Western Reserve University as a Fellow from 1934 to 1936, and then was honored as a Fellow of the American Council of Learned Societies at the University of Michigan, where he earned his Ph.D. in 1943. During his doctoral studies he made an important visit to the University of North Carolina in the summer of 1941, where he studied with Urban T. Holmes, Jr., and George Lane, and made friendships which would last and bear fruit over the next decades. His first faculty appointment was as Instructor of English Philology at Saint Louis University, and then he began his career association with Catholic University for which so many have reason to be grateful. He was appointed as Instructor in Sanskrit and comparative philology, and characteristically continued his studies under Leo Spitzer at the Johns Hopkins University as a Fellow from 1947 to 1950; at Catholic University one of his first colleagues was Helmut Hatzfeld, and he continued to meet and correspond with that great generation of scholars in philology, lexicography, textual studies, and linguistics in his wide range of languages and literatures.

From the postwar years until the present, Robert Meyer has been a member of the most active and select professional organizations, and has always been eager to share this insider's experience with his students and young colleagues, inviting them to take the fullest part in their profession. A list of conferences attended, papers delivered, formal and informal lectures invited and held, manuscripts read for publication, and all of the time-consuming activities that are so beneficial to others might require a small volume in itself. Suffice it to say that he has always been available to other workers in the vineyard, and the most welcoming friend and colleague, especially to newcomers unsure of their direction or their best abilities. It is seldom that a colleague did not become a friend after first meeting, and then a part of a worldwide network of correspondents and friends to whom a student or researcher might be sent with an almost medieval certainty of welcome and encouragement.

It should be emphasized that one of the best examples that Meyer has set for his students and colleagues is his working in a wide range of interests which come together sometimes in very surprising and provocative ways. From his early years in a farming region he acquired a countryman's deep knowledge of the seasons and cycles that ordinary bookmen too often know from print only. Adding to this a solid grounding in Greek and Latin, the literatures of the ancients and of the early Church, he came to medieval studies with an extraordinary workshop of tools and techniques which allowed him a profound sense of the living reality of a text, its author, and the author's culture. Textual criticism has recently acquired a surge of energy, and produces results which occasionally cause us to marvel at what would be seen as quite consistent and regular if the critic simply had a richer or firmer acquaintance with the history of textual studies. Then, too, it must be doubted if a single colleague or friend of Meyer has never seen him handle a book with the combination of familiarity and respect that is seen more commonly with curators and works of art; this is a treasured experience, even though historians seem to have just recently invented the study of material culture. For Meyer a text has a spiritual and a physical life, and both may be enjoyed and revered at once. On a sabbatical in 1959, he acquired the degree in Library Science which has been of such great benefit to both the Mullen Library at Catholic University and the Library of Congress and so the entire "republic of letters."

It is an honor to present this volume of essays to our friend and colleague, whose generosity over many decades has informed his chosen profession and vocation. We have chosen the title *Diakonia* in recognition of his ordination as deacon in 1971, when his ministry in service to his faith joined his profession and career under the same characteristic sign of generosity. It is a great satisfaction that retirement has not diminished his scholarly production, or his irreplaceable presence in our midst. He has often quoted a remark made to him by Werner Jaeger, the great historian of the ideal of education in Greece, about his own Festschrift: "I like this book because all my best friends and some of my best students are in it." We hope sincerely that *Diakonia* will play such a precious role when it joins Professor Meyer's personal library, which is an absolutely unique world already. The French national library was once called in a film "the whole world's memory." Something similar might be said of Robert Meyer's library as it welcomes its newest citizen: "the world's mind and heart and speech."

JOSEPH P. WILLIMAN

Tabula Gratulatoria

Claudia Russell Barquist

Elizabeth A. Beckwith

Barbara Beyenka, O.P.

J. Neville Birdsall

Gerda Blumenthal

Uta-Renate Blumenthal

David A. Butler, O.P., Ph.D.

The Catholic University of America
Library

Anthony J. Cavell

Giles Constable

Alessandro S. Crisafulli

Stanley M. Dahlman, Ph.D.

Bruno M. Damiani

Rt. Rev. Mark Delery, O.C.S.O.,
Abbot

George T. Dennis, S.J.

Dr. Charles Dowsett

E. Catherine Dunn, Ph.D.

Father Gerard Ellspermann, O.S.B.

Rev. Msgr. F. E. Gasbarre

Georgetown University Library

Francis T. Gignac, S.J.

George E. Gingras

Ellen S. Ginsberg

Patrick Granfield

Sidney H. Griffith

Rev. Lawrence R. Hennessey, S.T.

The Most Rev. James A. Hickey

The Rev. Edward F. James, Ph.D.

Thomas J. Mann

William J. McCarthy

Dr. Terrence J. McGovern

Frederick R. McManus

Professor Leo McNamara

M. B. McNamee, S.J.

Fr. Benedict Mary Meyer, O.S.B.

The Most Rev. Michael J. Murphy

Benedict Chiaka Njoku

Catherine O'Connor

Eric L. Ormsby

James W. Poultney

Boniface Ramsey, O.P.

Maria A. Rebbert

Kiffin Ayres Rockwell

Sally Rogers

Sister Mary Augustine Roth, R.S.M.

Nicholas B. Scheetz

Robert D. Sider

Michael Slusser

Josep M. Sola-Solé

Ruth Steiner

Sean Sweeney, S.M.A.

Louis J. Swift

Rev. Robert Trisco

Alberta Losh Vaughan

Carolyn J. Wall

Harry F. Williams

John F. Wippel

Francis J. Witty

Abbreviations

Titles of classical Greek works are abbreviated as in H. G. Liddell, R. Scott, and H. S. Jones, *A Greek-English Lexicon* (Oxford); titles of patristic Greek works as in G. W. H. Lampe, *A Patristic Greek Lexicon* (Oxford); titles of Latin works as in the *Thesaurus Linguae Latinae* (Leipzig).

ACW	*Ancient Christian Writers*, Westminster, Md.
BAC	*Biblioteca de Autores Cristianos*, Madrid
CCSL	*Corpus Christianorum, Series Latina*, Turnhout
CSCO	*Corpus Scriptorum Christianorum Orientalium*, Leipzig
CSEL	*Corpus Scriptorum Ecclesiasticorum Latinorum*, Vienna
DACL	*Dictionnaire d'archéologie chrétienne et de liturgie*, Paris
DS	*Dictionnaire de spiritualité ascétique et mystique, doctrine et histoire*, Paris
EETS	Early English Text Society, London
FOTC	*The Fathers of the Church*, New York
GCS	*Die Griechischen christlichen Schriftsteller der ersten Jahrhunderte*, Berlin
JbAC	*Jahrbuch für Antike und Christentum*, Münster
LCL	*Loeb Classical Library*, Cambridge, Mass.
LNPF	*A Select Library of Nicene and Post-Nicene Fathers of the Christian Church*, New York
LThK	*Lexikon für Theologie und Kirche*, Freiburg
PG	J. P. Migne, *Patrologia Graeca*, Paris
PL	J. P. Migne, *Patrologia Latina*, Paris
RAC	*Reallexikon für Antike und Christentum*, Stuttgart
SC	*Sources chrétiennes*, Paris
SLH	*Scriptores Latini Hiberniae*, Dublin
TS	Texts and Studies, Cambridge
TU	Texte und Untersuchungen zur Geschichte der altchristlichen Literatur, Berlin

PATRISTICA

GEORGE T. DENNIS, S.J.

Gregory of Nazianzus and the Byzantine Letter

SINCE HUMAN BEINGS first learned to write, they have, when separated by some distance, communicated with one another by written messages or letters. From ancient times rulers addressed letters to other rulers, and to their own subjects. But what concerns us in these pages are letters written by private individuals to other individuals. Many of these were practical, incised on wax tablets or penned on papyrus, and were erased or destroyed when they were answered or the business with which they dealt was no longer urgent. Many were personal, conveying news to a friend or relative. Most of those written in antiquity have not been preserved, one notable exception being those which Atticus retained from his correspondence with Cicero.

Fictitious or hypothetical letters, while much admired, were simply rhetorical exercises in which the author presented what he imagined the sentiments of Alexander or some other great man would have been on a certain occasion. These will not interest us here, nor will philosophical or literary essays in which the epistolary form is purely conventional. Letters of a practical nature, though, as well as personal ones, continued to be written and, although partly superseded by more instant forms of communication, are still written.

In late antiquity, noticeably in the fourth century of the Christian era, a different species, although not wholly without precedent, of letter writing developed and flourished.[1] The letter was still employed to

1. Not much has been written on this topic. See J. Sykutris, "Epistolographie," Pauly-Wissowa, *Real-Encyclopädie der klassischen Altertumswissenschaft*, suppl. Band, 5 (Stuttgart, 1931), 185–220.

3

convey a message to a distant friend, but it was evolving into a new literary genre. This sort of letter was meant to do more than bear a message. It became a vehicle to express feeling and emotion in a fairly formal, structured manner, with special rules of its own. It was the product, and at the same time the badge, of the intellectual elite. The letters they exchanged were small objets d'art, carefully articulated, circulated among a select group, collected, copied, and treasured. Education was the ticket for admission into this elite, an education in Greek grammar, rhetoric, and literature. Their education and their ability to express themselves perfectly, if somewhat artificially, in classical Greek, whether in oratorical or epistolary compositions, set these people apart and clearly distinguished them from the lower classes and, even more so, from the barbarians. Religious beliefs seem not to have affected membership in this exclusive group. In the fourth century both pagans and Christians belonged, as in later centuries clerics, monks, and lay persons together.

The Roman Empire in the East, battered by a series of tremendous shocks, particularly in the seventh century, almost went under, but, although greatly altered in shape and in spirit, managed to stay alive, and eventually came to flourish as what we now term the Byzantine Empire. Scholars have stressed the importance of this hiatus, this break in continuity, in the seventh century, and in general rightly so.[2] The empire and the civilization which emerged in the course of the eighth and the early ninth centuries differed significantly in many spheres: civil institutions, municipal life, religious practices, artistic expression. In one important area, however, there was genuine continuity. That was in the education of what we might call the upper classes, their literary interests, and the manifestation of these in their love for letter writing of high quality. There was also, it is true, a gap in literary activity during the turbulent seventh century. While education must have continued, we know very little about it, and no collection of letters dating from the seventh and eighth centuries has survived.[3] But when the turbulence

---

2. Most recently, C. Mango, "Daily Life in Byzantium," *XVI. Internationaler Byzantinistenkongress, Akten* I/1 (= *Jahrbuch der Oesterreichischen Byzantinistik* 31/1; Vienna, 1981), 337–354; "Discontinuity with the Classical Past in Byzantium," *Byzantium and the Classical Tradition*, ed. M. Mullett and R. Scott (Birmingham, England, 1981), 48–57; *Byzantium: The Empire of New Rome* (New York, 1980), 4–5; A. Kazhdan and G. Constable, *People and Power in Byzantium* (Washington, 1982), 117–139.

3. See P. Lemerle, *Le premier humanisme byzantin* (Paris, 1971), 9–108.

had passed, their basic interests and modes of expression had not changed to any significant degree. Photios, Psellos, Tzetzes, Kydones, and others from the ninth to the fifteenth centuries read more or less the same Greek classics as had Julian, Libanius, Basil, and Gregory; they learned and applied the same rules of grammar and rhetoric. One should, of course, make allowance for some ancient writings which may have been lost and for the addition of biblical and theological material. The tradition and practice of fine letter writing which had begun as a clearly defined art form in the fourth century was carried on by the Byzantine intellectual elite even beyond the fall of their empire in 1453.[4]

The men and women of late antiquity and of the Byzantine period wrote real private letters, much as we do today. But very few have come down to us for the simple reason that they did not think them worth copying. The sort of letters they delighted in composing and which alone were worth preserving were on a much higher level.[5] They were composed with a view toward eventual publication. At least a selection of them would, it was hoped, be of lasting merit and an object of admiration, not only for the addressee but also for future generations.

A letter of this kind had to rise above the ordinary routine of life. There had to be a touch of elegance, just as the poorest church had to have its bit of mosaic or gold ornamentation. The letter was to be brief and to the point, but also so finely crafted that the recipient would want to show it, rather read it, to his friends. It was not really prose in the modern sense of the word, nor was it, strictly speaking, poetry. It was, though, as Margaret Mullett has pointed out, the closest thing in Byzantine literature to lyric poetry, "a powerful, compressed emotional charge."[6]

Byzantine literature has often been harshly criticized, by Byzantinists as much as others, for being pedantic, artificial, and boring, and it must

4. See H. Hunger, *Die hochsprachliche profane Literatur der Byzantiner*, 1 (Munich, 1978), 199–239; J. Sykutris, "Probleme der byzantinischen Epistolographie," *IIIe Congrès international des Études byzantines* (Athens 1932), Compte-rendu, 295–310; N. Tomadakes, Βυζαντινὴ ἐπιστολογραφία. Εἰσαγωγή, κείμενα, κατάλογος ἐπιστολογράφων, 3d ed. (Athens, 1969); G. Karlsson, *Idéologie et cérémonial dans l'épistolographie byzantine* (Uppsala, 1962); V. Smetanin, *Epistolografija* (Sverdlovsk, 1970).

5. On the various levels see I. Ševčenko, "Levels of Style in Byzantine Prose," *XVI. Internationaler Byzantinistenkongress, Akten* I/1, 279–312.

6. M. Mullett, "The Classical Tradition in the Byzantine Letter," *Byzantium and the Classical Tradition*, 75–93, esp. 82.

be admitted that such judgments are not totally unfounded.[7] Recently, however, some scholars have begun to take a fresh look at that literature.[8] They have attempted to judge it upon its own merits and not simply according to modern tastes. This approach has particular validity when applied to letter writing. While we may not find the style and format to our liking, we must remember that, whatever else they may be, Byzantine letters were real letters written to real people. We cannot understand their role in Byzantine culture unless we try to form some appreciation of what they meant, on the personal level as well as the literary, to the people who wrote and who read them.

Educated Byzantines valued fine letter writing very highly and devoted a great deal of time and energy to it. Not only was it a worthy literary endeavor, but it was the bond that held them together, individually and as a group, and a very small group it was. From the fourth to the fifteenth centuries they were almost constantly composing their letters, becoming ever more proficient as time went on. About one hundred and fifty major collections of their letters are extant, according to Mullett's count, and these total some fifteen thousand letters, assuredly only a small portion of those written.

The formal letters written by the Byzantines may well be regarded as one of their greatest literary achievements. It was, moreover, although they themselves might be reluctant to admit it, the one field in which they surpassed their ancient models. The letters composed by such men as Psellos, Tzetzes, and Kydones are more varied in form and display more feeling and literary skill than those of Libanius, Synesius, and their contemporaries. Over fifty years ago one of the few scholars to busy himself with Byzantine letters, J. Sykutris, stated that, apart from religious poetry, "only in Byzantine epistolography does one find pieces which, according to absolute aesthetic standards, belong to world litera-

7. For example, see R. Jenkins, "The Hellenistic Origins of Byzantine Literature," *Dumbarton Oaks Papers* 17 (1963), 39–52; C. Mango, *Byzantine Literature as a Distorting Mirror*, Inaugural Lecture (Oxford, 1975); and my own unkind remarks in *The Letters of Manuel II Palaeologus* (Washington, 1977), xviii–xx, which may well require some revision.

8. At the Byzantine Studies Congress at Columbia University, 3–5 December 1977, A. Littlewood made an impassioned plea for the study and appreciation of Byzantine literature, while presenting a paper entitled "Artistry and Tradition in Byzantine Romantic Gardens," printed in *Byzantine and Modern Greek Studies* 5 (1979), 95–114; also see his "An Ikon of the Soul: The Byzantine Letter," *Visible Language* 10 (1976), 197–226; and the introductory comments of E. Hanawalt to a session on literature at the Byzantine Studies Congress at the University of Chicago, 15–17 October 1982, as well as papers delivered and articles by B. Baldwin and others.

ture."[9] Although long unnoticed, this judgment still appears valid. Obviously, though, as in any other branch of literature, not all letters were masterpieces; some were good, some merely average, and some worthless.

This literary genre, which the Byzantines exploited to the fullest, first flourished, as mentioned, in late antiquity, in the fourth century. The emperor Julian, called the Apostate, and the bishop Synesius were among the earliest and most notable practitioners. The most imitated was the orator Libanius, whose collected letters number over fifteen hundred. A thousand years later, to give just two examples, in his sixty-eight letters Manuel Palaeologus alludes to or cites Libanius' letters twenty-six times, and John Chortasmenos in his fifty-six letters cites them thirteen times, even composing a belated reply to one of Libanius' letters.

While the pagan Libanius served as a model, so did the Christian saints Basil and Gregory of Nazianzus. Gregory was the first, as far as we know, to prepare an edition of his own collected letters. More important, however, it was Gregory who set down the "rules" for good letter writing. These became the rules according to which Byzantine letters were judged. Again, a thousand years later Manuel Palaeologus could refer to these rules and in mock seriousness apologize for having transgressed them.

Although confused in the manuscript tradition, the correct order of Gregory's letters, as he compiled them into a collection, is now clear.[10] The first (Letter 52 in the edition) is his dedicatory epistle to his grand nephew Nikoboulos, who had requested him to collect his letters. The second (Letter 53) is a brief afterthought to the first. In third place (Letter 51) is a longer letter than usual, also in response to a request of Nikoboulos, containing advice on letter writing, the "rules" just mentioned. Fourth (Letter 54) is a bit of additional advice on the same topic. In the next letter (55) Gregory invites Nikoboulos to come and visit him.

The dedicatory epistle to Nikoboulos, written sometime in the years 384–390, reads as follows.

You ask the meadow to furnish flowers in autumn, and you would have

9. Sykutris, "Probleme der byzantinischen Epistolographie," 296.

10. *Saint Grégoire de Nazianze, Correspondance*, ed. and trans. P. Gallay, 2 vols. (Paris, 1964–1967); text only in *Gregor von Nazianz Briefe*, ed. P. Gallay (Berlin, 1969).

Nestor bear arms despite his advanced age. You do this now when you ask me for something cleverly written. For I have long ago given up the pleasures of life and of all speaking. Nonetheless, it is not the sort of labor which would call for Eurystheius or Hercules that you impose on us, but one which is quite mild and fitted to my abilities, that is, to make a collection of as many of my letters as possible for you. "Take now and place this ribbon around your" volumes.[11] This is not something erotic, but has to do with eloquence. It is not meant for show as much as to be useful and suited for our flock.

Some writers have certain distinguishing traits, to a greater or lesser degree, and others have other traits. What characterizes our writing is that it is instructive in its views and in its doctrines, wherever practicable. Furthermore, just as one can always see the father in a noble child, so it is with writing; a person who has produced some is usually recognized in his work just as clearly as though it were a matter of bodily characteristics.[12]

In return, you may pay us back by doing some writing yourself and by showing that you have profited from what we have written. We cannot request or demand a better recompense than this, or one more beneficial to those who ask or more fitting for him who provides.

Letter 51, in which Gregory instructs Nikoboulos in the art of writing letters, together with his brief note (Letter 54) on being laconic, reads as follows.

Some letter writers, since you also asked me about this, compose longer letters than are appropriate, whereas others write far too little. Both fail to attain the proper measure, just as some archers fall short of the target, while others shoot beyond it. All of them miss the mark, but for different reasons. The correct measure of a letter is simply what is needed. One must not write at great length when there is not much to discuss, or be very brief when there is a great deal. What then? Must we use the Persian yardstick to measure our skills, or should we use a child's ruler? We would end up writing so badly that we might as well not write at all. But should we not reproduce the shadows as they appear at noontime, or should we concentrate on those lines which begin right in front of us, but grow thinner as they recede until we can no longer determine where they end, but can only

---

11. Cf. Homer, *Iliad* 14.219.

12. The parent-child analogy applied to an author and his work was very common. St. Basil, e.g., wrote to Gregory: "I recognized your letter, just as men recognize the children of their friends by the parents' likeness appearing in them" (Letter 2; trans. R. Deferrari, *Saint Basil, The Letters*, 4 vols. [New York, 1926]). The Byzantines carried this a step further by referring to the author's teacher as the grandfather of the letter.

guess, and which become, to use an apt expression, likenesses of likenesses? It is necessary to avoid the distortion found in both extremes and to hit upon the proper measure.

This, then, is what I have to say about being concise. Now, what do I think about clarity of expression? As much as possible, the formal tone of a discourse must be avoided, and we should, instead, incline toward a conversational one. To put it succinctly, the best and most beautiful letter is the one which will win over the ordinary person as well as the educated man, the first inasmuch as it is within the grasp of the average person, the second inasmuch as it rises above the crowd. Such a letter should also be intelligible in itself. For it is just as inappropriate that a letter should need an interpreter as that a riddle be easily solved.

The third characteristic of a letter is elegance. We can maintain this quality if we make sure never to write anything harsh, unpleasant, or without embellishment, or anything, as they say, which is unadorned and not filled out.[13] Such would be the case if we left out maxims, proverbs, pithy sayings, even jests and riddles which sweeten the style. But we should certainly not make use of these in excess. The first extreme might be expected of a lad from the country, the other of one who does not know when to stop.

These elements ought to be used to the extent that purple thread is used in weaving cloth. We certainly allow figures of speech, but they should be few and kept within bounds. Antitheses, though, both of exactly equal and of nearly equal clauses, we leave to the sophists.[14] But if for some reason we do bring them in, we should employ them more in a playful manner than seriously.

Let me conclude my discussion with something I heard from a clever gentleman. He told of the time when the birds were trying to decide who should rule their kingdom, and they came beautifying themselves, each in a different way. The most beautiful thing about the eagle, he said, was that he did not think of himself as beautiful. In writing letters too this should be observed above all: avoid affectation and stay as close as possible to what is natural.

This concludes what I have to say to you about letters, here in the form of a letter from me. Perhaps, though, I ought not to be doing this, since I should be busy about more important matters. You will learn the rest by practice, for you are quick to learn, and people who are skillful in these subjects will teach you.

13. Dionysius of Halicarnassus, *On Thucydides* 23.
14. *Isokōla kai parisa*: see Diodorus Siculus 12.53.4.

Letter 54:

To be laconic is not, as you think, to write just a few words, but in a few words to talk about a great many topics. Accordingly, I can refer to Homer as extremely concise and to Antimachos as verbose.[15] How can I do this? One judges the length by the facts expressed and not by the number of letters.

According to Gregory, then, there are three characteristics of a good letter: conciseness (*syntomia*), clarity (*saphēneia*), and elegance (*charis*). He also urges the writer to avoid affectation and excessive use of rhetorical devices. Clearly Gregory did not simply invent these elements, but derived them from his analysis of what he and his literary friends looked for in one another's letters. At any rate, the advice given by Gregory was followed fairly closely and consistently by practically all Byzantine letter writers. A perusal of some editions of their letters should suffice to prove their adherence to what they termed the "rules" (*nomoi*) of letter writing. Hundreds, probably thousands, of Byzantine examples could be adduced to illustrate each one of Gregory's precepts, but there is no place for them in an article of such modest dimensions as this. In one way or another, of course, the rules would have been followed whether Gregory had codified them or not.

A speech could be lengthy, and often was, but not a good letter. This was expected to be brief and to the point. Gregory's notion of being concise reflects the classical Greek stress on proportion, proper measure (*metron*, *metrian*). Extremes were to be avoided. The Persian yardstick was supposedly so precise that it would be ridiculous to try to measure a person's skills with it, whereas a child's ruler would be too small to measure an object of any importance. The shadows at noon stand out so clearly that they cannot be missed, whereas other lines fade away and become so faint that they are barely visible. The letter writer, then, should neither limit himself to a few bold strokes, nor let himself become too imprecise and vague.

The brief letter (54) on being laconic simply underscores Gregory's views on being concise and is itself a perfect example of the subject he is discussing. In fact, most of Gregory's letters, as those of his contemporaries, Libanius in particular, are brief and succinct, and without any wasted words. St. Basil once replied to Gregory as follows: "[Your letter]

15. Antimachos (ca. 400 B.C.) composed the *Thebaid*, apparently a very lengthy epic, now lost.

was indeed strictly yours, not so much in handwriting as in the letter's peculiar quality. For though the sentences were few, they offered much thought. . . . Surely no trouble is involved in writing a laconic note, such as the letters which come to me from you invariably are." [16] Although the Byzantines, especially in later centuries, sometimes wrote longer letters, they strove to be concise, and had high praise for those whose letters were brief, to the point, and laconic.

Anyone who has read a sampling of Byzantine letters, or for that matter, Gregory's letters, may be taken aback at his emphasis on clarity as a hallmark of letter writing. For that does not strike the modern reader as their salient feature. But a closer look at Gregory's counsels may aid in understanding what he meant. First, he recommends that letter writers shun the formal tone of an oration, and, it must be admitted, Byzantine letters, although intended to be read aloud, generally do not sound like speeches. On the other hand, they do not sound much like an ordinary conversation. Undoubtedly, Gregory was thinking more of a polite, erudite discussion among very well educated persons. Attentive reading of Byzantine letters does reveal a style which, while it often impresses one as stilted and formal, actually does, as Gregory advises, incline somewhat toward a conversational tone.

Gregory next suggests that the letter should appeal to the ordinary or average person (*idiōtēs*, *hoi polloi*). But he must surely have realized that the ordinary man in the street (if that is whom he meant) would have great difficulty in comprehending heavily nuanced, rhetorical Greek, and this would be even more true in later centuries. Perhaps it is best to take this as a cautionary note against making the letter too recondite. It should be clear and intelligible, as he says, and not need an interpreter. But at the same time—and this the Byzantines were very faithful in observing—it should not be too clear. For then everyone could understand it, and nothing would set the educated persons apart from the others. There had to be some sort of riddle, some knot to be untied, some puzzle to be deciphered. If the language were too plain and straightforward, there would be little to hold the reader's interest or provide for his pleasure. But if there were some little challenge, if the reader had to make an effort to grasp the author's meaning, then he would come to appreciate the intricate craftsmanship of the letter, and he could look forward to discussing its complexities with his friends. There was,

16. Letter 19, trans. Deferrari.

then, a touch of studied obscurity in their letters which they seem to have enjoyed immensely, but which can be quite maddening to the modern reader or translator. Gregory's own letters are good examples of this, and almost every Byzantine letter has one twisted bit of syntax, one obscure metaphor, or one seemingly incomplete allusion. Clarity, then, there is, but a Byzantine clarity.

A letter was a gift to a friend, and so had to be prettily wrapped and presented with charm and elegance. There was no place for the ugly and the discordant. Some decoration was called for, as Gregory says, in the form of pithy sayings, proverbs, and jests. This too was carefully observed by Byzantine writers. Scarcely a letter was composed by them which did not include at least one proverbial expression, one cliché or classical allusion, one play on words, or one maxim.

Gregory also suggests that a good letter might well include jests and some pleasantry (*paidia*), elements which are abundant in his own letters and in those of his Byzantine successors. Sometimes jokes were made at the expense of the addressee, sometimes at that of a mutual friend. In the fourth letter of his collection, for example, Gregory takes all the characteristics which Basil had admiringly enumerated to describe his own country and very cleverly turns them against him. "Dealing with these topics now," he concluded, "would probably take up more space than it should in a letter, but less than one would expect in a comedy. Now, if you can bear this pleasantry in the right way, you will be doing well, but if not, then we shall pile on even more." Basil apparently took it in the right spirit, for in his next letter Gregory compliments him on being a good sport. Centuries later Michael Psellos enjoyed telling a friend (Letter 97) about a shipboard companion, the monk Elias, who knew all the prostitutes in Constantinople, and Manuel Palaeologus expressed his amusement (Letter 43) at the news that his sedentary friend Demetrius Chrysoloras had purchased a horse, which he would probably never mount. While much of their pleasantry and humor may strike us as labored and forced, it was expected and greatly appreciated by them, and it can, if we look closely, add another dimension to their personalities.

After explaining the three characteristics of a good letter, Gregory adds the recommendation that figures of speech, antitheses, and other rhetorical devices should be used sparingly, as purple thread is used in cloth to embellish or highlight but not to overwhelm the other colors and design.

Gregory concludes his brief treatise with an admonition to avoid affectation and to be as natural as possible. Did he observe this himself? Perhaps he thought he did, but his letters seem so elaborately worked out, so refined and recherché, that it is very difficult to regard them as "natural." Some later Byzantine writers, however, do appear less affected and seem more natural and spontaneous in their correspondence. But, in general, since they were composing their letters according to formal rules and in a language which was not the one they spoke, it was almost impossible for them to be truly natural, and perhaps we should not expect too much.

Nikoboulos presumably took Gregory's suggestions to heart and practiced and became proficient in the epistolary enterprise. And so did subsequent generations. They read the letters of Gregory and his contemporaries, and they continually labored over their own letters and subjected them to each other's critical scrutiny. Like Nikoboulos, the Byzantines were quick to learn, and they soon advanced beyond their teachers in the art of letter writing.

FRANCIS T. GIGNAC

Codex Monacensis Graeca 147 and the Text of Chrysostom's *Homilies on Acts*

IT IS A great pleasure for me to dedicate this article to Professor Emeritus Robert T. Meyer. I have known Dr. Meyer for many years and been associated with him in several areas. I welcome the opportunity to contribute to his Festschrift. The subject I have chosen is in an area well advanced by a friend of his and teacher of mine, the late Rev. Dr. Edgar R. Smothers, S.J., with whom he worked at the University of Michigan in the 1930s, in company with the late Professor Herbert C. Youtie.

Codex Monacensis Graeca 147 (henceforth Munich 147) is a parchment manuscript, well worn, with the ink now generally the same yellowish-brown color as that of Codex Michiganensis 14 (henceforth Michigan 14), but many folios are in quite black ink. Titles, lemmata of Acts, initials, and titles of the ethica are in a wine-red color different from that of the text. The writing of the text is very small and meticulous. There are two columns to the page. The pages are of folio size, numbering 420. The manuscript may be dated to the tenth century.

The title on folio 1 has been supplied on a panel of parchment pasted into a large square lacuna, in a cherry-red color like that of a modern red pen. Six lines of the text of Acts follow; on the original parchment, the first two are retraced in red over the original wine-red. The initial of the first word of Chrysostom is gilt. Signatures of quaternion gatherings may have been lost by trimming in many folios; this is confirmed by loss of prick points in the lower margins of the folios without signatures. This is not a complete proof, however, because folio 106 is written well

14

above the prick points, and folio 178 has neither signature nor prick points.

Pasted inside the front cover is a coat of arms with the inscription "Ex Bibliotheca Serenissimorum Utriusq[ue] Bavariae Ducum 1618." A second coat of arms follows, with the inscription "Ex Electorali Bibliotheca Sereniss[imorum] Utriusq[ue] Bavariae Ducum."

The binding may be Eastern. It is of wooden boards, with dark leather and no ribbing in the back, stamped with patterns on the back and sides.

The principal hand is very much like that of Michigan 14, the base manuscript of the rough recension of these *Homilies on Acts*, but is a little smaller, and occasional uncial forms, especially the lunate sigma, are admitted. A second hand, running from folios 25 to 105, has the peculiarity of hanging his letters from the ruling, while the first hand writes above it. The parchment of the entire section of the second hand is also somewhat heavier and coarser. There seems to be another change of hands, but not so well marked, between folios 169 and 170. The hand before 170 is freer and writes above the line; the hand of 170 and following is smaller, neater, and writes below the line. The hand of folios 106–169 seems the same as the one of folios 1–24. The hand from folio 170 on possibly changes again for a still neater hand, with the letters hung from the ruling; the new hand may begin at folio 250.[1]

The text of Chrysostom's *Homilies on Acts* contained in Munich 147 is that of the rough recension.[2] The existence of two ancient recensions of these homilies had already been assumed by Savile in order to account for the extraordinary diversity of manuscript readings.[3] These fifty-five homilies on the Acts of the Apostles came into printed literature in a version attributed to Erasmus, published in Basel in 1531.[4] Erasmus, however, seems to have translated only the first four homilies and left the rest to others.[5] The translation was based on the eleventh-century Paris

---

1. The above observations about the physical condition of the manuscript and the handwriting are based primarily on unpublished notes taken by Fr. Smothers in European libraries, July-October, 1952.

2. A manuscript of the rough recension can be identified readily by a different reading from the smooth (or printed editions) in the incipits of Homilies 4, 13, 19, 20, 23, 33, 42, 46, 54, and 55. In addition, Munich 147 has a different incipit of *Homily 26*.

3. H. Savilius, ed., *S. Ioannis Chrysostomi Opera Graece* viii (Eton: Norton, 1613), 625.

4. D. Erasmus, *Opera D. Ioannis Chrysostomi* (Basel: Froben, 1558), iii, cols. 437–804, which is probably a reprint of *Commentarium in Acta Apostolorum Homiliae Quinquagintaquinque*, printed at the Froben press in 1531.

5. E. R. Smothers, "Le Texte des Homélies de saint Jean Chrysostome sur les Actes des Apôtres," *Recherches de science religieuse* 27 (1937), 515 and n. 2.

Fonds grec 729, except for the last two homilies, which were based on three other Paris manuscripts, Fonds grec 725, 726, and 727.[6]

The *editio princeps* of these homilies in Greek was produced by Commelin in Heidelburg in 1603.[7] His edition was basically eclectic, as was Savile's and all editions since, but it appears that he mainly followed a text akin to that of Paris 729, from which, however, he occasionally departed in favor of readings deriving from a very different manuscript tradition; the individual manuscripts used by him have never been identified.[8]

Savile based the reedition of these homilies, a part of his magnificent edition of the complete works of Chrysostom, upon Commelin's text, which he corrected occasionally by incorporating readings from two manuscripts at his disposal, the eleventh-century New College 75-76 and the twelfth-century Paris Fonds grec 727.[9] These manuscripts differ greatly from Paris 729, which served as the basis of Commelin's edition, and represent a much rougher type of text. It was the extraordinary diversity of manuscript readings that led Savile to postulate two ancient recensions of these homilies.

Subsequently, Montfaucon collated for his 1731 reedition of these homilies the following manuscripts: Coislin 73, a fourteenth-century mixed text of the rough and smooth recensions; Paris 726, a thirteenth-century manuscript of the rough recension; and Paris 729, which had been Erasmus' manuscript of the smooth recension, as well as the edition of Savile.[10] But it seems that the basic text was Morel's 1633 reprint of Commelin's edition with an accompanying Latin translation.[11] Montfaucon, too, called attention to the great variety of manuscript readings

6. T. Fix in B. de Montfaucon, *S. Ioannis Chrysostomi Opera Omnia* (rev. ed.; Paris, 1834–1839), ix, 1; xiii, Epilogue, vi.

7. H. Commelin, *Expositio Perpetua in Novum Jesu Christi Testamentum* (Heidelburg, 1603), iii, 445–858.

8. H. Browne, *Chrysostom: Homilies on the Acts of the Apostles* (A Library of the Fathers of the Holy Catholic Church; Oxford, 1838–1885), xxxv, p. viii.

9. Savilius, *Opera* viii, 625–662. Savile's "copy" is no. 2773 in Madan and Crasten, *Summary Catalogue of Western MSS. in the Bodleian Library* ii, Part i, 536. Cf. also Browne (above, note 8), vii–viii. The New College manuscript is listed in *Codices Chrysostomici Graeci* I: *Codices Britanniae et Hiberniae*, ed. M. Aubineau (Paris, 1968), nos. 111–112.

10. B. de Montfaucon, *S. Ioannis Chrysostomi Opera Omnia* (Paris, 1717–1738), ix (1731), 1–416. The sources are indicated in the footnote on p. 1.

11. F. Field, *Homilies on Matthew*, Preface, sec. iii (*PG* 57: 3–4); Fix (above, note 6), xiii, Epilogue, iii.

in these homilies and despaired of listing all the variants without the apparatus being nearly as long as the text itself.[12]

The last complete publication of Chrysostom (apart from the Migne reprint) and that which exhibits the last reediting of the Greek text of the *Homilies on Acts* is the Fix-Dübner Benedictine revision of 1834–1839.[13] This is still basically the work of Montfaucon, with the addition of critical notes and a discussion of sources and of the problem of contrasting traditions, in which Fix indicated his preference for the smooth recension represented in Paris 729.[14] However, because they were unwilling to depart significantly from the text of Montfaucon, the Benedictine revisers produced an eclectic text like all editors before them.

The English translator Henry Browne was the first to reestablish a text based on a single tradition. In revising for the Oxford Library of the Fathers the translation of Chrysostom's *Homilies on Acts* prepared originally from Savile's text by J. Walker and J. Sheppard, Browne made a full collation of all the Paris manuscripts and a partial collation of the New College manuscript.[15] He came to the conclusion that an eclectic text fluctuating between the two traditions was inconsistent. One or another text had to be followed throughout, because of their inherent discrepancies. The rough recension was superior in sense and coherence; the smooth recension appeared to be a deliberate revision by a scribe who smoothed out the difficulties found in the original form of these homilies.[16] Browne therefore based his translation on the rough text, but never provided his proposed critical edition of the Greek text.

In a doctoral dissertation at the University of Michigan in 1932, Sharon Lea Finch added three more manuscripts to the rough recension: the eleventh-century Michigan 14; the Venice San Marco 594 (written in A.D. 1295); and the very late Vaticanus 548 (probably sixteenth century). Finch also showed that, at least in *Homily* 20, the text of the mixed recension was a conflation of the smooth and rough traditions.[17]

---

12. Fix (above, note 6), ix, p. vii.

13. B. de Montfaucon, *S. Ioannis Chrysostomi Opera Omnia* (rev. ed.; Paris, 1834–1839), ix (1837), 1–454.

14. Fix (above, note 6), ix, 62, note c, and esp. xiii, Epilogue, vi–vii.

15. Browne, *Chrysostom*, xxxv, p. vii.

16. Ibid., viii–ix.

17. S. L. Finch, "Codex Michiganensis and the Text of St. John Chrysostom's Homilies on the Acts of the Apostles" (Ph.D. diss., University of Michigan, Ann Arbor, 1932), esp. 25–33. An abstract, "The Text of Chrysostom on Acts," appears in *Transactions of the American Philological Association* 67 (1936), xxv.

In his doctoral dissertation of 1936, Edgar R. Smothers demonstrated the consistent superiority of the rough recension over the smooth in *Homily 16* by showing that the smooth was a thorough and deliberate revision of the rough, reflecting a tendency to impoverish the thought while smoothing the style.[18] This analysis effectively laid to rest any supposition that the homilies we have derive from two original recensions of a truly bicephalous tradition as if deriving from the notes of two stenographers or of successive deliveries, or that the smooth text in any way represents Chrysostom's own revision of the homilies for publication. Rather, the smooth version is a deliberate revision, probably posthumous, and therefore a sound edition should be established from rough recension manuscripts exclusively.

Smothers advanced this critical edition greatly by making a complete transcript of Michigan 14 as a basis for collations with other manuscripts of the rough recension, and collated New College 75-76. In 1952, he studied all the manuscripts of these homilies in Western European libraries and identified five more representatives of the rough recension: Athens, National Library 241 (tenth century); Florence, Laurentian Library, Pluteus IX-6 (eleventh century); Messina, San Salvatore 71 (A.D. 1064); Venice, San Marco 569 (eleventh century); and Munich 147. He presented a report of his work to the Second International Conference on Patristic Studies at Oxford in 1955.[19] Subsequent ill health prevented him from completing his project, and shortly before his death in 1970 he entrusted the critical edition to me.

In 1967, I had analyzed the biblical text of the Acts of the Apostles that served as the basis of Chrysostom's homilies and by a comparison of citations in two manuscripts of the rough recension (Michigan 14 and New College 75-76) and one of the smooth (Paris 729) found that the representatives of the rough recension almost invariably preserved the ancient readings, while the text in Paris 729 was repeatedly corrected in the direction of the medieval text that became the *Textus Receptus*.[20] In

18. E. R. Smothers, "The Twofold Tradition of Saint John Chrysostom's Homilies on Acts" (Ph.D. diss., University of Michigan, Ann Arbor, 1936), esp. 87–119. For a summary of this dissertation, see above, note 5.

19. E. R. Smothers, "Toward a Critical Text of the Homilies on Acts of St. John Chrysostom," *Studia Patristica* 1/1 (TU 63; Berlin, 1957), 53–57.

20. This was presented as a major theme paper to the Fifth International Conference on Patristic Studies and subsequently published as "The Text of Acts in Chrysostom's Homilies," *Traditio* 26 (1970), 308–315.

1971, I analyzed the relationship of Messina 71 with the other eleven manuscripts of the rough recension on the basis of a collation of all twelve manuscripts for *Homilies 16–21*.[21] The agreements and disagreements of Messina 71 with each of the other manuscripts of this recension enabled me to identify the largest subgroup and the main lines of derivation of these manuscripts, if not a hard and fast *stemma codicum*, which seems impossible because of the considerable degree of contamination among these manuscripts.

The main lines of derivation are the following:

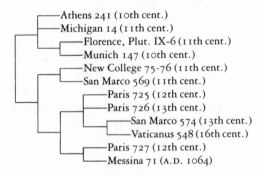

Athens 241 (10th cent.)
Michigan 14 (11th cent.)
Florence, Plut. IX-6 (11th cent.)
Munich 147 (10th cent.)
New College 75-76 (11th cent.)
San Marco 569 (11th cent.)
Paris 725 (12th cent.)
Paris 726 (13th cent.)
San Marco 574 (13th cent.)
Vaticanus 548 (16th cent.)
Paris 727 (12th cent.)
Messina 71 (A.D. 1064)

In this sampling of six homilies, Munich 147 has the closest textual affinity to the Florence manuscript. In the variants analyzed, these two manuscripts agree with each other 16 times against the rest of the manuscripts and another 72 times when supported by at least one other witness, among which Paris 727 is the most frequent, 47 times. In addition, Munich 147 is supported by other witnesses against the Florence manuscript a total of 40 times, including 7 times by Paris 727 and 5 times by San Marco 574. The Florence manuscript in turn is supported by other witnesses against Munich 147 a total of 19 times, including 9 times by Paris 727 and 5 times by San Marco 574. Thus, it seems that these two manuscripts, Munich 147 and Florence, Pluteus IX-6, can be derived from a common hyparchetype. Moreover, these two manuscripts never agree with any other manuscript or group of manuscripts against the rest in more than one significant variant from Michigan 14. Since Michigan 14 shows only 20 singular readings, compared with 49 for

21. F. T. Gignac, "Messina, Biblioteca Universitaria, Cod. Gr. 71 and the Rough Recension of Chrysostom's Homilies on Acts," *Studia Patristica* 12 (TU 115; Berlin, 1975), 30–37.

Munich 147 and 75 for the Florence manuscript, it seems that Michigan 14 is derived from a higher hyparchetype common to the Munich and Florence manuscripts. Munich 147 therefore is an extremely important witness to the text of the rough recension of Chrysostom's *Homilies on Acts*.

The singular readings of Munich 147 are found mainly in the earlier homilies, especially *Homilies 3–13*. The scribe has a tendency to explicitness of expression and emphasis, reflected in frequent additions of forms of *pas* "all" and in alterations of positive degrees of adjectives to the comparative or superlative degrees. He often strengthens connectives by the addition of another particle. He strives for clarity, adding explanations of words, frequently inserting *phēsin* "he says" parenthetically when a quotation is not obvious, and adding clarifying particles like *gar* "for" and *hoti* "because." He is also peculiar in punctuating as a question what occurs as a statement in other manuscripts and occasionally vice versa.

The text of Munich 147 is considerably longer than that of the base manuscript, Michigan 14. This results in great part from the fact that the scribe of Munich 147 commits frequent dittographies but relatively few haplographies, the latter almost always motivated by homoioteleuton. Moreover, although he occasionally omits a part of the text of Acts either in a lemma or in a subsequent quotation, he is more prone to add additional verses of Acts, even in paraphrase, and to repeat quotations, as well as to add personal disquisitions of his own on the text of Acts.

Orthographically, the scribe of Munich 147 generally follows classical norms. He elides regularly when other manuscripts do not, and often deletes a movable nu before a word beginning with a consonant and inserts one before a word beginning with a vowel, consistently so *in pausa*. But he often retains the nu before a word beginning with a consonant, as was the normal usage at his time. He also sometimes corrects movable sigma even through erasure to conform to the classical rule. He never employs iota subscript but occasionally writes iota adscript, even though he omits it in a following word or word-phrase. He also almost invariably corrects wrong accents. He tends to have classically correct spellings where most of the other manuscripts do not. Where Michigan 14 has a single rho, Munich 147 has a double rho. Where many other manuscripts have itacistic misspellings, Munich 147 has the correct spelling, except that the scribe has a tendency to misspell *ē* by *ei*. In this connection, he regularly uses the post-classical Attic *-ei* ending of the second person singular middle-passive, arising as a result of the general shortening of the long dipthong *ēi* to *ei*, rather than the classical Attic ending -*ēi*. He also confuses *o* and *ō*. But generally his orthography is a pleasure to read.

The analysis of the readings of Munich 147 in relation to the base manuscript, Michigan 14, and to those of other manuscripts of the rough recension brings us another step closer to the critical edition of Chrysostom's *Homilies on Acts*, to which Fr. Smothers devoted much of his life. It is hoped that, through our combined efforts, this edition so long in preparation may soon be in press.

SIDNEY H. GRIFFITH

Ephraem, the Deacon of Edessa, and the Church of the Empire

IT IS COMMON knowledge among patrologists that Ephraem the Syrian (ca. 306–373) was a religious poet, and a notable ascetic in the tradition of the early Syriac church. In fact, of all the writers in this tradition, Ephraem is the one with the most immediate name recognition among modern Western scholars. While his name is thus well known, opinions have nevertheless been varied among English-speaking readers about the quality of Ephraem's works. On the one hand, early in the present century, F. C. Burkitt wrote that "Ephraim is extraordinarily prolix, he repeats himself again and again, and for all the immense mass of material there seems very little to take hold of. His style is as allusive and unnatural as if the thought was really deep and subtle, and yet when the thought is unraveled, it is generally commonplace. . . . Judged by any canons that we apply to religious literature, it is poor stuff." [1] More recently, J. B. Segal echoed the same sentiment. While admitting that Ephraem was a master of Syriac style, Segal went on to say that "his work, it must be confessed, shows little profundity or originality of thought, and his metaphors are laboured. His poems are turgid, humourless, and repetitive." [2] In stark counterpoint to this negative chorus, Robert Murray has described Ephraem "as the greatest poet of

1. F. Crawford Burkitt, *Early Eastern Christianity* (London, 1904), pp. 95 and 99.
2. J. B. Segal, *Edessa, 'the Blessed City'* (Oxford, 1970), p. 89.

the patristic age and, perhaps, the only theologian-poet to rank beside Dante."[3]

While it is not particularly profitable to continue to engage in such broad characterizations of Ephraem's work, the striking divergence of impressions about his literary output recorded among English-speaking writers calls attention to the fact that until the recent work of Robert Murray and Sebastian Brock,[4] little concentrated attention has in fact been paid to Ephraem's thought in Britain or America, beyond the translation in the nineteenth century of a selection of his works, based on the old *editio romana*, and included in the Nicene and Post-Nicene Fathers.[5] Meanwhile, in European university circles a minor industry in Ephraem scholarship has been steadily growing in recent decades, as a brief glance at current bibliographies will confirm.[6] The catalyst that has been the principal motivation for these studies has been the appearance of modern critical editions of many of Ephraem's authentic Syriac works, and particularly those published over the last twenty some years by Dom Edmund Beck in the *Corpus Scriptorum Christianorum Orientalium*.[7] This achievement makes possible a new approach to Ephraem's thought, and even now new translations of his works into more felicitous English versions than were previously available are underway.[8]

The purpose of the present essay, which relies heavily on the studies

3. R. Murray, "Ephrem Syrus," *Catholic Dictionary of Theology* (vol. II; London, 1967), pp. 220–223. Murray reaffirmed his opinion in his *Symbols of Church and Kingdom: A Study in Early Syriac Tradition* (Cambridge, 1975), p. 31.

4. Murray's major work to date has been his *Symbols of Church and Kingdom*, which contains many translations of Ephraem's hymns. For Brock, cf. Sebastian Brock, *The Harp of the Spirit: Twelve Poems of Saint Ephrem* (Studies Supplementary to Sobornost, no. 4; London, 1975), and esp. the bibliog., pp. 70–72.

5. Cf. John Gwynn, ed., "Selections Translated into English from the Hymns and Homilies of Ephraim the Syrian, and from the Demonstrations of Aphrahat the Persian Sage," in P. Schaff and H. Wace, eds., *LNPF* (second series; London and New York, 1898), vol. 13, pp. 113–412. The *editio romana* is J. S. Assemani, ed., *Sancti Patris Nostri Ephraem Syri Opera Omnia Quae Extant Graece, Syriace, Latine* (6 vols.; Romae, 1732–1746).

6. The most complete recent bibliography is contained in Tryggve Kronholm, *Motifs From Genesis 1–11 in the Genuine Hymns of Ephrem the Syrian* (Lund, 1978), pp. 225–238. Cf. also M. P. Roncaglia, "Essai de bibliographie sur saint Ephrem," and Kh. Samir, "Complé-ments de bibliographie ephremienne," *Parole de l'Orient* 4 (1973), pp. 343–370; 371–391.

7. Cf. Kronholm, op. cit., pp. 225–226.

8. Following the lead of Murray and Brock (cf. n. 4 above), one may refer to the forthcoming work of Kathleen McVey of Princeton Theological Seminary, and the translation of Ephraem's *Paschal Hymns* being undertaken at the Institute of Christian Oriental Research, The Catholic University of America.

of the scholars who have been busily producing the critical editions of
Ephraem's works over the past generation, is to highlight an aspect of
his ecclesiology which has hitherto been somewhat neglected, viz.,
Ephraem's ideas about the organizational constitution of the church, and
its relationship to the newly Christian Roman empire. There are three
basic steps involved in this inquiry. The first of them is to review very
summarily the current scholarly consensus about Ephraem's own role in
the life of the church in Nisibis and Edessa. The second step will be to
gather together his remarks about church organization, and the role of
bishops in their dioceses, as well as his remarks about the Roman
emperors and their place in the Church. Finally, the third step consists of
an interpretation of Ephraem's ideas on these subjects in light of what one
knows from other sources about the efforts exerted in the fourth century
to establish the church of the empire.

I

In spite of his enormous literary output, not much is really known
about the details of Ephraem's life. There have been a number of studies
devoted to the legendary Syriac *Vita* tradition of the saint, but they have
mostly emphasized the unreliability of these accounts from the point of
view of modern historical documentation.[9] And it now seems clear that
even the Syriac *Vita* in fact owes a debt to notices about Ephraem which
first appeared in the works of the Greek historians of the church who
wrote in the fifth century, and particularly to Palladius and Sozomen.[10]
The *Vita* tradition in Syriac thereafter concentrated on magnifying
Ephraem's sanctity and orthodoxy with stories that had spiritual edification as their goal, and not mere biographical information.[11]

What is known with some certainty about the course of Ephraem's life
is soon told. He was born of Christian parents in the environs of Nisibis
around the year 306. Early on he came under the influence of James, the
bishop of Nisibis (303–338), and he continued afterwards to serve two
succeeding bishops of that city, Vologeses (346–361) and Abraham

---

9. Cf. particularly A. Vööbus, *Literary, Critical and Historical Studies in Ephrem the Syrian*
(Stockholm, 1958), pp. 11–93.

10. Cf. B. Outtier, "Saint Ephrem d'apres ses biographies et ses oeuvres," *Parole de
l'Orient* 4 (1973), pp. 11–33.

11. An account of the legends in the Syriac *Vita* tradition may be found in the introductory essay on Ephraem by J. Gwynn, in P. Schaff and H. Wace, eds., op. cit., pp. 120–152.

(361–363), in the capacity of deacon, preacher, exegete (*mpaśśqānâ*), and advisor. After the year 363, when Nisibis was surrendered to the Persians, Ephraem moved to Edessa and there served Bishop Barsai (361–371), and Bishop Vitus of the neighboring city of Ḥarrān, in the same capacity in which he had served the bishops of Nisibis. He reportedly died in Edessa on June 9, 373, with a reputation for holiness and heroic charity. [12]

This bare outline of Ephraem's life, virtually confined as it is to the list of bishops whom he served, underlines an important feature in Ephraem's biography. He was a bishop's man throughout his career, serving mainly in an academic capacity, interpreting scripture, preaching, and writing metrical compositions which were intended to be sung or recited publicly. Almost all of them have a strongly partisan strain, emphasizing that a major feature of Ephraem's pastoral ministry was to combat what he considered to be erroneous religious ideas, and to commend right thinking in the church. So strong is this role that modern scholars point to it as evidence that Ephraem could not have lived the life of a retired ascetic, as the Syriac *Vita* tradition insists. [13] He was actively engaged in an open struggle to win the allegiance of peoples' minds and hearts to true Christianity, which for him was that fostered by the bishops whom he served. The evidence for this assertion is to be read in the hymns, the *Carmina Nisibena*, which Ephraem composed in praise of his bishops, not only in Nisibis, but also in Edessa and Ḥarrān as mentioned above. [14]

An interesting theme in the earliest documents which take notice of Ephraem, all of them in Greek, and which will be of particular pertinence to the present inquiry, is his reputation among these Greek-speaking ecclesiastical writers for eloquence and intellectual perspicacity in discerning heretical ideas. Epiphanius of Salamis (d. 403), writing between 374 and 377, an arch-supporter of Nicea, was the first author to make such a reference to Ephraem, calling him in the *Panarion* "the wise

12. For the results of the modern scholarly study of Ephraem's biography, cf. in particular E. Beck, "Ephrem le syrien (saint)," *DS*, vol. IV, cols. 788–790; idem, "Ephraem Syrus," *RAC*, vol. V, cols. 520–531; R. Murray, "Ephrem Syrus, St.," *A Catholic Dictionary of Theology* (vol. II; London, 1967), pp. 220–223; and the summary, with extensive bibliography, in Nabil El-Khoury, *Die Interpretation der Welt bei Ephraem dem Syrer* (Mainz, 1976), pp. 13–20.

13. Cf. esp. Beck, "Ephraem Syrus," cols. 523–524.

14. Cf. E. Beck, *Des Hl. Ephraem des Syrers Carmina Nisibena I* (*CSCO*, vols. 218, 219 and 240, 241; Louvain, 1961 and 1963); I. Ortiz de Urbina, "L'évêque et son role d'apres saint Ephrem," *Parole de l'Orient* 4 (1973), pp. 137–146.

man among the Syrians." [15] In the *Lausiac History*, Palladius (d. 425) was more interested in Ephraem's reputation as an ascetic, although he did mention that the deacon of Edessa was "deemed worthy of the charism of natural knowledge, succeeded by the knowledge of God, and final beatitude." [16]

Later, Theodoret and Sozomen added to the accounts of Ephraem's cultivation of monastic ways statements about his intellectual acumen, as if they were indeed considerably impressed with it. Writing sometime between 441 and 449, Theodoret has the following to say about Ephraem: "Using the Syriac language, he radiated beams of spiritual grace. For, even though he had not tasted a Greek-language education, he sorted out the multifaceted errors of the Greeks, and he laid bare the weakness of every heretical malapropism." [17]

Writing his *Ecclesiastical History* in 443, Sozomen was even more impressed with Ephraem's accomplishments. He said:

He devoted his life to monastic philosophy; and although he received no instruction, he became, contrary to all expectation, so proficient in the learning and language of the Syrians, that he comprehended with ease the most abstruse theorems of philosophy. His style of writing was so replete with splendid oratory and sublimity of thought that he surpassed all the writers of Greece. If the works of these writers were to be translated into Syriac, or any other language, and divested, as it were, of the beauties of the Greek language, they would retain little of their original elegance and value. The productions of Ephrem have not this disadvantage: they were translated into Greek during his life, and translations are even now being made, and yet they preserve much of their original force and power, so that his works are not less admired when read in Greek than when read in Syriac. Basil, who was subsequently bishop of the metropolis of Cappadocia, was a great admirer of Ephrem, and was astounded at his erudition. The opinion of Basil, who was the most learned and eloquent man of his age, is a stronger testimony, I think, to the merit of Ephrem, than anything that could be indited in his praise. [18]

15. K. Holl, *Epiphanius (Ancoratus und Panarion)* (*GCS*, 3 vols.; Leipzig, 1915–1933), vol. II, p. 284, 18f.

16. C. Butler, *The Lausiac History of Palladius* (2 vols., TS, vol. 6; Cambridge, 1898 and 1904), vol. II, p. 126.

17. *PG*, vol. 82, col. 1189C.

18. *PG*, vol. 67, col. 1088. The translation here is by E. Walford, *The Ecclesiastical History of Sozomen, Comprising a History of the Church from A.D. 324 to A.D. 440* (London, 1855), p. 134.

Evident here are a number of themes which reappear in embellished form in the legends of the Syriac *Vita* tradition, principally St. Basil's enthusiastic approval of Ephraem.[19] What is more to the present point, however, is the accent which Sozomen put upon the surprising ability of Ephraem's works to be accommodated to the Greek. And in fact, Greek Ephraem did achieve a wide popularity, almost independently of the original Syriac works, and became the basis for translations of Ephraem's poems into many other languages.[20] What makes this popularity somewhat ironic is the insistence with which many modern scholars have in the past attempted to isolate Ephraem himself from direct contact with Greek thought, alleging that his theology is hellenophobic in principle. Robert Murray once even wrote, "Unlike Bardaisan, Ephrem probably knew no Greek, shows no debt to Greek philosophy, and expresses contempt for Greek thought."[21] And André de Halleux, who is careful to speak of "une osmose intellectuelle profonde entre les deux mondes,"[22] nevertheless keeps Ephraem and his fourth-century Greek ecclesiastical contemporaries worlds apart.

What fosters these attitudes about Ephraem's hellenophobia are his own words. He actually wrote such lines as, "Blessed is the one who has never tasted the poison of the wisdom of the Greeks,"[23] or, "the accursed dialectic is vermin from the Greeks."[24] But the proper target of his animosity was hardly Greek as such, anymore than it was Theodoret's target in his *Hellēnikōn Therapeutikē Pathēmatōn*, itself written with an obvious relish for Greek.[25] Paganism, and for Ephraem, the logic-chopping ways of philosophers and Arians, are clearly the enemies. As a matter of fact, both of the phrases cited above, which are generally the ones employed as evidence for Ephraem's hellenophobia, are quoted from

---

19. On this motif in Ephraem's *Vita*, cf. D. O. Rousseau, "La rencontre de saint Ephrem et de saint Basile," *L'Orient Syrien* 2 (1957), pp. 261–284; 3 (1958), pp. 73–90.

20. Cf. D. Hemmerdinger-Illiadou, "Ephrem grec," *DS*, vol. IV, cols. 800–815, and the extensive bibliography under "Ephraem Graecus," in M. Geerard, ed., *Clavis Patrum Graecorum* (vol. II; Brepols, 1974), pp. 366–468.

21. R. M. Murray, "Ephrem Syrus, St.," p. 221. Sebastian Brock voiced the same conviction in "Ephrem's Letter to Publius," *Le Muséon* 89 (1976), pp. 265–266.

22. André de Halleux, "Mar Ephrem Théologien," *Parole de l'Orient* 4 (1973), p. 54.

23. Edmund Beck, *Des heiligen Ephraem des Syrers Hymnen de Fide* (CSCO, vols. 154 and 155; Louvain, 1955), vol. 154, p. 7.

24. Ibid., p. 268.

25. Cf. P. Canivet, ed., *Théodoret de Cyr, Thérapeutique des maladies helléniques* (SC, no. 57, 2 vols.; Paris, 1958).

his *Hymns on Faith*, a collection devoted entirely to the combat against Arianism. [26] In them Ephraem again and again charges that the basic problem with Arianism is that its adepts have been seduced into doing research into divine things, in the dialectical manner of the academy, instead of remaining steadfast in biblical faith. And the dialectical method, in his view, as he said so clearly in the passage quoted above, comes ultimately from the pagan Greeks. Moreover, it has now been shown in numerous instances, particularly by Edmund Beck, that Ephraem was quite cognizant of many aspects of Greek thought. [27] One has every reason therefore to believe that he at least did research in Greek sources, even if he was not completely proficient in that language. In fact, as I shall be arguing, Ephraem was also doing everything in his power to bring the Syriac-speaking community into line with the "Church of the Empire," as Karl Baus has called it. [28] Accordingly, scholars are now adjusting their earlier statements about Ephraem's ignorance of Greek thought, and Robert Murray, regarding his own earlier statements, has recently written that "a certain *retractatio* is called for," [29] in the matter of Ephraem's alleged ignorance of things Greek.

It is curious to note in passing that while Sozomen wrote of Ephraem's language in such glowing terms, saying that "his style of writing was so replete with splendid oratory and sublimity of thought that he surpassed all the writers of Greece," [30] Philoxenus of Mabbūg (d. 523), in the heat of the christological controversies of more than a century later, was concerned about the inexactness of Ephraem's language. Philoxenus remarked in this connection, "Our Syriac tongue is not accustomed to

26. This conclusion was definitely established by Dom Edmund Beck in his *Die Theologie des hl. Ephraem in seinen Hymnen über den Glauben* (Studia Anselmiana, 21; Rome, 1949).

27. Cf. the sketch in E. Beck, "Ephraem Syrus," cols. 524–527, and also idem, "Ephraems Brief an Hypatios," *Oriens Christianus* 58 (1974), pp. 76–120; "Ephraems Rede gegen eine philosophische Schrift des Bardaisan," *Oriens Christianus* 60 (1976), pp. 24–68; "Bardaisan und seine Schule bei Ephräm," *Le Muséon* 91 (1978), pp. 271–333; "Die Hyle bei Markion nach Ephräm," *Orientalia Christiana Periodica* 44 (1978), pp. 5–30; *Ephräms Polemik gegen Mani und die Manichäer* (*CSCO*, vol. 391; Louvain, 1978).

28. Cf. Karl Baus, "The Development of the Church of the Empire within the Framework of the Imperial Religious Policy," in H. Jedin and J. Dolan, eds., *History of the Church* (vol. II; New York, 1980), esp. pp. 89–90.

29. R. Murray, "The Characteristics of the Earliest Syriac Christianity," in N. G. Garsoian, T. F. Mathews, and R. W. Thompson, eds., *East of Byzantium: Syria and Armenia in the Formative Period* (Washington, 1982), p. 9.

30. Cf. n. 18 above.

use the precise terms that are in currency with the Greeks."[31] Of course, by Philoxenus' day the Syriac-speaking church had already accommodated itself to the idea of participating in the "Church of the Empire," and the struggle then was to take part more fully in the theological debates of that church, with a view to advancing the establishment of one's own christological convictions, be they dyophysite or monophysite. Hence, as Sebastian Brock has expressed it, "The exigencies of the christological controversies of the time force Syriac writers like Philoxenus to abandon (or at least radically adapt) the native Syriac tradition of symbolic theology in the face of philosophically oriented Greek theology."[32]

In Ephraem's day, however, the project was to enhance and to strengthen "the native Syriac tradition of symbolic theology," to borrow Brock's phrase, but to do so with a view to confessing the faith of the "Church of the Empire," a subject to which one must now turn as the principal topic of the present essay.

II

Ephraem wrote no systematic treatise *De ecclesia*, to which one might have immediate reference in search of his ideas about how the church should be constituted in relationship to the empire. There is, of course, the collection of fifty-two *Hymni de ecclesia*.[33] However, these hymns cover a whole range of topics, only some of them having anything explicitly to do with the church *per se*, and none of them being particularly helpful in regard to the topic at hand. This circumstance instantly calls attention to the fact that the literary genre of most of Ephraem's works is not discursive prose, but poetry and song, and *Kunstprosa*. One must search for his basic ideas not in single-theme compositions, but over the whole corpus of his genuine Syriac works. The search is nevertheless rewarding, because the songs and poems have a definite didactic

31. A. De Halleux, *Philoxène de Mabbog, Lettre aux moines de Senoun* (*CSCO*, vol. 231; Louvain, 1963), p. 51. Quoted in the translation of S. Brock, "From Antagonism to Assimilation: Syriac Attitudes to Greek Learning," in N. G. Garsoian et al., eds., op. cit., p. 20.

32. Ibid.

33. Cf. Edmund Beck, *Des heiligen Ephraem des Syrers Hymnen de Ecclesia* (*CSCO*, vols. 198 and 199; Louvain, 1960).

function, a feature about which more should be said before pursuing the main topic in detail.

To the modern eye, the songs, hymns, and metrical homilies that make up the bulk of Ephraem's work do not appear to be a likely medium of official public discourse in the church. Rather, they seeem to be more suited to liturgy, and to the leisurely pace of contemplative prayer in community. And indeed, even until today, the liturgy is the setting in which one most often encounters Ephraem's compositions in Syriac-speaking churches. But there is another dimension.

Ephraem was a biblical scholar and a teacher. The Greek-speaking historians of the church, as noted earlier, not only recorded the memory of his elegant language, but also called attention to Ephraem's erudition, and celebrated the correctness of his doctrine. These accolades recall the fact that in the Syriac tradititon as well, and even among the hagiographic legends of the *Vita*, Ephraem is celebrated for his doctrine, and for his ability to express it convincingly in verse and song. His artistic talent, which is probably more responsible for his fame than his scholarship, was for writing didactic poetry to be used in the practical, day-to-day pastoral endeavor to foster correct thinking among the faithful, and to counteract the influence of heresies. Theodoret, Sozomen, and the Syriac *Vita* tradition all claim that Ephraem got his start in composition in an effort to counteract the influence of the doctrine of Bar Dayṣān, which is said to have been popularized in songs composed by a son, not too convincingly, but appropriately, named Harmonios.[34] Whether or not this is the true story of how Ephraem came to be a poet, it is a true depiction of how he used his poetry in service of the church's catechetical mission.

James of Sarūg (d. ca. 521), in his account of Mār Ephraem, "the teacher [*malpānâ*]," pays a considerable amount of attention to describing the care with which Ephraem taught his songs to choirs of men and women, with whom he even conducted rehearsals to insure the quality and correctness of their performance.[35] James accents the didactic charac-

---

34. Cf. *PG*, vol. 82, col. 1189; *PG*, vol. 67, col. 1089; T. J. Lamy, *Sancti Ephraem Syri Hymni et Sermones* (vol. II; Mechliniae, 1886), cols. 63–67. On the relationship between Bardayṣān and his son, cf. H. J. W. Drijvers, *Bardaiṣan of Edessa* (Assen, 1966), pp. 143–152.

35. Cf. P. Bedjan, *Acta Martyrum et Sanctorum* (vol. III; Paris and Leipzig, 1892), pp. 627ff. Cf. the study by Kathleen McVey, "Jacob of Serug on Ephrem: An Early Sixth Century Example of *sobria ebrietas* in Syriac," to appear.

ter of this exercise. In one image he calls Ephraem the second Moses, who in the time of battle repaired the breaches in the wall, "and took the side of doctrine [malpānûtâ], which had been overthrown."[36]

The hymns in which Ephraem inculcated the church's biblical doctrine are called madrāšê, that is to say, 'instructional hymns,' the Syriac term being cognate to the Hebrew word midraš, which similarly has to do with interpretation and instruction, particularly in the scriptures.[37] In his madrāšê Ephraem taught the exegesis of the scriptures, and catechized the faithful through the medium of song. He also composed metrical homilies, which were recited rather than sung in church, but their purpose was similarly didactic. Even the few prose works from his pen which have survived are very much on the order of Kunstprosa, being replete with rhymed cola, rhetorical figures, and measured cadences.[38] Only the surviving scripture commentaries are written in a straightforward prose style, but for the present purpose they are not particularly helpful.[39]

Here it will be useful to survey Ephraem's works under two broad headings, in order to gather up what may be found there, first of all, in reference to the Roman emperors, to the bishops, and to the relationship that should, in Ephraem's view, obtain between these two groups. Secondly, a quick review of Ephraem's reaction to the Arians will furnish an important element for piecing together his ideas about the "Church of the Empire." Since all of the references to Ephraem's works cited here are to metrical compositions, a certain lack of discursive consistency is to be expected. Nevertheless, the author's basic convictions should emerge fairly clearly.

A. Emperors

Most of the passages referring to emperors appear in the Carmina Nisibena, the diatribe Against Julian, and the Hymns on Faith. Accordingly, the present survey follows this chronological order of the works.

36. Bedjan, op. cit., p. 673.
37. Cf. R. Bloch, "Midrash," In W. S. Green, ed., Approaches to Ancient Judaism: Theory and Practice (Brown Judaic Studies, no. 1; Missoula, Mont., 1978), pp. 29–50.
38. Cf. S. P. Brock, "Ephrem's Letter to Publius," Le Muséon 89 (1976), pp. 261–305.
39. Cf. the list of commentaries ascribed to Ephraem in I. Ortiz de Urbina, Patrologia Syriaca (2d ed.; Rome, 1965), pp. 61–64. On his exegetical method, cf. C. Bravo, Notas Introductorias a la noematica de San Efren (Rome, 1956; L. Leloir, Doctrines et methodes de saint Ephrem (CSCO, vol. 220; Louvain, 1961); S. Hidal, Interpretatio Syriaca (Lund, 1974); and Kronholm, op. cit., n. 6 above.

In his *Carmina Nisibena* Ephraem says of Constantine (d. 337) and Bishop Jacob of Nisibis that they were a counterbalance to one another, as were Constantius (d. 361) and Bishop Vologeses, their successors. The kings provided laws, and the priests provided atonement.[40] Ephraem prayed, "May the priesthood be gentle, the kingship strong. Blessed be the One who has put together our twin benefits."[41] And his prayer expresses a commitment to the "Church of the Empire" which is unmistakable:

> Let the priests pray for the kings,
>   to be a protective wall for humankind.
> On the side of the kings let there be victory;
>   on the side of the priests faith.
> Victory will guard over the bodies,
>   faith over the souls.
> Let the kings bring an end to strife,
>   and the bishops bring an end to curious searching [ʿuqqābâ].
> May dialectic [drāšâ] and dispute come to an end.
> Blessed be the Son of the Pacifier of all.[42]

For Ephraem, the emperor's role was to support and protect the church. This much is also clear from what he says in his diatribe *Against Julian*, about the two emperors who preceded "the apostate." Here Ephraem speaks of Constantine and Constantius as "truth-loving kings" who "cultivated, adorned the earth,"[43] in the poet's words. And of Constantius he says that "he had entrusted his crown to the Knower of All," and that "for forty years his prayer had preserved his kingdom."[44] Obviously Ephraem intends to include the reigns of both Constantine and Constantius in this round number. In the hymn *De ecclesia*, which in all likelihood belongs among the hymns *Against Julian*, the poet assigns a cause for the irruption of the rule of the apostate, by citing the virulence of theological debate that had sprung up in the church in connection with the Arian controversy. Speaking of Constantine and Constantius he said:

40. Beck, *Carmina Nisibena I*, op. cit., vol. 218, pp. 58 and 59.
41. Ibid., p. 59.
42. Ibid.
43. Edmund Beck, *Des heiligen Ephraem des Syrers Hymnen de Paradiso und Contra Julianum* (CSCO, vols. 174 and 175; Louvain, 1957), vol. 174, p. 73.
44. Ibid., p. 88.

The kings who once gave shade,
    refreshed us in the heat.
We ate their fruit,
    but were ungrateful for their branches.
We had our heart's delight
    of good things and shade,
But our mouth became mad
    and attacked our Creator.
Wars in the shade
    we waged by our speculations;
[Now] He has withdrawn our shade
    to let us feel the heat.[45]

According to Ephraem, Constantine and Constantius had well ful-filled the role of emperor, which in the first stanza of the diatribe *Against Julian* he had described as "shepherding mankind, caring for cities, and driving away wild animals."[46] It may not be stretching matters too far to propose that the "wild animals" whom in Ephraem's view the emperor should drive away were heretics. Ephraem was indeed fond of describing the principal foes of the earlier years of his ministry as packs of wolves, foxes, and weasels. These were particularly the followers of Marcion, Mānī and Bar Dayṣān.[47] As for the Arians, with an obvious play on the similarity of their Greek name to the Syriac word *aryâ*, Ephraem likened them to lions.[48]

Twice more in connection with his reaction to the Arians Ephraem had occasion to refer to the Roman emperor. At one place in his *Hymns against Heresies*, mentioning among others the Aëtians and Arians, he celebrated the memory of the king who had summoned the council of Nicea, i.e., Constantine I.[49] Then in his *Hymns on Faith*, a collection devoted entirely to the anti-Arian campaign, Ephraem refers to the

45. Ibid., p. 70. The translation is from Murray, *Symbols*, pp. 110 and 111. That the hymn belongs among the *Against Julian* hymns is the judgment of Beck, *De Paradiso u. Contra Julianum*, op. cit., vol. 175, p. 61, n. 1. That it refers to the events designated here as the 'Arian controversy' is inferred from Ephraem's use of the term ʿ*uqqābayn* (Murray's "speculations"), which figures prominently in his description of that controversy elsewhere. Cf. below, n. 94.

46. Ibid., p. 71.

47. Cf., e.g., Edmund Beck, *Des heiligen Ephraem des Syrers Hymnen Contra Haereses* (*CSCO*, vols. 169–170; Louvain, 1957), vol. 169, p. 52.

48. Ibid., p. 95. Cf. Beck's note, ibid., vol. 170, p. 89, n. 12.

49. Ibid., vol. 169, p. 85.

Roman emperor again. This time his intention is to exculpate the crown, in spite of its imperial decrees against the Nicene party. Ephraem explains that in this matter "the crown is absolved, in that priests have put stumbling blocks in the way of the kings." [50] The best interpretation to put upon these words is that they refer to the Arianizing, or more correctly, the *Homoian*, anti-Nicene policies of the emperor Valens (364–378), who with his court bishop, Eudoxius, followed a program of putting sympathetic bishops in all of the sees of the east. [51] In fact, just a year after Ephraem's death, this policy was carried out even in Edessa. Earlier, in 371, Bishop Barsai had already been exiled while Ephraem, his *mpaššqānâ*, was still alive. [52] It is hard to imagine what Ephraem would have said about Valens if he had lived to see the full implementation of the emperor's policies in Edessa, which were carried out amid so much tumult. Prior to the event, however, it is clear from the phrase just quoted that Ephraem held Valens personally innocent in the overall campaign that was waged in his name. In view of Ephraem's exalted notion of the role of the Christian emperor, he may well have been reluctant to find fault with Valens, so soon after the catastrophe of Julian. Indeed, he had celebrated the arrival of the short-lived emperor Jovian (363–364) in almost ecstatic tones, singing: "The news of the new king comes thundering into the world." [53] It was an occasion now, as Ephraem went on to say, "for the former habits to be choked off between priest and righteous king." [54]

As Ephraem saw it, then, in the proper order of things, the emperor could even be viewed as a saint. A passage in the probably inauthentic collection of metrical *Homilies*, attributed to Ephraem in the manuscript tradition, may in fact not misrepresent the great man's opinion when it paints a verbal picture of the last judgment, in which the order of

50. Edmund Beck, *Des heiligen Ephraem des Syrers Hymnen de Fide*, op. cit., vol. 154, p. 271. In Beck's judgment, hymns 26–30 in the *Carmina Nisibena I* (op. cit., vol. 219, p. iv) refer to Valens' campaign in Edessa beginning in the year 365. Hymn 29 in this collection likens the affair to winter, brought on, in part, by wrong doctrine. Cf. Beck's version of hymn 29, strophe 17, ibid., p. 66, and Murray's reference to it in *Symbols*, p. 112.

51. Cf. Baus, art. cit., pp. 61–64.

52. Cf. the brief account, with references, in D. S. Wallace-Hadrill, *Christian Antioch: A Study of Early Christian Thought in the East* (Cambridge, 1982), pp. 89–91. For an account of Valens' *homoian* campaign, cf. Thomas A. Kopecek, *A History of Neo-Arianism* (2 vols., Patristic Monograph Series, no. 8; Cambridge, Mass., 1979), vol. II, pp. 421–440.

53. Beck, *Carmina Nisibena I*, op. cit., vol. 218, p. 57.

54. Ibid.

the heavenly court appears as proceeding from Christ, to Stephen and the martyrs, then to Paul and the doctors, and finally to "Constantine, the saint, and with him all the kings who had confessed the faith." [55]

B. Bishops and Emperors

It is clear both from his acquittal of Valens from blame in the emperor's anti-Nicene campaign, and from his own very explicit words on the subject, that for Ephraem the bishops are the real authorities in the church. Here is not the place to examine this issue in great detail, since other scholars have studied it specifically. [56] One may however mention the guiding principles of the matter, the first of which is Ephraem's view that God has established the bishop as the mind (re‘yānâ) of the church. He wrote very explicitly about Abraham, the bishop of Nisibis (361 – 363), that God had "undertaken to set him up as the mind in the midst of the great body of the church. His members surround him to purchase life from him, doctrine [yulpānâ], the new bread." [57] As a matter of fact, says Ephraem of this same Bishop Abraham, "He stands as the intermediary [meṣ‘āyâ] between God and humankind." [58] And it is clear that to teach is one of the bishop's primary functions in the church.

The bishop achieves his authority in the church, according to Ephraem, through the ritual laying on of hands in the apostolic succession. This concept was the linchpin of episcopal legitimacy for Ephraem, and he makes much of it in his *Hymns against Heresies*, claiming at one point that the tradition of the laying on of hands comes down in orderly succession (ṭûkāsâ) from God himself to Moses, through John the Baptist to Jesus, who "gave it to his apostles, and its tradition [yûbālāh] is within our church." [59]

The trouble with the heretics, even heretical bishops who had once received the imposition of hands in the true apostolic succession, some of whom had also subscribed to the council of Nicea, [60] says Ephraem, is that they have mixed poison with their doctrines. The poison may be in

55. Edmund Beck, *Des heiligen Ephraem des Syrers Sermones III* (*CSCO*, vols. 320 and 321; Louvain, 1972), vol. 320, p. 22 (ll. 513ff.).

56. Cf. Ortiz de Urbina, n. 14 above, and J. Molitor, "Die kirchlichen Aemter und Stände in der Paulusexegese des hl. Ephräm," in *Die Kirche und ihre Aemter und Stände: Festgabe Kardinal Frings* (Köln, 1960), pp. 379ff.

57. Beck, *Carmina Nisibena I*, op. cit., vol. 218, p. 46.

58. Ibid., p. 50.

59. Beck, *Contra Haereses*, op. cit., vol. 169, p. 84.

60. Ibid., p. 85.

the form of the dialectical inquiry of philosophy, noncanonical revelations and Acts of Apostles, or other such sources which are foreign to the Bible,[61] or it may be a matter of relying on only one portion of the Bible, or on one biblical theme.[62] Ephraem points out that the telltale sign of such heresy is that heretical groups generally go under the names of the teachers whose unique views they have adopted, as disciples of human masters, rather than under the name of Christ.[63] The true and only measure of right teaching for Ephraem is the Bible, with both testaments. There is no higher *magisterium* which he acknowledges, and by it even bishops are judged. As he says, "the true church . . . fits the whole of both testaments,"[64] and finally:

> Just as the body of the alphabet
>   is complete in its members,
> And there is no character to take away,
>   and none other to add.
> So also is the truth, which is written
>   in the holy Gospel,
>   in the characters of the alphabet,
> The complete measure, which is not susceptible
>   to less or more.[65]

According to Ephraem, then, the bishops are the teachers and the authorities in the church, and the emperors are its protectors. His vision is clearly reflected in a prayer he utters as the final strophe of the last hymn in his *Hymns of Faith*, almost all of which were composed to combat Arian ideas: "May our Lord give peace to both priests and kings. And in one and the same church may the priests pray for their kings, and may the kings have pity on their own cities; and may the inner peace that is in You, be for us an outer wall."[66]

The Arian controversy which pestered the church in one form or another throughout Ephraem's lifetime, was a major factor among the

61. Ibid., p. 85.
62. Ibid., pp. 9 and 10.
63. Ibid., pp. 79–80, 87–89. Ephraem had a problem in this matter of names. Some in Edessa called his own group "Palūṭians," because of their adherence to the community to which Bishop Palūṭ had belonged in earlier times. Ephraem disowned the name in forceful tones: "Let the ban be on anyone who is called by the name of Palūṭ, and not by the name of Christ." Ibid., p. 79. Cf. the discussion in the last section of this article.
64. Beck, *Contra Haereses* op. cit., vol. 169, p. 9.
65. Ibid., p. 78.
66. Beck, *Hymnen de Fide*, op. cit., vol. 154, p. 271.

circumstances in which the deacon of Edessa formulated his concept of the church of the empire. Accordingly, one must briefly review his reaction to this intellectual crisis as an important element in the context within which he enunciated his distinctive ecclesiological ideas. Contrary to what Walter Bauer thought, it is now clear that not only was Ephraem concerned to combat Marcionites, Manichaeans, and the followers of Bar Dayṣān,[67] but the Arians too were influential adversaries, who turned his attention precisely in the direction of concern for the faith of the church of the empire.

C. The Arians

Ephraem obviously knew about the Arians throughout his ministry. The first bishop whom he served, James of Nisibis, had attended the council of Nicea and subscribed to its decision. There is even a legend in the Syriac *Vita* that the bishop took Ephraem with him to the council. While this was probably not the case,[68] Ephraem certainly would have known from the beginning who were the adversaries whose teaching was condemned there, although in Nisibis their influence does not appear to have been overpowering. He mentions Arius, the Arians, or the Aëtians some half dozen times in two of his *Hymns against Heresies* (nos. 22 and 24), a work of his Nisibene period, composed, therefore, before the year 363. He calls Arius a heretic "of our own day,"[69] and says of the Arians and the Aëtians together that their trouble is that "they had become too captious."[70] But in the other four places in these two hymns he merely mentions their names.[71] It is quite clear that in the fifty-six *Hymns against Heresies*, the Arians were but a minor concern for Ephraem. He named them along with the Paulinians, the Sabellians, the Photinians, the Borborians, the Cathars, the Audians, and the Mesallians, for completeness' sake, in hymns in which the major purpose was to press the point that true Christians carry only the name of Christ, and not the name of any earthly teacher. From this point of view, in the *Hymns against Heresies*, the teachings of the Marcionites, the Manichaeans, and the followers of Bar Dayṣān appear to have posed the major intellectual

67. Cf. Walter Bauer, *Orthodoxy and Heresy in Earliest Christianity* (English trans., R. A. Kraft and G. Krodel, eds.; Philadelphia, 1971), p. 25.
68. Cf. Murray, *Symbols*, p. 30.
69. Beck, *Contra Haereses*, op. cit., vol. 269, p. 96.
70. Ibid., p. 79.
71. Ibid., pp. 84, 94, 95, 97.

and religious challenge in the Nisibis prior to the cession of the city to the Persians in 363. And the challenge continued thereafter in the Syriac-speaking world, for Ephraem vigorously attacked the three groups not only in these hymns of popular instruction, but also in a set of more scholarly and academic discourses, now called simply his *Prose Refutations*,[72] which he probably wrote later on in Edessa. Mānī, Marcion, and Bar Dayṣān had strong native ties to the Syrian world, and throughout his ministry Ephraem was engaged in one way or another in combatting their doctrines. Arius, Aëtius, and their followers and sympathizers, on the other hand, had their roots in the Greek-speaking cities to the west, and there in episcopal and imperial circles, a circumstance which increasingly alarmed Ephraem.[73]

Unlike the Manichaeans, who espoused a basically dualistic philosophy with Persian roots, or the Marcionites, who had jettisoned the whole Old Testament at the prompting of certain fairly vague Gnostic convictions, or even the followers of Bar Dayṣān, who were clearly motivated by nonscriptural, intellectual ideas which Ephraem always said were basically pagan, the Arians were a group clearly within the mainline Christian fold, and there they were causing strife (*ḥeryānâ*), in Ephraem's view due to the captiousness of which he had complained in his *Hymns against Heresies*.[74] Already in his *Homilies on Faith*, like the *Hymns against Heresies* a product of his Nisibene period,[75] Ephraem took note of this novel situation. He wrote, "While the outsiders [i.e., the Marcionites, the Manichaeans, and the followers of Bar Dayṣān] were not able to vanquish the victorious party, the party that had triumphed is being vanquished because it has fallen into battle with itself."[76]

Although Ephraem does not explicitly name the Arians in his *Homilies on Faith* it is clear from his customary anti-Arian vocabulary that he has them in mind when he attacks the group of those whom he presents as thinking that they can encompass the Godhead with their own methods of intellectual inquiry. This is to anticipate the charge he will level

---

72. Cf. C. W. Mitchell, A. A. Bevan, F. C. Burkitt, *S. Ephraim's Prose Refutations of Mani, Marcion and Bardaisan* (2 vols.; London, 1912 and 1921).

73. Cf. the account of encyclicals and councils, and countercouncils, especially in Antioch, in Kopecek, op. cit., n. 52 above, esp. vol. I.

74. Cf. no. 70 above.

75. Cf. Edmund Beck, *Ephraems Reden über den Glauben* (Studia Anselmiana, 33; Rome, 1953), p. 112.

76. Edmund Beck, *Des heiligen Ephraem des Syrers Sermones de Fide* (CSCO, vols. 212 and 213; Louvain, 1961), vol. 212, p. 19.

against the Arians with even greater force later on in his Edessan period. In the *Homilies on Faith*, he says to the adversaries, about the divine Son, "The inquirer is greater than that which can be subjected to inquiry. You call Him creator; will you then subject Him to inquiry like a creature?" [77] To do so, Ephraem goes on to say, is to debase the Son: "Through inquiry, you have belittled the Firstborn, who is greater than all." [78]

The root of the problem according to Ephraem is that the adepts of intellectual inquiry, or the dialecticians as one might call them, have abandoned the teaching of the scriptures, which for Ephraem, one will remember, is the sole reliable source of information about God. He writes about it in the *Homilies on Faith*, citing Peter's confession about Jesus in Matthew 16:16:

> Vainglory strives after the novel.
> It will not repeat what belongs to yesterday.
> The proud person considers it to be a degradation,
> To repeat the truth as it stands written.
> Seeking after hidden mysteries,
> He throws away the truth of the obvious.
> Simon gave you an image; imitate it.
> He was both Fisher and Image-maker.
> He has painted the model for the Churches.
> Everyone should copy his image on his own heart.
> Let each of us say of the Son,
> "You are the Son of the Living God." [79]

It is quite clear that Ephraem thought that proper faith required assenting to what is in the scriptures, and that one should not inquire further, using dialectical or rhetorical methods of analysis. He also makes this position clear in the *Homilies on Faith*: "If you ask about the existence of the Son, you may become acquainted with it in an instant. But if you ask about the 'how,' the question must wait until He comes." [80]

Furthermore, Ephraem makes it perfectly clear that for him vain intellectual inquiry is the peculiar fault of the educated classes, and specifically, as he will pointedly say when he takes up the question again

77. Ibid., p. 14.
78. Ibid., p. 15.
79. Ibid., pp. 9 and 10. The epithets 'fisher,' and 'image-maker,' turn on wordplay in Syriac, involving the roots *ṣ-w-d* and *ṣ-w-r*.
80. Beck, *Sermones de Fide*, op. cit., vol. 212, p. 48.

in Edessa, it is the fault of those who have tasted "the poisonous wisdom of the Greeks."[81] In his *Homilies on Faith*, however, he settles for such statements as this one: "Finding the Son belongs to the rude, searching for him to the educated."[82]

Finally, one must take notice of the fact that while he was still in Nisibis, Ephraem drew a connection between what was happening within the church with the Arian controversy, and what was happening in the civil life of the empire. Already in the *Homilies on Faith* he says:

> While the priests are fallen into strife over words,
> > the kings are set in battle.
> The external battle does not subside,
> > while the internal battle wages.
> One shepherd fights with another,
> > and the prelate with his brother in office.[83]

The easiest construction to put upon these remarks is that on the one hand Ephraem is referring to the Arian policies carried out among some bishops under Constantius, and on the other hand he is blaming this ecclesiastical strife for the rift between Constantius and Constans, and eventually even Julian's apostasy,[84] soon to erupt into the disastrous events which brought Ephraem to Edessa, to start his life anew.

Ephraem came into a profound conflict with the ideas of the Arians when he arrived in Edessa after the year 363, and became engaged there in the activities of the institution which would become the famous "School of the Persians." He was a partisan of the bishops of Edessa and Ḥarrān, Barsai and Vitus, both of whom in due course were troubled by the campaign of the emperor Valens and his court theologians to put anti-Nicene bishops in all of the important sees.[85] As a reaction to this state of affairs, and to Arian ideas of all colors, Ephraem composed his *Hymns on Faith*, a collection of eighty-seven hymns in all, in which, as in the earlier *Homilies on Faith*, he never once actually names the Arians, but

81. Beck, *Hymni de Fide*, op. cit., vol. 154, p. 7.

82. Beck, *Sermones de Fide*, op. cit., vol. 212, p. 43.

83. Ibid., p. 42.

84. Beck suggested the years 357/358 as a likely date for Ephraem's composition of the *Sermones de Fide*, citing changes in the religious policy under Constantius. Cf. Beck, *Ephraems Reden . . .*, p. 112. Cf. also Kopecek, op. cit., n. 52 above.

85. Ephraem alludes to these conflicts in his *Carmina Nisibena I*, op. cit., vol. 218, hymns 26 to 34, pp. 59–83. Cf. esp. Beck's notes to his German version, vol. 219, pp. 74–103.

in all of which he contends against Arian doctrines, as Dom Edmund Beck has shown in some detail.[86] In these hymns one finds the ultimate development of Ephraem's reaction to the Arian challenge, and a testimony to the issues that concerned him during the last decade of his life.

In the first place, as mentioned above, Ephraem is convinced that the emperor is personally innocent in the campaign to replace the Nicene bishops.[87] Rather, as he says in one place, the strife caused by churchmen has come to such a point that, with knife in hand, "women fall upon women, men upon their companions, and priests upon kings."[88] In this scenario the emperor almost appears as the ultimate victim in the affair, and Ephraem makes it clear in the very last two stanzas of this whole collection of poems that such is indeed his opinion. He wrote: "The priesthood, instead of praying for the kingdom, that battles might cease among humankind, has instructed them in a perverse warfare, which the kings have begun to wage with their own cities."[89]

There could hardly be a more explicit statement than this one on Ephraem's part in assigning blame for the emperor's ecclesiastical policies. And in the second place it is clear that according to Ephraem the basic mistake which the adversary bishops have made is to depart from the teaching of the scriptures, to enforce the doctrine of dialecticians, rather than simply to adhere to the whole Bible, in the peace and communion of all bishops. This was the conclusion he had reached already in his *Hymns against Heresies*, and in the *Homilies on Faith*, as mentioned above. Now, in his *Hymns on Faith*, Ephraem put a finer point on his anti-Arianism, rejecting the term 'creature' as a name suitable for the son of God: "It is insolence to call you by a name that is foreign to the one by which your father called you, who called you only 'my son,' at the Jordan river."[90]

At numerous places in the *Hymns on Faith* Ephraem makes it clear that for him the Bible is the only trustworthy teacher about God. Typical of his thought is the further remark he makes about names or terms to be applied to God's son: "I have left behind those that are not scriptural, and

86. Cf. Edmund Beck, *Die Theologie des hl. Ephraem in seinen Hymnen über den Glauben*, esp. pp. 62–80.
87. Cf. no. 48 above.
88. Beck, *Hymni de fide*, op. cit., vol. 154, p. 165.
89. Ibid., p. 271.
90. Ibid., p. 159.

have gone with ones that are scriptural, lest on account of the nonscriptural ones I should bring to nought the scriptural ones."[91] The target of
these remarks is the names 'creature,' or 'work,' which full-fledged
Arians, according to Ephraem, applied to the only begotten Son on the
basis of Proverbs 8:22: "The Lord created me, the first of his creatures."
Ephraem spends considerable time refuting the Arian interpretation of
this passage, especially in Hymn 53. The gist of his explanation is that
in seizing upon this single passage out of the whole scriptures the Arians
are guilty not only of missing the point here, but of doing violence to the
whole Bible as the rule of faith. On the one hand, says Ephraem,
Solomon is here referring to the Son's humanity. On the other hand,
everywhere else in the scripture the proper name 'Son' is used for the
second person of the Trinity.[92]

The Arians also commonly employed another proof-text from the
scriptures in defense of their position, viz., Mark 13:32: "As for the day
or hour, no one knows it, neither the angels of heaven, nor the Son; no
one but the Father." Ephraem addressed three hymns, 77, 78, and 79,
against their interpretation of this passage. The gist of his argument
once again is that the Arians have taken this passage in isolation from
other passages which stress the Son's divinity, and once again they have
confused what is said of the Son's humanity with what is said of His
divinity.[93]

According to Ephraem what led the Arians to use nonscriptural
names for the Son of God, and to search the scriptures for passages which
only at first sight seem to support their contentions, was their reliance on
human, academic methods of inquiry rather than accepting on faith the
revealed language of the scriptures. As we have seen, the academic
methods of inquiry which he had in mind are what he calls in one place
"the poisonous wisdom of the Greeks."[94] In another place he celebrates
the apostle Paul's triumph over the logic-chopping Greeks, in contrast
to the behavior of the insolent dialecticians (dārôšê) of Ephraem's own day
whose stock in trade, according to him, the Greek learning had become:
"The apostle was more subtle than these insolent men. He went right

91. Ibid., p. 200.

92. Cf. the hymn, ibid., pp. 164–167, and Beck's analysis of it in *Theologie . . . in seinen
Hymnen über den Glauben*, pp. 70–73.

93. Cf. the hymns, Beck, *Hymni de fide*, op. cit., vol. 154, pp. 234–245; and Beck's
commentary in *Theologie . . . in seinen Hymnen über den Glauben*, pp. 73–80.

94. Beck, *Hymni de Fide*, op. cit., vol. 154, p. 7.

into the very capital city of the Greeks. He spoke their own [language] to them to show them he knew how to. And when it was vanquished, he discarded their gear." [95]

A major purpose of the *Hymns on Faith*, as is evidenced by the hundreds of lines devoted to the effort, was to cultivate among the faithful a profound distaste for dialectics in religion, or indeed for any sort of philosophical inquiry governed by academic logic rather than by a fundamental faith in the scriptures. The simplest way to express Ephraem's attitude on this theme is to quote a stanza of his poetry in which almost every one of the detestable academic activities is mentioned, and contrasted with a laudable act of faith. In this instance Ephraem chooses as an example the act of faith exercised by the Magi, who on the Bible's account traveled a long distance to worship Christ, the newborn king. Ephraem taught his people to sing in the following way:

> Come, let us marvel at the men
> Who saw the king here below.
> They did not conduct an investigation [ᶜaqqebw],
> Nor did they engage in research [bᶜaw].
> No one of them opened a debate [draš].
> There shone there in silence,
> A pure act of faith.
> When he was here below, the Magi
> Did not venture to examine him [bṣâ ûhy].
> How can we then venture to examine him,
> Now that he has gone up and taken his seat,
> At the right hand on high? [96]

Most of Ephraem's negative words are here: 'investigation' (ᶜuqqābâ), 'research' (bᶜātâ), 'disputation' (drāšâ), 'examination' (bṣātâ). [97] He misses only one in this passage, which he uses with some regularity in the same context elsewhere, and that one is the word for 'rationalization' (hemsâ), which he generally uses in a verbal form in the *Hymns on Faith*, as in this line of prayer to the divine son: "Your birth is sealed within silence. What mouth would dare to rationalize it?" [98] All of these terms consti-

---

95. Ibid., p. 151.

96. Ibid., p. 33.

97. Cf. the virtually complete list of these words, along with their opposites, as they appear in the *Hymns on Faith*, in T. Jansma, "Narsai and Ephraem," *Parole de l'Orient* 1 (1970), pp. 60–66.

98. Beck, *Hymni de Fide*, op. cit., vol. 154, p. 49.

tute a *Wortfeld* of insolence as far as Ephraem is concerned. They define
the activities of academic philosophers or sophists, whose speech is
governed by schoolroom logic. Ephraem is not very impressed with
what they have to say, even about things which are the proper subject
matter of their inquiries. For example, he makes fun of the various
theories which the scholars propose about the soul, even about whether
or not it exists.[99]

In regard to God, Ephraem maintains, human speech is totally inadequate, however strictly it may be governed by logic. He says,

> The mighty nature is never spoken by any mouth.
> The mouth that wants to speak about what is ineffable
> Reduces to paltriness the greatness
> For which it is unfit.[100]

The problem is that God is beyond the reach of human thought. On this
theme Ephraem says:

> Thought is easier for us
> Than to speak a word.
> Thinking is what is capable
> Of reaching everywhere.
> When it comes to travel
> In Your direction, to search You out,
> Its path disappears in front of it.
> It is confused, forestalled.
> If thinking is thus overcome,
> How much more so speech,
> Whose path is an abode of contention?[101]

But God has not left his creatures without any way to approach Him.
According to their stations, all creatures, even the angels, learn about
God "by means of the symboling [*remzâ*] of the Spirit."[102] In the scriptures, and in nature itself according to Ephraem, God's Spirit has placed
the symbolic tokens, the mysteries (*râzê*) which disclose a glimpse of His
economy of salvation. "Your symbolic mysteries [*râzê*] are everywhere,"[103] says Ephraem in prayer to God. The only adequate response,

99. Ibid., pp. 3–4.
100. Ibid., p. 5.
101. Ibid., p. 13.
102. Ibid., p. 17.
103. Ibid., p. 12.

suitable to the powers of a human being, is then to attend to these mystic tokens of the one who is "imaged in likenesses, so that according to our own power we may come to learn of Him."[104] And such a response can only be silence (šetqâ) as far as inquiry and scrutiny are concerned, but it is a silence in which poetry and song should sing God's praises in terms of the mysterious symbols He has revealed, particularly in the scriptures.

For Ephraem then, the challenge of the Arians is met, not by conversation with them on their own terms, but by opposing the very idiom in which they raise their questions. For Ephraem it almost seems that the madrāšâ (or the metrical mêmrâ) is the only genre of human speech that is suitable to the issue of God-talk. One recalls that in the Syriac tradition the madrāšâ is hymnic poetry of an essentially exegetical character. It sings of the symbols, types, antitypes, and images which come from the scriptures, or from the natural world of creation. Its proper Sitz im Leben is the community at worship, the liturgy. In this idiom alone, utilizing scriptural language, is Ephraem willing to speak of the generation of the Son from the Father, and of how one might characterize the birth of God.

In the Hymns on Faith Ephraem puts forward in place of the philosophical discussion of the act of generation and its implications the ancient symbol of the sun, its rays, and its heat, as an image in which one may contemplate the wonder of the truth which God has revealed in the scriptures, that He is Father, Son, and Spirit. Throughout the collection of hymns, but especially in hymns 40, 73, and 74, he refines and fine-tunes this traditional image that had been, sometimes in slightly different form, used by the early Christian apologists as a way of explaining that triunity is not simply a contradiction in terms.[105] These are the only terms in which Ephraem is willing to address himself to the issues raised by the Arians. Earlier, as has been said, he chided them for forming a denomination, for misleading the emperors, for abandoning the whole program of the scriptures. When in Edessa he is forced to come to the point of it all, he responds with biblical exegesis and metaphor, but then only in poetry and song. It is not surprising finally, that it is at the end of his Hymns on Faith that one finds Ephraem's five hymns on the pearl, by his day already the favorite image of divine things for Syriac poets.[106]

---

104. Ibid., p. 25.
105. Cf. the study of Ephraem's deployment of this image in Edmund Beck, *Ephräms Trinitätslehre in Bild von Sonne/Feuer, Licht und Wärme* (CSCO, vol. 425; Louvain, 1981).
106. Beck, *Hymni De Fide*, op. cit., vol. 154, pp. 248–262.

They summarize his whole point of view. It is a classic instance in which the medium is most certainly the message.

Ephraem's confrontation with the Arians concerned much more than doctrine. In fact, one could almost say that it had little or nothing to do with doctrine. At the root of his concern was a vision of the church, and it came to expression in his view of the sort of public discourse that is legitimate in it. As he said over and over again in his *Hymns on Faith*, the act of faith in the revealed scripture, the whole Bible, constitutes the proper Christian response to God, to be celebrated in poetry and song, and worded in biblical terms. All other forms of discourse, and in particular the studied discourse of academic philosophers, have no place in the church.

When Ephraem contended with Marcionites, Manichaeans, or the followers of Bar Dayṣān, he was, in a certain sense, struggling with non-Christians for the allegiance of the minds of the Syriac-speaking people of Nisibis and Edessa. When he contended with Arians, he was struggling with Christians, who accepted the same Bible as he did and the same episcopal structure as he did, and who were devoted to the same "Church of the Empire" as was Ephraem himself. The struggle was over the public discourse of the church. Ephraem would allow only the kaleidoscopic language of biblical typology, which spilled over into metaphors and symbols borrowed from the natural order, but which never went beyond the contemplative, liturgical medium of poetry and song. Even the prose of his biblical commentaries served mainly to highlight the symbols and typologies embedded in the biblical narrative, and at the beginning of his commentary on Genesis he said that in this work he was merely "presenting in brief what we have presented at length in *mêmrê* and *madrāšê*." [107] To admit the language of the academy was to admit another measure of truth, and to attempt to state Christian convictions in nonscriptural, academic terms was to espouse non-Christian doctrines. For Ephraem, the Arians were the prime example of those who had given in to this temptation.

In the fourth century Ephraem was the casebook example of a conservative Christian who in a certain sense refused to accept modernity. The Greek education which Theodoret and Sozomen said he lacked was the symbol of the modernity he spurned. It was a question not of Greek

107. R.-M. Tonneau, *Sancti Ephraem Syri in Genesim et in Exodum* (*CSCO*, vols. 152 and 153; Louvain, 1955), vol. 152, p. 3.

language, but of inquiry measured by the rules of Greek speech, i.e., by academic logic, rather than by the whole imagistic world of biblical typology. After all, this rich world of symbolism was sung in Greek as well as in Syriac. One need only think of Melito of Sardis, or later of Romanos the Melode, or even of Greek Ephraem, so popular according to Sozomen. Even Arius found it useful to commend his peculiar views in a metrical composition. [108]

Ephraem was not unique because he wrote hymns, and preached in metrical homilies. His unique view was that poetry steeped in biblical typology is the only medium in which one may legitimately talk about God. He is pushed to this rather extreme view by his encounter with the Arians. He expressed it most insistently in his *Hymns on Faith*, which were, perhaps, among the last compositions to leave his hand. They afford us now a view into an earlier Christian world, which somehow knew that true religion could never be wholly rational by human standards. As Ephraem put it in prayer:

> My mouth is not adequate to You
>   and I rejoice in my inadequacy.
> For if somehow I should be adequate,
>   it would be a double-edged blasphemy.
> Human nature would be more exalted than God.
> This is too stupid! [109]

III

Everything studied thus far in Ephraem's metrical and midrashic compositions underlines the attention he paid to the life of the 'Great Church.' What is known of his biography puts an accent on his episcopal connections. More and more studies of his writings reveal his awareness of the intellectual developments in the Greek-speaking parts of the empire. He chose to live the latter part of his life under the Roman emperors, rather than under the great kings of Persia, as his move to Edessa after 363 testifies. Now, the survey of his works summarized above clearly demonstrates Ephraem's conviction that ideally there

---

108. Cf. G. C. Stead, "The Thalia of Arius and the Testimony of Athanasius," *The Journal Of Theological Studies* 29 (1978), pp. 20–52. The author provides references to earlier studies.

109. Beck, *Hymni De Fide*, op. cit., vol. 154, p. 55.

should be a close cooperation between the emperor and the bishops in the church, united in the confession of the faith of Nicea. Ephraem's pro-longed rebuttal of Arian ideas, especially in his *Hymns on Faith*, puts this conviction into high relief. And it is further supported both by the notice taken of him by such Greek writers as Epiphanius, Theodoret, and Sozomen, as well as by the popularity which his own compositions achieved in Greek translation. Therefore, it makes no sense at all to continue to think of Ephraem as a representative of some putative native church of Syria, which eschewed all ties with the Greek-speaking world. Rather, it can even be shown that Ephraem made an effort to translate certain exegetical formulae first elaborated in Greek, into the idiomatic requirements of the Syriac language, with its own preferred modes of religious discourse. It is no wonder, then, given all of this evidence of mutual concern, that as early as the first half of the fifth century, Sozomen was already positing a connection between Ephraem and Basil the Great.[110]

Ephraem was not alone in the Syriac-speaking world of the fourth century in promoting an almost Eusebian doctrine of the church of the empire. The 'Persian sage,' Aphrahat, Cyrillona, and later even Marûthâ of Maipherkaṭ can all be cited to support the idea that the church was meant to live under the protection of the kings of Rome until the second coming of Christ, an idea, characteristically enough for Syrian scholars, rooted ultimately in the exegesis of Daniel, chapters 7 and 8.[111] The fact that Christians in Persia later neglected the Roman theme, and assured the Persian kings of their loyalty, even reaching a certain accommodation with them,[112] in no way militates against the fact that in the fourth century, and even in the Syriac-speaking world, the idea of a Christian church, living in a Christian, Roman empire, awaiting the Second Coming of Christ, was an idea whose time had come. It probably played no small role in Ephraem's own move from Persian Nisibis to Roman Edessa after 363, and it is one more reason not to lose sight of the deacon of Edessa's persistence in communion with the Greek-speaking churches of the West, and his attention to their doctrine.

110. Cf. above, nn. 18 and 19.

111. Cf. Murray, *Symbols*, pp. 111–113, 241–246; and Francisco Javier Martinez, "Between Persia and Rome: Early Testimonies to the Support of the Roman Empire in Aphrahat and Ephrem," to appear.

112. Cf. S. P. Brock, "Christians in the Sasanian Empire: A Case of Divided Loyalties," in S. Mews, ed., *Religion and National Identity* (Studies in Church History, 18; Oxford, 1982), pp. 1–19.

Ephraem's ideas about the organization of the church in the empire, as schematic as they are in our reconstruction, since they are mined from hymns and poems, must be taken together with what one knows of other movements along the same lines in Edessa in the fourth century. In particular one must consider the *Doctrina Addai*, a product of the late fourth century in its present form.[113] Two pertinent issues in the *Doctrina* present themselves for attention here, namely, what one might call the Roman connection, and the account of the ordination of Palūt. But first one must briefly recall the general contents of the *Doctrina*.

It is well known that the *Doctrina* contains the story of the communication between Jesus and one of the kings Abgar of Edessa, and in addition, that it gives an account of the portrait of Jesus painted by Abgar's archivist, Ḥannān. Portions of this story appear in many early Christian sources, the earliest of them all being in chapter 13, Book 1, of Eusebius' *Ecclesiastical History*, where the author says, in Kirsopp Lake's translation, that there is "documentary evidence of these things taken from the archives at Edessa."[114] And further, regarding the correspondence between Abgar and Jesus which Eusebius quotes, he first says, "there is nothing equal to hearing the letters themselves, which we have extracted from the archives, and when translated from the Syriac they are verbally as follows."[115] Here Eusebius was obviously anxious to document the story. And even if his testimony turns out to be highly questionable, as far as it concerns the documentation for the establishment of the Church in Edessa, as Bauer has argued, the fact remains that in Edessa in the first part of the fourth century, there were people in the ecclesiastical establishment there who were already anxious to align themselves with the Great Church. To this much both Eusebius, and later the *Doctrina*, testify.[116]

Furthermore, the *Doctrina* in the form in which it has come down to us from the late fourth century has a much broader agenda than merely the story of the Abgar/Jesus correspondence. From there the author goes on to report three speeches delivered by the apostle Addai in Edessa,

113. Cf. I. Ortiz de Urbina, *Patrologia Syriaca*, p. 44. Texts and English translations are available in G. Phillips, *The Doctrine of Addai, the Apostle* (London, 1876), and, with the same text along with some variants, but a new English translation, in George Howard, *The Teaching of Addai* (Chico, Calif., 1981).

114. Kirsopp Lake, *Eusebius, The Ecclesiastical History* (2 vols.; Cambridge, Mass., 1926), vol. I, p. 87.

115. Ibid.

116. Cf. Bauer, op. cit., pp. 33–43.

when he was sent there after Jesus' ascension. They are: the story of Protonikē, the wife of Claudius Caesar, and of her finding of the true cross in Jerusalem; an apostolic kerygma; and a final testament to the Christians of Edessa, notable for its warnings against Jews, pagans, and dialectical inquiry into the teachings of the scriptures. In addition, the *Doctrina* contains an exchange of letters between Abgar and the emperor Tiberius, largely dealing with the desirability, in Abgar's view, of punishing the Jews for killing Christ.[117]

One recognizes immediately that among these themes are the characteristic concerns of the persons who were working to strengthen the "Church of the Empire." The first of them is the Roman connection itself, a point which Eusebius had been anxious to make in referring to Tiberius, in the fifteenth year of whose reign Jesus' public ministry began (Lk. 3:1), and whom Eusebius, quoting Tertullian, pictured as the first imperial protector of the church.[118] As for the story of Protonikē, who is portrayed as a proto–St. Helena in the *Doctrina*, it is not difficult to observe the Constantinian parallel that is here being read back into the earlier imperial court.[119] And even the warning against Jews captures a favorite Eusebian theme.[120]

Finally, running through the *Doctrina* at regular intervals are the names of Aggai, Palūṭ, Abšelāmâ, and Barsamyâ, who, according to the author, formed the first Christian hierarchy in Edessa after Addai himself. According to the *Doctrina*, before he died, Addai "called Aggai before all the congregation of the church, brought him near, and appointed him leader and ruler in his place. Palūṭ, who was a deacon, he appointed as presbyter, and Abshelāmâ, who was a scribe, he appointed as deacon."[121] At the very end of the *Doctrina* one finds the story about how Palūṭ became bishop of Edessa. The author explains that Aggai died as a result of the breaking of his legs on the order of one of the deceased Abgar's rebellious sons, and he goes on to say about Aggai:

117. Cf. Howard, op. cit., pp. 21–35, 39–63, 75–81, 83–97.

118. Cf. K. Lake, op. cit., vol. I, pp. 74–76 (1.10), 111–113 (2.2).

119. The story of Protonikē appears only in eastern sources, and in all probability is Edessan in origin. For orientation, cf. H. Leclercq, "Croix (Invention et Exaltation de la vraie)," in *DACL*, vol. 3, part 2, cols. 3131–3139. The story had a long life in Syriac sources. It appears in a sermon on the cross, integrated with the story of St. Helena, by Moshe bar Kēphâ, a Jacobite bishop of the late ninth century. Cf. Paris Syriac MSS 206 and 207.

120. Cf. R. M. Grant, *Eusebius as Church Historian* (Oxford, 1980), pp. 97–113.

121. Howard, op. cit., p. 81.

Because he died speedily and rapidly at the breaking of his legs he was unable to lay his hand upon Palūṭ. Palūṭ himself went to Antioch and received ordination to the priesthood from Serapion, Bishop of Antioch. Serapion himself, Bishop of Antioch, had also received ordination from Zephyrinus, Bishop of the city of Rome from the succession of ordination to the priesthood of Simon Peter who received it from our Lord, and who had been Bishop there in Rome twenty-five years in the days of Caesar who reigned there thirteen years.[122]

The historically attentive reader will notice immediately that something is wrong here, since Serapion was bishop in Antioch from 198/199 to 211/212, and Zephyrinus, the pope, reigned from ca. 198 until he died in the year 217. Here is not the place to study the historical question, which is a complex issue in its own right.[123] What is immediately clear in the quotation for the present purpose, however, is a concern for Palūṭ's relationship to the Great Church, the legitimacy of his ordination, and his position in the tradition of the laying on of hands, which, as one will remember, was a concern of Ephraem's with regard to bishops.

As mentioned above, Ephraem himself had an occasion to refer to Palūṭ in his *Hymns against Heresies*, written, one will remember, during his Nisibene period. It is clear from what he wrote that he had a definite position to espouse, in a church which was obviously still discussing the matter. Speaking of his adversaries, and their lack of convincing arguments, Ephraem wrote:

> See, their hands have slipped [*plaṭ*] off altogether,
> And there is no handle to grasp.
> They turn around and call us Palūṭians.
> But we have slipped [*plaṭn*] away from this
> and have rejected it.
> Let the ban be on anyone
> Who is called by the name of Palūṭ,
> And not by the name of Christ.
> The crucible of the ban has
> exposed those
> Who do not want to impose the ban.[124]

122. Ibid., p. 105.
123. Cf. Bauer, op. cit., pp. 17–22, and Segal, op. cit., pp. 62–87.
124. Beck, *Contra Haereses*, op. cit., vol. 169, p. 79. Cf. 1 Cor. 1:12 and 13.

From these last words one could take it that there were those in Ephraem's own party who gladly carried the name of Palūṭ, and who were reluctant to discontinue the practice. So Ephraem went on to explain:

> Nor did Palūṭ want
> People to be called by his name.
> If he were still alive, with every ban
> He would be issuing bans for this—
> He, who was a disciple of the
> Apostle who put on suffering, and
> was embittered
> About the Corinthians who abandoned
> The name of Christ and were called
> By the names of human beings. [125]

Ephraem was clearly in the camp of the author of the *Doctrina Addai* in its late fourth-century form. From this observation, and from all that has gone before, it seems reasonable to conclude that, far from being the last lonely Syrian to escape substantial influence from the Greek-speaking world of the Roman empire, as he is often portrayed, Ephraem the Syrian, especially in his Edessene period, when the Arians came to be among his principal adversaries, was in fact one of the most insistent champions of full membership in the emperor's church. It was due to his own success that after his time, the Syriac language itself, at least in the religious texts which are almost our sole witnesses for it, became more and more involved with Greek. [126]

125. Ibid., pp. 79 and 80.
126. Cf. Sebastian Brock's study of this development in his "From Antagonism to Assimilation . . .," art. cit., n. 31 above.

THOMAS HALTON

The Kairos of the Mass and the Deacon
in John Chrysostom

In *Homily 11 on 1 Timothy* John Chrysostom insists that deacons should have the same qualities as bishops for their ministerial role. Chrysostom takes up the exegesis of 1 Timothy 3:8:[1]

"Likewise the deacons." That is, they should have the same qualities as bishops. And what are these qualities? To be blameless, sober, hospitable, patient, not brawlers, not covetous. And that this is what he means when he says "likewise" is evident from what he says in addition, "grave, not double-tongued," that is, not hollow or deceitful. For nothing so debases a man as deceit, nothing is so pernicious in the Church as insincerity. "Not given to much wine, not greedy of filthy lucre,[2] holding the mystery of faith in a pure conscience." Thus he explains what he means by "blameless." And here he requires, though in other words, that he be "not a novice". . . . For would it not be absurd that when a newly purchased slave is not entrusted with anything in a house, till he has by long trial given proof of his character, yet that one should enter into the Church of God from a state of heathenism and be at once placed in a position of preeminence? (*PG* 62:553; cf. *LNPF* 13:441)

---

1. For earlier exegesis of 1 Tm. 3:8–13; cf. Ignatius, *Phil* 5.2 (*SC* 10:210, n. 1).
2. On avarice in deacons cf. Shepherd of Hermas, *vis.* 26: "The stones with spots are the deacons who administered their office wickedly and robbed widows and orphans of their livelihood; who made profit for themselves out of the ministry they received to administer." See also Chrysostom, *hom. 23 in Rom.*, PG 60:616.

It should be recalled that Chrysostom was an ordained deacon[3] in Antioch from ca. 380 to 386, when he was ordained priest, and it is clear from elsewhere in his voluminous writings that he saw the deacon[4] as indeed placed in a position of preeminence and nowhere more so than in his ministry in the Eucharistic celebration. As Ignatius of Antioch had put it so well: "Those who are deacons of the mysteries of Jesus Christ must please all men in every way. For they are not ministers of food and drink but servants of the Church of God" (*Trall.* 2.3).

Jean Daniélou,[5] in a well-known essay on the Kairos of the Mass in John Chrysostom, pointed out that the kairos (= favorable occasion) of the Mass has three chief meanings:

(i) the Mass is an exceptional occasion for prayer because it is not just the private prayer of the individual but the prayer of the community;

(ii) the presence of the angels gives the prayer of the Mass a special solemnity;

(iii) the Eucharistic kairos is a privileged moment in which prayer has an especially good chance of being heard because it is the offering of the body of Christ. It is this real presence of Christ, more than the presence of angels, more than the act of community, that gives the Mass its particularly solemn character.

---

3. For other aspects of the diaconate in Chrysostom cf. J. Lecuyer, "Saint Jean Chrysostome et l'Ordre du Diaconat," in *Mélanges Liturgiques . . . B. Botte* (Louvain 1972), 295–310. See also J. Lecuyer, art. "Diaconat," *DS* 3:803–810, especially "Les Fonctions du Diacre." In this tribute to a Celtic scholar and deacon it is appropriate to quote the duties of a deacon as listed by Gilbert of Limerick, papal legate to Ireland, ca. 1100 A.D., in his *De statu Ecclesiae* (*PL* 159:999–1000): "*Diaconorum* est dicere: *Exeant qui non communicant*; et: *Humiliate vos ad benedictionem*; et: *Humiliate capita vestra Deo*; et: *Ite, missa est*; et: *Benedicamus Domino*; et Evangelium legere et pronuntiare, sacrificia super corporalia statuere, sacerdoti ministrare, paschalem cereum benedicere; et in absentia presbyteri baptizare, et horas celebrare, stolam etiam super sinistrum humerum ferre, et indui dalmatica in solemnibus, id est, tunica amplis manicis. In festivis autem Quadragesimae induuntur diaconus et subdiaconus casulis in tota missa, nisi cum legunt." Interestingly, Gilbert's name may have been *Gillaeaspuic*, "the servant of the bishop"; cf. J. F. Kenney, *The Sources of the Early History of Ireland: Ecclesiastical* (New York, 1929; repr. 1966), 763.

4. For the diaconate prior to Chrysostom cf. "Diakonia, 1," *Theologische Realenzyklopädie* 8:621–629, and bibliog., 642–644.

5. Jean Daniélou, "Der Kairos des Messe nach den Homilien des heiligen Johannes Chrysostomos über die Unbegreiflichkeit Gottes," in Franz X. Arnold und Balthaser Fischer, *Die Messe in der Glaubensverkündigung* (Freiburg, 1953), 71–78 (= Jean Chrysostome, *Sur l'Incompréhensibilité de Dieu* 1, *SC* 28bis [Paris, 1970], 51–61).

In this brief tribute to a deacon friend it may be of interest to see how closely the deacon is associated by Chrysostom with these three aspects of the Mass.

In the *De incomprehensibili Dei natura* we read: [6]

If you happen to be in the marketplace at that very moment [*kairon*], if you happen to be at home, if you happen to be in the midst of unavoidable business, should you not break through all your bonds with more violence than a caged lion and come to participate in the community supplication? . . . That is why at this moment [*kairon*] the deacon makes the possessed [*energoumenous*] stand, and orders them to bend their heads only so that they may make their supplications by their bodily postures. (*SC* 28bis:224; cf. *FOTC* 72:113, trans. P. W. Harkins)

In Chrysostom's *On the Obscurity of the Prophecies* we read:

When in the assembly you hear the deacon ordering you, saying: Let us pray for the bishop, and the presbytery, and for help, and that the word of truth may be properly spread, and for those present, and for those absent, you do not refuse to obey the injunctions, but join earnestly in the prayer, and you know the power of your assembled prayer. Those who have been initiated in the mysteries know what I mean, for this has not yet been entrusted to the catechumens. (*PG* 56:182)

And in *Homily 2 on 11 Corinthians* we learn about the special prayer for catechumens: [7]

Therefore church law enjoins that there be prayers for the catechumens as well as for the faithful, for when the deacon says, "Let us pray earnestly for the catechumens," he stirs up the whole assembly of the faithful to pray for them, although the catechumens are still outsiders. For they are not yet of the body of Christ, they have not yet partaken of the mysteries, but are still separated from the spiritual flock. . . . Therefore they are excluded while those awesome prayers are being offered. . . . For the words "let us pray" are addressed not to the priests alone, but also to those who make up the laity, for when he says, "let us stand in order," "let us pray," he exhorts everybody to pray. (*PG* 61:399)

The reinforcement of the prayers of the Mass by the presence of angels is clear from the following:

---

6. For the full text and commentary see F. van de Paverd, *Zur Geschichte der Messliturgie in Antiocheia und Konstantinopel gegen Ende des 4 Jahrhunderts*, Orientalia Christiana Analecta 187 (Roma, 1970), 171.

7. On the prayer for catechumens see van de Paverd, 140 f.

What kind of hope of salvation will you have, tell me, at that moment, beloved? It is not men only who cry out with that most awesome exclamation, but the angels also fall at the feet of the Lord, and the archangels beseech Him. They have this favorable moment [*kairon*] as their ally, the oblation as their help. (*SC* 28bis:224; cf. *FOTC* 72:113)

And commenting on the deacon's instruction *Stand up straight*[8] he explains:

Know next to whom you stand, in what company you are going to call on God—with the Cherubim. Consider those who make up the choir with you, and this will suffice to alert you that though you are a body, and tied to a body, you have been deemed worthy to hymn the praises of the common Lord of all in the company of incorporeal beings. . . . As if you were standing beside the very throne of glory, transported thither with the Seraphim, offer your all-holy hymn to the God of glory and magnificence. That is why we are bidden by the deacon to stand up straight at that moment [*kairon*]. To stand up straight means nothing else than to stand in a manner befitting a man who is standing in the presence of God with fear and trembling, with a vigilant and attentive soul. (*SC* 28bis:260–262; cf. *FOTC* 72:132)

The deacon's role in calling for silence is dwelt on in *Homily III on II Thessalonians*. Criticizing the attention-getting, dramatic entrances made to Church by the wealthy—predictably, wealthy women ("she considers not how she shall hear the oracles of God, but how she shall surpass all the other women by her expensive clothes")—but, no less, wealthy men ("surrounded by his slaves, who thinks he is conferring a favor on us, on the people, perhaps even on God, simply by coming into the house of God"), he proclaims:

They think that when they come in here they come into our presence . . . they do not realize that they have come into the presence of God, that it is He who is speaking to them. For when the lector stands up and says: "This is the Word of the Lord," and when the deacon stands and imposes silence on all, he does not do so to confer an honor on the lector, but on Him who speaks to all through him. . . . We are ministers, beloved. We speak, not our own words, but the words of God; letters coming from Heaven are daily read. (*Hom. III on II Thess.*, *PG* 62:484; cf. *LNPF* 13:387)

---

8. Brightman places the deacon's call *orthoi stōmen kalōs* just after the kiss of peace and Offertory, at the beginning of the Anaphora; pp. 473 and 478, n. 16. Cf. van de Paverd, 242.

The deacon's task of general surveillance is referred to in *Adversus Judaeos* 1.4.8:

Do you take no notice of what the deacon continuously calls out at the mysteries? "Recognize one another," he says. Do you not see how he entrusts to you the careful examination of your brothers? (*FOTC* 68:16, trans. Harkins)

The deacon's role of watchman had already been defined in the *Apostolic Constitutions*:[9]

Let the deacon oversee the people, that none whisper, or doze, or laugh. [Similiter diaconus provideat, ne quisquam susurret vel dormitet vel rideat vel nutet.] (2.57.10, ed. Funk.)

The presence of angels at the prayer for the dead, which is introduced by the deacon and emphasizes the communion of saints, is dwelt on in *Homily 22 on Acts*:

Not in vain are the offerings made for the departed, not in vain the prayers, not in vain the almsgiving; all these things have been ordered by the Spirit, wishing us to give one another mutual assistance. . . . It is not for nothing that the deacon exclaims, "for those that are fallen asleep in Christ, and for those who make commemorations for them." It is not the deacon that utters these words, but the Holy Spirit; I mean the charism. What do you say? The sacrifice is at hand; all things are laid out in due order. Angels are there present, archangels, the Son of God is present. All stand with such awe, and in the general silence those stand by exclaiming. And do you think that what is done is done in vain? Then is not the rest also in vain, both the offerings made for the church, and those for the priests, and for the whole body? God forbid! But all is done with faith. What do you think of the offerings made for the martyrs, of the invocation made at that hour? Although they are martyrs, nonetheless "for the martyrs." It is a great honor to be named in the presence of the Lord when the Memorial is being celebrated, the dread sacrifice, the ineffable mysteries. (*PG* 60:111)

One of the deacon's chief functions was to exclaim "Holy things for the

---

9. See also *Homily 19 on Acts* (*PG* 60:156): "Just as our mouth is the mouth of our souls, though the soul has no mouth, so the mouth of prophets is the mouth of God. Listen and shudder. There in public view stands the deacon, exclaiming and saying, "Let us attend to the Reading." It is the common voice of the whole church, the voice which he utters, and yet none pays attention. After him the Reader begins, "The Prophecy of Isaiah," and still nobody pays attention."

Holy" after the Offertory, before the Communion.[10] In *Homily 17.8 on the Epistle to the Hebrews* we read:

These things have been given to the holy. This the deacon also proclaims when he calls on the holy; even by this call searching the faults of all. For, as in a flock, where many sheep are in good health, but many are full of the scab, it is needful that these be separated from the healthy, so also in the Church. Since some sheep are healthy and some diseased, by this voice he separates the one from the other. (*PG* 63:132)

In *Homily 3.4 on Ephesians* we read:

You hear the deacon stand up and say: "As many as are penitents, all pray." As many as do not partake are in penitence. Why, then, does he say, "Depart, you who are not qualified to participate"? Staying for the prayers is as forbidden to them as actually partaking of the Eucharist.[11] (*PG* 62:132)

In his second homily *On the Betrayal of Judas*, the real meaning of kairos is well expressed:

Accordingly, at the moment of sacrifice [*en tō kairō tēs thusias*] he called to mind no other commandment but brotherly reconciliation, showing that love is the greatest of the virtues. . . . Let us recall, then, those words, brethren, and that most awesome greeting [the kiss of peace].[12] For this kiss affects our minds and makes us all become one body and members of Christ, since we all share in the one body. (*PG* 49:391)

In his first homily *On the Betrayal of Judas* he writes:

It is now time [*kairos*] to approach the awesome, fearful altar. Let us all approach, then, with a pure conscience. For Christ is now present, adorning the altar. It is no mere man who makes these offerings become the body and blood of Christ. The priest merely stands, fulfilling a role and offering a prayer. But the grace and the power are God's which accomplish all these

10. On the ordination of deacons in the *Apostolic Constitutions* see I.-H. Dalmais, *Les Liturgies d'Orient* (Paris, 1959), 94–96.

11. For the deacon's role at the distribution of Communion cf. Justin, *1 apol* 65: "And when he who presides has celebrated the Eucharist, they whom we call deacons permit each one present to partake of the Eucharistic bread, and wine and water; and they carry it also to the absentees."

12. Cyril of Jerusalem, *catech. myst.* 5.2–3 lists two of the deacon's functions in the liturgy: presenting the water for the washing of the hands (5.2) and giving the invitation for the kiss of peace (5.3; cf. *SC* 126:146–148, *FOTC* 64:191–192).

things. This is my body, he says. This is the word which changes the substance of [*metarrythmizei*] [13] the offerings. (*PG* 49:380)

Finally, in *Adversus Judaeos* 111 he tells us:

And when the deacon bids you to pray all together, he also enjoins you in his prayer to ask for the Angel of Peace, and that everything which concerns you be blessed with peace. As he dismisses you from the assembly, he petitions [peace] for you and says: "Go in peace." [14] And without this peace, it is altogether impossible for us to say or do anything. For peace is our nurse and mother, she is very careful to cherish us and foster us. I am not speaking of what is merely called by the name of peace, nor of the peace which comes from sharing meals together, but of the peace which accords with God, the peace which comes from the harmony sent by the Spirit. (trans. P. W. Harkins, *FOTC* 68:68)

13. On the term see van de Paverd, 296, 301.
14. On the "Go in peace" see van de Paverd, 83, 404–406.

LAWRENCE R. HENNESSEY, S.T.

Diakonia and *Diakonoi* in the
Pre-Nicene Church

THE SECOND Vatican Council, in the dogmatic Constitution *Lumen gentium*, provided for the restoration of the diaconate in the Latin Church as a proper and permanent rank among the Church's ordained ministers. It further stipulated that this permanent ministry be opened to qualified candidates, both married and single.[1] On June 18, 1967, Pope Paul VI issued the *motu proprio Sacrum diaconatus ordinem*, which implemented the Council's provision for a permanent diaconate. The restoration was not made obligatory for the Latin Church; it was left, rather, to national conferences of bishops and other competent bodies to decide—with the approval of the Apostolic See—that the restoration was appropriate for the needs of their local churches.[2] The petition of the bishops of the United States for the restoration of the permanent diaconate was approved in October 1968 and implemented three years later.[3]

In providing for the restoration of the diaconate, the Council not only described this ministry as one of liturgy, of word, and of charity, but also explicitly exhorted contemporary deacons to imitate the diaconal spirit

1. Dogmatic Constitution *Lumen Gentium*, sec. 29 (21 November 1964): *Acta Apostolicae Sedis* 57 (1965), 36. The Council was even more explicit about the restoration of the diaconate in the Eastern Churches in communion with Rome: cf. the decree *Orientalium ecclesiarum*, 17 (21 November 1964): *AAS* 57 (1965), 81.

2. Paul VI (Montini), *Sacrum diaconatus ordinem*, (*motu proprio*: 18 June 1967): *AAS* 59 (1967), 697–704; cf. 698.

3. Cf. "Conditions for the Permanent Diaconate in the United States, in Response to the U.S. Bishops' Request," *Catholic Mind* 66 (Nov. 1968), 8; "Report of the U.S. Bishops' Committee on the Permanent Diaconate, Feb. 23, 1971," ibid. 69 (May 1971), 54–64.

of the early Church. Polycarp's letter to the Philippians is briefly cited to this effect.[4] While the Council's principal motive for the restoration of the diaconate was the needs of the contemporary churches, the link to the diaconal spirit of the early Church was not accidental. In fact, for both the Western and the Eastern Churches, the first three centuries of Christianity can legitimately be called the deacon's "Golden Age." At the time of the restoration, it seemed safe to say that the returning deacon's ministry would develop in substantial continuity with its early Christian antecedents.[5] Such a development, however, has not taken place. More than ten years after the restoration in the United States, the diaconate as a proper and permanent rank among the Church's ordained ministries is still experiencing significant problems of identity and of full integration into ecclesial life. Part of the difficulty results from a widespread misunderstanding of the deacon's role and the significance of diaconal ministry.[6] In light of this present situation, it seems that the contemporary perspective on the restored diaconate can be significantly deepened and enriched by a historical examination of this ministry's early Christian origins and spirit.

1. Classical and Judaic Antecedents

The Greek verb *diakonein* and its cognates *diakonia* and *diakonos* lie at the heart of early Christianity's self-understanding and of its understanding of Jesus. Prior to the appearance of Christianity, the words already had a long history in the classical Greek world. The verb *diakonein* is used first by Herodotus (4.154) in the concrete sense of 'to render personal service.' In ordinary use, this meant primarily waiting at table, but this concrete sense was expanded somewhat to include not only personal service rendered to someone, but service to others generally.[7]

4. *Lumen Gentium*, sec. 29: *AAS* 57 (1965), 36; Polycarp, *ep.* 5.2.

5. E. P. Echlin, "The Deacon's Golden Age," *Worship* 45 (1971), 37.

6. See, for example, the popular article by P. E. Ward, "The Permanent Diaconate after Ten Years," *America* 148 (1983), 475–477. Mr. Ward, himself a permanent deacon, cites problems such as conflict with the emerging role of the laity, changing views on ordained ministry, resistance by pastors and other priests, inadequate preparation of candidates, the need for education of other ordained ministers. The question is especially significant for the United States: according to the statistics of the International Center for the Diaconate, in 1982 there were 8,273 deacons worldwide; 62.8 percent of them were in the United States.

7. H. G. Liddell and R. Scott, *A Greek-English Lexicon* (rev. by H. S. Jones and R. McKenzie: Oxford, 1940), 398a.

In the classical Greek world, such personal service was not held in high esteem; it was the proper task of a slave (Plato, *Grg.* 491e). Only service to the state had any real value (Plato, *Lg.* 955c–d; Demosthenes 50.2). [8] The ideal of service to others was carefully circumscribed. For a Greek or Roman citizen consideration for service to those in need was limited to weaker fellow citizens; outsiders—slaves or resident aliens, i.e., metics—were not generally included.[9] In later Hellenism, when the significance of the *polis* had receded, there was a stronger cosmic awareness, which brought a sense of being a servant of God (Epictetus [ca.55–ca. 135 C.E.] 3.22.69; 3.24.65); yet, at the same time, the idea of service to one's neighbor withdrew into the background, and concrete obligations of this kind toward others almost completely disappeared. Nevertheless, despite the gulf between the Graeco-Roman ideal of service and the Christian ideal, the original classical sense of *diakonein* as 'rendering personal service; waiting at table' is still echoed in the theological and figurative meanings which New Testament writers give to this word.[10]

Diakonia, of course, is the noun which signifies the action or activity of *diakonein*. *Diakonos* is generally used as a noun in classical usage to signify a 'servant' (Herodotus 4.71, 72); or, in Hellenistic times, to designate an 'attendant' or 'official' in a temple or religious guild. *Diakonos* was also used as an adjective, meaning 'servile, menial' (Plato, *Plt.* 290c).[11] The Hellenistic usage of *diakonos* to mean an 'attendant' or 'official' in a temple or religious society points in the direction of later Christian use, despite the vastly different Christian sense.[12]

In Judaism, a much richer understanding of service prevailed. The two verbs most frequently used in the Hebrew Scriptures for service are *ʿābad* and *shērēt*. The verb *ʿābad* is used to signify 'labor,' and 'to serve another by labor,' for example, the service Jacob renders Laban for the hand of Laban's daughter, Rachel (Gn. 29:15, 18, 20). In addition, it also designates service of subjects to a king, or tributary subjection to a foreign king (e.g., 1 Sm. 11:1; Ez. 34:27). It is less frequently used for

8. H. W. Beyer, "*Diakoneō, diakonia, diakonos,*" *Theological Dictionary of the New Testament* 2 (Grand Rapids, 1964), 82.

9. J. B. Skemp, "Service to the Needy in the Graeco-Roman World," in J. I. McCord and T. H. L. Parker, eds., *Service in Christ: Essays Presented to Karl Barth on His 80th Birthday* (London, 1966), 20–21.

10. H. W. Beyer, 82–83.

11. H. G. Liddell and R. Scott, 398a–b.

12. J. B. Skemp, 19.

service to God (e.g., Ex. 3:12; 4:23), and only occasionally for Levitical service, and then generally of specific duties around the sanctuary (e.g., Nm. 3:7–8; 4:23, 26, 30). The verb *shērēt* also means 'to serve,' but with some different nuances. It is used for ministerial service as opposed to menial, for example, Joseph's service to Pharaoh (Gn. 39:4). By far its most extensive use is for service in worship of priests and Levites (e.g., Ex. 28:35; Nm. 3:6).[13] Of these two verbs, *shērēt* carries a more personal connotation of service to a person. Its participial form, *mᵉshārēt* is used substantively for 'servant,' for example, Joshua as Moses' servant (Ex. 24:13; 33:11; Nm. 11:28) and Elisha as servant of Elijah (1 Kgs. 19:21; 2 Kgs. 4:43). However, by far the most common word for servant is the noun *ᶜebed*. This word signifies household slaves (e.g., Gn. 39:17), subjects of a king (Ex. 7:28), and worshipers of God (2 Kgs. 9:7). It is used in the special sense of 'servant of Yahweh,' especially in the prophetic literature (e.g., Jer. 7:25; Ez. 38:17); to this same special sense belongs the designation of Israel as 'Servant of Yahweh,' most notably in the so-called Servant Songs (e.g., Is. 42:1; 48:6; 52:12).

The range of these Hebrew words indicates that nothing unseemly or demeaning was involved in service rendered at any level of Israel's social and religious life. This idea is carried over in the Septuagint translation of these terms. The verb *ᶜabad* is variously translated by *douleuein*, *latreuein*, and even *ergazesthai*; *shērēt* is translated most commonly by *leitourgein*, reflecting its cultic use; *mᵉshārēt* is variously *ho therapōn*, *ho leitourgos*, etc.; and *ᶜebed* is translated most commonly by either *pais* or *doulos*. Although the verbs *leitourgein* and *latreuein* appear mostly in cultic contexts, no embarrassment is felt in using stronger terms like *douleuein* and *doulos*. It should be noted that the Septuagint never uses the verb *diakonein*; *diakonia* and *diakonos* are both rarely used for both the *ᶜbd* and *shrt* roots.

The full scope of the Old Testament ideal of service is not exhausted by the words already mentioned. In fact the heart of the ideal was carried by another verb, *ʾāhab*, 'to love.' This verb was used in three major contexts: love of neighbor, of strangers, and of self; love of God for humanity; and love of humanity for God.[14] The growth of the concept of love

---

13. F. Brown, S. R. Driver, C. A. Briggs, *A Hebrew and English Lexicon of the Old Testament* (Oxford, 1972): *ᶜabad*, 712–713; *shērēt*, 1058.

14. E. Jenni, "*ʾhb*: lieben," *Theologisches Handwörterbuch zum Alten Testament* 1 (E. Jenni and C. Westermann, eds.: Munich, 1971), 67.

expressed by the verb 'āhab to the point of embracing these three contexts presupposes, of course, a long and complex development, which is outside the scope of the present study.[15] In the course of this development, however, love came to be understood as oriented to action; it was not only an inner disposition arising from experience or events, but also a conscious effort to act in behalf of the person loved or the thing preferred. The dimensions of this idea are clearly expressed in the commandment: "You will love your neighbor as yourself. I am the Lord" (Lv. 19:18). In this command, the attitude of love, which is expressed as the norm, arises not from a humanitarian spirit, but from divine command. Such a command made sense in terms of Israel's faith in God's love for her (e.g., Ps. 116:1). The scope of this command extended to one's neighbor and to resident aliens (Lv. 19:34; Dt. 10:18f.), but not to foreigners outside the community or the national boundaries.[16]

This ideal of love stood behind and informed the various kinds of social and religious service in the Old Testament; it is a decisive element, which helps distinguish the classical and Judaic concepts of service. Not only was the Old Testament concept of service grounded in a faith response to a divine command, its scope also reaches beyond one's kinsfolk and fellow citizens. Unlike the classical idea, service was a proper and dignified activity to be performed by all members of the community, according to their various roles and as needs arose.

In later pre-Christian Judaism, three obstacles arose, which tended to obscure this ideal of loving service. First of all, among the people influenced by the Pharisaic movement in the century and a half before Christianity,[17] a sharp distinction was drawn between the 'righteous,' i.e., careful observers of the Law, and the 'unrighteous,' i.e., public sinners, the religiously indifferent, Samaritans, and other nonobservers. This had the effect of dissolving the unconditional command of loving service, and gave rise to the attitude condemned by Jesus in the parable of the Good Samaritan (Lk. 10:25–37). Secondly, service came to be seen less and less as willing sacrifice for others, and more as a work of personal merit before God. Jesus censured this attitude in the story of

---

15. For a survey of this development, see J. Bergman, A. O. Halder, G. Wallis, "'āhabh," *Theological Dictionary of the Old Testament* 1 (G. J. Botterweck and H. Ringgern, eds.: Grand Rapids, 1974), 99–118.

16. Ibid., 105–106; 111.

17. Cf. A. Michel and J. Le Moyne, "Pharisiens," *Dictionnaire de la Bible: Supplement* 7 (Paris, 1966), 1022–1115.

the Pharisee and the Publican (Lk. 18:9–14). Finally, there also arose the
idea that service, especially service at table, should be withheld from the
unworthy. This factor played a role in early opposition to Jesus, because
of His habit of eating with tax collectors and sinners (Mk. 2:15–17;
Lk. 5:29–32; 7:36–50).[18] As serious as these three obstacles were, they
nevertheless served as foils to help the New Testament authors express
clearly the Christian ideal of loving service, the ideal of *diakonia*.

II. *Diakonein* and *Diakonia* in the New Testament

The command of love—expressed in Leviticus 19:18 by the verb
ʾ*āhab*—which represents the heart of the Old Testament concept of
service, is rendered by the Septuagint with the verb *agapān*. As happened in Old Testament religion, but now more extensively, the concept
of love, *agapān* and the noun *agapē*, suffuse the New Testament's ideal of
service. Jesus' own understanding of service grows out of the Old Testament command of Leviticus 19:18, which He is represented as linking
with the command of love for God in Deuteronomy 6:5; the two are then
called the greatest commandments (Mk. 12:28–31; Mt. 22:36–40).
For earliest Christianity, the two commandments constitute the divinely
willed ethical conduct of Jesus' followers. As has already been seen, Jesus
is seen as purifying the concept of service from the distortions it had
acquired in His own day (cf. Mk. 2:15–17; Lk. 10:25–37; 18:9–14;
5:29–32; 7:36–50).[19]

It goes almost without saying that Jesus' attitude towards service was
vastly different from the attitude of classical culture. Far from looking
down on service or considering it demeaning, Jesus, in fact, understood
loving service as the *sine qua non* of authentic discipleship (Mt. 10:38;
25:31–46, esp. 40 and 45). His astonishing act in the estimation of
service was precisely to reverse, in ethical estimation, the relation between serving and being served (Lk. 22, 26f.). Jesus is instituting a new
pattern of human relationships:[20] "I am among you as one who serves
[*diakonōn*]" (Lk. 22:27). The context of this idea is *diakonein* understood
as 'waiting at table.' In the Johannine tradition, this ideal of loving
service is preserved in the same context of table service, when Jesus

18. H. W. Beyer, 83.
19. Ibid., 84.
20. Ibid.

washes His disciples' feet (Jn. 13:1–17), although the verb *diakonein* is not used. However, *diakonein* is sometimes used in its original classical sense of 'waiting at table' (e.g., Mk. 1:31) without any special theological point being made.

It is, of course, the theological sense of *diakonein* and its cognates that is of primary interest to the New Testament writers. A brief outline of the range of usage of *diakonein* and *diakonia* can provide the basis for a fuller evaluation of the Christian understanding of loving service.[21]

The use of *diakonein* and *diakonia* in a theological sense can be arranged under two headings, the general technical use, and the specialized technical use:

(1) The general technical use of *diakonein* and *diakonia*.

Diakonein is used to describe Jesus' service to humanity (Mk. 10:45 = Mt. 20:28). It also refers to the practical service—preparing a meal, waiting at table—rendered to Jesus or to Jesus and His disciples (Mk. 1:31 = Mt. 8:15 = Lk. 4:39; Mk. 15:41 = Mt. 27:55; Lk. 8:3; 10:40; Jn. 12:2). Finally, it is used for service rendered to a fellow disciple or to the Church as a whole (1 Pt. 1:12; 4:10).

Diakonia is also used in the sense of service to the Church as a whole (2 Cor. 11:8), and also in the sense of practical service (Lk. 10:40). Its most extensive general technical use denotes a function or office within the Church or the activity of fulfilling it. In this sense it is used for the ministry of apostles, prophets, evangelists, etc. (e.g., Acts 1:17, 25; 20:24; 21:19; Rom. 11:13; 1 Cor. 12:5; 2 Cor. 4:1; 5:18).

(2) The specialized technical use of *diakonein* and *diakonia*.

In a more specialized technical sense, *diakonein* is used for service to the needy (Mt. 25:44); in reference to Paul's collection for the Jerusalem Church (Rom. 15:25; 2 Cor. 8:19f.); for service to the bodily and spiritual needs of fellow Christians (Heb. 6:10; 1 Pt. 4:11); and in reference to the supervision of communal meals (Acts 6:2). It is also used in reference to the discharge of the duties of *diakonos* (1 Tm. 3:10, 13).

The specialized use of *diakonia* generally runs parallel to the use of *diakonein*: for service to the needy (possibly: Rom. 12:7; 1 Cor. 16:15); for the daily distribution of food to the community (Acts 6:1); and for

---

21. For the outline that follows, see C. E. B. Cranfield, "Diakonia in the New Testament," in J. I. McCord and T. H. L. Parker, 37–39.

Paul's collection for Jerusalem (Acts 11:29; 12:25; Rom. 15:31; 2 Cor. 8:4; 9:1, 12, 13).

In both the general and the specialized technical senses of *diakonein* and *diakonia* there are strong echoes of the original classical sense of these words as 'rendering personal service; waiting at table; serving others generally.' It has already been seen how Jesus' revaluation of 'waiting at table' supported the institution of a new pattern of human relationships. The same change in evaluation applies almost everywhere else in the New Testament for both the general and the specialized uses of the word group. *Diakonein* and *diakonia* are used to cover the whole range of active Christian love; such loving service is at the heart of true discipleship. Its scope explicitly reaches beyond the community to every living person (Mt. 25:44).[22]

In Mark 10:43–45 (= Mt. 20:26–28), Jesus deepens the idea of service already expressed in Luke 22, 26f. and John 13:1–17. In the context, Jesus is speaking to His disciples about the question of status and precedence among themselves. He consciously opposes the example of secular princes' exercise of authority with His own idea of loving service. Jesus reminds the disciples that their concern is of a different order: it is the Kingdom of God, the age of glory. The path to this Kingdom leads through suffering and death. It is this fact which irrevocably shapes the attitude of all who follow Jesus into the Kingdom. The point of suffering and death is found in the service therein accomplished; this suffering makes the service sacrificial. This, claims Jesus, is the way to greatness (Mk. 10:43 = Mt. 20:26). In this context, Jesus does not stop at the picture of table service (cf. Lk. 22:26f.). *Diakonein* and *diakonia* are both understood as full and perfect sacrifice, of being for others—like Jesus—in life or in death. This is why the concept of *diakonein* and its cognates lies at the heart of early Christianity's self-understanding and of its understanding of Jesus. For what is true of Jesus Himself is also true of His servant (*ho diakonos ho emos*: Jn. 12:26). Authentic discipleship demands service—to God, to Christ, to neighbor, since it is one and the same as it was in Israel—even unto death (Jn. 12:25–26). Eternal life is the reward of this *diakonia*.[23]

22. H. W. Beyer, 85.
23. Ibid., 85–86.

III. *Diakonia* and *Diakonoi* in the New Testament

Consistent with the New Testament use of *diakonia* is the use of the noun *diakonos*, 'servant,' and later 'deacon' in the sense of an official minister in the community. Like the other two words in the word group, *diakonos* is used in both a general and a specialized technical sense.

In a general technical sense, *diakonos* is used in connection with service to God (Rom. 13:4; 2 Cor. 6:4; 1 Thes. 3:2); service to Christ (Jn. 12:26; 2 Cor. 11:23; Col. 1:7; 1 Tm. 4:6); service to the new convenant and to the Gospel (2 Cor. 3:6; Eph. 3:7; Col. 1:23); and finally, service to a fellow disciple or the Church as a whole (Mk. 9:35; 10:43 = Mt. 20:26; Mt. 23:11; 1 Cor. 3:5; Col. 1:25). The specialized technical use of *diakonos* is confined to its designation for the holder of a particular office (Phil. 1:1; 1 Tm. 3:8, 12). In Romans 16:1, Phoebe, a woman who collaborated with Paul in Cenchreae, is described as *ousan diakonon tēs ekklēsias*. This use of *diakonos* also seems to refer to a definite office; Romans 16:2 refers to her practical assistance to Paul and to others, service consistent with the office of *diakonos*.[24] As has already been noted, the verb *diakonein* is used in 1 Timothy 3:10, 13 in the sense of 'discharging the duties of *diakonos*.'

In the general technical use of *diakonos*, it does have, at least in one context, the straightforward sense of a 'waiter at table' (Jn. 2:5, 9). It also means 'the servant of a master' (Mt. 22:13), and this sense carries over to the designation of a Christian as a 'servant of Christ' (Jn. 12:26) and a 'servant' to fellow Christians (Mk. 9:35; 10:43; Mt. 20:26; 23:11). In a more figurative sense, the word describes the 'servant of a spiritual power,' both good (Eph. 3:6f.; Col. 1:23; 2 Cor. 3:6) and evil (2 Cor. 11:14f.; Gal. 2:17). The figurative use also describes an apostle as a servant of Christ (2 Cor. 11:23), and in a very special sense as a 'servant of God' discharging the *diakonia* with all of its attendant sufferings and difficulties (2 Cor. 6:3ff.). (In this sense, Paul usually prefers the stronger word *doulos*, 'slave' [e.g., Rom. 1:1; Phil. 1:1], to emphasize

---

24. C. E. B. Cranfield, 37, 39. The interpretation of Rom. 16:1 as referring to a definite office is much disputed. Nevertheless, Paul clearly teaches that each Christian is called to the Lord's service, and—according to his or her individual gifts (*charismata*)—entrusted with a particular ministry to be exercised in and for the community. Phoebe has a permanent and recognized ministry, as is clear from the use of the participle *ousan* and the designation of the place, Cenchreae. It is thus legitimate to see here at least the early stages of what became the ecclesiastical office of *diakonos*. Cf. E. Käsemann, *Commentary on Romans* (Grand Rapids, 1980), 410–411.

his total commitment to Christ and to the Father.) These figurative senses are also used for other apostolic collaborators (e.g., Timothy: 1 Tm. 4:6; Epaphras: Col. 1:7; Tychicus: Eph. 6:21; Tychicus: Col. 4:7). Paul describes himself as a 'servant of the Church' (Col. 1:25) in virtue of his divinely given commission. Finally, even the secular authorities are *diakonoi* of God (Rom. 13:1–4), because they hold their power from Him.[25]

Of particular interest for the developing life and internal structure of the Church is the emergence of the *diakonos* as an official of the community, entrusted with a specific office. Without going further into the details of the development of the Christian ideal of service—a task beyond the scope of the present study—the very centrality of the ideal for Christian discipleship makes it obvious that responsibility for the community's *diakonia* rested with every member. However, the very centrality of *diakonia* to the early community's self-understanding and its understanding of Jesus meant that the implementation of its responsibilities for loving service could not be haphazard or left to spontaneous good will. For example, the breakdown of fraternal love even in the context of the eucharistic assembly, which put the poorer members at a humiliating disadvantage (1 Cor. 11:17–22), evokes from the Apostle one of his sharpest condemnations (1 Cor. 11:27–30). This and other disorders caused him to emphasize the specific gifts (*charismata*) given to individuals for the sake of the community's integrity (1 Cor. 12:27–31). The community's life was not left to spontaneous good will. Gradually, various kinds of services, rooted in the ideal of Christian *diakonia* came under the care and direction of specific individuals, without, however, diminishing the responsibility of the whole community for the exercise of loving service. The emergence of the office of deacon is part of this larger evolution.

The first *diakonia* mentioned in the Acts as belonging to specific individuals is entrusted to "the Twelve"; it consists of being a witness to the resurrection of Jesus (Acts 1:15–26, esp. 17, 22, 25). This designation of twelve men is linked in Matthew and Luke with the eschatological function of judging the twelve tribes of Israel (Mt. 19:28; Lk. 22:28–30). The ministry of the Twelve thus seems to belong to the earliest years of the Jerusalem community, over which the Twelve exercised leadership and were responsible for the allocation of its funds (Acts

25. H. W. Beyer, 88–89.

2:14; 4:34–37). Their primary responsibility, however, was the proclamation of the good news (e.g., Acts 2:14–15; 3:12; 5:42). Despite their initial importance, the Twelve are not mentioned again after the death of Stephen (Acts 7:60); their ministry as a unified group quickly recedes. Persecution of the community (cf. Acts 12:19) may have led to their dispersal, while at the same time, the influx of Gentile converts would have called for a change in the structure of an exclusively Jewish community. In any event, while James remained behind in Jerusalem, Peter became a missionary (Acts 8:14; 10:23–24; 12:17).[26]

In the context of the ministry of the Twelve, an apparent extension of their ministry is also reported (Acts 6:1–7). According to Luke's source,[27] the rapid growth of the community created a serious difficulty in the daily *diakonia* of practical charity: the widows of the Greek-speaking Jews resident in Jerusalem were being neglected by the Aramaic-speaking Jews in the allocation of the community's fund for relief of the poor (6:1). The Twelve summoned the whole community to deal with the problem, asserting that their ministry of the word (*diakonia tou logou*) and their prayer had precedence over serving at tables (*diakonein trapezais*) (6:2–3). As a solution to the difficulty, they proposed the election of seven men from the Greek-speaking group—men "of good reputation, full of the Spirit and of wisdom" (6:3)—to carry out the daily *diakonia* for their own people. These men were then chosen by the community and presented to the Twelve. The Twelve prayed over them and imposed hands on them, thus designating them specifically for this *diakonia* of practical charity (6:5–6).[28]

Although the noun *diakonia* is used here in the sense of concrete personal service, and the verb *diakonein* is used in the sense of 'serving at table,' Luke does not call these men *diakonoi*. However, the passage (6:3) does recall the qualities required of *diakonoi* as listed in 1 Timothy 3:8ff., and Luke's readers may well have seen (even if anachronistically) the Seven as *diakonoi*, deacons in the later sense of 'holders of the office of deacon.'[29] They may well represent the incipient stages of the later office

26. A. Lemaire, "From Services to Ministries: *Diakonai* in the First Two Centuries," *Concilium* 80 (1972), 36–37.

27. On the complex and controverted question of the sources of Acts, see E. Haenchen, *The Acts of the Apostles: A Commentary* (Philadelphia, 1971), 81–90, and esp. 83–84 for the episode under discussion.

28. Ibid., 260–262. Cf. also G. Schneider, *Die Apostelgeschichte*, 1 Teil (Freiburg, 1980), 420–430.

29. Ibid., 262–263.

of *diakonos*, but it should also be noted that two of them—Stephen (Acts 6:8–10) and Philip (Acts 8:26–40; 21:8)—are reported as engaging in preaching, teaching, and even baptizing, just like one of the Twelve. In other words, the scope of their *diakonia* went beyond the ministry of practical charity. It would seem that no fixed delineation of ministerial roles existed at this early period. The importance of this passage for the development of the diaconate will be seen only later. Especially in the third century, it exercised a decisive influence on the structure of the office.

It has already been noted that the influx of Gentile converts would have called for a change in the organization of an exclusively Jewish community. It seems clear from the sources Luke uses in Acts that the exigencies of the Gentile mission created just such a new situation requiring new ministries within the expanding community. A strong impetus for this mission was assigned to the persecution in Jerusalem, which followed the murder of Stephen (8:1; 11:19). This persecution may also have prompted the relocation of the missionary effort in Antioch instead of Jerusalem (11:22ff.). In any event, Antioch became the center of the Gentile mission.

The Antiochene community at this time possessed a distinct group of leaders called 'prophets and teachers,' *prophetai kai didaskaloi* (13:1). When first spoken of, they are described as "worshiping the Lord [*leitourgountōn tō kuriō*] and fasting" (13:2). In the course of this "liturgical" service, an oracle was received from the Holy Spirit, designating Barnabas and Saul for special missionary work. The prophets and teachers fasted, prayed, and them imposed hands on the two, before sending them off (13:2–3). These prophets and teachers thus appear as the leaders of the community: they conduct its worship and preach and teach the word within it. According to the names mentioned (13:1), all the men designated prophets and teachers were Hellenists, i.e., Greek-speaking Jews.

Following their designation by the Holy Spirit and by the imposition of hands by the *prophetai* and *didaskaloi*, Barnabas and Saul are called 'apostles,' *apostoloi* (14:4, 14). Here 'apostle' is used for the first time in a technical sense, as an official representative of the community acting under the inspiration of the Holy Spirit, sent to proclaim the good news.[30] As official representatives of the Antiochene community, the two

---

30. A. Lemaire, 39.

apostles set out on the first missionary effort in Asia Minor, an effort directed primarily towards diaspora Jews (13:4–45). Under the pressure of increasing opposition, they gradually extended their mission to the Gentiles as well (13:46ff.). Towards the end of their mission, Barnabas and Saul are said to appoint (*cheirotonēsantes*) elders, *presbyteroi*, for each of the new communities they have founded (14:23). The report of these appointments is most probably an anachronistic insertion by the author of Acts.[31]

Nothing is said in Acts about the institution of *presbyteroi*. Without comment, James and the *presbyteroi* were said to be the leaders of the Jerusalem community (Acts 15:2, 4, 6; 21:18ff.). It was simply assumed that any Palestinian Jewish community would be organized with a college of *presbyteroi* at its head. It is probable that this organizational model was generally established in the new Jewish Christian communities in the diaspora.[32] Nevertheless, it seems initially to have been avoided in the communities founded by Paul, and only to have gained acceptance there after his death.

The first designation of specific individuals as *diakonoi* in the sense of 'office holders' occurs in a Pauline community. In the salutation of his letter to the Philippians, he singles out a definite group, which he calls *episkopoi kai diakonoi*, 'overseers and ministers' (Phil. 1:1). This letter was written most probably between 53 and 58, to a community Paul himself founded upon his arrival in Macedonia in 48/49. This group is certainly administrative, but nothing is said about its respective functions. Since the composition of this community was essentially Gentile-Christian, the antecedents of the *episkopoi* and *diakonoi* could well have been the administrative officers of the Hellenistic clubs and cult-fellowships.[33] Such an arrangement would have been easy to adapt to the new Christian purpose. One further point is worth noting: although the functions are not clear, the *diakonoi* are linked with the *episkopoi*. As the office of the *diakonos* continued to develop throughout the early

31. In this passage, Luke is apparently reading the ecclesial constitution of his own day back into the time of Paul. This is not the community organization which emerges from the genuine Pauline letters, which was more fluid and charismatic, e.g., at Corinth. So E. Haenchen, 436.

32. A. Lemaire, 41–42.

33. W. G. Kümmel, *Introduction to the New Testament* (Nashville, 1975), 322, 332. A. Lemaire, 43, suggests, on the basis of *Didache* 15.1, that these officers filled the office of the prophets and teachers of the Antiochene community. Since Antioch was the center of the Gentile mission, this suggestion is certainly possible.

Christian period it maintained a close and special link to the developing office of *episkopos*.

The next mention of *diakonoi* in the clear sense of 'office holders' is found much later in the Pastoral letters, which were written most probably at the end of the first or the very beginning of the second century.[34] Here again the *diakonoi* are linked with the *episkopoi* (1 Tm. 3:1–12), in a passage which sets out the qualities of character each kind of officer should possess, *episkopoi* first (3:1–7), then the *diakonoi* (3:8–13). The office of *diakonos* is apparently filled by both men and women (3:11). But, once again, the exact functions of the *episkopos* and the *diakonos* are not mentioned.

These letters apparently use the terms *episkopos* and *presbyteros* synonymously. In one passage using *presbyteroi* (1 Tm. 5:17), the functions of preaching and teaching were discharged by at least some of the *presbyteroi*. By this time, the "presbyteral" model inherited from Judaism has become more or less standard. The gradual codification of this model—consisting of two major offices: the *episkopos/presbyteros* and the *diakonos*—and its generalization reflect the ecclesial situation following the death of the first apostolic generation. New dangers have arisen: unsound teaching (Ti. 1:10–14), rivalry between *presbyteroi* (2 Tm. 1:15), and sinful abuses by community leaders (1 Tm. 5:20). The strong stress on qualities of character for ecclesial officers rather than on their functions indicates that one of the main problems facing the author of the Pastorals was precisely the unworthy behavior of these same officers.[35]

The development towards uniformity and the greater emphasis on the integrity of pastoral authority—at the expense of the service of the word and the more fluid and charismatic communal structures—continued in the period of the Apostolic Fathers. Although the specific responsibilities of the *diakonos* are not delineated, the diaconate does in fact emerge as a distinct office in the period covered by the New Testament writings. The specific responsibilities of this office most surely included the *diakonia* of practical charity, both within and outside the context of the community's formal liturgy. The original meaning of *diakonein*, 'to wait at table,' reflected quite clearly the sayings and example of Jesus. Following Jesus, earliest Christianity made this practical *diakonia* the symbol of all loving care for others. Precisely here was to be found the source of the

---

34. Ibid., 384–387.
35. A. Lemaire, 44.

living connection between the ideal of *diakonia* and the office of *diakonos*: the office came to be rooted in the service at the common meal—waiting at table—which was at the heart of the community's life, i.e., the Lord's Supper and the attendant *agapē*.[36] The next two centuries elaborated and deepened the sense of this connection between the community's worship and loving service. This New Testament ideal of *diakonia* came to be associated more and more explicitly with the office and person of the deacon.

IV. *Diakonia* and *Diakonoi* in the Second and Third Centuries

Throughout the second and third centuries, the Christian ideal of *diakonia* developed in profound continuity with its New Testament origins, especially as regards the connection between practical service and public worship.[37] Justin Martyr succinctly expressed it this way: "We have been taught that the only worship that is worthy of Him is not to burn what He has created for our nourishment, but to use it for our own good and for the good of those in need, and with gratitude to Him, to give thanks by solemn prayers and hymns . . ." (1 *apol.* 13).[38] True worship was not seen simply as ritual; the gifts offered were used for the community and for the poor. In Justin's description of the eucharistic assembly, a special collection was taken up among wealthier members for the express purpose of helping those in need, including orphans, widows, the sick, strangers, and prisoners (1 *apol.* 67).[39] Practical service (*diakonia*) to one's neighbor and to those in need was an expression of true worship of God, and was itself, in turn, embodied in the divine liturgy (*leitourgia*).[40] So closely associated are these two realities of service and worship that *diakonia* and *leitourgia* are used interchangeably.[41] The two realities were simply two dimensions of the one true Christian life.

Any attempt to separate practical service from worship was consid-

36. H. W. Beyer, 92.
37. Cf. G. W. H. Lampe, "Diakonia in the Early Church," in J. I. McCord and T. H. L. Parker, 49–64.
38. Justin, *1 apol.* 13: *PG* 6:345B.
39. Ibid., 429C.
40. G. W. H. Lampe, 49.
41. In Eusebius, *h.e.* 5.1.9: *pasē tē pros ton plēsion leitourgia*: K. Lake, *Eusebius: Ecclesiastical History* 1 (Loeb: London, 1975), 410. In the *Liturgy of James*: *ho themenos hēmas eis tēn diakonian tautēn*: B.-Ch. Mercier, "La Liturgie de saint Jacques," *Patrologia Orientalis* 26 (Paris, 1946), 194, line 2.

ered not only sinful, but even a sign of heresy. Ignatius of Antioch maintained that heretical opinions about the grace of Jesus Christ were manifest concretely in neglect of the very same needy who were the Church's special concern (*Smyrn.* 6.2).[42] Cyprian castigated the rich man who came to the liturgy without bringing an offering to be shared with the poor; such a rich man was thus partaking of the sacrifice provided by the *poor*—the proper evangelical order of things was sinfully reversed (*eleem.* 15).[43]

Beyond the context of the actual celebration of the Eucharist, the intimate connection between *diakonia* and *leitourgia* was extended to the *agapē*, a communal meal held apart from the Eucharist, but containing elements of public worship and practical charity. The *agapē* was an official function of the community. The bishop was supposed to preside, but if he was unable, then a presbyter or a deacon.[44] Each person present would receive a piece of bread blessed by the presiding minister, a ritual act clearly distinguished from the Eucharist.[45] The meal was accompanied by prayers beforehand and Scripture readings and hymn singing afterward.[46] The bishop might also give an exhortation or conduct a question-and-answer session.[47]

The motive for the *agapē* was clearly stated: it was to promote goodwill among the members of the community, but, especially, it was to help the poor.[48] Offerings from everyone were encouraged, and what was left over was distributed to the sick, widows, and the poor, under the supervision of a presbyter or deacon.[49] Since the *agapē* was another expression of both worship and practical service, conduct at the communal meal was carefully specified. To prevent abuses—a problem dating back to apostolic times (cf. 1 Cor. 11:17–21)—everyone was exhorted to eat moderately and to avoid drunkenness and carousing. Moderate

42. Ignatius, *Smyrn.* 6.2: K. Lake, *The Apostolic Fathers* 1 (Loeb: London, 1975), 258.

43. Cyprian, *eleem.* 15: ed. M. Simonetti, *Sancti Cypriani Episcopi Opera* (Turnhout, 1976), 64–65.

44. Ignatius, *Smyrn.*. 8.2: K. Lake, 260; Hippolytus, *trad. ap.* 26.11: G. Dix, *Treatise on the Apostolic Tradition of St. Hippolytus of Rome* (London, 1968), 48.

45. Hippolytus, *trad. ap.* 26.2: ibid., 45.

46. Tertullian, *apol.* 39.17–18: ed. E. Dekkers, *Tertulliani Opera* 1 (Turnhout, 1954), 152–153.

47. Hippolytus, *trad. ap.* 26.10: G. Dix, 47.

48. To promote goodwill: Clement, *paed.* 2.7.53.4: C. Mondesert and H.-I. Marrou, *SC* 108 (Paris, 1965), 110. To help the poor: Tertullian, *apol.* 39.16: E. Dekkers, 152.

49. Hippolytus, *trad. ap.* 26.1, 15: G. Dix, 45, 49.

eating also insured that some food would be left over, which could then be given away by the person hosting the *agapē*.[50]

Among the primary beneficiaries of the *diakonia* associated with the *agapē* and the Eucharist were Christians in prison, awaiting torture or death. They were cared for both by the community and by individual Christians, from their own private resources.[51] This special *diakonia* could even include provision for the *leituorgia*: Cyprian indicates that the Eucharist was celebrated in the prison for the benefit of the captives. So anxious were fellow Christians to help in this *diakonia* that they created a problem. Cyprian requested that they not go in crowds to the prison, lest they so incite the animosity of the prison authorities as to be forbidden all access to the captives. Thus, in the desire to do more, they would, in fact, lose the opportunity to do anything. For the same reason, Cyprian directed only one presbyter and one deacon to go at a time, and, by turns, a different pair was to go the next time (*epist.* 5.2).[52] During the time of persecution, Cyprian also urged his presbyters and deacons to maintain their special care for the poor, because those not dejected by poverty nor prostrated by persecution bore effective witness to the faith to other poor people.[53]

The strong communal dimension of the Church's *diakonia* in no way inhibited individual initiative. On this level, the Church maintained the traditions of Judaism, in which almsgiving occupied a key role.[54] The practice and Christian duty of giving alms was extolled by countless preachers and sometimes elaborated in a pastoral treatise, for example, Cyprian's *De opere et eleemosynis*. Such a discussion of almsgiving afforded an occasion to restate the true sense of *diakonia*: Everything we have we possess through the mercy of God. This is especially true of our salvation, an act of God's mercy occasioned by our sinfulness. We received this salvific grace in Baptism, but we continue to sin. Almsgiving washes away postbaptismal sins, because by giving alms we act in the way of our Baptism, i.e., we imitate the mercy God showed towards us (*eleem.* 1–2). Such works of mercy are thus necessary because of sin (4). They can even provide the occasion for dramatic displays of salvific grace:

---

50. Hippolytus, *trad. ap.* 26.7, 9: ibid., 46–47.

51. Tertullian, *mart.* 1: E. Dekkers, 3.

52. Cyprian, *epist.* 5.2: ed. G. Hartel, *S. Thasci Caecili Cypriani Opera Omnia* III, 2 (*CSEL*: Vienna, 1871), 479.

53. Cyprian, *epist.* 12.2: G. Hartel, 504.

54. G. W. H. Lampe, 52.

Christ, through Peter, restored Tabitha to life at the prayers of the widows she had helped with her alms (Acts 9:36–42: *eleem.* 6). To give away one's possessions is to acquire spiritual ones; in this sense, almsgiving insures salvation (7–8). Almsgiving will not impoverish us; it will multiply blessings (9). The point is that if we make Christ co-heir of our possessions, He will make us the co-heir of His kingdom. What we give to the least of our sisters and brothers we give to Christ, and, in this way, almsgiving actually makes God our debtor (13, 16). For the same reason, a rich man who refuses to give of his possession cannot offer true worship to God (15). On a more pedestrian level, Cyprian observes that alms given to God are safe from the tax collector (19); on a more sublime level, almsgiving in some small measure repays Christ for the price of His passion and blood (19, 23).[55]

In addition to the intrinsic value of a *diakonia* like almsgiving, another spiritual value of service arose from the relationship established between the giver and the receiver. Hermas explained the relationship in terms of mutual obligations: the rich man gives to the poor man of his more abundant material wealth; the poor man gives to the rich man of his more abundant spiritual wealth, by praying for the rich man.[56] The attitude reflected here was commonplace: the poor, undistracted by the cares of material wealth, were considered rich in spiritual resources; thus, they, too, had something of great value which they were expected to give.

Despite such an emphasis on mutual obligations, individual *diakonia* could easily be seen only as an occasion for the spiritual improvement of the giver, i.e., as a kind of spiritual exercise. The opposite tendency was also seen. A more inward spiritual exercise could be redirected outward: Hermas is instructed to fast on bread and water; the price of the food he would have eaten is to be given to the poor.[57] This was one way by which individual *diakonia* passed over again into its proper communal context. However, the authentic sense of *diakonia*, and especially its proper relation to *leitourgia*, were never left to mere chance or to spontaneous goodwill. The communal *diakonia* and the supervision of its individual forms were the responsibility of the Church's officers, in particular, of the *episkopos*, the bishop, and the *diakonos*, the deacon. As has been seen,

55. Cyprian, *eleem.*: M. Simonetti, 55–72.
56. Hermas, *sim.* 2.5–8: K. Lake, vol. 2, 144–147.
57. G. W. H. Lampe, 53; Hermas, *sim.* 5.3.7: K. Lake, vol. 2, 160–161.

many kinds of services and functions are called *diakoniai*, but the service of practical charity—especially to the needy and the poor—becomes more and more associated with one officer in particular, the *diakonos*, the deacon.

Throughout the first three centuries, the office of deacon developed in the closest relationship to the office of *episkopos*. This fact was true in the context of the dual ministry—where *episkopos* was synonymous with *presbyteros*, as regards the function of oversight—and also in the evolving tripartite ministry of *episkopos*, *presbyteros*, and *diakonos*.[58] The relationship was already present in Paul's Philippian community (Phil. 1:1) and remained the most distinctive characteristic underlying the shape of the early Christian diaconate.

In two of the earliest extrabiblical documents, the *Didache* and 1 *Clement*, both of which presuppose a dual ministry, the two officers are simply associated without further comments, as they are in the New Testament (Phil. 1:1, 1 Tm. 3:1–13; *Did.* 15.1–2; *1 Clem.* 42.4). In the letters of Ignatius of Antioch, on the other hand, the relationship receives special elaboration and emphasis, one using the typology of God the Father and Christ.[59]

To Ignatius, the deacons are his fellow servants (*sundouloi*: *Smyrn.* 12.2), who are most dear to him, entrusted as they are with the service (*diakonia*) of Jesus Christ (*Magn.* 6.1). In fact they are to be respected as Jesus Christ, even as the bishop is a type (*typos*) of the Father, and the presbyters are the council (*sunedrion*) of God and the college (*sundesmon*) of the Apostles (*Trall.* 3.1).[60] The relationship is described in the same spiritual—almost mystic—way in the following century in the Syriac *Didascalia*: "Let the bishop be honored by you as God, for the bishop sits for you in the place of God Almighty. But the deacon stands in the place of Christ; and do you love him" (2.26). This relationship should stand behind even everyday affairs: "And let the deacon be ready to obey and to submit himself to the command of the bishop . . . And be you [bishop

58. On the question of the evolution of the tripartite ministry from the earlier "presbyteral" model, see E. C. Jay, "From Presbyter-Bishop to Bishops and Presbyters," *The Second Century* 1 (1981), 125–162.

59. The present writer considers the letters to be authentic Ignatian writings. For a good summary of the most recent arguments for and against authenticity, see W. R. Schoedel, "Are the Letters of Ignatius of Antioch Authentic?" *Religious Studies Review* 6 (1980), 196–201.

60. Ignatius, *Smyrn.* 12.2; *Magn.* 6.1; *Trall.* 3.1: K. Lake, 264, 202, 214.

and deacon] of one counsel and of one purpose, and one soul dwelling in two bodies" (3.13).[61] Polycarp, too, uses the same God-Christ typology for these ministers (*ep.* 5.3), but with none of the elaboration found in Ignatius or the *Didascalia*.

The relationship between the bishop and the deacon was expressed concretely in a wide variety of ways, from teaching and liturgical functions to poor relief and common errands. It was clearly expressed in the rite of a deacon's ordination: the bishop alone imposed hands (or a hand) on the deacon; he was ordained not for the priesthood, but for service (*hypēresia*) of the bishop (*trad. ap.* 9.1–2).[62] This form of ordination did not vary.

As the bishop's assistant the deacon shared in the task of teaching. The *Didache* indicated that the bishops and deacons were responsible for the ministry (*leitourgia*) of the prophets and teachers (*didaskaloi*: 15.1),[63] the same responsibilities attributed to the leaders of the Antiochene community in Paul's time (Acts 13:1). Hippolytus may make reference to deacons instructing the assembly (*trad. ap.* 33.2); Origen actually specified the deacon's ministry as a ministry of the word (*hom. in Jos.* 2.1).[64] Deacons were an integral part of catechetical instruction, a role which was extended to preaching, as is clear from the second canon of Ancyra (314), which suspended lapsed deacons from liturgical and preaching functions. By the mid-fourth century, however, the function of preaching seems to have been withdrawn and confined to bishops and presbyters.[65]

One dimension of the essential connection between *diakonia* and *leitourgia* was concretely expressed in the deacon's role in the eucharistic liturgy and at the *agapē*. The deacons brought the oblation (*prosphora*) to the bishop for consecration (*trad. ap.* 4.2), a function also mentioned in the deacon's ordination prayer (*trad. ap.* 9.11).[66] The deacon then distributed the Eucharist, which was consecrated, although usage varied. In their capacity as eucharistic ministers, Ignatius described the deacons

61. *Didasc.* 2.26; 3.13: R. H. Connolly, *Didascalia Apostolorum* (Oxford, 1929), 86, 88; 148.

62. Hippolytus, *trad. ap.* 9.1–2: G. Dix, 15.

63. *Did.* 15.1: K. Lake, 330.

64. Hippolytus, *trad. ap.* 33.2: G. Dix, 60; Origen, *hom. in Jos.* 2.1: ed. A. Jaubert, *SC* 71 (Paris, 1960), 116.

65. G. W. H. Lampe, 58; Council of Ancyra (314), Canon 2: C. J. Hefele, *A History of the Christian Councils* (Edinburgh, 1894), 202.

66. Hippolytus, *trad. ap.* 4.2; 9.11: G. Dix, 6; 17–18.

generically as ministers "of the mysteries of Jesus Christ" (*Trall.* 2.3). In Justin's time they distributed both the bread and the cup, and brought the Eucharist to those absent (1 *apol.* 65, 67); while Hippolytus limited their role to auxiliary ministers of the cup, if enough presbyters were not present (*trad. ap.* 23.7). In Cyprian's church, they appear as ordinary ministers of the cup (cf. *laps.* 25).[67] At the *agapē*, deacons assisted in the distribution of the blessed bread both during the service and afterwards to the poor; they would also preside at this communal meal in the absence of the bishop and presbyters (*trad. ap.* 26.11, 15).[68] In addition, the deacons were also responsible for maintaining order in the assembly, both at the door and throughout the service, making sure everyone was properly placed and that no one whispered, laughed, or fell asleep (*Didasc.* 2.57).[69]

The deacon also had an important role in the rite of baptism as described by Hippolytus: deacons held the vessels contining the holy oils used in the rite (21.8), but most importantly, one of them accompanied the candidate down into the baptismal water (21.11).[70] The deacon, according to Hippolytus, could baptize in case of necessity (26.14); this is confirmed by Tertullian, who also observes that the ordinary minister is the bishop (*bapt.* 17).[71]

One further liturgical role for the deacon is worth noting. Because of the extreme circumstances of persecution, Cyprian allowed deacons to reconcile lapsed Christians to the Church, with the imposition of hands, provided no presbyter was available, the lapsed person was in imminent danger of death, and the lapsed person had obtained a "letter of peace" from a martyr (*epist.* 18.1).[72]

The deacon's assistance to the bishop was expressed not only in the context of *leitourgia*, but especially in the *diakonia* flowing from worship, the practical charity to the poor and needy. This was the other dimension to the essential connection between the two realities. The deacon's role in the distribution of food and provisions collected in the assemblies has already been noted. The deacon was also the bishop's special envoy: he

---

67. Ignatius, *Trall.* 2.3: K. Lake, 214; Justin, *1 apol.* 65, 67: PG 6:428A–B, 429B–C.

68. Hippolytus, *trad. ap.* 26.11, 15: G. Dix, 48–49.

69. *Didasc.* 2.57: R. H. Connolly, 120.

70. Hippolytus, *trad. ap.* 21.8, 11: G. Dix, 34–35.

71. Hippolytus, *trad. ap.* 26.14: ibid., 49; Tertullian, *bapt.* 17: J. G. Ph. Borleffs (Turnhout, 1954), 291.

72. Cyprian, *epist.* 18.1: G. Hartel, 523–524.

brought messages from one local church to another (Ignatius, *Phil.* 10.1); he had charge of community property and reported to the bishop whatever was deemed necessary; especially he notified the bishop about sick members of the community, that the bishop might visit them (*trad. ap.* 9.3; 30). The *Didascalia* assigned visitation of the sick to the deacon himself (3.13).[73]

The development of the office of deaconess was parallel to that of the deacons during this period. The technical term *diakonissa* did not come into general use until the fourth century; *diakonos* with the feminine article *hē* was used to designate the deaconesses. Since the office did not develop at this time in the Latin Church—the deaconal functions were apparently exercised by women in the role of widows—no technical vocabulary was used. However, Pliny, writing to Trajan from Bithynia, called the deaconesses *ministrae*, a term used for female attendants at pagan religious services (*epist.* 10.97.8). Clement of Alexandria used the expression *diakonoi gunaikes* (*str.* 3.6.59).[74]

The *Didascalia* gives the fullest description of the deaconess and her ministry during this period. Like the deacon, who was compared to Christ, the deaconess too was given a divine type: "the deaconess shall be honored by you in place of the Holy Spirit" (2.26).[75] It is interesting to note that in the trinitarian typology used here for the tripartite ministry, the presbyters—although considered to be higher in rank than the deacons—are not given a trinitarian referent. They are equated with the Apostles, a usage which reflects the binatarian typology of God-Christ used by Ignatius and Hippolytus.

The ministry of the deaconess as described in the *Didascalia* is directed specifically to women. Like the deacon, the deaconess too was a living link between the Church's *leitourgia* and *diakonia*. Her most important liturgical role was in the context of the baptismal rites. She assisted the women catechumens down into the water, and after the baptism, she anointed them with the holy oils. (In fact, if a deaconess was unavailable, special precautions had to be taken to insure modesty.)

73. Ignatius, *Phil.* 10.1: K. Lake, 248; Hippolytus, *trad. ap.* 9.3; 30: G. Dix, 15, 57; *Didasc.* 3.13: R. H. Connolly, 150.

74. On the ministry of widows in the Western Church, see R. Gryson, *The Ministry of Women in the Early Church* (Collegeville, 1976), 17–24. Pliny, *epist.* 10.97.8: *ancillae, quae ministrae dicebantur*: ed. M. Schuster and R. Hanslik, *C. Plini Caecili Secundi Opera* (Leipzig, 1958), 356. Clement, *str.* 3.6.59: ed. O. Stählin, *Clemens Alexandrinus* II (*GCS*: Leipzig, 1906), 220, 24.

75. *Didasc.* 2.62: R. H. Connolly, 88.

The deaconess was then responsible for the postbaptismal catechesis of the newly baptized women, a function which was a direct share in the teaching authority of the bishop. She also served the bishop in the practical *diakonia*. Deacons often could not visit the homes of Christian women without danger of serious scandal, so this home-visiting was done by the deaconesses. They also had particular care for the sick women in the community, especially in seeing to practical needs like bathing the sick. Nothing is said about the deaconess sharing in the wider administrative responsibilities of the deacon, and in this respect, her role appears circumscribed by, and confined to, the functions just mentioned (3.12).[76]

Because the office of deacon involved the administration and distribution of large sums of food, money, and provisions, it was open to abuse. Despite the high ideal of *diakonia* maintained by the Church, and the careful specification of moral and spiritual qualities for her ministers, there were those who seriously violated their trust. The need to specify ministerial qualities in the Pastoral letters (e.g., 1 Tm. 3, 1ff.) apparently points to just such a situation in the subapostolic generation. Later on, Hermas excoriated deacons who preyed on widows and orphans and enriched themselves at the expense of the poor entrusted to their care (*sim.* 9.26.2). Cyprian called attention to the crimes of the deacon Nicostratus, who had also defrauded the Church and the poor (*epist.* 52.1). In fact, warnings against avarice and exhortations to honest behavior for deacons are almost a commonplace throughout these centuries (e.g., *Didasc.* 3.13; *trad. ap.* 9.11). They also witness to the growing power of the deacons within the Church, which sometimes led to open confrontation between a deacon and his bishop, which, in turn, was seen as a serious breach in the divine order of things (Cyprian, *epist.* 3).[77] On the other hand, the senior deacon—later called the archdeacon (*archidiakonos*) and specially appointed by the bishop without regard to seniority—maintained such a relationship with the bishop that he ordinarily succeeded the bishop in the see, a practice said to be the norm at Rome during the third century.[78]

76. *Didasc.* 3.12: ibid., 146–148.

77. *Hermas, sim.* 9.26.2: K. Lake, vol. 2, 280; Cyprian, *epist.* 52.1: G. Hartel, 616–617; *Didasc.* 3.13: R. H. Connolly, 148; Hippolytus, *trad. ap.* 9.11: G. Dix, 17–18; Cyprian, *epist.* 3: G. Hartel, 469–472.

78. Athanasius provides an excellent example for the career of an archdeacon: Theodoret, *h.e.* 1.25: ed. L. Parmentier, *Theodoret: Kirchengeschichte* (*GCS* 44: Leipzig, 1911),

In order to prevent, insofar as it was possible, the promotion of
unworthy candidates to ordination, Cyprian, citing divine authority,
directed that all such ordinations take place before the whole assembly.
In this way, a suitable candidate could be chosen in the presence of the
people most acquainted with the candidate's life and actions. While
Cyprian's letter refers primarily to the ordination of bishops, he noted
that these apostolic precedents extended also to the presbyters and
deacons (*epist.* 67.4–5). It is still not clear whether the deacon was
elected to his office or appointed; the textual evidence is contradictory.
However, as Cyprian seems to suggest, there was apparently a public
scrutiny.[79]

Sometime in the course of the third century—quite possibly in the
second half—a very important change began to occur in the understanding of the diaconate as a permanent order in the tripartite ministry.
Instead of maintaining the integrity of the office in its own right, the
Church gradually came to see the diaconate as a lower rung in a ladder of
preferment—the diaconate became more and more a transitional step to
the priesthood.[80] One of the earliest indications of this shift is the
ordination prayer for deacons in the *Apostolic Church Order*, a late third-
century document: "Thus without blame in pure life, having served the
degrees of ordination, he may obtain the exalted priesthood" (24: Ethiopic text).[81] The origins of this development are obscure, but by the
fourth century, it was becoming generally accepted. It was given scriptural warrant on the basis of 1 Timothy 3:13, which was then interpreted to mean that a good deacon should normally be promoted to the
presbyterate.[82]

This attitude did not go unchallenged. The Arabic version of the
same *Apostolic Church Order* that signaled the change says nothing about
it when discussing diaconate ordination. Rather, addressing each minister, it insists: "Stand each one in the Order which is given him, and go

---

76–80. On the third-century practice at Rome: Eulogius Alexandrinus, *fr. Novat.*, ap.
Phot. cod. 280, *PG* 104:353C.

79. Cyprian, *epist.* 67.4–5: G. Hartel, 738–740. On appointment or election, Hippolytus, *trad. ap.* 9.1: G. Dix, 15, especially the discussion of textual variants. *Didascalia* 3.12
clearly speaks of appointment: R. H. Connolly, 146.

80. G. W. H. Lampe, 61.

81. *Apostolic Church Order* 24 (Ethiopic text): G. Horner, *The Statutes of the Apostles*
(London, 1904), 145.

82. G. W. H. Lampe, 61–62.

not beyond the limits which are its limits for him . . . Do not confuse
the ordination according to which each one of you was ordained to his
Order, nor take by force Orders which are not given to you and pass
beyond your own in an overbearing manner that you may possess what
belongs to another, over which you have no authority" (70: Arabic
text). Deacons, in particular, are reminded of the example of Stephen,
who never did anything unsuitable for deacons, but kept to the order of
deacons until the end, as was suitable for a martyr of Christ. If any
change does occur, it is clearly an exception, like the deacon Philip (Acts
8:26ff.), who was chosen for the priesthood directly by Christ (71:
Arabic text).[83]

The very tone of the opposition to change may very well point to a
more serious problem that contributed to the decline of the diaconate,
and may even have indirectly encouraged the change it sought to prevent. This problem was the growing resentment, during the third
century, of the presbyterate against the diaconate. One root of the
resentment can be traced to the interpretation of Acts 6:1ff. as the origin
of the diaconate, and to the gradual sacralization of the tripartite ministry. Irenaeus was apparently the first early Christian writer to interpret
Acts 6:1ff. as recounting the origin of the diaconate, with Stephen as the
first deacon (*haer.* 3.12.10; 4.15.1).[84] The most pervasive sacralization
of the ministry, although beginning with Tertullian, occurred with
Cyprian, who rooted his idea of ministry in a literal application of the
Old Testament priesthood to the Christian tripartite ministry.[85] When
these two trends converged, the diaconate was adversely effected. In
many larger sees, the number of deacons was restricted to seven. At
Rome, for example, the bishop, Fabian (235–250), divided the city into
seven districts, each under the control of a deacon; he was apparently
influenced more by Acts than by local Roman administration, which
had fourteen districts.[86]

Because the third century was a period of rapid growth in the
membership of the Church, the restriction on the number of deacons to
seven came at a particularly unpropitious time. In many cities, like

---

83. *Apos. Ch. Order* 70, 71 (Arabic text): G. Horner, 289, 293.

84. Irenaeus, *haer.* 3.12.10; 4.15.1: F. Sagnard, *SC* 34 (Paris, 1952), 236, 19;
A. Rousseau, *SC* 100 (Paris, 1965), 550, 20–21.

85. M. Wiles, "The Theological Legacy of Saint Cyprian," *Journal of Ecclesiastical History*
14 (1963), 144–145.

86. G. W. H. Lampe, 62.

Rome, a new minister, the subdeacon, quickly emerged to assist the deacon in his ministry.[87] Unlike the deacon, the subdeacon did not possess a special relationship to the bishop, nor to the presbyters, since he was not ordained. The office of deacon itself then grew in importance all out of proportion to the actual number of deacons. This was especially true of the senior deacon.

While this change was affecting the diaconate, the presbyterate was also in transition during this century. The more numerous presbyterate gradually assumed increasing administrative and liturgical functions, which in previous centuries belonged to the bishops and deacons. The presbyters became quasi-independent overseers of parishes or districts, where they were responsible for the *leitourgia* and the *diakonia* within them.[88] This was apparently the *locus* of presbyteral resentment against the deacons. The century became increasingly characterized by attempts to curtail the deacons and to emphasize their subordinate role. At the same time, the growth of the presbyterate apparently facilitated the growing reevaluation of the diaconate as a transitional ministry—a preparation for the priesthood—rather than a permanent order, as has already been seen. These changes in the diaconate attained legal status at the Council of Arles (314), which clearly subordinated the deacons to the presbyters, and forbade deacons to offer the Eucharist; at Neo-Caesarea (320), which restricted the number of deacons to seven on the basis of Acts 6:1ff.; and finally at the ecumenical Council of Nicaea (325), which sharply subordinated deacons to presbyters, and expelled nonconformists from the diaconate.[89]

The very finality of the Nicene canon simply set the seal on the end of an irreplaceable chapter in the history of the Church's ministry. The importance of this diaconal ministry can hardly be overestimated for these three centuries of the Church's life. The *diakonos* was the living link between the Church's *leitourgia* and the *diakonia*, through which she showed the meaning of practical Christian love. The witness continued to be effective, even after the vitality of the order had been eclipsed. The apostate Emperor Julian (361–363), in his attempt at a restoration of classical religion, admitted that the practical *diakonia*, linked to the

87. J. G. Davies, "Deacons, Deaconesses and the Minor Orders in the Patristic Period," *Journal of Ecclesiastical History* 14 (1963), 7.

88. G. W. H. Lampe, 57.

89. Council of Arles (314), Canons 15 and 18; Council of Neo-Caesarea, Canon 15; Council of Nicaea, Canon 18: C. J. Hefele, 193–194; 230; 426–427.

leitourgia, was the primary reason behind the success of the Christian mission. He urged every pagan—especially the pagan priest—to imitate this reality and prove his love: "a proof of his love for his fellows is his sharing cheerfully, even from a small store, with those in need, and his giving willingly thereof, and trying to do good to as many men as he is able."[90] In other words, for Julian, the best proof of one's love was to act like a *diakonos*.

In our own day, *diakonia* still lies at the heart of Christian self-understanding. The Church's identity is still inseparable from her *leitourgia*. Vatican Council II has issued a clear challenge in the present moment of the Church's life to reassert the vital connection between these two dimensions of authentic Christian life. The present attempts to restore the diaconate as a proper and permanent rank among the Church's ordained ministers may again provide just such a living link in the person of the *diakonos*.

90. Julian, *fr. ep.* 305B–D: W. C. Wright, *The Works of the Emperor Julian* 2 (Loeb: London, 1913), 336–339.

WILLIAM J. MCCARTHY

Resurrectio particulatim: Atomism and *Consolatio* in Prudentius' *Apotheosis*

PRUDENTIUS' WELL-CRAFTED and occasionally masterful poetry, a confluence of elements Christian and non-Christian, is just beginning to attract the sort of literary interest which was formerly reserved for the more traditional classics. Of the methods by which these works are interpreted, that which meticulously attends to the contexts from which words or phrases are drawn and into which they are set often may reveal much of the skill and purpose of an author. Not unreasonably may we anticipate that the Christian poet, thoroughly familiar with the tradition in which he is working, is also capable of subtle allusion in the service of his own themes.[1]

Nearly a century ago A. Puech noted that Prudentius modeled his *Apotheosis* on Lucretius' *De rerum natura*, the prototypical didactic (and polemic) poem of Latin literature.[2] Strangely, while agreeing that these poems share a general similarity of genre and tone, succeeding scholars have discerned but few ringing verbal echoes and have scrutinized the

---

1. Thus, this paper proceeds from the assumption that Prudentius, certainly one of the better students of the classics of Latin literature (in which all the later poets and rhetoricians were schooled as a matter of course), carefully exploits the received tradition in an effort to reformulate Roman culture as Christian culture.

2. *Prudence, Étude sur la poésie latine chrétienne au IVe siècle* (Paris, 1888), pp. 159–188, 219. Compare the similar (and equally general) observations of Puech's contemporary, G. Boissier, in *La fin du paganisme* (Paris, 1891), vol. 2, pp. 151ff. (= pp. 133ff. in the 1913 edition).

literary implications of none of these.[3] The purpose, then, of the present brief contribution, one offered in praise of and gratitude to the *honorandus*, is to demonstrate that within the ambient irony of a Christian poem which is both "Lucretian" and anti-Epicurean there is at least one specific borrowing (*particulatim* [1077]) which is quite pointed. Because the *Apotheosis* defends not only the divinity and humanity of Christ but also the "divinization" of the human body, a doctrine which is, of course, thoroughly un-Epicurean,[4] the astute borrowing of this atomistic term in the closing lines, where the poet expresses his hope and confidence in the resurrection, enhances our appreciation both of the irony implicit in the choice of poetic model and of the drama of the concluding *consolatio* addressed by the soul to the body.

A simplified version of Rank's organization of the poem provides us an adequate overview of its contents:[5]

3. C. Brakman ("Quae ratio intercedat inter Lucretium et Prudentium," *Mnemosyne*, n.s., 48 [1920], pp. 434–448), having cited a number of echoes and "coloristic" reminiscences of the one poet in the other (but only slightly supplementing the *index imitationum* of the *Apotheosis* [Cunningham's *CCSL* edition records none, Bergman's *CSEL* but one, and the *BAC* of Guillen and Rodriguez two]), concludes (p. 448) that "dubitare non possumus quin postremus poeta didacticus . . . studiosissime legerit et diligentissime pervolitaverit de Rerum Natura." G. B. A. Fletcher ("Imitationes vel loci similes in poetis latinis," *Mnemosyne*, n.s., 1 [1933–1934], pp. 202–203) also assembled a small group of unimposing reminiscences. Efforts to appreciate and to make good sense of the "Lucretian" properties of this Christian poem have been made by E. Rapisarda, "Influssi lucreziani in Prudenzio, un suo poema lucreziano e antiepicureo," *Vigiliae Christianae* 4 (1950), pp. 46–60; K. Smolak, "Die dreifache Zusammenklang (Prud. *Apoth.* 147–154)," *Wiener Studien*, n.s., 5 (1971), pp. 180–194 (esp. 182–185, 190–193); J. Fontaine, *Naissance de la poésie dans l'occident chrétien* (Paris, 1981), pp. 197–199.

4. The *locus classicus* of the Epicurean (as well as the Stoic) rejection of the resurrection is Acts 17:16ff. For its part, Christian polemic against Epicureanism, tending to draw on the arguments of the Stoa and the Middle Academy, condemns the philosophy for amorality, its perversely asocial character, its lack of scientificness, and, most of all, atheism (see W. Schmid, art. "Epikuros," *RAC* 5 (1962), cols. 792–799). Certainly the theme of life out of death in the *Apotheosis*, when set over against the chillingly atheistic atomism (according to which the only real life, the only true *amor*, is atomic) of the *De rerum natura*, obviates the irony of the latter serving as a model for the former. In this connection J. Fontaine (*Naissance*, p. 199) aptly remarks: "Ce mot [*apotheosis*] apparemment inquiétant résume donc, en réalité, l'essentiel de sa christologie qui fait l'objet du poème. On n'en comprendera bien le sens que dans la profession de foi finale du poète en sa propre résurrection. Cette profession contraste absolument avec le triomphe de la mort qui couronne le poeme lucrétien, et non moins avec la divinisation poétique d'Épicure."

5. R. G. Rank, "The *Apotheosis* of Prudentius: A Structural Analysis," *Classical Folia* 20 (1966), pp. 18–31.

proem (on the Trinity)	12 lines
preface:	
The difficulty of discerning the *recta fides* amidst false teachings.	56 lines
I. The majesty of God the Father:	
God is invisible, formless, impassible; the Son is the form by which He appears.	1–177
II. The fatherhood of God:	
God is a true Father and is distinct from the Son, not to admit which is to destroy both Father and Son.	178–320
III. The Jews:	
Their failure to see Christ as true God, true Temple; their fate as a consequence.	321–551
IV. The mystery of Christ:	
Christ was born of a virgin, truly a man and truly God.	552–781
V. The nature of the soul:	
The soul is not divine, but a divine creation. It is susceptible to sin through its union with the body. Christ's incarnation, suffering, and death have saved it.	782–951
VI. The Manichaean error:	
Christ, who is God, has a real body whose resurrection is the hope of man's own.	952–1084

While Rank recognizes the apotheosis of man himself as a "theme that is interwoven through the entire poem" (p. 27), he overlooks how skillfully Prudentius moves toward the climactic profession of confidence in the resurrection with which the poem concludes. We may note that the structure of the latter half (552–1084) follows an interesting pattern: Christ is not only human but also divine (IV), not only divine but also human (VI [952–1018 = 67 lines]); the human soul is not divine but has a divine origin, and has been saved through Christ's incarnation (V), and the human body, also God's creation, has been given a divine destiny through Christ's incarnation and resurrection (VI [1019–1084 = 66 lines]). The two major themes, one of the union of the two different natures in Christ and the other of the difference between man's two natures, are carefully interwoven, and thereupon resolved in the final lines. The ultimate "reconciliation" between soul and body in the general resurrection, that which is prefigured in Christ's, constitutes the crowning of the reconciliation between God and man. Pertinent to the resolution of these themes, and apropos of the poem's Lucretian model, is the subtle implication of an "atomistic" resurrection in the conclusion. But before we turn to the closing lines, let us first consider an echo of Lucretius in the opening lines of its sixth and final section.

The refutation of the docetist assault on the concrete reality of Christ's body begins with the ascription of a wryly phantasmal savior to the Manichaeans:

> est operae pretium nebulosi dogmatis umbram
> prodere, quam tenues atomi conpage minuta
> instituunt, sed cassa cadit ventoque liquescit
> 955   adsimilis fluxu nec se sustentat inani.
> aërium Manicheus ait sine corpore vero
> pervolitasse Deum, mendax fantasma cavamque
> corporis effigiem nil contrectabile habentem.[6]

[It is worthwhile to produce the shadow of a misty doctrine—a shadow which fine atoms in a very closely fitted structure comprise. But hollow it descends (sc. to the earth) and begins to disintegrate liquidly into the wind, very like the hemorrhaging of a weakened frame, nor does it hold itself together in the void. The Manichaean says that an insubstantial God without a true body flitted through this form, a God possessed of a false image and a hollow figure of a body which contained nothing tangible.]

(952–958)

The body of this Christ is, as we ought to expect of the Manichaean savior, insubstantial, some sort of a phantom;[7] yet, the description of it

6. In arriving at his interpretation of the final section of the *Apotheosis*, the author has been careful to compare the more recent but much maligned (see, for example, the scathing review by K. Thraede in *Gnomon* 40 [1968], pp. 681–691) edition of Cunningham (*CCSL* 126 [1966]) with those of Lavarenne (Les Belles Lettres, 1945), and Bergman (*CSEL* 61 [1926]). Although there are some minor differences in spelling and punctuation, these editors are, fortunately, in essential harmony with respect to the text of lines 952ff. Thus, citations of Prudentius in this paper contain no significant problematic readings, and are punctuated as deemed appropriate.

7. Because even the *editores antiquissimi* used the section titles we find in the *Apotheosis* (see Cunningham, p. xxiv), that of the final section is noteworthy: "Adversum fantasmaticos qui Christum negant verum corpus habuisse." This would indicate that here we are dealing with a very broadly defined "Manichaeism." Indeed, for Prudentius, as commonly during this period, the name of the heresy was "the *terminus technicus* for any form of dualism . . . [because it] was the most prominent and outspoken protagonist of a radically dualistic

is paradoxical. Or rather, perverse. Prudentius' intention in introducing the heretical doctrine is not to explain it accurately or fairly but to seek to lay the groundwork for a refutation. Thus, he deliberately confuses *dogma* with *umbra* (both are "misty"-—part of the satirical treatment[8]— so that we should not presume to dismiss the phrase *nebulosi dogmatis umbram* as hypallage) and immediately signals a less than earnest effort to explain the nature of the phantom. The pun of *umbram prodere* (the verb apparently also intending the sense of "project") is elaborated into the scathingly ludicrous notion of a divine savior, supposedly a being of light, who possesses a body which is a frail and sickly shadow (see note 10). The absurdity is compounded by the emphasis on the "airy" quality of the Manichaean Christ and, in consequence, that of man.[9] Most significantly, however, the very terms in which the composition of the unstable shadow is defined are at odds with the fundamental docetism of Manichaean soteriology because they are distinctly Epicurean (hence, ironically, the most materialist which ancient philosophy could offer), viz., *atomi* and *inane*.[10] Nonetheless, if the initial wit and sarcasm

---

concept of universe and man" (J. P. Asmussen, "Manichaeism," in *Historia Religionum*, vol. I, ed. C. Bleeker and G. Widengren [Leiden, 1961], p. 607). Nonetheless, it is clear that the vitriolic satire of the poem's final section is directed toward the fundamental (if scarcely unique) Manichaean revulsion from the material. As E. Rose (*Die manichäische Christologie* [Wiesbaden, 1979], p. 121) observes of the attitude of this heresy toward Christ, "Für die Manichäer war der blosse Gedanke, der göttliche Erlöser habe sich mit dem befleckten Fleisch verbunden, eine massive Schändung ihres Jesusbild, weshalb bei ihnen von einer Fleischwerdung der Logos keine Rede sein konnte."

8. A. H. Weston ("Latin Satirical Writing Subsequent to Juvenal" [Ph.D. diss., Yale, 1915], pp. 43–56) has long since made the case for Prudentius' skills as a satirist (for examples from the *Apotheosis*, see pp. 44–45), declaring in summary (p. 56): "He may be characterized . . . as the principal satirist of Christian Latin poetry, and rivalled only by Claudian of the other poets subsequent to Juvenal." A detailed exploration of the influence of satire on Prudentius was provided by S. M. Hanley in her dissertation ("Classical Sources of Prudentius" [Cornell, 1959], pp. 110–157), from which she subsequently developed the article "Prudentius and Juvenal," *Phoenix* 16 (1962), pp. 41–52.

9. Note that, having described the Manichaean Christ as *nebulosus* and *aërius* in his introduction of the heresy, Prudentius pursues this image and idea to absurd limits, and reaches the conclusion (1010–1018) that, if Christ deceived mankind *ventosa arte* (962), his phantom body (a kind of garment = *omne, quod est gestum* [Lavarenne: "toute notre enveloppe corporelle" (1017)] which the *tenues aurae* scatter) implies that the bodies of men are also not real (a point emphasized by the polyptoton of 1011ff.: *aërios . . . aërium . . . aëria . . . aëria*), that *sit fabula quod sumus omnes* ("all of us may be but a fiction").

10. Inasmuch as the *umbra* is without question made up of atoms, an allusion to its disintegration "in the void" as a result of instability would neatly round off this thumbnail "atomistic" parody of the (typically Gnostic) descent (= *cadit*) of a supermundane entity. However, the construe of *inani* as the locative of the Lucretian term *inane* involves a reevalua-

make the major points of the no less sarcastic and vituperative arguments to follow, it is important to bear in mind that atomism itself has been neither mocked nor rejected.

While the introduction to the Manichaean Christ provides an undeniable general reminiscence of Lucretius, we should be careful to note that, of the key terms *atomi* and *inane*, the former does not occur in the *De rerum natura*. Of course, Prudentius' fondness for Greek words may account for this substitution. For his part though, Lucretius, in avoiding the word, seems to have completely overcome the *patrii sermonis egestas* of which he complains (see 1.136–139, 830–833, and 3.258–260), for he meticulously shapes a range of equivalents or near-equivalents: *primordia, corpora, corpuscula, semina, elementa, figurae, materies* (or *materia*), and *particulae*.[11] Prudentius, then, whether or not he was much aware of

---

tion of the syntax and meaning of *fluxu*. First, so that *inani* may stand alone, we must reckon the principal caesura of line 955 to fall after *fluxu* (as it does more naturally) rather than after *adsimilis*, where Lavarenne and other editors place a comma (to indicate the caesura there) because they wish to take *adsimilis* with *ventoque* in line 954. While their maneuver is not unreasonable, it does force *fluxu* into the clause introduced by *nec*, a conjunction which normally takes first position. With the caesura after *fluxu*, we may take that noun as a poetical dative with *adsimilis*, and *ventoque* with *liquescit*. An appropriately pathological interpretation of the *fluxus* which the *umbra* suffers guides this construe. The noun, just as the verb *fluo* and the adjective *fluxus*, really ought never to be deprived of the fundamental sense of a "flowing" of some sort. In connection with the body, such "flowing" may pertain to one of its fluids (often menstrual blood or "seed"); and, in a sometimes related but more metaphorical sense, the "flowing" condition of the body indicates its enfeeblement, i.e., either its infirmity (due to disease, deprivation, adverse climate) or its slackness (brought on by luxury and indulgence). We see that the Manichaean shadow-body "flows" because it is an enfeebled structure of *tenues atomi*. Further, we interpret that, upon descending, "it begins to disintegrate liquidly (thus fully exploiting both the image and the inchoative suffix of the verb) into the wind" (= the dative of direction [see M. Lavarenne, *Étude sur la langue du poète Prudence* (Paris, 1933), p. 140]). Proceeding from these points, we may conclude that Prudentius, having already confused the *umbra* with its *dogma*, pursues his satiric treatment by describing its demise as a hemorrhaging (note that *fluxus* is used in this sense in the Latin Bible at Matthew 9:20) of its *tenues atomi* into the wind. *Adsimilis fluxu*, then, has been translated "very like the hemorrhaging of a weakened frame" in order that account be taken of the poet's apparent intention to apply to the *umbra* the literal and metaphorical senses which *fluxus* has in connection with the human body.

11. Concerning all these terms and their distinctions, see Katherine Reiley, *Studies in the Philosophical Terminology of Lucretius and Cicero* (New York, 1909), pp. 35–66 (on *particula* = ἄτομος [4.776, and possibly 3.708 and 4.261], see p. 59). More recent scholars have demonstrated the great precision with which Lucretius fashions and distinguishes his renderings of the term. For example, R. Keen ("Notes on Epicurean Terminology and Lucretius," *Apeiron* 13 [1979], pp. 63–69) astutely observes in connection with the translation *primordia* (pp. 63–64) that, because Epicurus (in the *Letter to Herodotus*) uses ἄτομος as an adjective (neuter [understood with σῶμα] or feminine [understood with φύσις]), the Latin

the fine shades of meaning which apparently distinguish these terms, at any event clearly had all at his disposal. If, in reference to the phantom savior, the Greek term (more exotic?) is preferred, the Latin *particula* plays an important role in his expression of belief in the resurrection and proves to be of special philological note to us. In the first place, it alone has an adverbial form, *particulatim*, which Lucretius uses (and only once). The word occurs in that section of the poem which argues against the survival of the soul after the body's death (3.417–829): [12]

540   quin etiam si iam libeat concedere falsum
           et dare posse animam glomerari in corpore eorum,
           lumina qui linqunt moribundi particulatim,
           mortalem tamen esse animam fateare necesse,
           nec refert utrum pereat dispersa per auras
545   an contracta suis e partibus obbrutescat,
           quando hominem totum magis ac magis undique sensus
           deficit et vitae minus et minus undique restat. [13]

[(Body and soul are observed to die gradually, and there is no concentration of soul within the dying body.) And indeed, even if it should be possible to concede that which is false and thus grant that the soul of those who are leaving the light, dying atom by atom, can be gathered together in their body, even so you would have to confess that the soul is mortal, nor does it matter whether it perishes by scattering through the air, or becomes stupified after it has withdrawn from its proper parts, since sensation wanes ever more swiftly everywhere throughout the whole person, and throughout less and less of life remains.]

(3.540–547)

Regarded strictly as the adverbial form of *particula* (and not of either *pars* [= *partim*] or *membrum* [= *membratim*], each of which adverbs is to be

___

term "does not represent 'atom' . . . but . . . the indivisible quality of those bodies." See also P. Grimal, "*Elementa, primordia, principia* dans le poème de Lucrèce," in *Mélanges P. Boyancé* (Rome, 1974), pp. 357–366, in which Lucretius' strict distinction between *primordia* (the "atoms") and *principia* (the "elements") is explored.

    12. The structure of the third book may be sketched as follows:

    A. Introduction: praise of Epicurus; a syllabus of the elements of this book's topic, the fear of death (1–93)
    B. The nature and structure of the soul (94–416)
    C. The proofs of the soul's mortality (417–829)
    D. The folly of the fear of death (830–1094)

    13. Here and throughout the Latin text is cited from the edition by C. Bailey (*Oxford Classical Texts*).

found in Lucretius), *particulatim* should refer here to the mortal decay of the body "atom by atom" rather than "part by part" or "limb by limb." [14] This atomistic interpretation is buttressed by our observation that the process of a slow bodily degeneration which is described here appears to be paired with a correspondingly gradual "clumping together" (*glomerari* implies the dense packing of many elements [= atoms]) of the soul. According to the theory rejected by Lucretius, then, as the body loses its soul (and the accompanying *sensus* and *vita*) *particula* by *particula*, its abandoned parts die. In this way we arrive at a neatly atomistic scheme which, even if Lucretius rejects the theory of the concentration of soul, takes much better account of his terminology.

Also philologically noteworthy is the infrequency of *particulatim*: despite the fact that it is not a great rarity in Latin prose, save for its occurrence in the above cited passage of the *De rerum natura*, the adverb is not found in poetry. [15] Thus, the recurrence at the end of the *Apotheosis*, in

---

14. Adverbs which terminate in *-im* returned into vogue in later antiquity following their fall into desuetude in the classical period. A. Funck ("Die lateinischen Adverbia auf *-im*, ihre Bildung und ihre Geschichte," *Archiv für lateinische Lexikographie und Grammatik* VIII [Leipzig, 1893], pp. 77–114) discussed at length the history and semantics of such forms, and furnished an extensive list (pp. 111–114). Brakman ("Quae ratio," pp. 445–446), for his part, took general note of the Lucretian *similitudo* which such adverbial forms (along with the infinitives in *-ier* and the use of Greek words) lend certain poems of Prudentius. The archaizing adverbs in *-im* are, however, not all that uncommon in Prudentius (see Lavarenne, *Étude*, pp. 422–423). Nonetheless, for our purposes the form *particulatim* is to be regarded as quite significant because it is unique (in Latin poetry) to Lucretius and Prudentius (see the following note), and it is a Lucretian term for "atom."

In addition, important to the point at hand is the question of how we are to understand *particulatim*. To this end the author, through a private communication, solicited the expertise of R. Newman, who is presently at work on the *particulatim* article for the *Thesaurus Linguae Latinae*. Prof. Newman was kind enough to disclose his (at this stage) preliminary findings concerning the semantic range of the adverb: of the two major divisions of the meaning, a distributive and a kind of limiting sense, the former "sometimes had a temporal notion attached (both Prudentius and Lucretius fall under this category)." Thus, we should understand *particulatim* (as an atomistic term) not in the sense of "atomwise" (or better, "as concerns atoms," if it should seem best to avoid a trend of modern colloquial English [compare "lengthwise," "leastwise," "moneywise," etc.]), but in that of "atom by atom," on the analogy of *guttatim* ("drop by drop," "in drops").

15. First found in Varro (e.g., *De lingua latina* 5.32), it is also absent from the works of Tertullian, whose *Adversus Praxean* is sometimes mentioned as a possible source for the *Apotheosis*. R. Newman (see the previous note) has assured the author, who himself had already failed to discover other occurrences of the adverb among all of the major (Lucretius, Vergil, Horace, Ovid, and Juvenal) and most of the minor poets from whom Prudentius borrows, that the Christian and the Epicurean "are the only two poets who use *particulatim*; it is otherwise strictly prosaic."

the same metrical position as in Lucretius' poem, should scarcely be counted as adventitious, especially if we take into account that this is arguably the Christian poet's most "Lucretian" poem. Let us then consider the new context.

To conclude his dismissal of the insubstantial Christ, Prudentius asserts God's love of man, body and soul (*tantus amor terrae, tanta est dilectio nostri* [1027]),[16] and then expressly recognizes his own self in Christ:[17]

> Christus nostra caro est; mihi solvitur et mihi surgit;
> solvor morte mea, Christi virtute resurgo.
> cum moritur Christus, cum flebiliter tumulatur,
> me video; e tumulo cum iam remeabilis adstat,
> 1050 cerno Deum. si membrorum fantasma meorum est,
> et fantasma Dei est . . .

[Christ is our flesh. For me he (or perhaps more specifically "his flesh") is dissolved and for me he rises. By my death I am dissolved, by Christ's power I rise again. When Christ dies, when tearfully he is buried, I see myself. And now when he emerges from the tomb and stands upright, I see God. If he is a ghostly image of my body, so too is he a ghostly image of God.]

(1046–1051)

Moreover, the future resurrection of the poet's own body (*nosco meum in Christo corpus consurgere* [see 1062ff.]) will be a complete restoration,

> debet enim mors victa fidem, ne fraude sepulchri
> 1075 reddat curtum aliquid, quamvis iam curta vorarit
> corpora; debilitas tamen et violentia morbi

16. The first half of this line is that of Vergil, *Georgics* 2.301, where, if its precise meaning is not uncontested (see W. Richter's commentary [Munich, 1957], p. 227), the agricultural context at least is certain. In borrowing the hemistich, Prudentius clearly has made it refer to the deep affection of the lofty for the lowly, and apparently means to have it combine the idea of God as the molder of man's clay with that of Christ as the one "planted" in it (compare God's mingling of Christ with *incorruptum solum* at 1038ff.). *Dilectio nostri*, then, is best taken to mean that love which God/Christ, human and divine, bears for "us," his lesser physical and spiritual creations.

17. The notion of Christ as a kind of mirror in which Prudentius sees himself (*me video . . . cerno deum*) contrasts, perhaps intentionally, with the figurative *speculum* of the past (3.972–975) offered the frightened and dying old man addressed by *Natura* at *De rerum natura* 3.931–977. There, as we might anticipate, the universal oblivion and mortality reflected in that mirror bears the image of both present and future. See T. Stork, *NIL IGITUR MORS EST AD NOS: Der Schlussteil des dritten Lukrezbuches und sein Verhältnis zur Konsolationsliteratur* (Bonn, 1970), p. 104.

> virtus mortis erat; reddet quod particulatim
> sorbuerat quocumque modo, ne mortuus omnis
> non redeat, si quod pleno de corpore desit.

[for conquered Death [18] must keep faith lest, by the deceit of the grave, he return something imperfect even though he now devours imperfect bodies; yet, feebleness and wracking disease were the peculiar strengths of Death. He shall return that which atom by atom he took away, however he took it away, lest the whole of the dead man not return if he should be lacking some portion of a whole body.]

(1074–1079)

In view of the already discussed infrequency of the word among the Latin poets, this recurrence of *particulatim* may be deemed a learned borrowing from Lucretius. We may also import its atomistic sense into the new context. By seeing himself in Christ, that is, his own resurrected body in Christ's, the poet leaves no doubt of an essential identity between the two. Neither is a phantom (note the echo of *fantasma* from 957 at 1051–1052), neither is anything less than true flesh. That the stuff of this flesh be atoms is both an idea not unwelcome in a poem of recognized "Lucretian" tone and a clever structural feature which ironically contrasts the skewered atomistic portrait of the Manichaean Christ at the opening of the final section with the gloriously imagined resurrection of the poet's own body at the end—where the now "Christianized" atomism inverts (inevitably) a basic Epicurean doctrine.

The views of the two poets on the condition of the soul vis-à-vis that of the body dying "atom by atom" differ radically. For Prudentius, the soul neither "clumps together" in the body (the view which Lucretius rejects) nor helplessly dissipates in the atmosphere as it departs (the accepted view). If in this case the manner of its departure is left unclear,[19] clear nonetheless is the fact that in the concluding lines the poet's "voice" is that of the soul addressing the body:

1080   pellite corde metum, mea membra, et credite vosmet
            cum Christo reditura Deo; nam vos gerit ille

18. Here (with Lavarenne ["La Mort, vaincue, doit avoir l'honnêteté de ne pas rendre . . ."]) we should regard death, already addressed at line 767, as a personified figure.

19. As a poet, Prudentius apparently felt free to embroider the manner in which this event takes place. Probably the most splendid vision is that of the death of Eulalia (*Peristephanon* 3.161ff.), whose soul departs her body in the form of a pure white dove making for the stars (*astra sequi*).

et secum revocat. morbos ridete minaces,
inflictos casus contemnite, taetra sepulchra
dispuite; exsurgens quo Christus provocat, ite.

[Banish fear from your heart, O parts of my body, (see note 22) and you yourself believe as well that you shall return with Christ who is God. For he puts you on and summons you back with himself. Laugh at the diseases which threaten you, scorn the disasters which befall you, spit with contempt on the vile tomb. Go forth to where Christ at his rising summons you.]

(1080–1084)

In general, because Prudentius deliberately discards the classical persona and thus is able "conventionally to begin his *opera* with literally himself in the *Proemium* and [to] end likewise with himself in the Epilogue,"[20] each of his poems is "personal" in a distinctly Christian manner. For him poetry is inextricably an expression of his soul's desire to attain heaven and the presence of God. His aspiration, then, is radically different from that of his classical models—the longing for imperishable *fama* among men.[21] At the conclusion of the *Apotheosis* this "personal" aspect assumes a particularly dramatic form in the address of the poet's soul to his moribund *membra*.

For Lucretius, the obvious mortality of the body provides a key sign from which to infer that of the soul. If the body, constituted of matter, dies, then the soul, material as well (though the stuff be very fine) is also mortal and it dies when does its proper vessel, the body. As a consequence of this conclusion, the Epicurean *consolatio*, whose cold eloquence concludes Book 3 (830–1094) of Lucretius' poem, must seek to remove the fear of death by promising that the results of the dissolution of body and soul are the absence of all sensation and complete oblivion.

Prudentius, on the other hand, assumes the immortality of the finely structured (see 868–869) soul, sprung from God's breath and God-like. The body, in its turn, was created by God's hand and then later, because

20. C. Witke, *Numen Litterarum: The Old and the New in Latin Poetry from Constantine to Gregory the Great* (Mittellateinische Studien und Texte 5; Leiden, 1971), p. 113.

21. Nowhere is this difference better expressed than in the closing lines of the "programmatic" *Praefatio*:

haec dum scribo vel eloquor,
vinclis o utinam corporis emicem
liber, quo tulerit lingua sono mobilis ultimo!

[While I write or recite my poems, O would that I might flash forth, free from the bonds of my body, to where my tongue, stirred by its final utterance, shall go!]   43–45

man had fallen into sin, was lovingly taken on (with the soul) by Christ. Such has he elevated the dignity of the formerly mortal body that ultimately all bodies will become the eternal partners of their proper souls, just as Christ's body is already the eternal partner of his divinity. The preeminent proof and guaranty of this divinization is, of course, the resurrection. In order to emphasize the real corporeality of Christ, Prudentius refutes the docetist/Manichaean view with an absurd "atom-ism," while at the conclusion of the poem, through his careful borrowing from Lucretius, he suggests a sort of Christian atomism, a *resurrectio particulatim* of the body which completely negates its *mors particulatim*, in order to underscore the completeness of that ultimate and eternal restoration.

If we infer that, because no part of it is to be lost to death, the body will come together again, just as it first will have perished, "atom by atom," "in atoms," then *mea membra*—better rendered "*parts* of my body" rather than simply "my body"—in line 1080 should be regarded as having a broad, atomistic sense. That is, *membra* refers to the body as the vast and presently ever-fracturing confederacy of atoms which is the soul's "brother" (see 827ff.).[22] Thus interpreted, Prudentius' self-consolation takes on an appropriately cosmic character in which the eternal reconciliation of human and divine in Christ is dramatically manifest in man (note that the body itself is "personified"). When, albeit previously dissolved, the *membra* are fully reconstituted on the Last Day, by following Christ to an eternal home with the soul, and God, among the stars,[23] this body will have realized for the hopeful soul the apotheosis

---

22. Although Lucretius does not use *membra* in the sense of *atomi*, his thoroughly atomistic thinking about all bodies always at least implies a regard for *membra* (human or otherwise) as an accident of atoms. See, for example, 3.967–969 (*Natura* is speaking [see note 17]):

> materies opus est ut crescant postera saecla;
> quae tamen omnia te vita perfuncta sequentur;
> nec minus ergo ante haec quam tu cecidere cadentque.

[There must be material (one of Lucretius' terms for *atomi*) so that future ages may grow, yet all that will follow you when life comes to an end. Like you, these things have passed away before and shall pass away no less again.]

It is especially apt for Prudentius to have an "atomic" body in mind at the conclusion of the *Apotheosis*. If, for Lucretius, the *membra* of the human body are real and permanent only at the atomic level, for Prudentius the complete restoration of *membra* in the resurrection proves that the sum of the "parts," the body which is the "brother" of the soul, is absolutely real and, in the end, eternal.

23. Belief, both popular and intellectual, in the aetherial or astral destiny of the soul recurs throughout antiquity. (See R. Lattimore, *Themes in Greek and Latin Epitaphs* [Urbana,

which Christ prefigures. Furthermore, because sensation is restored to the absence of oblivion (i.e., the body to the soul) in that blessed state, Prudentius' closing *consolatio* subverts, deliberately we may argue, the message of Lucretius' *consolatio* (and diatribe against the fear of death), and in particular the intended meaning of the well-known *sententia* of Epicurus with which he begins the final section of *De rerum natura* 3:[24]

nil igitur mors est ad nos neque pertinet hilum.

[Death, then, is nothing to us and has not a whit of relevance.]

(3.830)

1962], pp. 31ff., for a very useful diachronic overview.) Christians, and certainly Prudentius, add what pagans characteristically regarded with shock and scorn—an "astral destiny" of the body as well. Although at the end of the *Apotheosis* the poet is not explicit about where Christ will lead the newly resurrected body, we may compare *Cathemerinon* 3.196ff.:

credo equidem (neque vana fides)	spes eadem mea membra manet,
corpora vivere more animae;	quae redolentia funereo
nam modo corporeum memini	iussa quiescere sarcophago
de Flegetonte gradu facili	dux parili redivivus humo
ad superos remeasse Deum.	ignea Christus ad astra vocat.

[And indeed I believe—nor is it an empty faith—that bodies live in the manner of the soul; for even now I call to mind that a God with a body returned from Phlegethon to the heavens with an easy step. The same hope awaits my flesh which, smelling of its burial spices and bidden to rest quietly in the tomb, Christ, its leader, risen from the very same earth, summons to the fiery stars.]

See K. Thraede ("'Auferstehung der Toten' im hymnus ante cibum des Prudentius [*Cath.* 3.186–205]," in *Jenseitsvorstellungen in Antike und Christentum: Gedenkschrift für A. Stuiber* [*JbAC* Ergänzungsband 9 (1982)], pp. 68–78) for an appreciation of Prudentius' reworking of traditional themes, especially the Vergilian *descensus* in *Aeneid* 6, in the closing strophes of this poem.

24. This grim *sententia* (ὁ θάνατος οὐθὲν πρὸς ἡμᾶς [Κύριαι Δόξαι 2, at Diogenes Laertius 10.139; *Epistula ad Menoeceum* 125 = von der Muehll, p. 45, line 19]) is attributed to the sophist Prodicus at *Axiochus* 369b; however, Epicurus, who likely drew, in part at least, on Platonic ideas put forth most explicitly at the conclusion of the *Apology* and in the *Phaedo*, may rightly be judged its originator. (See J. P. Hershbell, *Pseudo-Plato, Axiochus* [Ann Arbor, 1981], pp. 14ff.) In any event, regardless of the true originator, Lucretius almost certainly intended the *sententia* to be taken as one of his master's. We may note that it rather abruptly introduces the third book's final section, a compelling combination of *consolatio* (see T. Stork, *NIL IGITUR* [pp. 25–42 on the dictum]) and diatribe (see B. Wallach, *Lucretius and the Diatribe against the Fear of Death* [Amsterdam, 1976], pp. 11–109 [pp. 11–20 on the dictum]) in which the preceding scientific arguments against the soul's survival give way to the more dramatic rhetorical devices (prosopopeia, for example). The fact that Lucretius' purpose in this section, to prosecute a more emotional disuasion of his audience from the fear of death, nicely parallels the purpose of the brief but empassioned self-consolation which concludes the *Apotheosis* suggests that here again, as in the use of *particulatim*, Prudentius had his eye on the third book of the *De rerum natura*.

The *consolatio* genre, the modern pioneer in whose study was C. Buresch (*Consolationum a Graecis Romanisque scriptorum historia critica* [Leipziger Studien zur klassischen Philologie 9.1; Leipzig, 1886]), has been conveniently reviewed recently by R. C. Gregg in *Consolation*

Through the voice of the immortal soul to its mortal (but only for a time) body the *topos* of the nothingness of death "to us" takes on a completely Christian coloring. Weak and contemptible, Death, in effect, no longer exists, and in that sense it is "nothing to us," soul and body.

Philosophy: Greek and Christian Paideia in Basil and the Two Gregories (Patristic Monograph Series 3; Cambridge, Mass., 1975), pp. 1–50.

MICHAEL SLUSSER

The Corban Passages in Patristic Exegesis

FROM THE EARLY DAYS of monasticism family attachments were seen as
a threat to the ascetic life: "But the Devil, the hater and envier of good,
could not bear to see such resolution in a young man, but set about
employing his customary tactics also against him. First he tried to make
him desert the ascetic life by putting him in mind of his property, the
care of his sister, the attachments of kindred. . . ."[1] Renunciation of
family stands out as an ascetical requirement in some passages of the *Life
of Pachomius* also; for example, when the young Theodore's mother came
to the monastery armed with letters from her bishop to find her son,
Pachomius asked Theodore if he wanted to meet her.

Theodore replied, "If I go out to meet her, will I not be found at fault before
the Lord for having transgressed his commandment which is written in the
Gospel? If the answer is no, I will go; if that is going to be a weakness [on
my part], God forbid that I should see her. I would not spare her even if it
were necessary to kill her, just as the sons of Levi of old acted by an order the
Lord gave them through Moses. God forbid that I should sin against him
who created me, because of love for parents according to the flesh." Our
father Pachomius replied, "If you wish to obey the Gospel's commandment,
am I going to make you transgress it? It would never occur to me to urge you
to do that. . . ."[2]

---

1. Athanasius, *v. Anton.* 5, in the translation by Robert T. Meyer: St. Athanasius, *Life of
St. Antony*, ACW 10 (New York: Newman, 1950), 22. Dr. Meyer's splendid translations and
notes for that work and for Palladius' *Lausiac History* have earned him lasting gratitude from
students of early monasticism.

2. The Bohairic *Life of Pachomius* 37, trans. Armand Veilleux, *Pachomian Koinonia* I
(Kalamazoo: Cistercian Publications, 1980), 60–61.

Later Theodore equates a desire to visit one's parents with outright denial of the Gospel.[3] It is true that the first Greek version of the *Life* gives a less rigorous picture,[4] and other signs of mildness can be seen elsewhere in early monastic literature,[5] but it still seems that the monks took very much to heart the drastic admonition of Luke 14:26: "If anyone comes to me and does not hate his own father and mother and wife and children and brothers and sisters, yes, and even his own life, he cannot be my disciple."

But what about that other saying of Jesus where he disputes with the Pharisees and scribes about their traditions? "For Moses said, 'Honor your father and your mother'; and, 'He who speaks evil of father or mother, let him surely die'; but you say, 'If a man tells his father or his mother, What you would have gained from me is Corban' (that is, given to God)—then you no longer permit him to do anything for his father or mother, thus making void the word of God through your tradition which you hand on" (Mk. 7:10–13 = Mt. 15:4–6, RSV). To a modern reader, the drastic separation exemplified by Theodore and mirrored in countless other citations of Luke 14:26 or its parallel, Matthew 10:37, is not very far from the practice which Jesus condemns here. While one's parents may expect their children to rally around and support them in their old age, one not only can but must refuse to do so in the name of God's prior claims.[6] The monks, especially those of the Pachomian communities, were great readers of and meditators on the Bible;[7] did they never feel the conflict between these words of Jesus? Did others in the church not raise a question when they came to the Corban passages?

My search for patristic interpretations of these passages has turned up surprisingly little. One cannot attribute the sparsity of comments to the relative unpopularity of the gospel according to Mark, because the story

3. Bohairic *Life* 63, ibid., 83–84.

4. First Greek *Life* 37, ibid., 323, where Pachomius adds, "'But if someone meets his relatives not as his relatives but as members of Christ whom he loves as he loves all the faithful, he does not sin.'"

5. Basilius Steidle, "Das Wiedersehen des Mönches mit Mutter und Schwester in der alten Mönchserzählung," *Erbe und Auftrag* 35 (1959), 10–20, uses the above story to show there was no absolute prohibition against seeing one's mother, and gives many other instances. Also see Irénée Hausherr, "Le moine et l'amitié," in *Le message des moines à notre temps* (Paris: Fayard, 1958), 207–220.

6. Another text employed in this regard was Matthew 8:21–22.

7. See Armand Veilleux, "Holy Scripture in the Pachomian Koinonia," *Monastic Life* 10 (1974), 143–153, which is a translation of chapter 5 of part II of his *La liturgie dans le cénobitisme pachômien du 4e siècle* (Rome: Herder, 1958).

appears in almost the same terms in the more heavily used gospel according to Matthew. In general, such comments as have turned up do not suggest that the Corban story created any tension or conflict in the church with regard to asceticism.

Many appeals to the passages pay no attention at all to the injunction to honor one's parents. In the controversies over Gnosticism, for instance, Ptolemy invokes the Corban story as evidence for the differing origins of various strata in the Old Testament, while Irenaeus cites it to show that Jesus taught that the Law and the Prophets really did stem from his Father.[8] A later use portrayed the Pharisees in the account as the prototypes of all who distort or override Scripture in bad faith for their own purposes. For Clement of Alexandria, it is those who have distorted true philosophy;[9] for Athanasius, it is his persecutors;[10] for Apollinaris, it is those who despise spiritual things and are absorbed by the bodily.[11] John Chrysostom and Theodore of Mopsuestia content themselves with straightforward exposition, while Peter of Laodicea draws a moral about not overlooking major duties for the sake of fine points.[12] Jerome takes over from Origen (to whom we shall return) a simple historical explanation, but he specifies what was meant by "honor": "Honor in scripturis non tantum in salutationibus et officiis deferendis quantum in elemosinis ac munerum oblatione sentitur. . . . Praeceperat dominus uel imbecillitates uel aetates uel penurias parentum considerans ut filii honorarent etiam in uitae necessariis ministrandis parentes suos."[13] This stress on temporal needs matches the context of the Corban problem.

According to John Cassian, the monk Archebius tried to fulfill the Lord's precept in the Corban passage by seeing to his mother's financial well-being, while still refusing to meet her face to face.[14] That was one way of dealing with potential conflict. Another way of harmonizing the conflicting demands involved moralizing in some fashion the very dras-

---

8. Ptolemy, *ep.* 4.11–14 (= Epiphanius, *haer.* 33.4); Irenaeus, *haer.* 4.9.3.

9. Clement of Alexandria, *str.* 6.7.59.2.

10. Athanasius, *fug.* 2.

11. Apollinaris, *fr.* 79, ed. J. Reuss, *Matthäus-Kommentare aus der griechischen Kirche*, TU 61 (Berlin: Akademie-Verlag, 1957), 24.

12. John Chrysostom, *hom.* 51 *in Mt.*, ed. F. Field (Cambridge: University Press, 1839), II, 70; Theodore of Mopsuestia, *fr.* 79, Reuss, ed. cit., 124–125; C. F. Georg Henrici, ed., *Des Petrus von Laodicea Erklärung des Matthäusevangelium* (Leipzig, 1908), 169–172.

13. Jerome, *in Matth.* 2, on 15:4–6, ed. Émile Bonnard, Saint Jérôme, *Commentaire sur S. Matthieu*, T. I (Paris: Cerf, 1977), 320–322 and n. 85.

14. John Cassian, *inst.* 5.38. See Steidle, art. cit., 14.

tic terms of Luke 14:26 and Matthew 10:37, as when John Chrysostom acknowledged how wicked it would have been for Jesus to order us to hate without qualification; rather, if and when someone wants to be loved more than Jesus, we are to hate them in that respect.[15] It would extend this paper excessively to try to survey all the interpretations of Luke 14:26 and its parallel, Matthew 10:37, but Gregory the Great's treatment is an example of one which comes close to facing the conflict of duties:

We may well question how we are ordered to hate our parents and those near us in the flesh, since we are commanded to love even our enemies. And indeed concerning one's wife the Truth says, "What God has joined let man not separate," and Paul says, "Men, love your wives just as Christ loves the church." See, the disciple says our wife is to be loved, although the Master says, "Whoever does not hate his wife cannot be my disciple." Surely the judge does not decree one thing, the herald announce something different! Or can we both hate and love at the same time? But if we weigh the force of the precept, we may by distinguishing be able to do both, so that we may love those who are linked to us in fleshly kinship and whom we know as neighbors, and by hating and fleeing those who block us on the divine path we may become oblivious of them. For we love the worldy-wise as if by hating him, not listening when he would steer us wrong. But the Lord, in order to show that this hatred toward those near and dear does not proceed from lack of feeling but from charity, goes on to say, ". . . but even his own soul." Therefore we are told to hate our neighbors, and also to hate our own soul; so it follows that we ought to hate our neighbor by loving him, and thus hate him as ourself. For we really hate our own soul when we do not yield to its fleshly desires, when we break its appetite, when we fight back against what it wants. So the things which are brought to a better condition by being spurned are as it were loved by being hated. Thus doubtless ought we to make a distinction in hating those who are near us, so that we might both love in them what they are, and regard with hatred what they do to block our way to God.[16]

Didymus the Blind also blunts the Matthew 10:37 saying,[17] using two of the same devices which we have seen employed by John Chrysostom. He first restricts the force of the verb: "If someone should hate his father, it is

15. John Chrysostom, *hom. 35 in Mt.*, Field, ed. cit., I, 491.

16. Gregory the Great, *in euang.* 2.37.2.

17. Didymus of Alexandria, *Ps.* 26.10, ed. Michael Gronewald, *Didymos der Blinde, Psalmenkommentar (Tura-Papyrus)*, T. II (Bonn: Rudolf Habelt, 1968), 242–246.

not as his father but as impious that he hates him"—and will love him in so far as he has raised him in piety. Then like John he underlines the comparative element, "more than me," and says, "'Hate' here is meant only as not preferring something to God." Didymus likewise observes that this admonition is especially adapted to times of persecution.

Only four of the authors I have examined do anything with the Corban passages which goes beyond what we have already seen.

Origen, after giving an explanation of the practice of Corban which he says he owes to "one of the Hebrews," applies Jesus' words in Matthew 15:4–6 in a way which suggests that he sees them as concretely relevant in the church of his own time: "So even if one of those we call presbyters, or some leader of the people, would rather that people gave to the poor in the name of the community, rather than to the donors' own family (even if these happen to lack the necessities of life and the donors cannot do both), such a one would rightly be called a brother of those Pharisees who abrogated the word of God through their own traditions and were convicted of hypocrisy by the Savior." A *fortiori* such leaders would not dare take anything from the poor fund for themselves, after reading this passage and the story of Judas (Jn. 12:6).[18]

Cyril of Jerusalem in his prebaptismal catechesis deals with the apparent conflict between the dominical sayings. His affirmation of the priority of one's parents' claims may be due to the context: the catechumens are being trained in basic morality, and relatively few of them at this time will have to have broken with their families in order to become Christian. Cyril says,

For the Lord did not say, "Whoever loves father or mother is not worthy of me," lest out of ignorance people might draw a wrong inference from what was rightly written; but he added, "more than me." For when our fathers on earth purpose things contrary to the Father in heaven, then we have to follow this saying. But when we, carried away by folly and forgetful of all the good they have done us, spurn them even though they do not stand between us and piety, then that saying will apply which says, "Let whoever speaks against father or mother die!"

For the first piety and virtue of Christians is to honor those who bore us, to requite the labors of those from whom we sprang, and with all our might to do what will comfort them; for even if we gave them back all we could, we could never reciprocate the gift of birth.[19]

18. Origen, *comm. in Mt.* 11.9.
19. Cyril of Jerusalem, *catech.* 7.15–16.

Though the only part of the Corban story Cyril quotes is the threat from Exodus 21:17, he makes it clear that in some contexts at least the Decalogue was seen as the general rule, the demands of Luke 14:26 as a rather dangerous exception.

Didymus the Blind explains Jesus' reaction to the Pharisees in Mark 7:9–13 in the usual historical way, but calls attention to the reciprocal obligations of parents from Ephesians 6:4, and adds a wry remark, "Therefore when the Word of God comes, who doesn't want to be honored out of the neediness of parents, nor for fathers to live in less dignity than their children or vice versa, he makes the aforementioned accusations."[20] This remark, while it does not set the opposed sayings against each other, suggests that Didymus was well aware of the concrete conflict.

Cyril of Alexandria does make the conflict explicit:

One must, one really must, honor those who gave us life, not destroy the Law as regards them out of piety towards God. Therefore one ought neither to neglect the things befitting God for merely human reasons, nor on God's account to disregard human beings out of hand; but rendering the utmost in charity to the principle of all things, namely, God, and in second place to our neighbor, we should immediately also convey to those who effected our birth the honors most fitting to them.[21]

Another fragment presents similar sentiments:

Although God ordered us to honor our parents and warned of danger to the disobedient, you [the Pharisees] tell children not to honor their parents, if perchance from generosity they wish to do this; but "If they should ask you for something, say to them 'What you might have received, know that you would be robbing God of it, for I have undertaken to give it to God in sacrifice.'" And on the one hand it is necessary to honor God more than one's parents, but [I say that] we must also demand that people remember the honor due to parents, for children ought not to offend against their own parents under the pretext of giving something to God.[22]

Various hypotheses could be proposed for the seemingly conflict-free atmosphere in which patristic exegetes read the Corban passages. I doubt if there is enough evidence to reach a sure conclusion. But the

20. Didymus of Alexandria, *Trin.* 2.24.
21. Cyril of Alexandria, *fr.* 182, Reuss, ed. cit., 212–213.
22. Cyril of Alexandria, *fr.* 183, ibid., 213.

whole matter may be placed in better perspective if we reflect that for many who pursued the ascetic life their families were a support, not a hindrance, especially if the ascetic was well-to-do. Forsaking the world in this way was quite similar to the *otium* sought by many others of their class who wanted to devote themselves to the things of the spirit. John Chrysostom's mother made a strong case for his remaining at home, concluding with this assurance:

Of course, if you have reason to complain that I distract you with worldly cares and make you manage my property, then pay no attention to nature's laws or education or custom or anything else, but shun them as traitors and enemies. But if, on the contrary, I do everything to provide you with plenty of leisure for the pursuit of this kind of life, then let this bond, if nothing else, keep you by my side. Even if you argue that you have a thousand friends, not one will let you enjoy such freedom as this, for there is nobody who cares for your reputation as I do.[23]

In the discussion between John Cassian and Abba Abraham it comes out that Cassian is supported by his family at home; Abraham says that he too could have been in that situation, but mindful of the Lord's command in Luke 14:26 he preferred to earn his own living with his hands.[24] When ascetics clung to the parental support system and the prospects for inheritance, Luke 14:26 would have conflicted not with God's command to honor one's parents, but with the self-interest of the half-committed young ascetic. That may be part of the reason why so little is said about the conflict in patristic exegesis of the Corban passages.

---

23. John Chrysostom, *sac.* 1.21–22, in the translation by Graham Neville, *St. John Chrysostom, Six Books on the Priesthood* (Crestwood, N.Y.: St. Vladimir's Seminary Press, 1977), 40.
24. John Cassian, *conl.* 24.1–2 and 12.

MEDIEVALIA

E. CATHERINE DUNN

The Myroure of Oure Ladye:
Syon Abbey's Role in the Continuity
of English Prose

JUST A HALF CENTURY AGO R. W. Chambers wrote an essay on the tradition of English devotional prose from Alfred to Thomas More. The work, which has become a classic of modern literary scholarship, was an introduction to a Renaissance biography of More, and a critical analysis of his spiritual writing against its historical background.[1] Detached from this matrix the essay was reprinted in its own right and has become a major force to reckon with in any later exploration of medieval English prose style. Perhaps the strongest challenge to it has been that of William Matthews,[2] who indicated that the ascetical treatises like the *Ancrene Wisse* and Hilton's *Scale of Perfection* constituted only a small stream of English composition, and that other varieties of prose like travel literature and chivalric romance were quite distinct from the spiritual instruction in content and style. Matthews' most formidable proposition was that the only "continuity" of English prose was linguistic, i.e., the solid structure of the language itself, underlying all the types of written expression. Chambers' central thesis, however, was not seriously threatened by this attack, for he had traced the *dominant* form of the prose, an elegant, thoroughly polished, and learned style that England alone

1. R. W. Chambers, *On the Continuity of English Prose from Alfred to More and His School*, EETS (London: Oxford University Press, 1932, repr. 1957).

2. W. Matthews, *Later Medieval English Prose* (New York: Appleton-Century-Crofts, 1963), Introduction.

could claim in a vernacular medium at this period of European history. Addressed to nuns, who were usually not proficient in Latin, this English literary tradition was a *Kunstprosa* cultivated by generations of spiritual directors and chaplains responsible for the education and guidance of women in religious life.

Chambers singled out as the leading characteristics of this prose its lucidity and simple elegance.[3] His critical judgment was the intuitive response of a cultivated British man of letters to a refined medium of communication, with its gentle rhetoric of persuasion to righteous living in a spirit of devout, even mystical, prayer. He found these techniques already in the late Anglo-Saxon homilies of Aelfric, in the thirteenth-century rule for anchoresses, and in the fourteenth-century mystics represented by Richard Rolle, Juliana of Norwich, and Walter Hilton. Chambers did not subject this prose tradition to a statistical, formal study, preferring his literary taste to the methodical analysis of diction, sentence structure, and paragraph rhythms. A reader in our time, accustomed to the Formalist criticism of the mid-century, is likely to sense a real lacuna in Chambers' essay, a need for a set of objective criteria to ground subjective response and to indicate complexities in the prose tradition beyond his interests. The *Ancrene Wisse*, for example, may be simple and homely in its metaphorical use of English country life for teaching of spiritual lessons; Juliana of Norwich may have a characteristic brevity of sentence structure in simple, paratactic clauses coordinately arranged; but on the other hand, Walter Hilton has complex sentence patterns that can truly be called Ciceronian; and Syon Abbey's *Myroure of Oure Ladye* has a flexibility and range of modes from the simplest to the grandest that give it a significant place in fifteenth-century style. This last-named treatise may, indeed, be the best example of the prose tradition in its versatility, and with such a proposition in mind, perhaps one can come to understand the role of Syon in the "continuity of English prose."

Chambers made only a passing reference to Syon, saying that special mention should be accorded to the Bridgettine nuns there, for whom the *Myroure* was composed.[4] This brief allusion is comparable to his slighting of Malory's *Morte Darthur*, excluding it from the mainstream he was studying in the "continuity." Neither of these pieces has the lucidity and

---

3. Chambers, p. cxv.
4. Ibid., p. cxxxii.

simple elegance that he regarded as the hallmarks of the tradition, but each would have made a genuine contribution to his thesis if he had addressed himself to them. Here we can consider only the *Myroure*.

Syon Abbey, a religious house in the London area, was the product of the Lancastrian monarchy.[5] The English royal family became interested in the religious order of the Bridgettines when Philippa, daughter of Henry IV, married Eric XIII of Sweden in 1406. Baron Henry Fitzhugh, a member of the northern Scrope family, but a supporter of Lancastrian rule, accompanied the wedding party to Sweden. While there he laid plans for an English branch of the Bridgettine community, and later did much of the diplomatic and financial work that finally brought the undertaking to realization. Henry V became the monastery's actual founder and patron, bestowing royal property at Twickenham and later at Isleworth for the building of the new community. He was following an English royal custom in founding a religious house at the time of his accession to the throne.[6] The community, in imitation of the Swedish pattern established by St. Bridget at Vadstena, consisted of sixty nuns, with a small corps of clerics and laymen to serve the spiritual and managerial needs of the contemplative women, with their properties.

The story of Syon's early days has been detailed a number of times, covering the dedication of its first building by Henry V in 1415, before the French expedition that led to Agincourt; the first profession of novices in 1420; and the laying of the cornerstone for a new building complex by John, duke of Bedford, in 1426, after Henry's untimely death.[7] For present purposes, it is of more significance to concentrate upon the cultural ambience of the community and the literary distinctions of its members and patrons. As a royal foundation and a London institution, it played an extremely important role in the national life, serving as both a model and a sign of English vitality and aspiration. The

5. Ibid., p. cxli.

6. See the master's dissertation of Mary Elizabeth Jellen, "Syon Abbey as a Literary Center in Fifteenth Century England," Catholic University of America, Washington, D.C., 1970.

7. For the institutional history of Syon Abbey, see the Introduction to *The Myroure of Oure Ladye*, ed. John H. Blunt, EETS, e.s., 19 (1873) (New York: Kraus Reprint, 1975), pp. xi–xiv; Margaret Deansley, ed., *The Incendium Amoris of Richard Rolle* (Manchester: Manchester University Press, 1915), pp. 91–130; John R. Fletcher, *The Story of the English Bridgettines of Syon Abbey* (South Brent, Devon: Burleigh Press, 1933), pp. 16–25; David Knowles, *The Religious Orders in England* (Cambridge: Cambridge University Press, 1955), II, 176–181.

brief period after Henry IV's victory at Shrewsbury, and the short reign of his oldest son, constituted a small renaissance on English soil in the domains of literature, music, and theology.[8] One needs no better testimony to the quality of Lancastrian leadership than the establishment of Syon Abbey, and its remarkable success during the fifteenth century, even through the years of civil strife. This religious house drew to itself some of the best-educated and most cultivated men and women of the country, including many Oxford and Cambridge alumni.[9] Contemplatives already in religious life as hermits and anchoresses found themselves drawn to Syon. The solitary life of mystical contemplation, flourishing in late medieval English spirituality as an individual quest, opened itself to the new foundation at London, where the anchoritic life was refashioned into a community pattern under a Rule and obedience to an elected abbess.[10]

The library of the new foundation became a fine collection of Latin and English books of spirituality. The masculine members of the joint establishment had their own library, the manuscript catalogue of which survives today in the library of Corpus Christi College, Cambridge.[11] Hope Emily Allen speaks of Syon as "a great centre of Rolle's influence," where autograph copies of his works were gathered, perhaps because Baron Fitzhugh's family, the Scropes, had been sympathetic and friendly to Rolle in the fourteenth century.[12] The abbey was fortunate in its patronage by booklovers who could afford to pay for the laborious and expensive work of copying the manuscripts. John, duke of Bedford, who became England's regent at the death of Henry V, was a generous donor, presenting to the community two handsome books containing the Latin office of the Blessed Virgin, the fundamental prayer structure prescribed by St. Bridget for nuns of her order. In addition, he presented "unam legendam"[13] to the Syon sisters, and these three volumes became the

8. Manfred Bukofzer, *Studies in Medieval and Renaissance Music* (New York: Norton, 1950), p. 76; Emmet Hannick, *Reginald Peacock* (Washington: Catholic University of America Press, 1922), p. 58; Chambers, pp. cxv–cxvii.

9. "Syon," *New Catholic Encyclopedia* (New York: McGraw-Hill, 1967), XIII, 892.

10. Helen Gardner, "Walter Hilton and the Mystical Tradition in England," *Essays and Studies by Members of the English Association* 22 (1936), 113.

11. Blunt, p. 83. It is MS C.C.C. 251.

12. Hope Emily Allen, *Writings Ascribed to Richard Rolle* (New York: D. C. Heath, 1927), p. 216, and her edition of *English Writings of Richard Rolle* (Oxford: Clarendon Press, 1931), p. 83.

13. Blunt, p. xvii.

substance of the work known as *The Myroure of Oure Ladye*, in English translation, the Bridgettine breviary as used by the women religious.

The presence of texts in the library, precious as such gifts may be, is not of itself evidence for a cultivated reading audience. There are, however, explicit indications of a lively interest in the literature of mysticism and the devout life among the Syon nuns. Late in the century Dame Joan Sewell, of the Syon community, received a gift of Hilton's *Scale of Perfection* (the printed edition of Wynkyn de Worde, 1494) annotated by the donor, a Carthusian monk named Greenehalgh. The gift was made because the Syon sister was known as a devotee of mystical writing, particularly of Richard Rolle's work.[14] There is, moreover, additional evidence of a cultivated reading audience from the *Myroure* itself. It contains an essay on reading, prefixed to Part 2, under the running title "How ye shall be gouerned in redyng of this Boke and of all other bokes." The method of meditative reading advocated there is much in the spirit of the *lectio divina* prescribed in the *Rule* of St. Benedict, although the writer does not cite such an original. He makes practical suggestions for the choice of reading material, e.g., that a person should not select a severe ascetical treatise at a time when he or she is suffering from melancholy or tribulation.[15] He distinguishes clearly between books that are directed to the understanding, with a cognitive approach, and those that are meant to stir the emotions with an affective appeal (pp. 69–70). He indicates that the Bridgettine office and its lectionary move freely back and forth from cognitive to affective address, and it is clear that he envisions not only the community recitation of this office but also an individual program of frequent private reading.

The clerics who served as confessors and spiritual directors for the nuns of Syon took considerable pains to supply their library with vernacular versions of Latin spiritual writings. These English translations were made anonymously and the problem of authorial identification is a difficult one. For some of them there is no known candidate for authorship and no certainty that they were actually written at Syon itself. But the several texts closely associated with literary activity at the monastery have an affinity of genre and style suggesting a small "school" or coterie of writers, most probably under royal patronage. This literature is contemporary with the work of John Lydgate, a Benedictine monk also

14. Chambers, pp. cxxvi–cxxvii and cxxxii.
15. *Myroure*, p. 69.

residing in the London area, a prolific writer likewise encouraged by the royal family. [16] The Syon texts, however, have a different focus from that of Lydgate and his imitators. The focus is in the revelations of two great feminine mystics, St. Bridget of Sweden and St. Catherine of Siena, whereas the Lydgate coterie was much interested in the French allegorical writing of Guillaume de Guilleville, the Cistercian pilgrimage-of-life literature. It is entirely appropriate that the spiritual reading given priority at Syon should be feminine in its origins, psychology, and manner of expression. The sisters of this community were simply having their turn at sharing in the long tradition of religious writing for English women, a personnel presumed to have no ready command of Latin linguistics. It is Chambers' great achievement to have perceived this serious concern with the spiritual formation of women, out of which grew, as a by-product of major importance, the continuity of English prose.

One well-known example of this translation enterprise at Syon was the *Dialogo* of St. Catherine, the Sienese mystic of the late fourteenth century. Known as *The Orcherd of Syon*, this work contains a direct address to the sisters of the community. [17] It gives to them not a translation of Catherine's Tuscan Italian account of her visions, but a careful, literal version of the Latin. Scholars have not yet determined whether the Middle English is based on Raymund of Capua's Latin rendering, but this view is favored by Sister Denise Mainville, who says that Raymund's work itself involved a difficult task of translating Catherine's colloquial Italian composition into a formal Latin idiom. [18] The Middle English of this celebrated mystical work has not called forth enthusiastic critical estimates of its prose style. Rev. Thomas Dibdin, a nineteenth-century bibliophile, has probably made the most accurate comment, observing that the language and thought of the *Orcherd* are "of obscure nature." [19] Phyllis Hodgson ventured only the opinion that "the prose of the translation merits attention in its own right," [20] and she made no stylistic

16. See Walter Schirmer, *John Lydgate: A Study in the Culture of the Fifteenth Century*, trans. Ann Keep (Berkeley and Los Angeles: University of California Press, 1961). The duke of Bedford was patron for a set of texts that he sponsored as English translations of French moral allegories (pp. 120–129).

17. *The Orcherd of Syon*, ed. Phyllis Hodgson and Gabriel Liégey, EETS 258 (1966), I, vii.

18. Mainville, "'The Orcherd of Syon': An Introduction," *Traditio* 14 (1958), 283.

19. Quoted by Sister Denise, p. 274, n. 23.

20. Hodgson, "*The Orcherd of Syon* and the English Mystical Tradition," *Proceedings of the British Academy* 50 (1964), 249. Jeremy Finnegan's essay "Catherine in England: The Orcherd

analysis. My judgment is that the English translator's extreme care to reproduce the expression of the Latin has given the prose a ponderous cast.[21] The work is thus an important contribution to Syon's awareness of Continental mysticism but not a distinguished piece of English prose. The complex sentence structure certainly excludes it from the simple lucidity that R. W. Chambers valued so highly. The hypotactic arrangement of subordinate clauses suffers from a lack in medieval English syntax of inflected relative pronouns by which complex Latin periods can deploy several dependent clauses in an evolving periodic structure moving to a climax. This poverty of English connectives marks the prose of even a great English writer like Chaucer and accounts for the predominance in Middle English prose of a paratactic arrangement of short, coordinate, independent clauses in a serrated form avoiding subordination.[22]

One may therefore turn from the *Orcherd* to the English version of St. Bridget's *Revelationes* for a second indication of Syon's translation activity. This material is very complex and the total corpus of the accounts written by the saint is enormous. Editions vary in their contents, and translations are likely to be selections rather than complete works. Bridget recorded her visions and the instructions received in them, immediately after their occurrence, and composed these accounts in Swedish. She reported that her mandate was to give the vernacular versions to her confessor, Peter of Skänninge, for translation into Latin, and then to submit the latter text to a Spanish theologian, Alphonse, for approval of the doctrinal contents.[23] Syon Abbey had a Latin text of the complete *Revelationes*, transcribed in 1427 from the original in the Swedish monastery at Vadstena.[24] An English translation of excerpts is extant at Princeton University Library, and has been edited in the EETS series by William Cumming.[25] Phyllis Hodgson considered that neither

---

of Syon" (*Spirituality Today* 32 [1980], 13–24) is a study of her thought and avoids evaluation of the prose style.

21. Sister Denise (p. 270) remarks on this exact rendering of Latin style and sentence structure, but seems to regard the closeness of rendition as a positive contribution to the sustained English prose that results.

22. Matthews, Introduction, pp. 12–16.

23. See A. J. Collins' edition of *The Bridgettine Breviary of Syon Abbey* (Worcester: Stanbrook Abbey Press, 1969), Introduction, p. xviii, for the identification of St. Bridget's confessor, and of Alphonse as the Spanish bishop Alfonso da Vadaterra.

24. The manuscript is extant as British Museum MS Harley 612.

25. *The Revelations of Saint Birgitta*, ed. William P. Cumming, EETS 178 (1929).

this version (the so-called Garrett manuscript) nor the other six translations still extant were likely to have been made at the Abbey itself.[26] Cumming evaded this problem of identifying the translator but considered it likely that the Syon Latin manuscript was used, even if it was loaned out for the purpose of translation.[27]

Cumming also expressed his critical opinion that the text was superior, in a stylistic sense, to any of the other English versions, all of which are independent one of another. He observed that the English follows the Latin carefully, even to awkwardness at times, but regarded the prose as generally simple and direct, with some excellent passages, retaining much of the pictorial power of Bridget's imagery in the translation.[28] I am not inclined to agree with this favorable estimate. Like the *Orchard of Syon*, the text is historically important for its transmission to English readers of a powerful Continental work. The prose, however, reads very awkwardly as "translation English" and cannot easily be regarded as an example of the elegance that Chambers admired.

William Matthews, in arguing his case against "continuity," insisted that Middle English writers achieved no theory of translation and no practical set of techniques for handling alien syntactic structures in their native vernacular.[29] I would argue that each individual achieved his own style in the struggle with the alien idiom—some forging a fine English prose, others, like the translator of this Garrett manuscript, failing to do so.

The *Revelationes* of St. Bridget became available to the sisters at Syon in a second way, however, by the translation of the Bridgettine breviary into English, together with an introductory essay that draws freely upon various visions of the Swedish saint. This work is the *Myroure of Oure Ladye*, completed in the early years of the Abbey, at least before 1450.[30] Identification of the translator has been a long-standing problem and the names of possible candidates include monks of Syon—Thomas Ismaelita, Clement Maidstone, Thomas Fishbourne, Richard Whytford— and also a prominent benefactor of the order, Thomas Gascoigne, closely identified with Oxford University. John Blunt, in editing the text for the

---

26. Hodgson, "*The Orchard of Syon* and the English Mystical Tradition," p. 237.
27. Cumming, pp. xx–xxi.
28. Ibid., p. xxii.
29. Matthews, p. 6.
30. Blunt, p. viii.

EETS in 1873, favored Gascoigne, and this learned man has been the strongest candidate,[31] known as a generous donor of books to Syon Abbey and a frequent user of its library. He has several literary works to his credit, including a theological dictionary and an account of the conflict between Archbishop Scrope and King Henry IV. His thought was much influenced by the writings of St. Bridget, and he was interested also in the life of her associates at the Vadstena Abbey.[32] Most significant of his achievements, perhaps, is his position as vice-chancellor of Oxford (1434–1439) and chancellor (1442–1445). Very recently, however, a Swedish editor of the Bridgettine breviary has bypassed Gascoigne and asserted categorically that the *Myroure* was translated into English by Thomas Fishbourne, first confessor general of the Bridgettines at Syon.[33]

Whoever may have translated the text, the *Myroure* is a version of the canonical hours as chanted by the nuns of the order, along with the Proper parts of Masses celebrated in honor of Mary. This work, substantially a book of hours with a lengthy introduction on monastic community prayer, is to be distinguished from the "Little Office of the Blessed Virgin," as Eric Colledge points out,[34] for it is the full Bridgettine breviary of Marian offices, through which the sisters progressed each week. (The masculine members of the community chanted in their own chapel not a Marian breviary but the regular office of the Church according to the Sarum Use.)[35] The Psalms, which form a substantial element in the Hours, nevertheless are missing in the *Myroure*, as the writer indicates they are available in English Bibles and also in Richard Rolle's special translation.[36] The *Myroure*, then, is a complex work, differing from other Syon translations like the *Orchard* in its freedom from a

31. Ibid., p. ix. Winifred Pronger, in an untitled article on Gascoigne in the *English Historical Review* 53 (1938), 625, considers Gascoigne not to be the translator. Collins strongly favored Thomas Fishbourne, but remained uncertain (pp. xxxvii–xl).

32. Pronger, pp. 618–625; Blunt, p. 9.

33. Den Heliga Birgitta och den Helige Petrus av Skänninge, *Officium Parvum Beate Marie Virginis*, ed. Tryggve Lundén, 2 vols. (Upsala: Acta Universitatis Upsaliensis, 1976), I, cx. (The text is in Latin, with modern Swedish translation; and introductory material is in Swedish, with an English summary of it on pp. cv–cxii.)

34. Colledge, "A Syon Centenary," *Life of the Spirit* 15 (1960–1961), 308.

35. F. Procter and E. S. Dewick, eds., The Syon *Martiloge in Englysshe* (London: Henry Bradshaw Society Publications, vol. III, 1893), p. ix, say that in 1414 the London diocese substituted the Sarum Use for the old use of St. Paul's.

36. *Myroure*, "The Fyrste Prologue," p. 3.

compelling need to retain the precise sense of a mystical revelation, and therefore in its freedom to become an English prose of stylistic ease and persuasive beauty.

The most striking feature of the *Myroure* is the flexibility of its sentence rhythms and patterns of embellishment. In this supple quality of the prose it differs from the other classics of devotional writing in the English tradition. It cannot be easily classified or typed, as can Juliana of Norwich's *Revelations* or Walter Hilton's *Scale*, as an example of "estilo culto" or of "Ciceronianism."[37] Nor does it establish its mode fundamentally in one of the style levels familiar to the Latin rhetorical tradition as *humile*, *medium*, and *grande*. Moreover, it completely avoids the type of ornamentation that the fifteenth-century writers spoke of as "aureation," the gilding of simple, Anglo-Saxon diction with long polysyllabic coinages, deliberately imported from Latin or French bases.[38] The *Myroure* does, however, preserve an *address*, a way of approaching the taste and interests of the feminine reading audience, that places the work firmly in the continuity of the English prose classics. It seems to recapitulate various forms of development from a prose affiliated to the Old English poetic hemistich, through a style of short, paratactic, balanced clauses, and including the complex periods of an adapted Ciceronian rhetoric—all of these modes available in one or another English exemplar like Aelfric's homilies or the *Ancrene Wisse*. This ability to draw at will upon all of the tactics used by cultivated translators of Latin prose gives to the *Myroure*'s author a role as creative adapter of stylistic modes, just as Syon Abbey itself became a repository and recapitulation of Western European spirituality at the close of the Middle Ages.

Each of the above propositions would need a detailed study that cannot be made in a short essay like the present one.[39] It is, perhaps, feasible to deal with the process of address and its adjustment of stylistic modes under broad, comprehensive categories with illustration from the

37. The best discussion of Latin prose style in vernacular imitations is still that of Morris Croll, originally an introduction to an edition of Lyly's *Euphues*, but reprinted in the collection *Style, Rhetoric and Rhythm: Essays*, ed. J. M. Patrick et al. (Princeton: Princeton University Press, 1966).

38. Schirmer, pp. 73–77, discusses aureate style.

39. Rhetorical studies in the English department at the Catholic University of America are closely related to the work of the late Professor J. Craig La Drière, whose methodology of "voice and address" has been expanded and applied by his students and colleagues.

two major parts of the *Myroure*. The translator of this Bridgettine material adopted a different stance for each of his tasks, viz., of teaching,
admonishing, and moving the hearts of his readers. Style is a function of
"address,"[40] and whether the writer was thinking formally in terms of
the Ciceronian ends of discourse (*docere*, *delectare*, and *movere*)[41] or not, he
displayed a fine adaptability to each of his separate pedagogical aims. As
indicated above, he distinguished between literary composition directed
to the understanding and that making an appeal to the emotions, advis-
ing the sisters to adjust their response to each method and, above all, to
recognize that the "office" they chanted varied frequently from cognitive
to affective appeal throughout its range.

Parts 1 and 2 of the book are best studied separately for their *stylisti-
que*. The first is an expository essay on divine service, defining the nature
and manner of the Church's official prayer, commonly known as the
canonical "hours" or the Divine Office. The twenty-four chapters of this
scholastic lecture are the best illustration within the *Myroure* of a cognitive approach to the reader—informative, analytical, occasionally pre-
ceptive. The style is simple, with declarative sentences, often lacking
hypotaxis or subordination of clauses, and the diction is intellectual,
factual, and objective, often Anglo-Saxon rather than Latinized. The
analytical tendency to divide and subdivide genera into species betrays
the manner of a philosophy professor. Once in a while there is an
interruption of the expository line for an anecdote or an *exemplum* such as
a homily might contain.[42] The speaker has assumed the role of lecturer to
a class, presumably of novices in the religious community of Syon.
Although many of the newly professed women may have been fairly
advanced in age, and experienced in the anchoritic life, it is highly
probable that they lacked experience and training in monastic community prayer of the liturgical hours.

Within this part of the *Myroure*, fundamentally written in the *genus
humile* of the stylistic levels, a typical passage occurs in chapter 2, in
which the author explains why there are seven definite times for liturgical prayer and why each "hour" occurs just when it does. He explains that

40. La Drière, "Voice and Address," in *Dictionary of World Literature*, ed. Joseph Shipley,
rev. ed. (New York: Philosophical Library, 1953), p. 443.

41. Cicero discusses the three functions of the orator in terms of fitness or decorum in
Orator 21.69–71 (see the edition of P. Reis [Lipsiae: Teubner, 1932], pp. 23–24).

42. See, e.g., p. 34 of the *Myroure* (the story of King Robert) and pp. 64–65 (the
encounter of the desert Fathers with some pagan philosophers).

major events in the life of Christ occurred at certain times of the day or night and are recalled in one of the official prayer intervals. The hour of none, apparently recited before the midday meal, has definite associations: "At howre of none, oure lorde Ihesu crist cryed, & gave out his soulle by dethe, the same houre a knyght openyd our lordes syde with a spere, & smote thorugh his herte, where out came water to our baptym, & blode to our redempcion. And on Ester day he apperyd the same howre to saint peter" (p. 13; I have normalized the spelling of "u" and "v" in the modern way). He details the memories honored and celebrated at each time of liturgical prayer, without any effort to create an emotional resonance in the language, even where the allusion is to the Passion of Christ. Lucidity is the need and simplicity is the means.

Even within the long stretches of this "low style," however, there are short passages of quickening enthusiasm and deliberate adornment. Chapter 12 deals with the values of chanted song as prayer and the following chapter gives a historical sketch of sacred chanting from the time of Moses' emergence from the Red Sea leading the Israelites in a song of victory and praise. In these sections the author is not so much instructing the readers as persuading them to love their community prayer and appreciate its possibilities for stirring the heart to contrition, raising it above melancholy, overcoming obstacles and enemies, and pleasing God.[43] Because he is listing these advantages in a series and elaborating on each one, the pattern of sentence structure takes on a serial character, short, paratactic units one after the other in coordinate arrangement. The deployment of these units in measures of equal length (what the Greek rhetoricians called *isocolon*) is noticeable, together with a parallelism of syntactic structures preserved throughout the series (*parison*). Occasionally the balance of these measured parts is emphasized by similarity of phonemic quality in corresponding words (*paromoion*). The total effect of such a passage is one of swelling and growing intensity. It is a kind of florid speech, a *genus medium*, that belongs to medieval Latin prose at its most characteristic. This effect has been designated as *estilo culto* when it is deliberately created in a vernacular idiom, but it is fundamentally a set of techniques known in ancient Greek and Latin prose and practiced assiduously by medieval Latin writers for centuries.[44] An example of this consciously structured rhythm and musical sound

43. *Myroure*, pp. 32–34.
44. Croll, pp. 242ff.

patterning occurs in the fourth reason given for the efficacy of chanted prayer:

The forthe profyt of holy chyrche songe ys, that yt dothe away undyscrete hevynes. . . . And Isodore saith that devoute syngyng in holy chyrche conforteth hevy hartes, and makyth soulles more gracyous, yt refresshet them that ar wery and tedyous, yt quyckeneth them that are dulle, and yt sturryth synners to wayle theyr synnes. For though the hartes he sayth of flesshely people be harde; yet when the swetnes of that songe soundyth in them, theyr soulles ar sturred to the affeccyons of pyte.[45]

This style is rather familiar to historians of English prose as Euphuism, but here it should not be judged as a "precious" affectation in John Lyly's Renaissance mode. The very sparseness of passages like this one calls attention to them as momentary embellishment rather than as pervasive manner. The alliterative repetition of "s" phonemes in this illustration is confined to the final sentence and is dropped quickly, before it can become alienating rather than attractive.

While Part 1, the introductory essay, thus flows along in a generally simple and informative exposition, occasionally rising to a more florid manner in passages of persuasive enthusiasm, Part 2, the translation of the Office itself, gives the writer an opportunity not only for the low and middle styles but also for some measure of the *genus grande*. This highest level of prose style is again an infrequent phenomenon, occurring as a kind of modulation or a regular rise and fall of intensity. Here the most detailed commentary occurs in the office of matins, for the author has psalms, hymns, anthems, and three lengthy lessons to work with on each day of the week. The lessons, which he calls "storeys" (although they are not narratory), constitute the *legend* or lectionary that St. Bridget received, in her own account of it, directly from an angel.[46] They deal with the excellence of Mary in various aspects, e.g., the joy of the Holy Trinity in her and the love of the angels for her.[47]

The principle of address operates in this commentary of Part 2 on a macrostylistic scale, i.e., the ornateness seems to occur not in a concluding sentence of a passage, but rather in long "blocks" or intervals

---

45. *Myroure*, p. 33. Comparable passages occur on p. 6, "The Fyrste Prologue"; p. 37, beginning at l. 5; p. 55, l. 29; p. 64, l. 29; p. 97, l. 5.

46. Tryggve Lundén bypasses the question of an angel's dictation, and instead indicates the theological sources of this material, e.g., in the *Speculum Virginum* (p. cxi).

47. *Myroure*, First Prologue, pp. 4–5, outlines the contents of the legend.

associated with quasi-lyrical pieces, like the "Te Deum" of matins, the "De Profundis" of tierce and the "Magnificat" of vespers. There is much expository writing in this second part, but even this expository manner has features differing from the simple didacticism of Part 1. The inter-action, therefore, of cognitive and affective address throughout the office commentary is more complex than in the introductory essay.

The lessons of matins, as mentioned above, are a lengthy treatise on Mariology, divided into three lessons for each day of the week. They explicate the Blessed Virgin's status, role, and vocation as they relate to Scriptural events (both Old and New Testament) like the Creation, the Exodus, or the Incarnation. The didactic manner here is sometimes low-key, but often the mystery involved in the Marian role is so profound as to defy the effort to reduce it to simplicity. The writer must have recognized that he was not here dealing with an introductory orientation to the liturgy addressed to novices, such as he had offered in Part 1. He seems to have judged the intellectual capacity and level of maturity to be very elevated at Syon; there could be no greater tribute to the cultured women of that community than the adjustment of his language to these theological mysteries without flinching from the difficulty of the task. The lessons of the Sunday matins, on Mary's relation to the Trinity, and those of the Saturday, on her bodily Assumption into heaven, are prob-ably the best illustrations of the colossal task here undertaken,[48] but they do not lend themselves easily to quotation. A passage in the Friday matins, however, may illustrate the type of theological reflection used by the commentator. It deals abstractly with one of Mary's prerogatives, her degree of knowledge about her Son's future sufferings. The writer spends a couple of pages on the thought that she knew the meaning of the Old Testament prophecies about Christ's sufferings to come, and knew the implications more profoundly than did the prophets themselves: "*Et vere*," he says, picking up the text of the lesson, "And veryly yt is to beleve [to be believed] wythoute eny doute that she understode by the inspyracyon of the holy goste all that the speches of the prophetes bytokened or mente more perfytly. then [*sic*] the same prophetes. that of the same spyryte spake the wordes by mouthe" (p. 245). The density of the linguistic texture here seems to call for a compensatory release into a more affective mode, and the depiction of Christ's Passion in these Friday

48. *Myroure*, Sunday matins, pp. 102–113; Saturday matins, pp. 260–271.

lessons balances the reflective commentary with pictorial images of vivid realism suggesting the language of the English Passion plays.

The Invitatory Psalm (94) of matins, chanted at the beginning of the Office each day, and the commentary upon it, are perhaps the best revelation of the writer's flexibility and the ease of his movement among style levels. The Invitatory is a mutual call of the religious community members one to another, urging them to be present, in the full sense of the word, to the liturgical prayer they have come to perform. Its theme is "Venite," the opening word of the Psalm: "Venite, exultemus Domino, jubilemus Deo salutari nostro."[49] The translator pauses on one word or phrase at a time, and quietly explicates it in a simple, didactic manner: "*Venite* that ys. Come ye. To whome speke ye; they that ar presente, ar come alredy. they that ar absente; may not here you. whome bydde ye come and whyther: Oure lorde ys over all presente and ever more redy to here them that pray in chyrche but all ar not come to hym. that ar come to chyrche. For he sayeth of some that worshyp hym with theyr mouthes. that theyr harte is farre from hym" (p. 84).

As he advances through the five verses of the psalm, he rises at times above this *humile* style to a greater floridity, as he urges the community to sing joyfully, picking up the Latin "exultemus," "jubilemus," and "adoremus." As the exultation turns to serious admonishment in the final verses, he observes that the psalm had begun in joy but ends in fear, as it refers to the Israelite ancestors in the desert who had heard the Lord's voice but had hardened their hearts against it. The verses of the psalm encourage a profound reflection on life, for they speak of God's power and lordship over all the earth—the heights, the depths, the sea, and the dry land. As the commentator catches this vision of the world his expression assumes not only an affective language but a high degree of complexity in sentence patterning. Here it is not the small correspondences of clause length, phrase, and individual sounds that strike the reader, but rather the kind of hypotactic building of clauses into a compound-complex periodic structure that gathers paradoxical ideas into a delicately suspended unity of thought. He seems to reach a *genus grande* for a time as he

49. The reader may find Karl Young's text of Christmas matins in the Roman liturgy, reproduced for those studying the medieval liturgical drama, helpful in understanding the way in which the Ninety-fourth Psalm was normally chanted with repetition of its antiphon after each of the psalm verses (*The Drama of the Medieval Church* [Oxford: Clarendon Press, 1933], I, 50–51).

contemplates, *Quia in manu eius fuerunt omnes fines terre / Et altitudines moncium ipse conspicit.*

And the hyghnesse and depnesse of mounteynes he beholdeth. As hygh as a mounteyne is to the beholdynge of him that standeth bynethe; as depe ys yt to the syghte of hym that standeth above & loketh dounewarde. then a mounteyne ys bothe hyghe and depe. for they that make them selfe depe and lowe to god. by mekenesse. he beholdeth by hys mercy and lyfteth them up. and maketh them hyghe mounteynes by hys grace. And therfore sayeth the prophete here that the hyghnesse, and depenesse of mounteynes he beholdeth. (p. 86)

His rapture seizes the phrase "altitudines moncium" as he catches the two contrasted meanings of depth and height present in the Latin word, and creates balance, antithesis, and climactic movement, in the grand manner.

In the scope of the *Myroure* there is, in summary, a whole range of oratorical effects and a frequent modulation of style to meet the requirements of address as they arise. The translator, whether Thomas Gascoigne or Thomas Fishbourne, has drawn upon the stylistic resources of the Latin rhetorical tradition and achieved a copiousness understood and honored in that tradition. *Copia* is the characteristic of this work, rather than the simple lucidity that Chambers had distinguished in the continuity of English prose devotional literature. The writer is master of a simple, low style when he judges that his readers need initiation into community liturgical prayer, as though they were novices in search of instruction. He commands also a style of considerable floridity when his own enthusiasm for this form of prayer overflows into a joyful or earnest exhortation to love of the Marian office. In the more abstruse passages devoted to the vocation and role of Mary he becomes involved in hypotactic, complex sentences in order to probe mysteries and make precise comparisons and distinctions. At times he intervenes in this doctrinal analysis and rises to a sustained eloquence as he catches the rapture present in a psalm or a hymn that he is explicating, and achieves a grand manner. He demonstrates the riches of elegant diction, cognitive and affective, in the tradition of English devotional prose, and he also recapitulates its various prose rhythms at will, thus transmitting to later writers like Caxton, Malory, and More both the spiritual treasures of a contemplative prayer and the rhetorical craftsmanship of a great literary tradition.

VERLYN FLIEGER

Naming the Unnameable:
The Neoplatonic "One" in Tolkien's
Silmarillion

IN PHILOSOPHY AND theology, as in all else, the more things change, the more they are the same. Recent directions in metaphysical speculation, the revalidation by theoretical physics of the primordial Big Bang with its attendant concept of a developing universe, the mid-century synthesis of Western with Eastern mystical thought, all are part of the same phenomenon—the renewal of interest in the meta-physical nature of the universe. None of this is new; it can be found in the myth-imagery of Hinduism and the early science of Heraclitus. It is rediscovery rather than discovery, but that need not devalue the freshness and creativity with which a new age approaches an old idea and gives it new expression.

Much of the philosophical and theological speculation of the late twentieth century can be rediscovered in part or in embryo in the teachings of the Neoplatonists from Augustine to Abelard. A central idea, indeed a major element, in Neoplatonic thought is the concept of God as the One, the Monad beyond human knowing or naming. It appears prominently in the works of two otherwise dissimilar figures, Plotinus, the third-century Aristotelian systematizer of Platonic thought, and pseudo-Dionysius, the unidentified sixth-century ecclesiastical mystic whose speculations influenced the theological tradition of the West for over a thousand years.

Given an age as theologically and philosophically fragmented as the present one, it is perhaps not surprising that the most vivid and popular presentation of the idea of the One should appear neither in learned philosophical argument nor in abstruse scientific journals, but in the fiction of the master of modern fantasy, the Oxford philologist J. R. R. Tolkien. The fictive and imaginative character of Tolkien's work has tended to obscure its theological content, which is only of late beginning to be seriously examined. His first major effort, *The Lord of the Rings*, although it had great popular success, was ostentatiously neglected by the members of Tolkien's own profession, and generally regarded as children's literature. As with Swift's *Gulliver's Travels*, Tolkien's imaginary world with its little people overshadowed the seriousness of his theme, which was nothing less than the Fall, the interpenetration of good and evil, and the relationship between man and God.

Much of the early misreading of *The Lord of the Rings* has been corrected by the publication, nearly three decades late, of its parent mythology, *The Silmarillion*. Tolkien's whole *mythos* now emerges clearly as a theological, though not specifically religious, work, deriving from but independent of Judaeo-Christian mythology. More important, *The Silmarillion* deals directly with what *The Lord of the Rings* only alludes to, and that obliquely—the God-figure of Tolkien's mythic world, his relationship to creation and to his creatures, and his part in the unfolding of human history.

Tolkien's stated intention was to create a mythology for England,[1] drawing on the motifs, patterns, and heroic figures of the mythologies of northern Europe, chiefly the Scandinavian, Celtic, and Finnish which he knew and admired. His mythic world, therefore, is a hodgepodge of all of these, populated by elves, dwarves, wizards, demigods, nature spirits, and shape-changers as well as ordinary mortals. The overarching idea which unites these seemingly random elements into a coherent whole is Tolkien's God-figure, Eru, drawn not from any national or ethnic mythology, but from the arcane reaches of Plotinian and Dionysian explications of the nature of God. Examination of Tolkien's presentation of this God-figure will show both its relationship to and its differences from its Neoplatonic antecedents.

Pat upon introduction of the One arises an unsolvable problem for all three. Plotinus, Dionysius, and Tolkien, whatever their chosen mode of discourse, be it philosophy or fantasy, are forced to use words. They are

---

1. J. R. R. Tolkien, *The Letters of J. R. R. Tolkien*, ed. Humphrey Carpenter with Christopher Tolkien (Boston: Houghton Mifflin Co., 1981), p. 144.

confined to the separable and limited vocabulary of human language to talk about inseparable, unlimited being. They must express the inexpressible. Plotinus acknowledges the problem explicitly, the other two implicitly. Plotinus cautions his reader that he is and must be speaking "incorrectly." [2] For even the statement that the One "is" embodies contradiction; the addition of the verb is an admission of duality to express singularity.

This problem admitted, all three writers go on to affirm, each in his own way, the oneness of the One, its indivisibility and its incomprehensibility to the divided human mind. The One, says Plotinus, is self-constituted, perfect, the source of all yet separate from and beyond that which comes from it. [3] Dionysius, mystical rather than logical, describes a God beyond comprehension, of whom he says: "the boundless Super-Essence surpasses Essences, the Super-Intellectual Unity surpasses Intelligences, the One which is beyond thought surpasses the apprehension of thought, and the Good which is beyond utterance surpasses the reach of words. Yea, it is an Unity which is the unifying source of all unity and a Super-Essential Essence, a Mind beyond the reach of mind and a Word beyond all utterance, eluding Discourse, Intuition, Name, and every kind of being." [4]

Dionysius' very wordiness and repetition bespeak the impossibility of what he attempts, the description of what is beyond description, the characterization of what is beyond character. Tolkien's approach to the problem is a different one. Where Plotinus explicates and Dionysius describes, Tolkien states, and in stating creates. The opening words of *The Silmarillion* "There was Eru, the One, who in Arda in called Ilúvatar," [5] declare at once the unity, the preexistence, and the limited human perception of his God-figure. The first three words are striking in their simplicity: "There was Eru," a plain declarative in the past tense singular of the verb "to be," coupled with no place and no time other than the indeterminate pre-present, plus a single noun with no modifier, no Dionysian superlative, no embellishment. Rather than try to explain the unexplainable, Tolkien presents his reader with subject and predi-

2. John N. Deck, *Nature, Contemplation, and the One* (Canada: University of Toronto Press, 1967), p. 10.

3. Deck, p. 10.

4. Dionysius the Areopagite, *The Divine Names and The Mystical Theology*, trans. C. E. Rolt (London: SPCK, 1977), pp. 52–53.

5. J. R. R. Tolkien, *The Silmarillion* (Boston: Houghton Mifflin Co., 1977), p. 15.

cate, the minimum necessary to put his meaning into a literate sentence. And he adds, as his only explication, "the One."

Where Plotinus and Dionysius both use the colorless, well-nigh meaningless pronoun "It" to refer to the Monad, Tolkien signs his primordial essence Eru, a word neither then nor subsequently explained, followed almost immediately by "who in Arda is called Ilúvatar." Eru is clearly not a name, but it is glossed by a name, and the difference is worth examining. Given Tolkien's profession, his thorough grounding in the history and derivations of words, an intentional connection between his fictive Eru and the hypothetical Indo-European root *er-*[1], "to set in motion,"[6] is not unlikely. Granting the connection, the use of Eru followed by "the One" would suggest Tolkien's God-figure as the motionless generator of motion, beyond movement (since allness cannot go beyond itself) but giving rise to movement. Eru, Prime Mover, is the essential nature of the One.

Ilúvatar is another matter, and here again Tolkien's choice of verb is important. Eru is *called* Ilúvatar. Ilúvatar is name, not essence. *The American Heritage Dictionary* defines *name* as "a word or words by which any entity is designated and distinguished from others." Ilúvatar is a characterizing epithet signifying an aspect by which Eru can be distinguished, if not known. It is a name for the unnameable, and thus akin to Dionysius' concept of Divine Names, which, he says, "refer in Symbolical Revelation to Its beneficent Emanations."[7] The beneficent emanation is explained not in Tolkien's text, but in the index of names at the end of the volume, where Ilúvatar is translated "Father of All."[8]

With this concept human perception enters the picture. Tolkien says by means of one name what Dionysius writes a treatise to explicate, that no human mind can apprehend the entirety of the One. "Father of All" is a partial perception, an emanation of Eru seen from the perspective of human generation. Not the One, not Prime Mover, but Father, a word with domestic as well as theological overtones, one common to many mythologies. God the Father is one aspect of the Christian Trinity. Greek Zeus Pater becomes Jupiter, both carrying the same father-god meaning. Odin, chief god of the Norse pantheon, has the epithet *al-faðir*,

---

6. "Indo-European Roots," in *The American Heritage Dictionary of the English Language*, ed. William Morris (Boston: Houghton Mifflin Co., 1969).

7. Dionysius, p. 56.

8. Tolkien, *The Silmarillion*, p. 336.

"All-father." It is a popular concept to characterize the relationship of the supreme being to the humanity which worships it. But such a designation is of necessity built from human perception, derived from and reflecting a human model. Tolkien's addition of an epithet for Eru, and of this particular epithet, signals his reader that this mythology, like all mythologies, is to be seen as from the inside, from the point of view of those whom he calls the Children of Ilúvatar, the elves and men who are the chief peoples of his world.

Like Plotinus and Dionysius, Tolkien develops the concept, carrying oneness into multiplicity without dividing it. Plotinus gives the One a conscious self-identity which he calls Nous, from which flows the logos intellectually articulated as logoi, plurality, separate beings who produce contrariety and thus conflict.[9] In similar vein, Dionysius distinguishes Heavenly Hierarchies, first among which are angels, whom he describes as "things rational and intellectual" which "participate," that is, have a part in, the "self-perfect and pre-eminently perfect wisdom, above all reason and mind," of the One.[10]

Once again, Tolkien creates where his predecessors explain. His opening sentence continues beyond the simple first clause, compounding it as Tolkien compounds his Prime Mover. "There was Eru, the One, who in Arda is called Ilúvatar; and he made first the Ainur, the Holy Ones, that were the offspring of his thought, and they were with him before aught else was made." Here is creation, beginning, the firstness before which only Eru was. Tolkien uses the word "made," which suggests conscious creation, but he also uses the term "offspring," suggesting progeny, but also implying self-contained action, self-motivated springing away. As "offspring" of Eru's thought, the Ainur are aspects of whole mind, differentiations of Eru's undifferentiated nature. They are divided parts of that which is undivided, thoughts springing outward from the mind, assuming life of their own. As parts, they express, but cannot encompass, the whole, "for each comprehended only that part of the mind of Ilúvatar from which he came, and in the understanding of their brethren they grew but slowly."[11] This is Plotinus' contrariety, Dionysius' "thing

---

9. Deck, pp. 57, 58.

10. Dionysius the Areopagite, "On the Heavenly Hierarchy," in *The Works of Dionysius the Areopagite*, Part I (Merrick, New York: Richwood Publishing Co., 1976, repr. from 1897–1899 ed. published by James Parker and Co., London), p. 17.

11. Tolkien, *The Silmarillion*, p. 15.

rational and intellectual," the multiple products of the one mind from which arise conflict, energy, and tension.

It is the Ainur, not Eru, who actually create Tolkien's world. They sing its plan in the Great Music which they make from the themes Eru propounds to them, and from that plan fabricate the material world. The rest of Tolkien's vast mythology is enacted without Eru, involving chiefly the Ainur and the Children of Ilúvatar. Father of All he may be, but he has no further role in the action. With one notable exception—when the Holy Ones call upon Eru to put down rebellious humanity—the One remains above and beyond the world, working only in and through his personified aspects, the Ainur. He remains throughout the Unknown God, unknowable and unreachable in his oneness, perceivable and approachable only to the extent by which the part can represent the whole.

In an age which distrusts myth even as it hungers for it, Tolkien's fantasy speaks to the heart rather than the mind, bypassing the rational intellect in favor of the intuition and the imagination. His fictive mythology, an outgrowth as well as an expression of Western speculative theology, may serve to point a way, to make it easier for all of us, as Eliot says, "to arrive where we started and know the place for the first time." [12]

12. T. S. Eliot, "Four Quartets," in *The Complete Poems and Plays* (New York: Harcourt, Brace and Co., 1950), p. 145.

LOUIS J. SWIFT

Defining *Gloria* in Augustine's
City of God

THE DICHOTOMY WHICH Augustine establishes in the opening lines of his *City of God* between the *gloriosissimam ciuitatem Dei* and the *ciuitatem terrenam* sets the tone for the whole apology and is a particularly apt introduction to the first five books of this *magnum opus et arduum*.[1] The celestial city, he argues, is founded not on the presumptuous efforts of man but on the gratuitous act of God who "resists the proud but gives grace to the humble" (Jas. 4:6). The *ciuitas terrena*, on the other hand, is the work of the *superbi* who arrogate power to themselves and who glory in that spirit of mastery which is summed up in Vergil's line "Parcere subjectis et debellare superbos" (*Aen.* 6.853). In exercising dominion over others, Augustine claims, the founders of the earthly city take what belongs to God and in the very act of asserting their power become slaves themselves to the *libido dominandi*.

The contrasts outlined here between the two *ciuitates* (i.e., pride/humility, self-sufficiency/dependence, domination/subservience) assume very concrete form in the first five books of Augustine's work, where the theme is the relationship between the *ciuitas Dei* and the *ciuitas Romana*,[2]

---

1. The relationship between this preface and the work as a whole is discussed at length (with copious bibliography) by K. Thraede, "Das antike Rom in Augustins *De Civitate Dei*," *JbAC* 20 (1977), 103–132.

2. For Augustine's tendency in the whole first half of the *City of God* to identify the Roman state with the *ciuitas terrena* see H. Hagendahl, *Augustine and the Latin Classics* (= *Studia Graeca et Latina Gothburgensia* XX.II [Göteborg, 1967]), 409–412. The complexities of Augustine's thinking on this matter are well known and are succinctly summarized in R. A. Markus' comment: "Augustine's identification of the Roman state with the earthly city

and where the argument is directed toward two quite specific aims.[3] In
these books Augustine seeks to demonstrate first that Rome's material
growth and prosperity owed nothing to the worship of pagan deities (or
conversely that physical disasters such as Alaric's sack of Rome were not
caused by the rise of Christianity) and, second, that the development of
Roman *imperium* was the result of divine providence. On both these
points Augustine could scarcely avoid dealing with the issue of *gloria*,
which was an inseparable, pervasive, and all-but-controlling force in
Roman society.[4] From what he has to say on this theme in the first five
books of *The City of God* we can understand more clearly what separates
the celestial and the terrestrial cities and what kind of interplay there is
between them in the world of time, where perforce they are linked
together.

A few prefatory comments are in order about traditional Roman
views of *gloria* and the role it played in social, civic, and political life.
"All of us," says Cicero in a typical remark, "are driven by a zeal for
praise, and the best men are attracted most of all by glory."[5] Defining the
term quite simply as "the good reputation one enjoys among good men"
(*bona fama bonorum* [*Sest.* 65.139]), the orator suggests that *gloria* is the
most desirable of human blessings (*Phil.* 5.18.49–50; *Arch.* 11.28),
that the Romans surpass all other races in pursuing this kind of personal

---

is as clear in his writings as is his refusal to abide by this identification. His logic is the logic
of later antique rhetoric rather than modern formal logic" (*Saeculum: History and Society in the
Theology of St. Augustine* [Cambridge, 1970], 59).

3. Augustine's purposes here are reiterated in various ways in the *City of God* itself and in
other works. See, for example, *civ.* 2.2; 3.1; 4.1–2; 5 *praef.*; *retract.* 2.69; *epist. ad Firmum*;
epist. 169.1 and 184 A.5. Ultimately the specific goals of the first five books should be seen
in the larger context of Augustine's overall purposes and developing ideas about the two
cities. On this latter point see A. Lauras and H. Rondet, "Le thème des deux cités dans
l'oeuvre de Saint Augustin" in *Études Augustiniennes* (Paris, 1953), 99–160. For a good recent
survey of the historical and intellectual milieu of the *City of God* see T. D. Barnes, "Aspects of
the Background of the *City of God*," *University of Ottawa Quarterly* 52 (1982), 64–80.

4. For the importance of this dimension of Roman life see, among others, A. F. von
Müller, *Gloria Bona Fama Bonorum: Studien zur sittlichen Bedeutung des Ruhmes in der
frühchristlichen und mittelalterlichen Welt* (= *Historische Studien*, Heft 428 [Husum, 1977]),
28–38; A. D. Leeman, *Gloria: Cicero's Waardering van de Roem en Haar Achtergrond in de
Hellenistische Wijsbegeerte en de Romeinse Samenleving* (with English summary), Rotterdam,
n.d.; and especially U. Knoche, "Der römische Ruhmesgedanke," *Philologus* 89 (1934),
102–124.

5. "Trahimur omnes studio laudis, et optimus quisque maxime gloria ducitur" (*Arch.*
11.26 [ed. Clark]); cf. Tacitus' statement to the same effect: "nam contemptu famae con-
temni uirtutes" (*ann.* 4.38 [ed. C. D. Fisher]).

renown (*Manil.* 3.7), and that it is the one consolation man has for his own mortality.[6] Cicero reflects a long-standing tradition when he claims that there can be no true *gloria* apart from service to others[7] (a point that is implied in the Roman aphorism that glory is the *umbra uirtutis*)[8] and that by winning glory one provides both a model and a stimulus to later generations. Thus, it is appropriate to speak of a *hereditas gloriae* (Cicero, *off.* 1.22.78; 1.33.121; *epist.* 9.14.4) and to acknowledge, in the words of Sallust, that "the glory of [one's] forebears is a light to posterity" (*Iug.* 85.23).[9] "The memory of [others'] accomplishments," says the historian, "stirs a flame in the heart of noble men, and that passion is not assuaged until they have achieved equal fame and glory through their own virtue" (*Iug.* 4.6). Meritorious acts, of course, entail discipline, effort, and suffering, and the amount of glory achieved is directly proportionate to the amount of difficulty involved.[10] In all instances great care is required to prevent one's placing one's own personal glory above the law or above the common good, for without such vigilance what results is *nimia cupiditas gloriae*, which is nothing less than a kind of sickness or disorder in the soul.[11]

When Augustine deals with *gloria* in the early books of the *City of God*, he seems to be using the term in three different senses.[12] The first of these appears in chapters 14–15 of Book 3, where *gloria* is intimately bound up with *libido dominandi* and with moral decline in the life of the state.[13] Following the lead of Sallust (*Catil.* 2.1–2) Augustine argues

6. *Phil.* 14.12.32: "Brevis a natura uita nobis data est; at memoria bene redditae uitae sempiterna. Quae si non esset longior quam haec uita, quis esset tam amens qui maximis laboribus et periculis ad summam laudem gloriamque contenderet?" (ed. Clark).

7. *Phil.* 1.12.29: "Est autem gloria laus recte factorum magnorumque in rem publicam fama meritorum quae cum optimi cuiusque tum etiam multitudinis testimonio comprobatur" (ed. Clar). Cf. *Marcell.* 8.26.

8. See Cicero, *Tusc.* 1.45.109, and consult A. Otto, *Die Sprichwörter und sprichwörterlichen Redensarten der Römer* (Leipzig, 1890), 155.

9. Cf. Q. Curtius, 4.14.25: "Ite alacres et spiritus pleni ut quam gloriam accepistis a maioribus posteris relinquatis" (ed. Bardon).

10. Cf. Cicero, *de orat.* 3.4.14; *Rhet. her.* 4.25.34; Seneca, *de prov.* 3.9.

11. Cicero, *fin.* 1.18.59–60, *Tusc.* 4.79, *off.* 1.20.68–69.

12. For important studies dealing with various aspects of this topic see von Müller, op. cit., 58–73; V. Hand, *Augustin und das klassisch römische Selbstverständnis* (= *Hamburger Philologische Studien* 13 [Hamburg, 1970]), 16–22; W. Kamlah, *Christentum und Geschichtlichkeit*, 2d ed. (Stuttgart, 1951), esp. 281–301, and F. G. Maier, *Augustin und das antike Rom* (Tubingen, 1955), esp. 125–145.

13. Augustine seems not at all consistent in his views about when and if moral decline occurred in the development of the Roman state. In 3.14 he quotes Sallust to the effect that

that men of the earliest times had lived *sine cupiditate*, but that with the advent of Cyrus and the outbreak of wars among Greek nations *libido dominandi* became sufficient reason for taking up arms, and the belief became widespread that "the greatest glory resided in the greatest empire" (3.14). As a victim of this "lust for mastery" which "afflicts many evils on the human race and wears it down,"[14] Rome triumphed over her mother city Alba Longa and "praised her own crime with the name of glory." Such renown, the bishop suggests caustically, is typical of the gladiatorial contests and serves only to hide the endless slaughter of kinsmen and allies.[15]

The *libido dominandi* which is viewed here as the vitiating element in the pursuit of glory waxed strong in Roman society, Augustine suggests, after the destruction of Carthage. It sprang up in *superbissimis mentibus* as a result of the absolute power which longevity in office conferred on particular individuals, and that longevity was itself an outgrowth of the ambition that arose in a society corrupted by avarice and luxury. It was to forestall such a disastrous chain of events by means of external threats, Augustine claims, that Scipio Nasica argued against Cato's famous dictum *Carthago delenda est*. Nasica "thought that fear [of Carthage] would act as a curb on lust and that lust, being curbed, would not run riot in luxury and that the restraint of luxury would bring avarice to an end, and that with these vices out of the way virtue would flourish and increase. . . ." (1.31).[16]

---

the seeds of such decline were sown after the time of Cyrus; earlier (2.18) he had suggested that vices existed from the very beginning, and in 5.12 he will contend that, despite the truth of this latter statement, there were a few men in the early days who attained glory and honor by the path of virtue. For a thoughtful analysis of how Augustine reevaluates Sallust's ideas see G. F. Chesnut, Jr., "The Pattern of the Past: Augustine's Debate with Eusebius and Sallust," in J. Deschner et al., eds., *Our Common History as Christians: Essays in Honor of Albert C. Outler* (New York, 1975), 69–95. It seems to me, however, that Chesnut's assessment of Augustine's attitude toward Roman *uirtus* is overly pessimistic.

14. And which Augustine believed was especially virulent in the Roman people. See 1.30.

15. 3.14. Cf. Thraede, op. cit., 125. In 5.17 the bishop takes a slightly different slant on such conquests but still insists on the emptiness of human glory: "Nam quid intersit ad incolumnitatem bonosque mores, ipsas certe hominum dignitates, quod alii uicerunt, alii uicti sunt, omnino non uideo, praeter illum gloriae humanae inanissimum fastum in quo perceperunt mercedam suam, qui eius ingenti cupidine arserunt et ardentia bella gesserunt" (*CCSL* 47 : 150).

16. With a few changes I have followed the translation of the *City of God* by G. MacCracken and W. Green in the Loeb series.

The inescapable connection that Augustine sees here among *auaritia*, *libido dominandi*, and *superbia* is clearly articulated in a well-known passage of the *De Genesi ad litteram* (11.15.19), which was composed not long before these early books of the *City of God*. Commenting on the fall of the angels, Augustine suggests that the line from Ecclesiasticus "Pride is the beginning of all sin" (10:13) and the text of 1 Timothy 6:10 "Avarice is the root of all evil" are tantamount to the same thing if one understands avarice not as the love of money but more generally as that vice by which one "desires something more than he should for the sake of his own promotion and out of love for his own concerns." It was avarice, in fact, that caused the fall of Satan, "who, to be sure, loved not money but his own personal *potestas*." [17] The opposite of such *auaritia/superbia* is *caritas*, which "does not seek its own" (1 Cor. 13:5), i.e., "does not rejoice in its own excellence and thus is not puffed up by its own achievement." Augustine then goes on to define these *duo amores*, as he calls them, by contrasting their individual characteristics. The one (*caritas*) is social, the other (*auaritia*) private; the one looks out for the common good for the sake of the celestial society, the other subordinates that good to its own power *propter adrogantem dominationem*; the one is subject to God, the other vies with him; the one prefers truth to empty praise, the other is *auidus laudis* in every way possible; the one rules in the interests of the governed, the other for its own private gain. [18]

The two loves described here are not precisely those that separate the

---

17. Cf. *in epist. Ioh*. 8.6: "Certe radix omnium malorum auaritia est: inuenimus et in superbia auaritiam esse, excessit enim modum homo. Quid esse auarum esse? Progredi ultra quam sufficit" (*PL* 35:2039). For the passage under discussion see the comments of A. Solignac, S.J., "La condition de l'homme pécheur d'après saint Augustin," *Nouvelle Revue Théologique* 78 (1956), 370–371.

18. 11.15: "Hi duo amores—quorum alter sanctus est, alter immundus, alter socialis, alter priuatus, alter communi utilitati consulens propter supernam societatem, alter etiam rem communem in potestatem propriam redigens propter adrogantem dominationem, alter subditus, alter aemulus deo, alter tranquillus, alter turbulentus, alter pacificus, alter seditiosus, alter ueritatem laudibus errantium praeferens, alter quoquo modo laudis auidus, alter amicalis, alter inuidus, alter hoc uolens proximo quod sibi, alter subicere proximum sibi, alter propter proximi utilitatem regens proximum, alter propter suam—praecesserunt in angelis, alter in bonis, alter in malis . . ." (*CSEL* 28:347–348). On *superbia* as the source of sin see, among others, W. J. Green, *Initium Omnis Peccati Superbia* (Berkeley, 1949); Solignac, loc. cit.; D. J. Macqueen "Augustine on *Superbia*: The Historical Background and Sources of His Doctrine," *Mélanges de Science Religieuse* 34 (1977), 193–211, and the same author's "*Contemptus Dei*: St. Augustine on the Disorder of Pride in Society and Its Remedies," *Recherches augustiniennes* 9 (1973), 227–293.

two cities in the later books of the *De ciuitate Dei* (e.g., 11.33; 12.1; 14.13 and 28), where the difference between the *iusti* and the *iniqui* is presented in more metaphysical terms (i.e., *amor Dei* vs. *amor sui*). Here the contrast is rather between the social and self-sacrificing character of *caritas* and the self-aggrandizing dimension of *auaritia*, which looks out for its own interest at the expense of others.[19] It is the *gloria* that springs from the second of these *amores* (*auaritia/superbia*) that Augustine decries in Rome's wars of conquest, and it is this type of *gloria* that leads him in the preface to counter Vergil's *debellare superbos* with the words of the Psalmist "Deus superbis resistit, humilibus autem dat gratiam."

The *gloria* that is typical of the *ciuitas Dei* is of another kind, as Augustine's discussion of the Christian apostles and martyrs in Book 5 makes clear. In assessing their achievements Augustine works with the Ciceronian definition of glory (i.e., "the favorable judgment of men who think well of other men" [5.12]) but redefines some of its constituent elements. He rejects Cicero's notion that only those activities which are held in high esteem by society at large can give rise to glory. The apostles won distinction for themselves by preaching the name of Christ in places where it was disdained or even detested: "Amid curses and reviling, amid bitter persecutions and cruel tortures, they were not deterred from preaching man's salvation in spite of all the raging of man's hatred" (5.14). Such actions, Augustine assures us, merited for the apostles not only "the glory of their own conscience," as St. Paul would have it (2 Cor. 1:12), but "great glory in the Church of Christ." Augustine then goes on to define *gloria Christiana* in a way that reflects both a continuity with traditional Roman concepts and a sharp departure from them. Referring to the Apostles he says,

They did not rest in that glory as if it were the goal of their virtuous endeavor. Instead they ascribed that very glory to the glory of God, by whose grace they were such as they were. And with that tinder they set fire to those whom they taught, so that they also burned with the love of him who had made them, too, such as they were. For their master had taught them not to be good for the sake of human glory. . . . But again lest they should take this in the wrong sense and be afraid to please men and so, concealing their goodness, should be of less help to others, he showed them what their aim ought to be in attracting attention: "Let your works so shine

19. See Lauras and Rondet, op. cit., 113.

before men that they may see your good deeds and glorify your father who is in heaven" [Mt. 5 : 16]. (5.14)[20]

Whereas the Roman might be expected to find fulfillment in the recognition accorded him in his own lifetime and in the expectation of living on in the memory of posterity, the Christian ascribes the glory he receives to the source of his power, thereby stirring others to a love of that same source. This amounts to transforming one's own subjective glory (i.e., the renown an individual attains through virtuous acts) into an objective glory (i.e., praise of God for enabling one to perform such acts). The reason for this change, Augustine argues, is that the perspective of Christian heroes is different from that of their Roman counterparts. As dwellers in an earthly city the latter were concerned about a kingdom on earth, and because for them there was no eternal life but only a continuous cycle of generations of men, the only thing they could love was a glory that would survive their death on "the lips of those who sang their praises." The Christian's destiny is an eternal city where no man is born or dies (5.16), which is "as far removed from [Rome] as heaven is from earth, eternal life from temporal joys, solid glory from hollow praise, the company of angels from that of mortals" (5.17). There God himself is "life and salvation and sustenance and richness and glory and honor and peace and all good things" (22.30).[21]

Thus, *gloria* is for Christians a reality outside time in which they expect to participate in a conscious way but is also a reality in time by which men are assisted toward that final goal. Following Matthew's words about letting one's light shine before men (Mt. 5 : 16) Augustine argues that by means of their own temporal glory individuals should become an example for others who might glorify the Father, turn to

20. "Non in ea tamquam in suae uirtutis fine quieuerunt, sed eam quoque ipsam ad Dei gloriam referentes, cuius gratia tales erant, isto quoque fomite eos quibus consulebant, ad amorem illius a quo et ipsi tales fierent accendebant. Namque ne propter humanam gloriam boni essent, docuerat eos magister illorum. . . . Sed rurus ne hoc peruerse intellegentes hominibus placere metuerent minusque prodessent latendo, quod boni sunt, demonstrans quo fine innotescere deberent: 'Luceant,' inquit, opera uestra coram hominibus, ut uideant bona facta uestra et glorificent patrem uestrum, qui in caelis est" (*CCSL* 47 : 148).

21. *Civ.* 22.30: "Praemium uirtutis erit ipse [Deus], qui uirtutem dedit eique se ipsum, quo melius et maius nihil possit esse, promisit. Quid est enim aliud quod per prophetam dixit: 'Ero illorum Deus, et ipsi erunt mihi plebs,' nisi: 'Ego ero unde satientur, ego ero quaecumque ab hominibus honeste desiderantur, et uita et salus et uictus et copia et gloria et honor et pax et omnia bona'? Sic enim et illud recte intellegitur quod ait apostolus: 'Ut sit Deus omnia in omnibus' [1 Cor. 15 : 28] (*CCSL* 48 : 863). Cf. 14.28.

him, and become what they (i.e., the Christians) are (5.14).[22] Such a view is not far removed from the ideas of Sallust and Cicero on the paradigmatic character of *gloria* which we saw above, although in their case the underlying assumptions and the final good belong to a different order of reality.

The two kinds of *gloria* we have dealt with thus far are rather easy to differentiate and to describe. Between them is a *tertium quid*, which is more difficult to categorize but equally important to Augustine's thought. After arguing at length in the first four books of the *City of God* that the growth of Roman *imperium* had nothing to do with honoring pagan deities, Augustine attempts to explain in Book 5 that this development was, in fact, part of God's providential design.[23] In historical terms that providence works through human motivation, and no less than Cicero or Sallust (*Catil.* 7.6), Augustine suggests that what lay behind Rome's rise to power and what inspired its heroes was ultimately *cupiditas gloriae*: "Hanc [i.e., gloriam] ardentissime dilexerunt, propter hanc uiuere uoluerunt, pro hac emori non dubitauerunt; ceteras cupiditates huius unius ingenti cupiditate presserunt. Ipsam denique patriam suam, quoniam seruire uidebatur inglorium dominari uero atque imperare gloriosum, prius omni studio liberam, deinde dominam esse concupiuerunt" (5.12 [*CCSL* 47 : 142–143]).

What follows in Augustine's text is a brief delineation of the accomplishments provoked by this passion for renown, accomplishments which Augustine acknowledges were "laudibilia scilicet atque gloriosa secundum hominum existimationem." Though the underlying motive here is still *dominatio*, Augustine's remarks on the growth of empire in this part of his work are descriptive rather than polemical and are largely free of the trenchant criticism of Rome's wars that we saw earlier.[24] He

22. On this point cf. Augustine's sermon *De Bono Uiduitatis* 22 (*PL* 40 : 448–449) and consult von Müller, 63, 70–71, and L. Buisson, *Potestas und Caritas: Die Päpstliche Gewalt in Spätmittelalter* (= *Forschungen zur Kirchlichen Rechtsgeschichte und zum Kirchenrecht*, Bd. II [Koln, 1958], 129–130). Augustine returns to this theme of the *exemplum* a little later (5.19) where he discusses what the truly virtuous man does in the face of praise. This individual, having no desire to rule, is concerned only with leading others to the celestial city, "ideoque instat ardenter ut potius ille laudatur a quo habet homo quidquid in eo iure laudatur" (*CCSL* 47 : 155).

23. 5.11: "Nullo modo est credendus [Deus] regna hominum eorumque dominationes et seruitutes a suae prouidentiae legibus alienas esse uoluisse" (*CCSL* 47 : 142).

24. For Augustine's treatment of *gloria* in this part of the *City of God* see the helpful comments of Thraede, op. cit., 138–139 with notes.

follows Sallust in recognizing that the *imperium Romanum* expanded through the arts of conquest, and then he makes an interesting comment: "Has artes illi tanto peritius exercebant quanto minus se uoluptatibus debant et eneruationi animi et corporis in concupiscendis et augendis diuitiis et per illas moribus corrumpendis, rapiendo miseris ciuibus . . ." (5.12 [*CCSL* 47:144]). Following Sallust again, Augustine introduces here an old theme in Roman historiography, i.e., the corrupting effects of avarice on a society which was originally motivated by noble aims,[25] and he harks back with some satisfaction to the heroes of an earlier day who pursued glory *per bonas artes* (i.e., the path of virtue).[26] These individuals, he argues, were motivated by *ambitio* ("a vice, which comes close to being a virtue") rather than by *auaritia*, and though few in number they managed important affairs and should be considered good men "according to their own standards."

The theme of a pristine era when Rome's leaders were free of avarice is reiterated in the next chapter, where Augustine attempts to explain why God willed that the empire should come into being: "Idque [i.e., regnum] talibus potissimum concessit hominibus ad domanda grauia mala multarum gentium qui causa honoris laudis et gloriae consuluerunt patriae in qua ipsam gloriam requirebant, salutemque eius saluti suae praeponere non dubitauerunt, pro isto uno uitio, id est amore laudis pecuniae cupiditatem et multa alia uitia conprimentes" (5.13 [*CCSL* 47:146–147]). And again in chapter 15, where the topic is God's justice in granting empire to men who practiced virtue according to their own best lights, he focuses on the absence of *auaritia*: "Sic et isti priuatas res suas pro re communi, hoc est, re publica, et pro eius aerario contempserunt, auaritiae restiterunt, consuluerunt patriae consilio libero, neque delicto secundum suas leges neque libidini obnoxii; his omnibus artibus tamquam uera uia nisi sunt ad honores imperium gloriam" (5.15 [*CCSL* 47:149]).

Throughout these comments on Roman worthies who practiced a

25. For the origins of this theme see A. W. Linott, "Imperial Expansion and Moral Decline in the Roman Republic," *Historia* 21 (1972), 626–638. See also G. Bonamente, "Il *metus Punicus* e la decadenza di Roma in Sallustio, Agostino ed Orosio," *Giornale Italiano di Filologia* 27 (1975), 137–169, where additional bibliography can be found.

26. "Hae sunt illae bonae artes, per uirtutem scilicet, non per fallacem ambitionem ad honorem et gloriam et imperium peruenire; quae tamen bonus et ignauus aeque sibi exoptant; sed ille, id est bonus, uera uia nititur. Uia uirtus est, qua nititur tamquam ad possessionis finem, id est ad gloriam honorem imperium" (5.12 [*CCSL* 47:144]).

high degree of virtue (*pro suo modo*, though it be)[27] there runs a consistent thought. Such men, Augustine argues, resisted the vice of avarice; that is, they were willing to sacrifice their own good for the good of others, their own private immediate benefit for the welfare of the community at large. In short, while pursuing personal temporal glory they were, in fact, placing limits on their own *amor sui*, and it is precisely this fact which distinguishes them both from those who are totally subject to the *libido dominandi* and from the Christian faithful. From this perspective, then, it seems appropriate to speak of three types of glory, since there are, in fact, three types of *amores* (i.e., that of the *superbi*, that of the *boni sine fide*, and that of the *sancti*). Augustine's more typical view that all men are governed by one of two *amores* (i.e., *amor sui* or *amor Dei*) and thus preoccupied with one or the other of two types of *gloria* does not easily accommodate a *tertium quid*, but it is clear that there are individuals who fall outside the categories of *sancti* or *superbi* and who practice a kind of natural virtue[28] for which they receive a temporal reward.[29]

As one might expect in an apologetic work designed both to demonstrate the uniqueness of the Christian perspective and to gain a sympa-

---

27. "Sed per quosdam paucos, qui pro suo modo boni erant, magna administrabantur atque illis toleratis ac temperatis malis paucorum bonorum prouidentia res illa crescebat. . . . Paucorum igitur uirtus ad gloriam honorem imperium uera uia, id est, ipsa uirtute, nitentium etiam a Catone laudata est. Hinc erat domi industria, quam commemorauit Cato, ut aerarium esset opulentum, tenues res priuatae. Unde corruptis moribus uitium e contrario posuit, publice egestatem, priuatim opulentiam" (5.12 [*CCSL* 47:146]).

28. Whether the concept of natural virtue has any proper place in Augustine's thought is a much discussed issue. For opposing views on the matter see Maier (loc. cit.) and J. Straub, "Augustins Sorge um die *regeneratio imperii*," *Historisches Jahrbuch* 73 (1954), 36–60. Their differences on this point are part of a much larger disagreement about Augustine's attitude toward Rome as a temporal power. Maier contends that Augustine is fundamentally and pervasively negative on this score; Straub argues for a more positive oulook on the bishop's part. See also Thaede (op. cit., 141–145), who attempts to strike a middle ground on the issue. On the matter of natural virtue, it is difficult to gainsay the kind of evidence found in Augustine's letter to Marcellinus (*epist.* 138.17) dated 412 A.D.: "Deus enim sic ostendit in opulentissimo et praeclaro imperio Romanorum quantum ualerent ciuiles etiam sine uera religione uirtutes ut intellegeretur hac addita fieri homines ciues alterius ciuitatis cuius rex ueritas, cuius lex caritas, cuius modus aeternitas" (*CSEL* 44:144–145). But see Maier, op. cit., 69–75, and F. Paschoud, *Roma Aeterna* (= *Bibliotheca Helvetica Romana* VII [Rome, 1967]), 263–275. A thoughtful and comprehensive study of the whole question of pagan virtues is that of J. Wang Tch'ang-Tche, S.J., *Saint Augustin et les vertus des paiens* (Paris, 1938).

29. Augustine quotes or paraphrases Mt. 6:2 ("they have received their reward") several times in this vein when he is trying to show that temporal power was God's just recompense for those who practiced virtue *sine fide*. Cf. 5.15 and 17 and see Thraede, op. cit., 139.

thetic hearing from an audience preoccupied with what Peter Brown calls *litterata uetustas*,[30] Augustine's attitude toward these heroic figures is at once begrudging and full of admiration. Speaking of them in chapter 13 of Book 5 he says in a well-known comment: "Men who do not obtain the gift of the Holy Spirit and bridle their baser passions by pious faith and by love of intelligible beauty at any rate live better because of their desire for human praise and glory. While these men are not saints, to be sure, they are less vile [*minus turpes*]." Elsewhere, the bishop insists that such virtues, motivated as they are by human glory and oriented to a temporal reward,[31] are not to be compared with the *uera uirtus* which springs solely from Christian faith (5.19), and he does not hesitate, as we have seen (5.13), to call the love of human glory a *uitium*. Nonetheless, he can also speak of a *ueram licet humanarum laudum gloriam* (5.19),[32] and his descriptions of men like Regulus, Torquatus, Fabricius, Lucius Ualerius, and other noble *maiores* (5.18) suggest that these individuals were more than paper heroes to be dismissed or treated lightly.[33] What sets them apart from others is a resistance to the kind of *auaritia/superbia* that we have seen above and a readiness to sacrifice their own interests for the benefit of others. If this is not true virtue (*uera uirtus*) in the Augustinian sense of the term, it is analogously so and, thus, worthy of commendation. What is more, Augustine frankly acknowledges that love of human glory can scarcely be eradicated from the heart of man (5.14) and, indeed, in the case of individuals wielding power, its absence

---

30. I.e., an antiquarian interest in their religious past as found in the literary monuments. See Brown's *Augustine of Hippo* (Berkeley, 1969), 299–312. E. Fortin provides an attractive and more subtle analysis of what the bishop was attempting to do in his attack on bookish religious ideas of pagan contemporaries. Fortin suggests that in place of a frontal assault on civil religion, which could prove to be excessively harmful in a time of political instability, Augustine chose to "take issue with an archaic religion for the sake of demonstrating, if only by implication, the fundamental defect of contemporary pagan religion or, for that matter, of any form of civil religion" ("Augustine and Roman Civil Religion: Some Critical Reflections," *Revue des Études Anciennes* 26 [1980], 255).

31. Such glory is consistently spoken of as *humana* (5.16) or *hominum* (5.18), or as *terrena gloria* (5.15). For additional references see Hand, op. cit., 20 with notes.

32. Without some distinction regarding the nature of human glory, there would be no point to Augustine's remarks (following Sallust) that some of the ancients pursued *gloria* by the *uera uia* but others through *dola atque fallacia*. See 5.12 and 19.

33. In citing such *exempla* Augustine was following a long-standing Roman tradition. See V. Pöschl, "Augustinus und die römische Geschichtsauffassung," *Augustinus Magister* II (1954), 957–963, and III, 206, and for his assessment of these heroes see Maier, op. cit., 84–93, and A. Calderini, "Riflessi di storia antica nel 'De Civitate Dei,'" *S. Agostino: Pubblicazione commemorativa del xv centenario della sua morte* (Milan, 1931), 405–421.

can be a dangerous thing: "The man who disregards glory but is eager for rule surpasses wild beasts in vicious cruelty or in luxurious living. There have been Romans of this type, who, though they had lost interest in their reputation, were, nonetheless, not free from lust for domination" (5.19).[34] Thus, for all its limitations and for all the criticisms Augustine leveled against it, temporal glory had a laudable role to play in promoting *uirtus* and restraining *uitium*.[35]

It is partly for these reasons that Roman heroes who sought and won glory for themselves could serve as paradigms for those who seek another kind of glory. "Let us consider," Augustine says to his Christian audience, "what great things those Romans disregarded, what they endured, what passions they subdued, all to get glory in the eyes of men" (5.17), and "if in serving the glorious city of God we do not cling to the virtues that they clung to in serving the glory of the earthly city, let us be pricked to our hearts with shame" (5.18).

What separates the Christian from the pagan is not the pursuit of glory but the definition of the term and the conditions that govern its pursuit. If pagan and Christian glory are ultimately incompatible, the proportion that describes the relationship between the two in the world of time is not simply *malum* to *bonum* but human to divine, temporal to eternal, terrestrial to celestial. Thus, it is not enough to focus only on the ways in which Roman heroes in their pursuit of human glory fell short of Christian *uirtus*. Roman preoccupation with *gloria* could have salutary effects even in a Christian context, and for this reason Augustine's treatment of the theme is not just a measure of the gulf that separates the author from his pagan audience but a sign of the common ground on which they both stood.

34. The most prominent example, of course, was Nero, "cuius fuit tanta luxuries ut nihil ab eo putaretur uirile metuendum; tanta crudelitas ut nihil molle habere crederetur, si nesciretur" (*CCSL* 47:155). For Augustine's comments on this emperor see J. Rougè, "Néron à la fin du IVe et au début du Ve siècle," *Latomus* 37 (1978), 77–79.

35. For the positive effects of *cupiditas gloriae* and for Augustine's views on the superiority of the Roman *imperium* over earlier realms see the comments of E. von Ivánka, "Römische Ideologie in der *Civitas Dei*," *Augustinus Magister* II, 411–417.

HARRY F. WILLIAMS

The Hidden Meaning of Chrétien's
Conte du Graal

BEHIND THE GLITTERING facade of Chrétien's romances, superficially tales of love and adventure, lies at least one subsurface meaning, otherwise we must accept them as merely series of loosely connected episodes joined only for entertainment, a viewpoint long ago abandoned by connoisseurs. Conservative exegetes, seeking the author's intentions, discern in these stories literal and figurative levels.[1] Besides, the medieval reader was accustomed to seek reality beyond the veil of literature, it would seem. A story's bipartite planes are intimated in the exordium of the *Chevalier de la Charette*, where the author attributes to Countess Marie of Champagne the *matiere et san* ("meaning and plot") and to himself only his *painne et antancion* ("trouble and time").[2]

Never is the underlying idea openly stated; it must be inferred by

---

1. Jean Frappier (*Chrétien de Troyes—L'Homme et l'oeuvre* [Paris: Hatier-Boivin, 1957]) saw in the *Conte du Graal* (pp. 185–186) three levels of meaning (psychological, moral, religious). Robertsonians distinguish four; see Urban T. Holmes and Sister M. Amelia Klenke, *Chrétien, Troyes, and the Grail* (Chapel Hill: University of North Carolina Press, 1959). A religious level, provocative as it is, presents certain problems and discounts the Gauvain section; see Paul Imbs, "L'Élément religieux dans le *Conte del Graal* de Chrétien de Troyes," in *Les Romans du Graal dans la littérature des 12ᵉ et 13ᵉ siècles*, Colloques Internationaux du Centre National de la Recherche Scientifique, Strasbourg, 1954 (Paris: C.N.R.S., 1956), pp. 31–58, esp. p. 53, and Roger S. Loomis, "The Origin of the Grail Legends," in *Arthurian Literature in the Middle Ages* (Oxford: Clarendon Press, 1959), pp. 274–294. The four-level argument falls by its own weight; see *The Sower and His Seed*, ed. Rupert T. Pickens, French Forum Monographs 44 (Lexington, Ky.: French Forum, Publishers: 1983), p. 149.

2. Urban T. Holmes, *Chrétien de Troyes* (New York: Twayne Publishers, 1970), pp. 87–88. Cf. Jean Frappier, *Le Chevalier de la Charrette (Lancelot), Roman traduit de l'ancien*

retrospective conceptualization.[3] Chrétien prefers to mystify with both language and themes. Such authorial strategy promotes more audience participation, a constant preoccupation of medieval romance writers, particularly. The real import of all his fiction still fuels lively discussion,[4] but no romance incites more debate concerning its inner meaning than does his *Conte du Graal*, the subject of theories, in excess of two dozen, which seek to elucidate its obvious symbolism and calculated ambiguity.[5] Such characteristics lend themselves to multivalent interpretations which will continue to proliferate, but no hypothesis advanced by others seems more cogent than my own.[6]

Here, we seek guidance for a penetration of the meaning of the *Conte du Graal* by first viewing it telescopically, then relating it to our author's total literary production, as basis for discussion of clues provided by the story's prologue to arrive at a hypothesis whose confirmation is found in the adventures of Perceval and Gauvain.

To the uncritical eye, Chrétien's Grail story presents, after an unusual prologue, a kaleidoscopic series of experiences undergone by two successive heroes whose lives and fortunes are subtly intertwined and eventually are affected profoundly by an enigmatic adventure, as each journeys through antithetical worlds.

First we accompany the naive boy Perceval, who, impelled by the expressed desire to become a knight, leaves the Waste Forest to enter the Arthurian world (from which his family had been exiled by cataclysmic events), only to be engulfed later by the supernatural Grail community.

---

français (Paris: Champion, 1962), p. 19. Mention is made of *sans ne painne* in the *Charette* (v. 23); of *entente et paine* in *Graal* (v. 62).

Our references to the *Graal* are to the edition of William Roach (Geneva: Droz, 1959); to the other works of Chrétien, Foerster's edition, *Christian von Troyes sämtliche erhaltene Werke* (Halle: Niemeyer, 1884–1899).

3. See Donald Maddox, "The Prologue to Chrétien's *Erec* and the Problem of Meaning," in the *Jean Misrahi Memorial Volume, Studies in Medieval Literature*, ed. Hans R. Runte, Henri Niedzielski, and William L. Hendrickson (Columbia, S.C.: French Literature Publications Co., 1977), pp. 160, 167.

4. The most recent discussion of all Chrétien's Arthurian romances is L. T. Topsfield, *Chrétien de Troyes: A Study of the Arthurian Romances* (Cambridge: Cambridge University Press, 1981). Douglas Kelly, *Chrétien de Troyes, An Analytic Bibliography* (London: Grant and Cutler, 1976) is a superb guide.

5. See the *Jean Misrahi Memorial Volume*, pp. 140–145, Joseph J. Duggan, "Ambiguity in Twelfth-Century French and Provençal Literature: A Problem or a Value?" and Harry F. Williams, *The Sower and His Seed*, pp. 146–154.

6. Theory first broached (and from a different viewpoint) in "The Numbers Game in Chrétien de Troyes' *Conte du Graal (Lancelot)*," *Symposium* 31 (1977), 72.

Then we follow the accomplished knight, Gauvain, who is implicitly attracted more by amatory dalliance then by chivalric exploits, as he leaves Arthur's court to wander in a kind of Waste Forest before he arrives at the Castle of Marvels in a land "whence no knight can return," vv. 6602–6603, which analogically recalls the Grail Castle.[7]

Despite the attention paid to chivalry and love, we feel intuitively that Chrétien no longer poses in his last romance the problems faced in his previous ones; we have here a different orientation. He wrote at least five romances (if we leave aside *Guillaume d'Angleterre* of debated authenticity, for it breathes a different spirit and poses a chronological problem). A conspicuous trait of Chrétien is a penchant for harmony and order involving both individuals and society; he is a concerned observer of the human condition in both its positive and its negative aspects.

Although a virtuoso in composition, he treated remarkably few themes in his various works. Common to both *Erec* and *Yvain*, reduced to their simplest terms, are the same principal themes and problems (viz., the relative roles of love and chivalry in a young man's life), although these tales exhibit vast surface differences. He claims in the *Cligés* to have written an earlier *Tristan* story, yet the *Cligés* itself is fundamentally a Tristan tale. So, for the second time, apparently, he treated twice, although in different ways, identical problems, a procedure consonant with medieval emphasis more on form than on subject matter. It is not unreasonable, therefore, to seek connections between the *Charette* and *Graal* stories.[8]

Each of those poems was commissioned by a patron; both lack the customary conclusions of Chrétien; they bear descriptive and suggestive titles (a characteristic shared by his *Le Chevalier au Lion*); only these two designate King Arthur's country as Logres; in them alone is a litter used for transportation. Other parallels between them include extraordinary use of suspended or denied explanations; mysterious geoscenic backgrounds; a bipartite structure (as opposed to the triptych appearance of *Erec* and *Yvain*); the respective heroes do not begin their primary quest at Arthur's court; each of the three heroes remains unmarried. Moreover,

7. See Omer Jodogne, "L'Autre Monde celtique dans la littérature française du 12ᵉ siècle," L'Académie Royale des Sciences, des Lettres, et des Beaux Arts de Belgique, Classe des Lettres et des Sciences Morales et Politiques, *Bulletin* 46 (1960), 584–597.

8. For some contrasts, see Nathan Lyons, "Chrétien's *Lancelot* and *Perceval*: Some Contrasts in Method, Style, and the Nature of Love," *The Missouri Univ. Review* 21 (1964–1965), 313–318.

each story follows first a straight line and unfolds at a fast pace which becomes, in the second part, more leisurely and involuted. Both Lancelot and Gauvain are tested by a perilous bed. Both fight at a ford, experience a combat delayed, suffer a humiliating experience, and each must cross a sinister river; the author abandons them while they are imprisoned.

Lancelot and Perceval fall into a love-trance; they share action with Gauvain (as did Yvain); both resist the advances of a seductive hostess, exhibit a unique singleness of purpose, seem cast in a messianic role. The career of each (and of Gauvain) is affected by meeting a father and son (Grail King, Fisher King; Garin, Herman [at Tintagel]; Bademagu and Meleagant); each travels over a stone pass; their very names play a role in their respective stories; and Arthur's cup, stolen by the Red Knight, functions like the abduction of Guenevere. Their main theme seems identical: the protagonist leaves the everyday world to spend time, for a specific purpose, in a mysterious land which must have been, in the author's mind, a heteroclitic Otherworld. They cross and recross the boundary between life and death; they are involved in a kind of resurrection. Although often warned of the dangers, Lancelot and Gauvain, in their respective stories, consciously penetrate this other realm, Lancelot in successful search for his abducted mistress, Guenevere, whom he frees and thus illustrates courtly love; Gauvain out of curiosity liberates the enchanted castle but becomes thereby a prisoner in it. Perceval unconsciously enters the Otherworld, he is not warned, and he fails to fulfill his mission: to answer the questions about the Grail and the Lance, i.e., to discover the meaning of Life and Death. Perceval is ignorant of his destiny; are we not all? The future is unknown except for the fact that people are mortal and ultimately they experience death, yet still one goes on, from experience to experience, and fails to be unduly disturbed by the inevitable end. After Perceval's failure to penetrate the mystery of Life and Death, Gauvain is charged with seeking the key to Death (the Lance) and he too fails, but their actions illustrate the existence of faith, the fact that hope is eternal, that man will continue to dream of solving, and continue to fail to solve, the ultimate riddle of humankind. Lancelot succeeds (as did Hercules, certain Celtic heroes, and Christ); Perceval and Gauvain fail (as did classical Orpheus and Perseus). Such numerous correspondences and this fundamental contrast between the *Chevalier de la Charette* and the *Conte du Graal* must point to the message of each.

The *Chevalier de la Charette* in addition to being predominantly an exposition of courtly love, involves a victorious mission in a hostile region ("whence no stranger returns," v. 645) strongly reminiscent of the Celtic Otherworld. Might not the Perceval story be a failed Otherworld quest, with the love interest subordinate? Such a reversal of viewpoint is typical of *Erec* and *Yvain*; to cite but one example, the Knight with the Lion is responsible for the disharmony in his married life whereas Enide bears that responsibility in the earlier story. Chrétien's attitude is not always positive: Calogrenant fails and Yvain triumphs at the fountain; Cligés does not reconcile chivalry and love service; Gauvain fails and Lancelot succeeds in the *Chevalier de la Charette* poem. While writing this romance, Chrétien was obviously absorbed in Celtic mythology and so he had Lancelot complete successfully his Otherworld mission. Later, influenced more by Christian tradition, and doubtlessly familiar with mythical Orpheus' failure to accomplish his quest in the Underworld, he has his new heroes, Perceval and Gauvain, involved less in love casuistry or high chivalric deeds and more in eschatology. As in the *Chevalier de la Charette*, the basic problem posed in the *Conte du Graal* seems to be the eternal one of Life and Death.

This problem is subtly indicated not only by Chrétien's total literary production, but also in the prologue to his Grail story by such *topoi* as number symbolism, significant evocations of individuals, and meaningful upheaval of the old social order.

In the exordium to the *Conte du Graal*, Chrétien's references to Holy Writ create immediately an atmosphere antithetical to that of the *Chevalier de la Charette*, as much as to say: Celtic mythology is here subordinate to Christian dogma. And he contrasts basic qualities of two questers—the virtues of the living Christian, Philip of Alsace, who furnished the book which inspired this romance, and the vices of the dead pagan Alexander the Great. This expressed hierarchy of two different worlds recalls to the attentive reader the unmentioned fact of Philip's interest in the material life of his country and the spiritual life of Christians everywhere (twice he went on crusade to the East and eventually died there)[9] and Alexander's sowing, throughout the known world, of death and destruction. Thus is set up a dichotomy that will be continued throughout the romance. Do not Perceval and Gauvain reso-

9. Holmes, *Chrétien de Troyes*, pp. 18, 161.

nate with Philip and Alexander?[10] The underlying message is undoubtedly dyadic in nature.

Initial verses present curious repetitions of two concepts clamoring for
attention: sowing and charitableness. One interpretation of charity
might well be here: "Be charitable to this work." The concept of the first
verb used (*semer*) is repeated, literally or figuratively, six times (and three
more in the introductory scene). Such insistence surely recalled to medieval audiences the biblical parable of the sower, which contains the
injunction: "He that hath ears, let him hear. . . . Take heed, therefore,
how ye hear."[11]

I hear in the *Conte du Graal* Chrétien's account of a quest doomed to
failure, just as Alexander lacked the qualities necessary to enter Christian heaven. The hidden message, clued in part by the parable cited, is
this: all generations, both sexes, any individual, the young and the
mature, are all involved in a Dance of Death, all journey to a common
end. Observe therefore the principal Christian virtues, of which charity
is the greatest, and seek not to unriddle the eternal enigma of Life and
Death. This ultimate secret is withheld from mortals.[12] This theory is
corroborated by both the Perceval and the Gauvain parts of the story.

The exuberant life of the immature country boy Perceval is abruptly
changed by his first encounter with merchants of death—five knights in
search of five others riding with three girls. He learns then from his
mother that his father and two brothers died in the service of chivalry
and that she wanted to shield him from the same fate. The story begins
with reference then both to life and death and to a troubled world.

The disharmony in Perceval's life is but one item in the disoriented
social order sketched in the romance. At the death of Uterpendragon
(father of Arthur), people were killed, impoverished, disinherited, and
exiled. At that time, we learn later, Uter's wife went to Roche de
Canguin where she welcomes, with her daughter and granddaughter,

10. Both crossed oceans; Perceval and Gauvain meet their supreme adventures near a
forbidding river. Note, however, that Tony Hunt (*Romania* 92 [1971], 359–379) considers
the *Graal* prologue as purely rhetorical, a *benevolentiae captatio*, which furnishes no positive
indication of the sense of the romance.

11. Matthew 13:3–9; Mark 4:3–14; Luke (esp.) 8:5–18, and (in reduced form)
Galatians 6:7. "A listener [or reader] must condition himself to understand the message of a
text," says Calogrenant in Chrétien's *Yvain* (vv. 150–174).

12. Representations of contemporary life, in all of Chrétien's romances, are obvious even
to the casual reader, but equally present, although less noted, is the theme of death in all its
forms, including attempted suicide, which medieval society commonly regarded as heinous.

her grandson Gauvain. Since Perceval was two years old at the time of his exile, and since the Grail King (Perceval's uncle) had retired to the inner room 11, 12, 15, 20 years before Perceval's visit (the time varies in the MSS), and since Perceval is now about 14 years old, inasmuch as he is ready for knighthood, then the Grail family was probably displaced at the same time as Perceval's was. The Waste Forest, the Grail Castle, and the Roche de Canguin would then be fragments of the previous Arthurian world; perhaps even the Hermit Uncle went to his hermitage then. Arthur too was certainly affected, and he may be considered in exile, if not dead, at least spiritually, since he is so strangely apathetic toward the Red Knight. But life went on in the various places of exile, as Christians are taught to expect life after death, although this fictional otherlife is corporeal rather than spiritual. Only an afterlife could restore order to such social fragmentation in life.

The atmosphere of Christian life and death in the Grail Castle is suggested by the procession's form (a cross), and by its passage into the inner room to serve the holy man a single wafer, his only nourishment. This wafer recalls Christian communion, symbolic of the body of Christ. The procession passes between the bed and the fire, each of which suggests both life and death. The Grail objects are of white or red colors (symbols of life and death). The Grail Castle questions [13] suggest symbolically life and death: whom does the Grail serve? (the Grail King, says the Hermit later) and why does the Lance bleed? (question unanswered). At table the diners eat flesh of dead animals. Contrastive are the castle life in the evening and the dead atmosphere next morning when Perceval finds himself alone.

Little effort is required to interpret the Blood-on-the-Snow scene as symbolic of life and death. Even Perceval's ecstasy is a kind of death, and death threatens the three successive knights who try to dispel his revery. The colors involved here, which recall to Perceval the complexion of Blanchefleur, remind us not only of her mortality but also of the Grail scene and of the Red Knight.

Spiritually dead, Perceval meets near the Hermitage three women and

---

13. Critics commonly ignore analogous questions in the Gauvain section. Guiromelant asks (and answers) whether Gauvain inquired who she (the old queen) is and whence she came (v. 8729): Arthur's mother who came to reign at Roche de Canguin when Uter died. Here again, life and death are evoked. Another deemphasized analogy: the consequences of Perceval's failure to ask the Grail questions and why the inhabitants of the Castle of Marvels await a liberating knight (v. 7574).

ten knights, thirteen people who came to worship on Good Friday, anniversary of the death of Christ. They remind us of the Waste Forest scene: five knights in pursuit of five others and three girls. In or near the Castle of Marvels are met particularly the three queens and five men besides mysterious Silverleg and newly-arrived Gauvain: boatman, Guiromelant, Orguilleux du Passage à l'Étroite Voie, Greoreas, and his nephew; the reader is left to wonder whether these are the eight people sought initially by the five questing knights. This and other tantalizing questions are no more elusive than the mystery of life and death.

The Christian context of this life-death theme extends then from the prologue through the successive lessons provided by the mother, Gornemant, and the Hermit Uncle, i.e., the entire Perceval story, whereas the Gauvain section, except for the use of empty formulas, conspicuously lacks it, as did Alexander the Great, of course. The theme's context is now less religious but the theme continues to be dominant.

The prologue's contrastive views of two individuals mirror the separate careers of Perceval and Gauvain. Actions and character of each predispose the audience to accept without undue disappointment their fate. Failure [14] of the two heroes in their primary quests was anticipated by the failure of Alexander to measure up to Philip, as well as by the catastrophe which struck Uter's realm, and by secondary quests of our protagonists: knighthood by Arthur and reunion with mother; finding the maid of Montesclaire and fighting contracted but postponed duels.

The three generations evoked in the prologue and initial scene (Alexander, Philip, and Perceval; Uter, Arthur, Perceval) are reflected by three at the Grail Castle (Grail King, Fisher King, and the latter's niece) and at the Castle of Marvels (Uter's wife [who died 60 years before], Lot's wife [dead for 20 years], and the latter's daughter). Even at the Hermitage are multiple generations apparently (Hermit, priest, and acolyte). Such insistence on generations as well as genealogies must surely be accounted for in the meaning, as much as the evocation of both life and death.

Three women influence Perceval's life strongly: his mother (close and afar), the Tent Lady (before and after the Grail scene), Blanchefleur (in fact and in retrospect). Three others serve the tale's economy: the Laughing Girl, his girl cousin, the Loathly Damsel. Male figures who further his development are Arthur, Gornemant, and the Hermit Uncle. Infor-

14. Three of the people Perceval meets qualify their opinion of his potential success (mother, Laughing Girl, Gornemant): vv. 520–521; 1039; 1488–1490.

mative (again in different ways) are twice three individuals or groups: the questing knights, the Red Knight, Orguilleux de la Lande, charcoal seller, Clamadeu and Enguigeron, the Grail people. This last group includes the two men rulers and one corporeally absent but psychologically present woman (niece), and the Grail procession consists of three boys, two girls. At Blanchefleur's Castle is both a convent and a monastery. Rulers meeting Gauvain at the Castle of Marvels are three women, and five men are in its orbit. Pilgrims at the Hermitage include both sexes. Gauvain encounters on his travels as many women as men. This staging of both sexes must be significant for the whole story. [15]

The relentless march of time is shown not only by the multiple generations depicted but also by glimpses into a past and a future of Arthur, Perceval, Gauvain, the Grail Castle, and the Castle of Marvels. This aspect of time is prefigured in the prologue by comparison of Count Philip and King Alexander and verbally underscored later by the mother, the *cousine*, the Loathly Damsel, and Guiromelant. Arthur's world was of course disturbed by the upheaval in Uter's Kingdom which Perceval's mother recalls. One of the questing knights tells Perceval in the Waste Forest that Arthur knighted him five years previously. The charcoal seller tells the boy that Arthur has just defeated Rion des Iles. At story's end Arthur is being summoned to witness Gauvain's combat with Guiromelant. Past, present, and future merge meaningfully.

Perceval learns from his mother part of his ancestry. Later meetings with other relatives reflect parts of his prehistory: Fisher King, Hermit Uncle, and girl cousin. His Hermitage experience is a projection into the future. [16] Perceval's wandering five years in vain search of the Grail Castle suggests eternity, as does his circuitous route (the Hermitage is a pendant to the Waste Forest).

Gauvain is challenged by three enemies who defer combat: Escavalon whose father Gauvain had killed, Greoreas the rapist whom Gauvain had forced to eat with dogs for a month, with this hands tied behind his back, and Guiromelant who lost a cousin to Gauvain and a father to Gauvain's father. Is not life a deferral of death?

15. Might the numbers three symbolize Perceval and his brothers, and Gauvain's family members in the Castle of Marvels?

16. As brilliantly advanced by Rupert T. Pickens, *The Welsh Knight: Paradoxicality in Chrétien's Conte del Graal*, French Forum Monographs 6 (Lexington, Ky.: French Forum, Publishers, 1977), p. 136. The logic of this construction is a question not previously addressed.

Gauvain's final quest and ultimate fate (like that of the historical Alexander) in the *Conte du Graal* is clearly in the land of the dead, one aspect of the Celtic Otherworld. Perceval's adventure at the Grail Castle is not so explicitly depicted, but it is mysterious, enigmatic, unreal, and is sufficiently analogous with the Castle of Marvels to be considered as located in the Otherworld. The most cogent etymology of Perceval's name, which is closely bound to his Grail adventure, is Perce-val,[17] he who pierced the vale. He entered and left the Otherworld without restoring the harmony of his family or of the world. Why? This liberating role is reserved in Christian thought only to Christ.

Instead of one hero succeeding and the other failing, as in the *Chevalier de la Charette*, now both fail although in different degrees. Gauvain has a measure of success, for he does dispel the enchantments of the Castle of Marvels, but he is now a prisoner there, and he never finds the Bleeding Lance. His mission may be termed failure in success; Perceval's, on the other hand, may be called success in failure, for his *échec* at the Grail Castle is transcendental. His career and Gauvain's remind us to accept with biblical Job certain tests whose reason is known only to God.

Gauvain is Perceval's double.[18] The former's career forms both contrast and complement to the latter's. Perceval goes upward, as indicated in part by the three sets of lessons he gets, from zero to infinity, and Gauvain goes downward, from infinity to zero. Perceval the boy leaves his mother in the Waste Forest to find in Gornemant a father figure whom he quickly leaves at the height of his reputation. Gauvain goes from Arthur's court, the pinnacle of chivalry, and suffers through situations, each more ridiculous than the preceding one, to find at the end his mother, whom he wants to leave but cannot. Perceval goes from a matriarchal milieu to a patriarchal one; Gauvain does the reverse. To the

17. Readers of the King James version of the Bible are familiar with the expression "valley of death," but it occurs in neither the canonical nor the apocryphal Vulgate Bible. However, Chrétien was familiar with the *Aeneid* (he mentions Lavinia and Aeneas in his Grail poem) where the hero crosses a valley on his way to the underworld rendezvous with his father. See James D. Bruce, *The Evolution of Arthurian Romance*, 2d ed. (Gloucester, Mass.: Peter Smith, 1958), I, 251, n. 35. Both Perceval and Gauvain go down to the mysterious castles. And Perceval's mother said (v. 562) "by the name one knows the man." See William A. Nitze and Harry F. Williams, *Arthurian Names in the Perceval of Chrétien de Troyes— Analysis and Commentary*, University of California Publications in Modern Philology 38 (1955), 287.

18. Cf. Barbara N. Sargent, "L'Autre chez Chrétien de Troyes," *Cahiers de Civilisation médiévale* 10 (1967), 199–205.

three male members of Perceval's family who are dead and from whom no more is heard contrast three female dead relatives of Gauvain who inhabit the Castle of Marvels. The immature Perceval and the mature Gauvain are, in a different way, as contrastive as Philip and Alexander in the prologue; it might be argued that Gauvain's career begins where Perceval's leaves off. This viewpoint on the two heroes also suggests the author's intention.

Each of the three preliminary abodes which Perceval and Gauvain respectively pass [19] represents a stage in his upward or downward spiral. Perceval travels quickly and alone from Arthur to Gornemant to Blanchefleur; Gauvain goes slowly and always with a companion past Tintagel, Escavalon, Galvoie. Both the Grail Castle and the Castle of Marvels give the impression of being suspended in time, with infinite past and future. Hither will come both men and women. Through the Grail Castle will doubtlessly pass individuals like Perceval who will be close to the great mystery. In the Castle of Marvels will be permanent residents like Ygerne and later her grandson Gauvain. The disharmony in this romance could be removed only by a resurrection. [20]

So, our hypothesis, kindled by patterns of Chrétien's art and strengthened by resemblances between his *Chevalier de la Charette* and his *Conte du Graal*, is supported by subsequent reflections of motifs found in the latter's prologue. Confirmation of our theory results from post-prologue expressions and motifs, implicit or explicit, when subjected to logic or analogy.

Despite the voluminous research already devoted to the *Conte du Graal*, scholars have not noted sufficiently, in print at least, certain structural details of importance. Perceval left his mother, met the Tent Lady, fought the Red Knight near Arthur's court, received instruction from Gornemant, succored Blanchefleur, and then arrived at the Grail Castle. His adventures after that high point are analogous to the prior

19. Perceval enters each and dines with the Tent Lady, Gornemant, then Blanchefleur, and, later, the Grail King and the Hermit Uncle, whereas Gauvain enters none and dines with no one (alone he accepts wine in the Castle of Marvels and unspecified food, it seems). Foulon's article then might have shown this contrast: "Les Quatre Repas de Perceval," *Mélanges de philologie et de littérature offerts à Jeanne Wathelet-Willem* (Liège: Marche Romane, 1978), pp. 165–174.

20. For the meaning of Chrétien's romances, it matters little whether the inspirational source of any episode is Celtic (Judeo)-Christian, Oriental, ritualistic, or whatever; what matters is the use made of sources by our author.

sequence. He left his *cousine* (whom he made unhappy as he had done his mother), met the Tent Lady again (and "repaired" the wrong he had done her), fought near Arthur's court Keu (whose arrogance reminds us of the Red Knight), acquired knowledge and aided others from a five-year experience as Knight Errant (compare the Gornemant and Blanchefleur episodes), and then came to the Hermitage (which is analogous to both the Grail Castle and the Waste Forest). Such a route suggests his career is ended; further adventures of his would be superfluous; Chrétien never intended to return to Perceval's story (the most defensible interpretation of vv. 6514–6518: "De Percheval plus longuement / Ne parole li contes chi, / Ainz avrez molt ançois oï / De monseignor Gavain parler / Que rien m'oiez de lui conter").[21] He had gone from real life to a symbolic death after a brief visit to the Otherworld.

His post-Grail experiences are introduced by a proverb (as the romance had begun with another): v. 3630, "Les mors as mors, les vis as vis," which Perceval utters after guessing his name and learning from his cousin about his mother's death. Significantly the cousin does not challenge the name he divines, only its qualifier "li Galois." Since she knew the significance of the Grail Castle, she must have known the import of his name and realized that he had come close to the dividing line between life and death, and now knew the meaning of mortality, which young people find difficult to comprehend.

Perceval disappears from the story after agreeing to stay at the Hermitage through the weekend, doing penance for his confessed sins. He took communion on Easter Sunday and presumably departed the next day. The only other explicit mention of confession and communion is when Greoreas demands them (vv. 6971–6979). Our author is so fond of tripling motifs that we may expect another reference to these Christian activities. Such an occurence is implicit in the position of the Hermitage episode. It takes place in the middle of Gauvain's four main adventures. Perceval reached his Hermit Uncle only after wandering for five years and after we learn about Gauvain's experiences at Tintagel and at Escavalon, which last only a couple of days. Such arching of the two careers must surely mean that we are to apply the Hermitage adventure to both heroes. Each has now finished his earthly destiny without knowing it.

At the end of the romance, Arthur is summoned to the tourney to be

---

21. See William Roach, "Transformation of the Grail Theme in the First Two Continuations," *Proceedings of the American Philosophical Society* 110 (1966), 160–164.

held at Roche de Canguin. This will mark the third entry on the scene of the King. There is no doubt he will come to the land of the dead, for his time will have arrived to join his relatives already there. And there is no other place except the Otherworld for Perceval to be, since his career is obviously over.

In the *Conte du Graal*, Chrétien de Troyes devotes his talents to the problem of life and death. The teachings of man, woman, or church cannot deliver us from human bondage nor enable us to penetrate the final mystery. No other theory of the meaning of our story explains so satisfactorily as this one the careers [22] of Perceval and Gauvain.

22. For some similarities between the two careers, see Norris J. Lacy, "Gauvain and the Crisis of Chivalry in the *Conte del graal*," *The Sower and His Seed*, pp. 155–166, esp. n. 10, and for many contrasts, Antoinette Saly, "L'Itinéraire intérieur dans le *Perceval* de Chrétien de Troyes et la structure de la quête de Gauvain," *Voyage, quête, pèlerinage dans la littérature et la civilisation médiévales*, *Senefiance* 2 (Aix-en-Provence: CUERMA, 1976), particulièrement pp. 357–360.

JOHN F. WIPPEL

Some Issues concerning Divine Power
and Created Natures according
to Godfrey of Fontaines

THE DECADES IMMEDIATELY following upon the death of Thomas
Aquinas in 1274 witnessed a growing interest in questions relating to
God's power and its implications for created being. Thomas himself had
devoted considerable attention to issues centering around divine power.[1]
Even greater attention was directed to such topics by leading thinkers at
Paris and Oxford in the later decades of the thirteenth century and
onward into the fourteenth century.[2] Various reasons might be offered to
account for this. For instance, the Condemnation of 219 propositions by
Bishop Stephen Tempier at Paris in March 1277 reflects such concern on

1. See, for instance, L. Moonan, "St. Thomas Aquinas on Divine Power," in *Dio e
l'economia della salvezza* (*Tommaso d'Aquino nel suo settimo centenario*: Atti del Congresso Inter-
nazionale [Roma-Napoli—17/24 Aprile 1974]), vol. 3 (Naples, 1976), pp. 366–407;
M. A. Pernoud, "The Theory of the *Potentia Dei* according to Aquinas, Scotus and Ockham,"
Antonianum 47 (1972), pp. 69–95; J. F. Wippel, "The Reality of Nonexisting Possibles
according to Thomas Aquinas, Henry of Ghent, and Godfrey of Fontaines," *Review of
Metaphysics* 34 (1981), pp. 729–758.

2. In addition to the last two items mentioned in the preceding note see the other
secondary sources cited by Pernoud, as well as A. B. Wolter, "Ockham and the Textbooks:
On the Origin of Possibility," *Franziskanische Studien* 32 (1950), pp. 70–96/repr. in
J. F. Ross, ed., *Inquiries into Medieval Philosophy* (Westport, Conn., 1971), pp. 243–273 (on
Henry of Ghent, Scotus, and Ockham); K. Bannach, *Die Lehre von der Doppelten Macht Gottes
bei Wilhelm von Ockham: Problemgeschichtliche Voraussetzungen und Bedeutung* (Wiesbaden, 1975),
with extensive discussion of Henry of Ghent, Thomas Aquinas, and Duns Scotus as well as
Ockham. For a later illustration see the account of Gabriel Biel's thinking on divine power in
H. A. Oberman, *The Harvest of Medieval Theology* (Cambridge, Mass., 1963), pp. 30–56.

the part of the bishop and his commission. And this in turn may also be an expression of an important concern of the newly developing Neo-Augustinian philosophical current which was coming to the fore at that time and which would both contribute to and profit from the consequences of the Condemnation itself.[3]

Be that as it may, here I shall concentrate on one important figure from this period of transition—Godfrey of Fontaines. He seems to have already been engaged in formal studies at the University of Paris by the early 1270s, and served as Regent Master of Theology in that same University from 1285 until ca. 1303/1304. As I have indicated elsewhere, his philosophical thought stands out as perhaps the purest version of Aristotelianism to be developed during the period running from the death of Aquinas until the ascendancy of Duns Scotus around the beginning of the fourteenth century.[4] But this notwithstanding, we find various questions relating to divine power scattered throughout his most important contribution to philosophical and theological thought—his fifteen Quodlibetal Questions.[5]

In turning to Godfrey's texts, it should be noted that those with which we shall be concerned are all quodlibetal disputations. This means that the questions were posed for the Master, here for Godfrey himself, by others who were in attendance at these solemn disputations. Precisely because such questions were not fixed in advance by Godfrey himself they reflect the issues and concerns of the students and other Masters who were present at these disputations. Among such questions proposed for Godfrey's determination I have here singled out three: (1) Whether God

3. For this see J. Wippel, "The Condemnations of 1270 and 1277 at Paris," *The Journal of Medieval and Renaissance Studies* 7 (1977), pp. 169–201; F. Van Steenberghen, *Maître Siger de Brabant* (Louvain/Paris, 1977), esp. chap. III: "Entre les deux condamnations (1271–1276)"; R. Hissette, *Enquête sur les 219 articles condamnés à Paris le 7 mars 1277* (Louvain/Paris, 1977); Hissette, "Etienne Tempier et ses condamnations," *Recherches de Théologie ancienne et médiévale* 47 (1980), pp. 231–270. On condemned propositions relating to divine power see Bannach, *Die Lehre*, pp. 98–111; Wippel, "The Condemnations," p. 188; Hissette, *Enquête*, pp. 43–87. For a good overview of the Neo-Augustinian philosophical movement of the later thirteenth century see F. Van Steenberghen, *La philosophie au XIIIe siècle* (Louvain/Paris, 1966), pp. 456–471.

4. See J. Wippel, *The Metaphysical Thought of Godfrey of Fontaines: A Study in Late Thirteenth-Century Philosophy* (Washington, D.C., 1981), p. 385. For Godfrey's life and works see pp. xv–xxxiv.

5. His Quodlibets date from 1285 until ca. 1303/1304. They have appeared in *Les Philosophes Belges* in volumes 2, 3, 4, 5, and 14, and will be cited hereafter as follows: PB (for *Les Philosophes Belges*) followed by numbers indicating the volume and the page.

can change ("transubstantiate") a spiritual nature into a corporeal nature (Quodlibet 5, qu. 1); (2) Whether God can convert one accident into another (Quodlibet 9, qu. 1); (3) Whether God can restore as numerically the same a motion from the past (Quodlibet 6, qu. 2). Because of their close interrelationship, questions 1 and 2 will here be considered together.

I

Godfrey's treatment of the first issue has occasioned some difficulty for the few twentieth-century scholars who have concerned themselves with it. Thus Maurice De Wulf refers to a peculiar theory of "transubstantiation" which Godfrey has added to the classical theory of substantial change. In De Wulf's view the classical theory of generation is sufficient to allow for natural changes, and Godfrey's additional kind of change should be eliminated from cosmology. Robert Arway comments that De Wulf has cited two texts from Godfrey's Quodlibets—Quodlibet 5, qu. 1, and Quodlibet 10, qu. 1. But, he comments: "The first is capable of a more traditional interpretation than the 'bizarre' theory proposed by M. De Wulf. The second text does not mention the question in point." [6] While Arway is correct in noting that the theory in question is not mentioned in Quodlibet 10, qu. 1, it does receive considerable attention in Godfrey's Quodlibet 9, qu. 1. And as will become clearer below, if one reads the discussion in Quodlibet 5, qu. 1, in light of the follow-up discussion in Quodlibet 9, qu. 1, it will be difficult to give to either the "more traditional interpretation" mentioned by Arway.

At the beginning of Quodlibet 5, qu. 1, Godfrey briefly recalls the reorganization he would have been expected to impose upon the haphazard order in which questions had been raised on the first day of this quodlibetal disputation. (He would, in fact, have already imposed his organizing plan at his oral determination during the second day of this disputation.) [7] Certain questions had been raised about God, and others

---

6. M. De Wulf, *Etude sur la vie, les oeuvres et l'influence de Godefroid de Fontaines* (Brussels, 1904), p. 121. Also see De Wulf's *Histoire de la philosophie médiévale*, 6th ed., vol. 2 (Louvain, 1936), p. 295; R. Arway, "A Half Century of Research on Godfrey of Fontaines," *The New Scholasticism* 36 (1962), pp. 206–207, n. 37.

7. For a brief introduction to the Quodlibet see my "The Quodlibetal Question as a Distinctive Literary Genre," in *Les genres littéraires dans les sources théologiques et philosophiques médiévales* (Actes du Colloque international de Louvain-la-Neuve 25–27 mai 1981), R. Bultot, ed. (Louvain-la-Neuve, 1982), pp. 67–84. See pp. 72–73 on the Master's obli-

about creatures. Concerning God questions were raised which have to do with what is essential to him, and others with what pertains to him in terms of the divine persons. Regarding the first of these—questions dealing with what is essential to God—two had to do with divine power. The first of these asked whether God could change ("transubstantiate") a spiritual or angelic nature into a corporeal substance, such as wood or a stone, or whether God could proceed in converse fashion and change a corporeal substance into one that is spiritual.[8]

Godfrey refers to one argument which had been offered in support of the claim that God can change an angel into a body. To produce something from nothing is greater than to transubstantiate or change one being into another, since there seems to be greater distance between nothingness and something than between any being and any other being. But God can produce something from nothing. Therefore he should be able to change any being into any other being, including a stone into an angel.[9]

Godfrey then recalls an argument which had been offered against this same possibility. God cannot do that from which something impossible follows. But something unfitting and impossible would follow from the transubstantiation of an angel into a body. If an angel should be changed into a stone, just as the accidents of bread remain when bread is changed into Christ's body in the Eucharist, so too, the accidents of such an angel could remain without their subject. But then the very intellect and will of the angel would remain without the angelic substance which serves as their subject.[10]

In setting the stage for his own response to this question, Godfrey distinguishes three kinds of change. A first kind involves only one

gation to impose an appropriate organizing plan upon the various questions raised during the first day's disputation. For more on the quodlibetal disputation see the valuable introductions in P. Glorieux, *La littérature quodlibétique de 1260 à 1320*, vol. 1 (Paris, 1925), pp. 11–95; *La littérature quodlibétique*, vol. 2 (Paris, 1935), pp. 9–50.

8. PB 3 : 1. Note in particular: "Primum erat utrum Deus posset transsubstantiare naturam spiritualem sive angelicam in substantiam corporalem, puta in lignum vel lapidem, vel e converso."

9. Ibid.

10. PB 3 : 1–2. The argument goes on to suggest that this would also lead to positing the existence of an angelic intellect and will without the appropriate acts of understanding and willing. Apparently the point is that since the angel would no longer exist, and since the angel (as the subject of action) could not therefore act, there could be no subsequent acts on the part of the surviving angelic intellect and will.

positive terminus and lacks any common subject. Here Godfrey has in mind creation and annihilation. It is in this way that every creature may be said to be "changed" by God from nothingness to being, if we take the term "change" broadly. And, adds Godfrey, by his absolute power God could reduce any creature to nothingness or annihilate it.[11]

A second kind of change involves two positive terms and a subject which is common to both. In this case that which undergoes the change remains in terms of something which was intrinsic to it in the thing into which it has been changed. When one takes change in this sense, comments Godfrey, God cannot change one material nature into another nature which is not also material. Nor by such change could God produce an angel from a stone so that something which was intrinsic to the stone would remain in the angel. Godfrey, it should be noted, does not admit of matter-form composition in angels.[12] But, continues Godfrey, by such change God could immediately convert any body into any other body which shares in the same kind of matter. Thus from a stone he could immediately produce an ass, or a lion, or anything else of this sort. For support Godfrey turns to Augustine's *Literal Commentary on Genesis*, Bk. 7, chaps. 10 and 16.[13]

In addition to these, continues Godfrey, there is a third kind of change, which he describes as transubstantiation. This has two positive termini but no common subject. In such change one complete thing is changed into another existing thing and not accidentally but rather substantially or in terms of that which it is in itself. The question raised in Quodlibet 5, qu. 1, has to do with this kind of change—whether by this kind of change God can transform an angel into a stone or, for that matter, a stone into an angel.[14]

---

11. PB 3:2. Note Godfrey's terminology in the following remark: ". . . et hac trans-mutatione omnis creatura a Deo est ex nihilo ad esse transmutata, large de transmutatione loquendo, et posset Deus potentia absoluta quamlibet in nihilum redigere."

12. For more on Godfrey's rejection of matter-form composition of angels and of human souls see my *The Metaphysical Thought*, pp. 275–285.

13. The correct reference should rather be to Bk. 7, chap. 12 (*PL* 34:362). Cf. chap. 20 (*PL* 34:365). As Godfrey's text indicates, Augustine there notes that there were certain philosophers who held that every body could be changed into every other body; but Augustine knows of no one who holds that a body could be changed into a soul and become an incorporeal nature.

14. PB 3:2. Note the following from Godfrey's description of this kind of change: ". . . et haec dicitur transsubstantiatio qua scilicet res aliqua non accidentaliter sed substantialiter secundum illud quod est in aliam iam existentem transit et convertitur . . ."

The reader may wonder how this third kind of change is to be distinguished from change of the second kind, that is, from ordinary substantial change. In change of the second type there are two positive termini, and this is also true of change of the third type. But in change of the second kind there must also be a common subject, for instance, prime matter in the case of substantial change. In change of the third kind there is no such common subject. Rather one entire substance, including both its matter and its form, is changed into another entire substance. Not even the prime matter of the old substance remains as such in the new. [15]

Godfrey's defense of this as a third and distinctive kind of change seems to have been inspired, at least in large measure, by his reflections on Eucharistic transubstantiation. Thus he immediately comments in passing on one unacceptable theory of Eucharistic transubstantiation. According to this view, in Eucharistic transubstantiation the bread is not annihilated for the simple reason that the accidents of bread remain. Godfrey has some difficulties with this explanation. First of all, nothing pertaining to the essence or substance of the bread would remain. If appeal to the remaining accidents is the only way of accounting for the fact that the bread is not annihilated, this explanation ends, in fact, by implying that all that pertains to the essence of the bread has been annihilated. Moreover, it is not in order to avoid saying that the bread is annihilated that one must hold that the accidents of bread remain. The accidents are held to remain for a very different reason, in order to account for the fact that that into which the substance of bread has been changed—the body of Christ—may continue to be present in sacramental fashion where the substance of the bread had originally been present locally. [16]

If Godfrey's general theory of transubstantiation seems to have arisen in large measure from his consideration of Eucharistic transubstantiation, he does not restrict his third kind of change to the case of the Eucharist. He rather seems to view this as a more general kind of change, of which Eucharistic transubstantiation would be only one species. And

15. The importance of this point will become clearer below, in light of certain restrictions Godfrey applies to this kind of transubstantiation. Precisely because the prime matter found in the terminus *ad quem* is not identical with that of the terminus *a quo*, change of this type is not reducible to change of type two, according to Godfrey, even if he will also insist that matter must be present in both termini.

16. PB 3:2–3.

he uses the unacceptable theory of Eucharistic transubstantiation just mentioned as the occasion to offer some additional precisions about his more general theory of transubstantiation.

First of all, in transubstantiation of this kind, if one terminus can be completely transformed into another, the converse should also hold. The terminus *ad quem* should be capable of being transformed by the same process into the terminus *a quo*. Secondly, change of this kind is not to be reduced to Godfrey's first kind of change or to annihilation for a very different reason from that offered by the unacceptable account of Eucharistic transubstantiation. It is not because the accidents of bread remain that the bread is not annihilated in the case of the Eucharist. It is rather because that which the bread was in terms of its substance or essence has now been completely transformed into something else—the body of Christ. In fact, argues Godfrey, even if the entire bread in terms of its substance and its accidents were to be changed into the body of Christ, the substance of the bread would still not be annihilated; for that into which the substance of the bread had been changed would itself remain. So too, the fact that the accidents of an angel could not remain if the angel were to be transformed into a stone does not of itself show that such change is impossible. Such a change would not thereby amount to the annihilation of the angel and the subsequent creation of the stone, since the substance of the stone into which the angel had been transformed would itself remain. If such change is impossible, it must be for some other reason.[17]

With these reflections in mind, Godfrey develops the contrast between his third type of change (transubstantiation), and change of the second kind (normal generation). There can be no transformation of a stone into an angel or, conversely, of an angel into a stone, by the second kind of change because the two termini, the angel and the stone, do not share in any common nature or subject. Some such common nature or subject is required if that which is changed is to remain in terms of something which was intrinsic to it in the new substance into which it has been changed.

In other words, for substantial change or change of this second kind to

---

17. PB 3:3. Note in particular: ". . . nam in huiusmodi transmutatione videtur esse convenientia terminorum, et sicut unus potest converti in alium, ita e converso. . . . Quia ergo hoc non impedit quin possit substantia angeli converti in lapidem, possibile est hoc fieri, si aliud non obsistat."

occur, the same prime matter must be present in both termini. But this is not true of Godfrey's third kind of change. As we have already seen, Godfrey holds that the presence of such a common subject is not required if such change is not to be reduced to a case of annihilation. The fact that the terminus *a quo* has been transformed into the terminus *ad quem* is of itself enough for him to account for this. The terminus *ad quem* itself does remain. This is so even though nothing which was present in the old substance actually remains as such in the new. Unlike change of the second type, in change of the third kind not even the same prime matter of the old subject will remain in the new. This will hold even in cases of such transubstantiation of one matter-form composite into another matter-form composite. To illustrate this Godfrey compares the possible transubstantiation of a stone into a piece of wood, on the one hand, and the possible transubstantiation of the stone into the heaven on the other. One could no more say that the matter of the stone remained in the piece of wood than that its matter remained in the heaven, whether one holds, as Godfrey seems to, that there is no matter in the proper sense in heavenly bodies, or whether the matter found there is of another kind. [18]

From this line of reasoning it would seem to follow, as Godfrey notes, that a stone could be changed into an angel and vice versa. The terminus *a quo*, the stone, would remain in the terminus *ad quem* only in the sense that the former would have been changed into the latter. And since God has power over every being, it seems that he could change any created entity into any other created entity without annihilating the former; for the entity into which the first created entity had been changed would itself remain. In other words, such change would terminate not in nothingness but in a completely different being. [19]

At this point, however, Godfrey introduces some qualifications. While the first is not surprising, the second may prove to be so for the reader. Godfrey begins by observing that God could not change anything into himself; for such change requires that both termini be capable of under-

18. PB 3:4. For presentation and discussion of Godfrey's position concerning matter-form composition of heavenly bodies see *The Metaphysical Thought*, pp. 285–291.

19. PB 3:4. Note especially: "Secundum hoc ergo videtur posse dici quod lapis posset in angelum transmutari et e converso. Solum enim in hoc dicitur manere conversum, quod entitas sua fit illa, et quia Deus habet potestatem super totum ens, quamlibet entitatem creatam videtur posse in aliam transmutare sic quod transmutatum non adnihiletur, quia manet illa entitas in quam est conversum."

going change, and that either can be transformed into the other. Such will not hold for God, since God cannot be changed into anything else.[20]

Godfrey comments that Eucharistic transubstantiation, which we accept only on religious grounds, is supernatural and completely surpasses human understanding. Even so, if we cannot understand how it comes to pass, it cannot be so opposed to the natural order that it implies contradiction. For that which is contradictory can be done by no power.[21] (Here, if only in passing, Godfrey seems to be committing himself with respect to another contested point. In agreement with Thomas Aquinas but in opposition to Henry of Ghent, Godfrey holds that if something is self-contradictory, it simply cannot be done in itself and therefore God cannot do it. Henry had reasoned that it is because God cannot do that which is self-contradictory that it cannot be done.)[22]

This leads Godfrey to his second qualification. As we have already seen, transubstantiation as he is here defending it is not to be reduced to annihilation because when it occurs what is changed in some way remains in that into which it has been changed. But for this to be possible Godfrey now comments that the terminus *a quo* must in some way be potentially the terminus *ad quem*. If the mode of production or transubstantiation will itself be supernatural, the termini must at least have this in common with one another—that one is in some way the other in potency. Godfrey is led to this conclusion because it seems unlikely to him that any active power could transform one thing into another if the former is completely incapable of becoming the latter. And if one thing is to be capable of being transformed into another by such a process—by transubstantiation—Godfrey reasons that in some way each will have to be composed of matter. So surprising is this qualification that one writer concludes that Godfrey now seems to have given up his third and distinctive kind of change.[23]

20. Ibid.

21. ". . . id est modo qui contradictionem includat, quia hoc nulli potentiae subici potest" (ibid.).

22. For discussion see my "The Reality of Nonexisting Possibles . . . ," pp. 735–738 (Aquinas), pp. 748–749 (Henry), pp. 756–757 (Godfrey). Note that this is Henry's later position (of Quodlibet 8, qu. 3). In his earlier Quodlibet 6, qu. 3, he had held that while things are possible in themselves only because God has the power to do or make them, the absolutely impossible simply cannot be done; therefore God cannot do it. On this also see the helpful discussion by A. B. Wolter, "Ockham and the Textbooks . . . ," in *Inquiries into Medieval Philosophy*, pp. 244–247.

23. PB 3:4–5. See K. Plotnik, *Hervaeus Natalis OP and the Controversies over the Real Presence and Transubstantiation* (Munich-Paderborn-Vienna, 1970), p. 36: "After discussing

This, however, does not seem to be the case; for Godfrey will continue to insist that nothing that was intrinsic to the old substance or entity, not even its matter, will be present in the new entity into which it has been transformed. But he has now introduced a major restriction: only if there is matter (and therefore matter-form composition) in both termini will such transubstantiation be possible. As the reader can easily infer, this restriction will also lead Godfrey to reject, if somewhat tentatively, the possibility of a stone's being transubstantiated into an angel or vice versa, an angel's being transubstantiated into a stone. But one may wonder why Godfrey has introduced this restriction.

In developing his thinking on this point, Godfrey considers two possible situations—the transubstantiation of a previously existing thing into one that did not previously exist; and the transubstantiation of one previously existing thing into another which did previously exist.

As regards the first possibility, Godfrey comments that things which share in matter can be converted into one another by purely natural agency, but only according to a certain order. Thus a stone is potentially an ass, and a plant, but only according to a certain ordered sequence. In other words, according to the natural order a stone cannot be changed immediately into an ass. Its matter would not yet be properly disposed to receive the form of the ass. Here Godfrey is speaking of natural change, or change of the second type. But since God can act upon things in immediate fashion without observing any such ordered sequence, he can immediately produce a body from any other body which shares in matter. Thus if God were to produce a new ass from a stone, the stone would not be said to be annihilated; for the entire stone would in some way remain in the ass into which it had been converted. This would be so by reason of the matter of the stone into which its form would have been resolved.[24]

Although Godfrey could be clearer concerning this point, here he seems to have shifted to change of the third kind, or transubstantiation.

---

third kind of change at considerable length, Godfrey actually seems to reject it and conclude that one thing can be changed into another only if they both share in matter." What should be made clear is that Godfrey still defends the possibility of one material thing's being *entirely transformed* (transubstantiated) into another material thing. This, he maintains, would be very different than for the latter to be produced from the former by generation. Since Plotnik also finds Godfrey's general theory of matter extremely complex "if not inherently contradictory" (pp. 37–38), the reader may consult my discussion of this in *The Metaphysical Thought*, pp. 261–274.

24. PB 3:5.

If, as he continues, a not-yet-existing angel were to be produced from a stone, the stone could not be said to remain in the angel in any way. The stone could only be annihilated since it could not remain in the terminus *ad quem* by reason of anything which had been intrinsic to it. The newly produced angel would lack all matter. Godfrey's reason for drawing this conclusion is his conviction that the stone would not have been in potency in any way whatsoever to be changed into or to become the angel. Hence he concludes that one must reject the possibility that God could convert or transubstantiate a previously existing stone into a not-yet-existent angel, or, in other words, that he could produce an angel from a stone. There could only be creation of the angel after the existence and corruption or annihilation of the stone.[25]

Godfrey next turns to the second possible situation. Perhaps God could transform a previously existing entity into another one which already exists. If this kind of change is not to be reduced to an annihilation of the first substance, Godfrey reasons once more that the first substance must be converted into something to which it was previously in some way in potency and which is of such a nature that it could be made from the first substance if that substance (the latter) did not already exist. In fact, he suggests that the latter substance must be potentially though not actually the same in kind as the former insofar as it is subject to natural agency, and even potentially the same numerically insofar as it falls under divine agency. (In support of the last point he notes that by divine power something can even be annihilated and then restored so as to be numerically the same as it was previously! Godfrey's point seems to be that if such restoration is possible, then it must also be possible for the terminus *ad quem* of transubstantiation [as he here understands it] to be retransformed by divine power into the terminus *a quo*.)[26]

Godfrey's first reason for making this claim is that such change through transubstantiation must not be reduced to the annihilation of the first substance. His second reason seems to be that he wishes to reinforce another qualification already mentioned. Nothing can be converted into something else by the kind of transubstantiation he has in

---

25. Ibid.

26. ". . . et quod sit in potentia illud idem in specie virtute naturali, et idem numero virtute supernaturali, qua potest etiam aliquid adnihilari et idem numero reparari" (ibid.). See Part II below of this study for Godfrey's discussion of God's ability to restore a permanent being, as distinguished from a successive one, so as to make it numerically identical with its former self. It seems to be something like this which he here has in mind.

mind unless that into which it is transformed can also be reconverted back into the first entity. For this to be possible, suggests Godfrey, both must share in matter of the same kind. He finds support for this claim in Boethius' *Liber de duabus naturis et una persona Christi*, chap. 8. There Boethius writes that not everything can be converted or changed into everything; the corporeal cannot be changed into the incorporeal; neither can an incorporeal thing be changed into something bodily. Only those things can be changed or transformed into one another which have in common one and the same kind of matter. In sum, therefore, Godfrey concludes that something bodily cannot be changed into something spiritual.[27]

After making another reference to Eucharistic transubstantiation,[28] Godfrey returns to the specific question posed in this quodlibetal disputation. A stone is not even potentially of such a nature that a nonexisting angel could be produced from it, nor, conversely, is an angel of such a nature even potentially that a nonexisting stone could be produced from it. So, too, it seems to follow that a stone could not be transformed into an already existing angel nor could the converse occur without the annihilation of the terminus *a quo*. But annihilation would not be true conversion of one thing into another.[29]

Godfrey does comment here that he does not wish to speak definitively about this matter. When it comes to understanding what is

27. "Ita ergo nullo modo fieri potest ut corpus [according to MSS C and P for *incorporea*] in incorporalem speciem permutetur; quorum enim communis nulla est materia, nec in se converti nec permutari possunt" (ibid.). For Boethius see his *Contra Eutychen et Nestorium*, chap. 6 (rather than chap. 8), in Boethius, *The Theological Tractates, The Consolation of Philosophy*, ed. H. F. Stewart, E. K. Rand, and S. J. Tester (Cambridge, Mass., 1978), p. 108:20–26. Cf. p. 112:66–68.

28. PB 3:5–6. "Et quia Deus potuit ab initio corpus suum ex materia panis, quae secundum suam essentiam praeexistebat, producere; ita potest etiam substantiam panis eandem in idem corpus iam existens convertere, et sic conversa non debet dici annihilari." See Godfrey's remark somewhat farther on: "Si autem sic ponatur quod corpus in spiritum non possit transmutari, remanet dubium quomodo fiet conversio substantiae panis in corpus Christi, si in eo non sit aliqua forma substantialis alia ab anima in quam oportet substantiam panis converti, quae tamen est substantia a materia abstracta, posito quod tota substantia panis composita ex materia et forma substantiali per se convertatur in totum corpus Christi compositum etiam ex materia et forma substantiali." Godfrey declines to go into this issue in the present context. For discussion and background see Plotnik, pp. 34–38. Also see his "Transubstantiation in the Eucharistic Theology of Giles of Rome, Henry of Ghent, and Godfrey of Fontaines," in *Wahrheit und Verkündigung, Michael Schmaus zum 70. Geburtstag*, vol. 2 (Munich-Paderborn-Vienna, 1967), pp. 1073–1086.

29. PB 3:6.

subject to divine power, the human intellect is severely limited. His response to the opening argument which had been offered in support of the possibility of transubstantiation of an angel into a body is worth mentioning. The argument maintained that to produce something from nothingness is greater than to convert something which already exists into something else. In reply Godfrey concedes that this is true of that kind of change whereby something material is changed into something else which is material and not yet existing, as for an ass to be made from a stone. It also holds for the case where something already existing is converted into something else which already exists. But this reasoning does not apply to the transformation of something material into something immaterial or the converse, because no contradiction is involved in creation or in the production of something from nothingness. But contradiction does seem to be involved in such a proposal.[30]

In sum, therefore, in Quodlibet 5, qu. 1, Godfrey has proposed and at least tentatively defended a rather unusual view of transubstantiation. Transubstantiation differs from creation and annihilation in that it presupposes two positive termini. It differs from ordinary substantial (or accidental) change in that there is no common subject or substratum which would have existed in the terminus *a quo* and which would continue to exist as such in the terminus *ad quem*. In the case of the kind of transubstantiation which Godfrey has in mind, the entire substance of the terminus *a quo* would have been converted by divine intervention into a new substance, the terminus *ad quem*.

Even so Godfrey has qualified his theory to some extent. Although God has direct and total control over the entire being of the terminus *a quo*, not even by divine power can anything whatsoever be changed into anything whatsoever. As a first restriction, nothing apart from God can be changed into God. In addition, Godfrey has suggested that for one thing to be converted into another by transubstantiation, the two must have something in common—the possibility that the first can be transformed into the second and, conversely, that the second can be transformed into the first. For this possibility to be verified it seems that both termini must share in matter, and even in matter that is in some way one in kind. The different kinds of matter which some such as Thomas

---

30. Ibid. Note in particular: "Super hoc tamen nihil assero, quia quae divinae potentiae sunt subiecta, non potest humanus intellectus perscrutari."

Aquinas had posited in heavenly bodies and earthly bodies would not be sufficient for this, Godfrey has implied.[31]

As we turn from Godfrey's discussion of this in Quodlibet 5 of 1288 to his later Quodlibet 9, qu. 1, of ca. 1293/1294,[32] we find him continuing to defend the same position. This time the question explicitly proposed for his determination is slightly different: Can God convert one accident into another?[33] In setting the stage for his reply, Godfrey refers again to his general theory of transubstantiation. He begins by placing this question within the broader background of his earlier discussion in Quodlibet 5. He notes that we are again dealing with the possibility of transforming one nature into another, and by the kind of process which involves two positive termini in actuality without the presence of any common subject in the two termini. Such change implies that one terminus is converted in terms of its total being into another terminus, and in total fashion. And such change is not to be equated with or reduced to annihilation precisely because that into which the terminus *a quo* has been converted—the terminus *ad quem*—itself remains.[34]

Godfrey notes that in his earlier discussion (in Quodlibet 5, qu. 1) he had touched on two different ways of approaching this issue. According to one approach, it would seem that any accident could be changed into any other accident. The fact that through natural change one thing can be changed into another only if the two things share something in common is due to the limited character of any natural agent. Such agents require some kind of subject which receives their action, for they do not have power over the totality of a thing's being. This is why such natural change presupposes some common subject which receives the change and which is essentially and in the same respect present in both termini. Accordingly, in natural change one whole is not changed as such or as a whole into something else. It is rather in terms of some factor which remains in both termini that the one is changed into the other and therefore that the former is not annihilated. Even in the natural order, and presumably in accord with the order required for matter to

31. For Aquinas' defense of a different kind of matter in heavenly bodies see T. Litt, *Les corps célestes dans l'univers de saint Thomas d'Aquin* (Louvain/Paris, 1963), esp. pp. 54–90.

32. For discussion and some suggested revisions in Glorieux's dating of Quodlibets 8 through 14 see my *The Metaphysical Thought*, pp. xxiv–xxviii.

33. "Utrum Deus possit unum accidens in aliud convertere" (PB 4 : 181).

34. Ibid.

be properly disposed so as to receive a new form, anything material can be changed into anything else which is also material. But in the natural order something material cannot be changed into something immaterial.[35]

But, continues Godfrey as he now directs his attention to change of the third kind (transubstantiation), in this type of change the terminus *a quo* is not transformed into the terminus *ad quem* by reason of any factor which remains intrinsically present and identical with itself in both termini. It is not because of the continuing presence of any such common subject that such change is not annihilation, but because the terminus *a quo* is changed in terms of its entire being into something else which remains in existence. When one approaches the issue of transubstantiation (taken broadly as Godfrey's third kind of change) in this way, it seems that the only requirement for such change will be that both termini involve some kind of being which is created and capable of being changed in terms of its entire being into something else, at least by the Creator. Since an infinite agent has power over every created entity, it will be able to change whatever being is found in one created nature into the being which is present in any other, just as it produces every creature from nothingness. According to this line of reasoning, therefore, it would seem to follow that God can change any creature into any other creature. And it would seem to follow that God can change any accident into any other accident.[36]

But now, as we have already seen him doing in Quodlibet 5, qu. 1, Godfrey approaches the same question from a different side. Even such change should not be thought to go beyond the natural course of events to such an extent that it implies contradiction. It seems to be more in accord with reason to hold that things cannot be converted into one another even by transubstantiation unless they really do share in some intrinsic principle in such fashion that one is of such a nature as to be capable of becoming or being made the other. And this in turn seems to presuppose the presence of something which is common to both and which is indifferent to each in the sense that it is each in some way, that is, potentially. Thus a stone in actuality is potentially a piece of wood, and vice versa. If of their natures they were so different from one another that the one was not potentially capable of becoming the other, in no way

35. PB 4 : 181–182.
36. Ibid.

could one which did not yet exist be produced from the other. One would have to be completely annihilated and simply succeeded by the other.[37]

By considering the general question of transubstantiation from this approach, Godfrey reintroduces the restriction we have already noted in his discussion in Quodlibet 5, qu. 1. It seems that not anything whatsoever can be converted into anything else whatsoever, not even by divine power.[38] If one thing is to be converted into another even by Godfrey's third kind of change, the two termini must at least share in matter which is of the same kind in all material things, and in which matter all material forms are already present virtually and potentially. It is by reason of their matter that all material things are one in some sense and of such a nature that they can be changed into one another in the natural order through change of the second type. But the matter itself of one cannot be changed in terms of its essential being into another matter by purely natural agency. Because God himself is the cause of the very being of matter, his action touches its very essence. Hence God can transform the matter of one such entity into the matter of another such entity.[39]

When one turns from the case of matter to the possible conversion of forms into other forms, however, it might seem that the common presence of matter will not be enough to account for this. One form simply considered in itself is not of such a nature as to be potentially another form. Nor is one angel of such a nature as to be another angel in potency. Nor, for that matter, is anything material of such a nature as to be potentially something immaterial. Hence, it seems to follow once more that one material being can be converted into another material being through such transubstantiation, but not that a material being can be converted into something immaterial.[40]

---

37. PB 4: 182–183.

38. PB 4: 183. Here again Godfrey reasons that it does not seem possible for for a not-yet-existing angel to be produced from a stone by any agent, nor does it seem possible for a stone to be transformed into an already existing angel. In each case this is because the two termini do not share in any common matter by means of which one could be said to be the other potentially, or to be capable of being transformed into the other. By the same token, because of the presence of matter of the same kind in each, it does seem to be possible for a calf which does not yet exist to be produced from a stone, and for a stone to be transformed into an already existing calf.

39. Ibid.

40. Ibid. In support of the final point Godfrey again refers to Augustine's *Literal Com-*

Still, forms seem to present a special problem. Simply considered in themselves, forms, whether substantial or accidental, differ essentially from forms of other species. How, then, can one material being be transformed in terms of its entire being (including both its matter and its form) into another material being (including both its matter and its form) if the two differ in species? To deny that such can be done would compromise Godfrey's general theory of transubstantiation, and would also raise some difficulties in accounting for Eucharistic transubstantiation. In addressing himself to the problem of Eucharistic transubstantiation and to what he regards as an inadequate effort by Giles of Rome to resolve it,[41] Godfrey develops his more general explanation of how one substantial form can be converted into a new substantial form by transubstantiation. The ultimate foundation for action and hence for conversion taken in the active sense is an agent's form. Thus if action is properly assigned to a composite whole as its agent, this is ultimately by reason of the form of that agent. In like fashion, reasons Godfrey, conversion taken in the passive sense seems to arise from the matter of the thing which can be transformed into something else. If this is so, it seems that a form considered simply in itself is not directly and as such transformed into anything else. It is transformed only insofar as it is united with matter in a composite.[42]

Godfrey insists that it is because of the presence of matter that any matter-form composite can be transformed into any other matter-form composite, whether or not the two are identical in species. Even in the

---

mentary on Genesis, Bk. 7 (see n. 13 above). If one material thing can be transformed into another by transubstantiation, this will be because of the common presence of matter in both termini. One may still wonder, however, whether the substantial form of one can be transformed into the substantial form of the other.

41. PB 4: 183–184. In brief the Eucharistic problem reduces to this: If one substantial form cannot be converted into a specifically distinct substantial form, how can one hold that the substance of bread including both its matter and its substantial form is changed into the substance of Christ's body, including both the matter and the substantial form of the latter? Giles holds that the form of bread cannot be changed into the form of Christ's body, which for Giles is the soul of Christ. Hence it can only be changed into the matter of Christ's body. See Plotnik, *Hervaeus Natalis*, pp. 26–30 (on Giles), pp. 34–37 (for Godfrey's efforts to resolve this theological difficulty). The problem arises for those who defend unicity of substantial form in man, such as Thomas Aquinas and Giles. Godfrey himself was inclined to accept unicity of substantial form in man on philosophical grounds, but had some reservations because of theological considerations. On this see my *The Metaphysical Thought*, pp. 314–347.

42. "Ita etiam videtur quod tota ratio conversionis passivae erit ex materia ita quod forma in nihil per se convertitur, sed ut est coniuncta materiae" (PB 4: 184).

purely natural order a new instance of fire can be produced or generated from water because of the presence of matter in the water. By reason of its matter water is potentially fire. If such is true in the natural order, then it seems that by divine power the entire water can be converted into an already existing instance of fire, and this in terms of both the matter and the form of the water. The water will not be annihilated but will remain in terms of both its matter and its form insofar as the fire remains into which the water has been converted or transubstantiated.[43]

Godfrey now generalizes. It seems that any material entity both in terms of its matter and in terms of its substantial form can be converted by divine agency into another preexisting material entity in terms of the matter and the form of the latter. The possibility for such transubstantiation viewed passively or from the side of the being which can be so transformed follows from the presence of matter in it as well as in the being into which it is to be transformed.[44] As regards the possible transubstantiation of one substantial form into another, Godfrey does seem to defend this as a possibility, but restricts it to the transformation of material entities into other material entities. In such transformation not only the matter but the substantial form of the first will be converted into the matter and the substantial form of the second.[45]

Then Godfrey takes up the case of the possible conversion of accidental forms into other accidental forms. As a first qualification, he seems to hold that if accidents in some way share in matter, they can be converted into other accidents which share in matter of the same kind. Thus one substance-accident composite could be transformed into another substance-accident composite by such a process of transubstantiation. Because each is composed of matter and form, transubstantiation of the substance of the first into the substance of the second is possible. Moreover, the accidents of the former could be converted into the accidents of the latter as well. Presupposed for this would be the fact that in each case there is a subject for the accidents in question, and a subject which is itself composed of matter and form.[46]

43. PB 4:184–185.
44. PB 4:185.
45. "Sic ergo videtur posse poni quod materiale secundum formam et materiam tum ratione materiae potest converti in alterum materiale praeexistens etiam secundum materiam et formam, tum etiam ratione formae" (ibid.).
46. "Ex hoc autem ulterius patet quomodo accidentia possunt in accidentia converti; quia accidentia quae communicant in identitate materiae possunt in accidentia quaecunque alia quae communicant in eadem materia converti, ut scilicet compositum ex substantia et

As an illustration Godfrey again notes that water could be converted by such a process into fire both in terms of its matter and in terms of its substantial form. Moreover, an accident such as the coldness found in the water could be turned into an accident such as heat which inheres in the fire. Such conversion would apply both to the total reality of the substance or subject of the water and to its accidents as well. With this thought in mind, he even suggests that such could happen (although it normally does not) in Eucharistic transubstantiation. Not only would the entire bread be transformed in terms of its substantial being into the body of Christ. Even the accidents or species of bread which normally remain without their subject would be transformed so that nothing of the bread would then remain apart from the body of Christ. Everything originally pertaining to the bread, whether substantial or accidental, would have been transformed into the body of Christ.[47]

One might wonder about the species of bread which do remain without their substantial subject in normal Eucharistic transubstantiation as Godfrey understands this. Could such species or accidents be directly converted into other accidents by divine power? Godfrey mentions this problem in passing but does not offer any detailed reply. He limits himself to the comment that one should say of such Eucharistic species what is said about the corruption of such accidents and the way in which something may be produced from them and nourished by them.[48] His point seems to be that one must admit that such species or accidents

---

accidente, ratione tamen subiecti, in compositum ex alio accidente et subiecto ratione etiam ipsius subiecti convertatur" (ibid.). The final observation in my text—that the subject itself must be composed of matter and form—is not as explicitly stated by Godfrey as one might wish. But it seems to be implied both by his demand that the accidents in question share in matter, and by the example he offers in illustration in the immediately following context.

47. Ibid. Note in particular: "Et sic aqua posset in ignem converti secundum materiam et formam substantialem; et frigidum in calidum secundum substantiam et formam accidentalem."

48. PB 4 : 185–186. If Duns Scotus' representation of Godfrey's position in the latter's Quodlibet 11, qu. 3, were correct, there he would have held that when the Eucharistic species undergo rarefaction or condensation, completely different quantities are thereby introduced, and so much so that nothing of the prior quantity remains in the one which follows. Hence in this case there would be motion without a subject. Moreover, this kind of motion can be brought about even by a created agent. One might be tempted to connect this view with the present inquiry concerning the possibility that one separately existing accident might be converted into another. However, as I have indicated elsewhere, I strongly doubt that the first point in Scotus' interpretation of Godfrey's Quodlibet 11, qu. 3, is correct. See my "Godfrey of Fontaines on Intension and Remission of Accidental Forms," *Franciscan Studies* 39 (1979), pp. 316–355, esp. pp. 346–353. For a different view concerning Scotus' interpretation of Godfrey see Edith Sylla, "Godfrey of Fontaines on Motion with

are transformed in some way when the Eucharist is consumed, even though they have been kept in existence apart from their substantial subject, the bread.

Before leaving Godfrey's discussion of this in Quodlibet 9, qu. 1, it may be helpful to note his reply to an objection which might be raised against the possibility of one accident's being transformed into another. Accidental forms are simple beings and therefore have nothing in common with other accidental forms. In replying Godfrey again distinguishes between accidents insofar as they inhere in a material subject, and accidents insofar as they are sustained in being by divine power without their appropriate subject. As regards the latter, Godfrey's explanation merely repeats the comment mentioned in the preceding paragraph. As regards the former, however, he notes that the same thing should be said of accidental forms which inhere in a subject as of substantial forms. Substantial forms are also simple, but they are present in a composite. As present in a composite a substantial form can be transformed because of the presence of matter in the terminus *a quo* into a new substance consisting of a new substantial form and a new prime matter. So too, accidental forms are present in a composite—of a substantial subject and the accidental form in question. Hence accidental forms can be converted into other accidents by reason of some such subject, presumably because this subject itself can be transformed into another substantial subject with other accidents.[49] And the ultimate

---

respect to Quantity in the Eucharist," in *Studi sul XIV Secolo in Memoria di Anneliese Maier*, ed. by A. Maierù and A. Paravicini Bagliani (Rome, 1981), pp. 122–131; but see p. 141, n. 114, for some qualifications.

49. PB 4:186–187. Here he also presents and then criticizes an argument which might be offered to show that any form which exists apart from matter might be transformed into another by divine power: With respect to the kind of change which involves the production of something from nothing, any being can be converted in such fashion by divine power into any other. As an opening argument in support of such change, Godfrey had recounted the claim that no less is required to produce something from nothing than to convert any being into any other (PB 4:181). Apparently against both of these lines of reasoning, he now counters that in some cases less is required to produce something from nothing than to convert a being into another. For while the former does not imply contradiction, the latter seems to in certain instances. Nor can one validly argue that there is no greater "distance" between any two creatures than between nothingness and a creature. There can be no valid comparison between these two kinds of "distances," since between any two creatures there is a true distance; but such does not really obtain between nothingness and a creature. Hence in certain cases there can be repugnance between two creatures, while there is no repugnance between nothingness and something except with respect to the kind of agent which can act only on preexisting matter.

reason why such a substantial subject, and therefore why its accidents, can be so transformed by divine agency is the fact that any such subject must be composed of matter and form.

In sum, therefore, Godfrey continues to defend his general theory of transubstantiation in Quodlibet 9, qu. 1. His restriction of the possibility of such transformation to substances composed of matter and form does not mean that he has reduced change of this type to normal substantial change (change of the second type). Moreover, such transformation or transubstantiation of substances does not occur in the natural order. It requires divine agency. As regards the possible transformation of one accidental form into another, this too presupposes the presence of the original accident in a substance-accident composite. It also presupposes that the accident which is to be so transformed as well as the accident into which it is to be transformed both share in matter. Godfrey's views concerning the possibility of God's converting one accident which exists apart from its substantial subject into another such accident remain unclear from his present discussion. What does remain clear, however, is his conviction that for any kind of change or transubstantiation to take place, it must not entail that which is self-contradictory. What is self-contradictory cannot be done, and therefore not even God can do it.

II

In addressing himself to the third question singled out for consideration in our study, Godfrey reveals something more of his reasons for refusing to admit that an infinitely powerful being can do that which is self-contradictory. Thus in Quodlibet 6, qu. 2, he was asked to determine whether God can restore as numerically the same a motion from the past. In replying he comments that God, whose power is infinite, can do whatever can be done. But anything can be done which is not opposed to being taken universally. And this, says Godfrey, is that which does not entail contradiction.[50] Though he makes this remark only in passing, his position seems to be that the principle of noncontradiction itself expresses in logical fashion something which rests on being. To put this in more ontological terms, the principle of noncontradiction really states that being is not nonbeing. Given this fundamental opposition between

50. PB 3 : 110. Note in particular: "Possibile est autem fieri id quod enti universaliter non opponitur; hoc autem est quicquid contradictionem non importat."

being and nonbeing, one can be certain that the two cannot be identified, not even by God.

Given his view that God cannot do that which is self-contradictory, Godfrey now applies this to the present issue. If the restoration of something from the past in such fashion that it would be numerically identical with its former self entails self-contradiction, it cannot be done, not even by God. But, continues Godfrey, such restoration would be contradictory for things whose being consists in process (*in fieri*) and in succession, or whose being is not completely simultaneous and whose various essential and quantitative parts cannot be realized simultaneously but only successively. Motion, continues Godfrey, is something whose being is necessarily successive rather than simultaneous. Therefore, God cannot restore a past motion so as to make it numerically the same as it was previously.[51]

In developing this reasoning, Godfrey comments that the unity of something such as motion includes in its definition continuous duration. Interruption in the existence of such a thing disrupts its unity. When any such motion ceases to exist (or is interrupted), it cannot be continuous with a motion which comes into being at a later time. This is so because the interruption has occurred and an intervening time has been interposed. Given this, if a motion previously existed and then was brought back into existence, it could not be measured by one and the same time. Therefore any new motion must be numerically different from any preceding one. Motion itself is divided and numbered according to the numbering and division of time. Hence a preceding part of a given motion cannot be identified with a subsequent part of the same motion, nor can the two be measured by the same part of time. This is so even though the two parts may be parts of a motion which enjoys unity by reason of the continuity of its parts with one another. But just as no preceding time can be identified with a following time when interruption has occurred, the same must hold for motion.[52]

Godfrey argues that this is so because things such as motion and time are so constituted of their respective parts that when one part exists, say of a motion or its corresponding time, another and succeeding part cannot exist. All such things can enjoy being only in continuous and

51. Ibid. Note his conclusion: ". . . quare motum eumdem numero non potest reparare Deus."

52. PB 3:111.

successive becoming. Since the existence of one part of a given motion excludes the simultaneous existence of another part of that same motion, a part which has passed cannot be restored again as numerically the same. Otherwise the prior part and the posterior part would be simultaneous, and something would be simultaneously present in different spaces and in different times, and would be simultaneously moved by numerically distinct motions.[53]

To illustrate this Godfrey suggests that we think of a body moving from point A through point B to point C. If God could restore as numerically the same this motion from A through B to C, he could also restore as numerically the same the first part of the motion (from A to B) after it had ceased to exist. Suppose that the moving body were now moving from B to C. At the same time because of God's restoration of it, it would also be moving from A to B. The part of the motion which took place in the past would exist now, but in a space and time which was past. But, protests Godfrey, all of this is impossible and entails combining things which are incompatible with one another (*incompossibilia*). In sum, therefore, Godfrey concludes that it is not possible for the same motion to be restored so as to be numerically identical with its past self.[54]

Before leaving this question Godfrey draws an interesting contrast between successive entities such as motion or time, on the one hand, and what he refers to as permanent beings, on the other. Unlike successive entities, permanent beings do not directly and necessarily include the kind of unity which is based only on the continuity of successive duration. Their being does not consist in process or in becoming in such fashion, nor do their parts unite to constitute them as wholes in such successive fashion. Rather each exists in itself in terms of its completed being. Because of this, Godfrey concludes that it would not be repugnant for such entities taken in terms of their total being and in terms of their various parts to enjoy existence at different points in time. Hence it would not be repugnant for such beings, after being corrupted, to be restored as numerically the same as they were before their corruption.[55]

Godfrey does qualify his conclusion by observing that permanent beings come into existence in the natural order only by means of the kind

53. Ibid. Note in particular: "Huius autem ratio est quod talia sic constituuntur ex suis partibus quod una existente alia non potest existere, quia omnes habent esse in continuo et successivo fieri."
54. Ibid.
55. Ibid.

of successive motion through which natural agents produce their effects. Since such motions cannot be restored so as to be numerically the same, it follows that even permanent beings cannot be so restored by purely natural agency. Nor for that matter could they be brought into existence by divine agency by the same natural motion through which they were originally produced. But since God can produce them without using intermediary causes and without having recourse to motion at all, God can restore such beings so as to make them numerically the same.[56]

III

In all of the cases examined in this study, Godfrey has consistently defended divine power, on the one side, and the integrity of the principle of noncontradiction, on the other. The latter has served as a control for his applications of divine power to particular problems. If something entails self-contradiction, it cannot be done by any agency. Therefore God cannot do it. On the other side of the coin, if something does not entail self-contradiction, even if it cannot be done by natural agency, it can be done by God. The difficulty is to determine when a proposed application of divine power entails contradiction. It is to decide this that Godfrey has directed his skills in answering each of the quodlibetal questions considered here.[57]

56. PB 3:111–112.

57. See Godfrey's remark in Quodlibet 5, qu. 2: "confiteor tamen Deum posse omne illud quod contradictionem non includit, licet non intelligam omnia quae facere potest" (PB 3:8). There he is considering the question "Utrum Deus possit ex materia [corporis] corruptibilis producere aliquod corpus incorruptibile."

HUMANISTICA

BRUNO M. DAMIANI

Didacticism in Cervantes' *Galatea*

A CAREFUL READING OF *La Galatea* suggests that Cervantes was less concerned with the trappings of pastoral than with the novel's transcendental and ultimately didactic message, as evidenced by the author's preoccupation with death, the transitoriness of life, and the fugacity of time. In its didactic import *La Galatea* is connected with a wave of "medievalism" that extended, in some of its aspects, to the seventeenth century. If *La Galatea*, as the rest of the pastoral, celebrates the human power to love and to accomplish great deeds, it also underscores human weakness and fallibility. Skeptical of human love, Lenio looks upon feminine beauty as vain and mortal; he warns man against attachment to the transitory beauty of woman, which will destroy him, while love of divine beauty would improve him: "la caduca y mortal belleza, que los destruye, que no la singular y divina, que los mejora" [1] (I, 124). Indeed, love based on ephemeral physical beauty can lead only to suffering and death: "Pues deste amor o desear la corporal belleza, han nacido, nacen y nacerán en el mundo asolación de ciudades, ruina de estados, destruición de imperios y muertes de amigos" (II, 45). In Book II, that substantial part of Mireno's song which begins with the verse "Abatida pobreza, causadora" (I, 182) reflects not only the desire to flee the artificiality of the court but also man's weariness of the things of this world. Accordingly, Belisa warns: "dejad la vana afición, engendradora de afrenta" (II, 239); she also observes, "Llamando dulces tan amargas penas / paso la corta fatigada vida" (II, 88). It is this pessimistic view of life which leads

---

1. Textual references are to *La Galatea*, ed. Juan Bautista Avalle-Arce (Madrid, 1961), vols. I and II.

Darinto to proclaim, "es una guerra nuestra vida sobre la tierra" (II, 34),
words which evoke Heraclitus' famous dictum, "Omnia secundum
litem fiunt," cited in the prologue of *La Celestina*, and which bring to
mind even more directly the similar passage in Job (7 : 1).[2] Darinto's
statement is qualified immediately with the observation that "en la
pastoral hay menos [guerra] que en la ciudadana, por estar más libre de
ocasiones que alteren y desasosieguen el espíritu" (II, 34). Lauso's song,
recalled by Damón, emphasizes a skeptical view of the human condition
and of the world; Lauso remarks upon "la humana condición, flaca,
doliente, / en caducos placeres ocupada," and "el falso, el menti-
roso / mundo, prometedor de alegres gustos"; he deplores "la voz de sus
sirenas, / . . . [que] cambia su gusto en mil disgustos"; the world is "la
Babilonia, el caos que miro y leo / en todo cuanto veo," and pleasure
". . . nos convierte / en pocas horas en mortal disgusto" (II, 37). The
same view of the present world as toilsome and vile is voiced by Shake-
speare's heroine Cleopatra as she asks: "Shall I abide / In this dull world,
which in thy absence is / No better than a sty?" (*Antony and Cleopatra*
IV. 13).

La Galatea stresses the transitoriness of all things, including misfor-
tunes: "los males . . . todos son mortales" (II, 230). Marsilo speaks of
man's "vanas confianzas" (II, 230), while other rustics refer to life as "un
sueño, un pasatiempo, un vano encanto" (II, 178), a "mortal bajeza" (II,
182), and a "mar incierto" (II, 146). Life is seen as a frail ship moving
aimlessly in the stormy sea (II, 102). Significantly, Teolinda's promises
have been blown away like sand (I, 99), and Timbrio sows his hopes on
sand (I, 172).

Silerio underscores the ephemeral nature of life by asking: "De la
instabilidad, de la mudanza / de las humanas cosas, / ¿cuál será el
atrevido que se fíe?" (I, 124; cf. Eccl. 2 : 11). Following his turbulent life
of love, danger, and frustrations, Silerio sees himself "cansado ya y
desengañado de las cosas deste falso mundo en que vivimos . . ." (I,
187). *Desengaño*, as theme, is foreign to the pastoral ideal of man's idyllic
communion with nature,[3] yet it appears here and in the *Arcadia* of Lope
de Vega as a striking means of depicting man's growing insensitiveness, a
"death," symbolically speaking, to the things of this world. Silerio's
disillusionment, which is temporary, serves the function of introducing a

---

2. See *La Galatea*, ed. J. B. Avalle-Arce, II, 34, n. 12.
3. J. B. Avalle-Arce, ed. cit., I, 187, n. 187.

moral message into the novel when the shepherd concludes: "he acordado de volver el pensamiento a mejor norte, y gastar lo poco que de vivir me queda en servicio del que estima los deseos y las obras en el punto que merecen" (I, 187). Thus, Silerio embraces the penitent life in the hermitage, "hasta que el cielo le tenga y se acuerde de llamarme a mejor vida" (I, 187).

There is hardly an element in *La Galatea* untouched by the sense that all is relative. Sex, rank, fortune, the ages of characters, and nature itself are all seen as variables rather than as constants. This is true as well of time, which moves relentlessly to bring man to his ultimate end. Time, seen as the "consumidor y renovador de las humanas obras" (I, 16), is an obsession for most rustics of the Arcadian fields, who comment on how "Vuele el tiempo presuroso" (II, 229); who speak of the "vïolento curso del tiempo" (II, 208); or who look upon life as a "Día que al medio curso se escurece, / y le succede noche tenebrosa, / envuelta en sombras que el temor ofrece" (II, 179). Orompo dramatizes further the fleeting quality of human concerns and the rapid passing of time: ". . . el bien se aleja / con tal ligera corrida, / que forma quejas la vida / de que la muerte la deja" (I, 224). The message that the passage of time leaves none untouched is captured in the verses that follow: "Con alas vuela el tiempo presurosas, / y tras sí la esperanza / se lleva del que llora y del que ríe" (I, 124).

Caught in the conflict between freedom to love and filial obedience, Galatea herself contemplates the brevity of human pleasures as she contrasts them with the seemingly eternal hours of her suffering: "Breves horas y cansadas / fueron las de mi contento; / eternas las del tormento, / mas confusas y pesadas" (II, 133). Anguished by the conflict at hand, Galatea anticipates with resignation everyone's ultimate destiny: "Ya triste se me figura / el punto de mi partida, / la dulce gloria perdida / y la amarga sepultura"; "Mas todos estos temores / que me figura mi suerte, / se acabarán con la muerte, / que es el fin de los dolores" (II, 134). The initial refrain of Teolinda's lament underscores the loss of hope, so frequently experienced by shepherds; the flight of time; and the imminence of death: "Ya la esperanza es perdida, / y un solo bien me consuela: / que el tiempo, que pasa y vuela, / llevará presto la vida" (I, 61). The only consolation is that time moves the begrieved Teolinda closer to the end of her suffering: ". . . en esta amorosa escuela / mil males me martirizan, / y un solo bien me consuela" (I, 61). The "martyrdom" suffered by Leonida is further dramatized by the rhetorical question: "¿Quién hay que no se consuma / con estas ansias que tomo . . . ?" (I, 61).

The shepherds' concern with the passage of time, however, is also a source of consolation. All-subduing time will have its influence on sorrow and will soften pain and dull the sharp edges of grief (I, 16). "Time, after all, is a lenient god," the chorus assures Electra (Sophocles, *Electra* 179). Furthermore, time gives meaning both to what has gone before and to what is to come. It is significant indeed that one of the best sonnets in *La Galatea* is the one dedicated to "time."

The consideration of *La Galatea* as an important example of mythopoetic literature in which pastoral fiction is understood as conscious allegory[4] is particularly relevant to an understanding of Cervantes' treatment of death. Consonant with his ostensible intention of intermingling "razones de filosofía entre algunas amorosas de pastores" (I, 8), Cervantes gives his novel a moral tone. We see this early in the work, in Lisandro's first song (I, 33–34), an apotheosis of his dead beloved. Here, the traditional pastoral motif of elevating the beloved to divine status is expressed in a crescendo of praise and hope that makes this song one of the most inspiring of its kind in secular poetry:

> Goza en el sancto coro
> con otras almas sanctas,
> alma, de aquel seguro bien entero,
> alto, rico tesoro,
> mercedes, gracias tantas
> que goza el que no huye el buen sendero;
> allí gozar espero,
> si por tus pasos guío,
> contigo en paz entera
> de eterna primavera,
> sin temor, sobresalto ni desvío;
> a esto me encamina,
> pues será hazaña de tus obras digna.
> Y pues vosotras, celestiales almas,
> veis el bien que deseo,
> creced las alas a tan buen deseo (I, 34).

To think of death is to forsake sin, to leave aside corruption, to contemplate the afterlife. The view of death not as a terminal phenome-

4. See Louis Edward Cox, Jr., "The Pastoralism of Cervantes' *La Galatea*" (Ph.D. diss., Johns Hopkins, 1974), p. 7.

non but rather as a new beginning is implied when Lisandro affirms that "En la muerte de Leonida comenzó mi desventura, la cual se acabará cuando yo la torne a ver" (I, 53). Belief in a divine and perfecting afterlife of the mortal nature of mankind finds splendid expression in Elicio's song of Neoplatonic love: "Un bello rostro y figura / aunque caduca y mortal, / es un traslado y señal / de la divina hermosura" (I, 82). Life is seen as a "mar insano" and death as a "dulce región maravillosa" (II, 179), a special "región" which appears again in Lauso's song: "Meliso, digno de immortal historia, / digno que goces en el cielo sancto / de alegre vida y de perpetua gloria" (II, 177). The unbending devotion shown by the shepherds to the famed shepherd Meliso (a pseudonym for Diego Hurtado de Mendoza) can well serve to illustrate the view expressed by Theodore Spencer that though the emphasis on death did not increase after reaching its climax shortly before the middle of the sixteenth century, "it can hardly be said to have suffered a decline, and as the convention of fame became widespread toward the end of the period, the necessity of contemplating death remained in the background as part of the universally accepted doctrine." [5] Lamenting Meliso's death, Tirsi also laments death's swiftness: "¡Oh muerte, que con presta violencia / tal vida en poca tierra reduciste!" (II, 178).

Death intimidates man and makes him humble, as Elicio suggests at the tomb of Meliso: "Que aquello que contemplo agora, y veo / con el entendimiento levantado, / del sacro tuyo sobrehumano arreo, / tiene mi entendimiento acobardado, / y sólo paro en levantar las cejas / y en recoger los labios de admirado" (II, 182). The redeeming value of death is exemplified in Elicio's verses: "Desta mortal, al parecer, caída, / quien vive bien, al cabo se levanta, / cual tú, Meliso, a la región florida" (II, 182). In gratitude for this devotion to the dead Meliso, the muse Calliope promises wisdom and guidance to the gathered rustics: "guiaré vuestros entendimientos" (II, 188).

Although "Todo concluye y fenece" (II, 230), in him who loves well faith is permanent. Therefore Marsilo can say, ". . . mi fe nunca fue muerta, pues se aviva con mis obras" (II, 231), a paraphrasing "a lo profano" of the words in James 2:26. This thought is reiterated later in the same song: "todo el bien desaparece; . . . sola la fe permanece" (II, 231). Cervantes' serious and responsible treatment of the theme of death is illustrated again in the final chapter of *Don Quijote* and in the brief but

5. Theodore Spencer, *Death and Elizabethan Tragedy* (New York, 1960), p. 53.

deeply moving prefatory paragraph "To the Reader" which he composed
on his deathbed for his posthumous novel, the *Persiles*. In the latter
instance, Cervantes presents death as "sweet," though mortal nature
awaits its coming reluctantly and with glimmerings of hope that life on
earth may yet be prolonged.[6] Yet death is for Cervantes the *janua vitae*,
the door to a fuller life: "¡Adiós gracias, adiós donaires, adiós regocijados
amigos; que yo me voy muriendo, y deseando veros presto contentos en
la otra vida!"[7]

The thought of death "enriches the sense of the precariousness and
preciousness of life,"[8] and Cervantes' concern with it and with the
ephemeral nature of life and human endeavor in *La Galatea* reveals an
underlying philosophy in which order and purpose are reasserted beneath a seemingly bland content. In contrast to Alberto Tenenti, who
analyzes Renaissance Christianity as a movement which is turned toward
the present, one in which death is no longer the beginning of a new life,[9]
Cervantes presents a view of death as the end of strife and the beginning
of peace, as a transition to everlasting life—a "lesson" which he seeks
ever to communicate to his reading audience.

6. Otis H. Green, *Spain and the Western Tradition: The Castilian Mind in Literature from "El
Cid" to Calderón* (Madison, Milwaukee, and London, 1968), IV, 122.

7. Miguel de Cervantes Saavedra, *Obras completas*, ed. Angel Valbuena Prat (Madrid,
1960), p. 1529.

8. Philippe Ariès, *The Hour of Our Death*, trans. from the French by Helen Weaver (New
York, 1981), p. 330.

9. Alberto Tenenti, *Il senso della morte e l'amore della vita nel Rinascimento* (Turin, 1957),
p. 52.

GEORGE E. GINGRAS

Louis Bertrand and the Popularization of Patristics: The Vision of Early Christian North Africa

Pour restituer une image vivante et complète du passé, quelquefois même—
quand les documents sont rares—la seule image possible, l'historien est obligé
de faire appel à des facultés qui sont celles mêmes du romancier: l'imagination
représentative et la sympathie intellectuelle.[1]

THE PUBLICATION IN the spring of 1913 of his life of Augustine inaugu-
rated a new phase in the career of the many-faceted writer who was Louis
Bertrand. His reputation among the general public he owed to his
novels, especially those dealing with life among the European immigrants to colonial Algeria, and to a series of travel narratives recounting
his journeys through North Africa, Greece, and the Near East.[2] A

1. Louis Bertrand, "Une Evolution nouvelle du roman historique," *La Revue de Paris* (15
mai, 1921), 330.
2. The author of some seventy volumes, Louis Bertrand (1866–1941) is best remembered among today's reading public for his biographies of Augustine and Louis XIV (1924),
but his most original work was done at the outset of his career: the novels of Algeria (*Le Sang
des races*, 1899; *La Cina*, 1901; *Pépète le bien-aimé*, 1904; *La Concession de Mme Petitgand*,
1912), Marseille (*L'Invasion*, 1907), and the Lorraine (*Mademoiselle de Jessincourt*, 1911); plus
the early travel narratives (*Le Jardin de la mort*, 1905; *La Grèce du soleil et des paysages*, 1908;
and *Le Mirage oriental*, 1910). A Lorrainer by birth, he lived the greater part of his life along
the Mediterranean, whose therapeutic effects constituted one of his major themes. The rich,
neopagan sensibility manifested in his early writings was eventually tempered by his return
to Catholicism, his adoption of a conservative political and social ideology, and his rigidly
intellectualistic aesthetics. In 1925 he was elected to the *Académie française*. Albert Memmi
(*Anthologie des écrivains français du Maghreb* [Paris: Présence Africaine, 1969], 57–59) and
Jean Déjeux (*La Littérature algérienne contemporaine* [Paris: PUF, 1975], 20–25) consider

masterful stylist who could transpose into a rich, oratorical prose his impressions of awesome desert landscapes and colorful street scenes, he was particularly admired for the evocative power of his descriptive art. But he could also discipline his prose into an incisive instrument of critical analysis, as a small but impressive body of scholarly works had already shown.[3] Trained at the *Ecole Normale Supérieure* and for nearly a decade a professor at the Lycée of Algiers, Bertrand was an accomplished Latinist, solidly grounded in the methods of historical criticism. When he finally abandoned academic life to make his way as a writer, he carried over into his new endeavors a fidelity to his scholarly formation tempered only by a desire to make accessible to as large a public as possible the fruits of his research. It was in this spirit that he wrote the *Saint Augustin*, his first attempt at biography and the first of several books he would devote to the theme of early Christian North Africa.

It was a theme he would approach from various angles—as hagiographer, translator, martyrologist—and in a number of different genres—biography, critical essay, historical novel, romance. Besides the *Saint Augustin*, which enjoyed considerable success in France and abroad—an English translation by Vincent O'Sullivan,[4] for example,

---

Bertrand to be a forerunner of the Algerianist school and a major influence on its writers of the twenties and thirties. He has been the subject of several books, including David C. Cabeen, *The African Novels of Louis Bertrand: A Phase of the Renascence of National Energy* (Philadelphia: Westbrook, 1922); Maurice Ricord, *Louis Bertrand, L'Africain* (Paris: Librairie Arthème Fayard, 1947); Marie J. Cousins, *Le Sentiment chrétien dans l'oeuvre de Louis Bertrand* (Montréal: Fides, 1947); Warren F. Wilder, "The Concept of 'Latinité' in the Works of Louis Marie Emile Bertrand" (Ph.D. diss., Boston University, 1960); and Louis A. Maugendre, *La Renaissance catholique au début du XXe siècle*, T. VI: *Louis Bertrand (1866–1941)* (Paris: Beauschesne, 1971). For my review of the latter volume, see *French Review* 46 (April 1973), 1016–1017.

3. See in particular his doctoral dissertations, *La Fin du classicisme et le retour à l'antique* (1897), a work described by Roger Laufer as still the most comprehensive study of the neoclassicizing movement in French literature, and the complementary Latin thesis, *Raphaëlis Mengsii de antiquorum arte doctrina cujus momenti in Gallicos pictores fuerit* (1897); his editions of two hitherto-unpublished early Flaubert manuscripts, *La "Première" Tentation de saint Antoine de Gustave Flaubert (1849–1856)*, brought out by Fasquelle in 1908, and "La Première *Education sentimentale*," which appeared in the *Revue de Paris* from December 1910 through February 1911; and his *Gustave Flaubert* (1912), consisting of the critical essays he had devoted to Flaubert's art and thought over nearly a decade and a half of careful study of the latter's novels, correspondence, and notebooks.

4. Vincent O'Sullivan (1868–1940), American-born and British-educated (Oscott; Exeter College, Oxford), was by turns a poet, essayist, novelist, and dramatist. A friend of Dowson, Beardsley, and Wilde, he did most of his writing before World War I, a notable exception being his *Aspects of Wilde*, published in 1936; from 1919 until his death, he lived

appeared as early as 1914—he produced over the next twenty years three more works centered around the bishop of Hippo and his times: an anthology of selections in translation, *Les plus belles pages de saint Augustin* (1916); a volume of essays, *Autour de saint Augustin* (1921); and an imaginative study entitled *Celle qui fut aimée d'Augustin* (1935), which dealt with Augustine's companion of many years and the mother of his son Adeodatus. But Bertrand's interests went beyond the Age of Augustine to encompass other periods of the North African Church: in 1918 he wrote *Sanguis martyrum*, a historical novel situated in the mid-third century during the persecution of Valerian; and in 1930 *Les martyrs africains*, a series of dramatic portraits of those who had witnessed for their faith, from the martyrs of Scillium in 180 under Commodius to Saint Salsa, whose death at Tipasa took place sometime during the last years of the reign of Constantine. Finally, the relationship of North Africa's Christian heritage to the contemporary Church was a subject he treated from time to time in articles and lectures, notably in his addresses to the Eucharistic Congresses held at Carthage in 1930 and at Algiers in 1939. Taken as a whole these works project a vision of early Christian North Africa that deserves to be studied not only as a reflection of an individual writer's interpretation of a particular historical moment, but as an example of the complex dialectical process out of which a literary theme slowly takes shape. It will be the purpose of this article to trace the genesis and elaboration of a North African Christian thematic in the writings of Louis Bertrand, with a view both to defining from what perspective he has tackled such a subject and to evaluating how adequately he has realized its rich potential.

The origins of the theme antedate the *Saint Augustin* by nearly two decades and are rooted in the motif of renewal which underlies all of his North African writings, be they antiquarian or contemporary, fictional, historical, or polemical. That Bertrand did not initially articulate that motif in primarily Christian referential terms is evident from his early Algerian works, which tend to emphasize a neopagan vitalism at the expense of more spiritually regenerative forces. From the outset, however, his notion that the North Africa of his day was a land of resurrection had latent within it a potential Christian dimension which came sud-

continuously in France, teaching, lecturing, and translating. For a brief but excellent biographical sketch, see Alan Anderson's introduction to *Opinions*, a collection of O'Sullivan's essays on writers of the 1890s, published by the Unicorn Press in 1959.

denly into focus as a result of visits made to the site of the old Roman colony at Tipasa in 1895 and, again, in 1898. With its antique ruins set amid a magnificent natural landscape, Tipasa has symbolized for more than one modern writer the triumphal struggle of life to rise out of death.[5] In Bertrand's case it proved to be a particularly effective symbol, since it brought together in perfect fusion both the natural and the supernatural dimensions of that struggle, allowing him to move easily from one order of values to another. In 1895 at the time of his first visit, it was as a naturist celebrating the cyclical rebirth of life that he interpreted the message of Tipasa, describing the way sea, sand, and gently sloping hills appeared to merge there in an act of natural love as an embodiment of the female principle of revivification. Three years later, however, the archaeological remains of an early Christian presence having made their influence felt, there arose out of the ruins of the necropolis and basilica of Saint Salsa a cry of hope in a different kind of rebirth. It was expressed in an inscription carved on a wall of the ancient baptistery, affirming that, through the waters of the sacrament, man will receive the gift of life and enjoy a vision of the heavenly kingdom: "Si quis ut vivat quaerit addiscere semper, hic lavetur aqua et videat caelestia regna."[6]

This irruption into Bertrand's consciousness of a pristine evangelical faith in eternal life was eventually to have a profound effect on his writing. When he attempted, however, to thematize the message of Tipasa in his second novel, *La Cina*, published in 1901 and situated in the Algeria of the Dreyfus affair, he encountered serious structural problems. Its primitive title, *Le Baptistère*, suggests that he had originally intended to center his action around the regenerative powers of a religious faith grounded in the moral climate of the early Church. But the forces of renewal in the Algeria of the 1890s were hardly those of primitive Christianity; rather, they were the instinctive forces of a dy-

5. See Albert Camus, "Noces à Tipasa," in *Noces* (Paris: Gallimard, 1950), 11–27. A youthful text, it was first published in a limited edition in Algiers in 1938.

6. For Bertrand's reaction to Tipasa, see his letter to Joachim Gasquet, dated Tuesday, April 12, 1898, in *Terre de resurrection*, préface et notes par Maurice Ricord (Paris: Editions de la Nouvelle France, 1947), 74–79; his reference to the inscription on the baptistery is to be found on p. 77. How significant was the experience of Tipasa for Bertrand may be gauged by his repeated allusions to it in subsequent works, notably in *Sur les routes du sud* (Paris: Arthème Fayard, 1936), 203–222, where he devotes a whole chapter—"Le Soleil parmi les ruines et les chefs-d'oeuvre"—to a recollection of his visits there with Stéphane Gsell, the historian and archaeologist who introduced him to the Africa of antiquity.

namic nature that enterprising men were molding into the building blocks of a new society and that Bertrand proceeded to objectify in the person of his heroine, Félicienne Colonna, "La Cina," after whom he ultimately retitled the novel. Under their impact, the primitive resurrection motif associated with Tipasa receded into the background and was confined to a single chapter—appropriately entitled "Le Baptistère"—where it functioned as a metaphor for a reawakening of faith in the novel's uncharismatic hero.[7]

Failure to recapture the sensibility of early Christianity in *La Cina* cannot be attributed solely to the fact that contemporary fiction may have been an uncongenial vehicle for such a theme. It had something to do with Bertrand's mind-set at that stage in his writing. As evidence, we need only cite the minor role he gave to Christian antiquity in his *Jardin de la mort*, published four years later in 1905. This travel narrative, probably the most eloquent expression of his neopagan sensibility, was the work of a true "pèlerin de la beauté antique."[8] Everywhere, as he moved among the monuments of Roman Africa, the Christian presence faded before the splendor of the secular culture, and the ethos of a dying paganism alone seemed to appeal to him. In the gladiators' barracks at Cherchell, for example, not far from Tipasa, he remained unmoved by the pious tale of the martyrdom of a young girl from Rusuccuru, gored by a savage bull and devoured by a leopard! It was the gladiator who attracted Bertrand, with his prodigious way of life, "à la fois héroïque et frivole, poétique et absurde," existing only to please the crowd.[9] And

---

7. As an example, I cite this passage from chapter five of *La Cina*, where the hero, Michel Botteri, reflects on the ruins of Tipasa: "Maintenant qu'il était pris de plus en plus par les ruines chrétiennes, de nouveaux liens l'y attachaient. Le Catholicisme vague qu'il avait apporté des brumes natales trouvait une nourriture substantielle dans l'enseignement positif qui se dégageait de ces pierres. Peu à peu il refaisait en lui l'atmosphère morale des temps évangeliques. Sur chacune des tombes qu'il foulait était écrite la certitude de la résurrection, la confiance dans l'avénement prochain du royaume de Dieu." There is an unmistakable poignancy to Michel's desire to relive, if only vicariously, that moment when the Church could still express its pristine confidence in the resurrection amidst a setting suggestive of an idyllic pastoral Christianity. Unfortunately, in the dynamics of the novel, it represents an ineffective yearning on the part of a character destined to have no lasting impact on the course of events, and ultimately smacks of historicism.

8. Ricord, *Bertrand l'Africain*, 313.

9. The Catholic novelist Emile Baumann, a lifelong friend and correspondent of Bertrand, was troubled by this passage, as we can see from a letter dated 30 October 1905: "Il y a un paradoxe (p. 191) que j'ai peine à comprendre: les gladiateurs préférés aux martyrs chrétiens! Je ne m'explique pas que vous mettiez le culte faux de l'art, le cabotinage poussé jusqu'à la dérision sanglante de la vie, au goût des plaies hideuses et du massacre profession-

amid the ruins of the ancient colony's baths, no evangelical message of renewal was to be heard, only the mysticoerotic strophes of those pagan vespers, the *Pervigilium Veneris*: "Cras amet qui numquam amavit, quique amavit, cras amet."

By 1911, a shift in perspective had set in, and he was now more disposed to the idea of enlarging the range of his North African material to include among its motifs subjects rooted in the Christian milieu of the Late Empire. Two distinct but interrelated factors will account for Bertrand's change in outlook: (1) the need to revitalize a flagging Algerian thematic, which, since *Le Jardin*, had yielded little new material; and (2) a desire to give a more overt artistic expression to the faith he had rediscovered five years earlier in Jerusalem, and which, so far, had found only the most discreet manifestation in his writing. The suggestion that he undertake a biography of Augustine gave him just the opening he had been seeking.[10] His decision to go ahead with the project would prove to be a watershed in his career.

It was Paul Bourget who perhaps best summed up the achievement of the *Saint Augustin*, when he noted that Bertrand had rejuvenated the psychological biography by joining to a scholarly reading of the document the vision of the novelist.[11] That Bertrand had a novelist's interest in his subject is undeniable; to the poet Joachim Gasquet he confessed: "c'est l'âme lyrique et sentimentale de mon personnage—le jeune homme voluptueux, inquiet, romantique déjà—qui m'attire."[12] But the novelist's hand can be detected not only in a flair for a certain type of character but in the very composition of the work. The methodological approach of Bertrand the biographer resembled the techniques of the writer of realistic fiction: defining a milieu, establishing hereditary and environmental influences, introducing racial, geographical, climatic

---

nel, plus haut que le cri intérieur de la foi, que la beauté d'un groupe de victimes, chantant des psaumes quand les loins rugissent. . . . Cette fin du monde antique eut toutes les tares de notre décadence, et notamment la perversité esthétique" (cited in L.-A. Maugendre, *La Renaissance catholique au début du XXe siècle*, T. V.: *Emile Baumann (1868–1941)* [Paris: Beauchesne, 1968], 145). It is one of the ironies of Bertrand's evolution as a person and a writer that he would one day depict the heroic ideal of martyrdom in a spirit akin to that of Emile Baumann.

10. Louis Bertrand, *Mes Ambassades* (Paris: Arthème Fayard, 1953), 78.

11. Bourget's judgment will be found in an unpublished letter addressed to Louis Bertrand, dated October 30, 1913. Bourget's letter is in a private collection.

12. Undated letter of Louis Bertrand to Joachim Gasquet, probably written sometime in 1912, and published in *Terre de résurrection*, 152.

forces operative in molding a temperament. His familiarity with the North African landscape, in particular his experience with transposing into fiction and travel narrative its unique topographical features, enabled him to convey an authentic image of the world in which Augustine came to manhood. His Augustine was first and foremost a Romanized African, not so different in his passionate temperament from the neo-Latin immigrants whom Bertrand had known in turn-of-the-century Algiers. He was much more, of course; and the fact that through reason, will, and grace he had mastered that temperament and channeled it into one of the most genial sensibilities that Latin Christianity had produced was the governing idea of Bertrand's volume.

As substantial as were the contributions of the novelist to the making of that volume, by no means has Bertrand written a romanticized or fictionalized life of Augustine. His biography stands as a solid work of popular scholarship, firmly anchored in a knowledge of both primary and secondary sources. André Mandouze, for example, places it among a select group of lives of the saint published in this century, "qui, par leurs qualités scientifiques, leur talent ou leur originalité de point de vue, ont pu faciliter l'accès à l'étude d'Augustin ou ont contribué à le faire connaître dans le monde entier du public cultivé ou même du grand public." What especially distinguishes works of this kind from a host of popularizations, Mandouze adds, is their authors' "efforts de situer les *Confessions* par rapport à l'ensemble du contexte augustinien." [13] Interestingly, this very point had long before been made by Louis Bertrand, who recognized the danger of relying solely on the *Confessions* or on Possidius' *Vita* as sources for an authentic portrait of Augustine: "Il y en a d'autres, Dieu merci: les Dialogues philosophiques, les Sermons, les Commentaires sur les Psaumes ou les Evangiles, la Correspondance, et ça et là, les controverses et les traités théologiques. . . . c'est surtout dans les premiers de ces livres que j'ai cherché à retrouver ou à surprendre le vrai caractère de mon héros." [14] This statement is significant both for what it tells us about the genre of the *Saint Augustin* and for what it tells us about

13. André Mandouze, *Saint Augustin: L'Aventure de la raison et de la grâce* (Paris: Etudes Augustiniennes, 1968), 22–23 and n. 3, p. 23.

14. Louis Bertrand, *Les Plus Belles Pages de saint Augustin* (Paris: Arthème Fayard, 1916), 11. Subsequent references to this work will appear in the body of the article with the abbreviation PBP and appropriate page number. The citation is taken from the preface to *Les Plus Belles Pages*, the bulk of which was republished in *Autour de saint Augustin*, under the title "Réponses à quelques objections."

Bertrand's approach to his sources. He has written, it would seem, a heroic rather than a spiritual or intellectual biography; and, in his choice of material, he has obviously tended to valorize one category of texts over another, downplaying, for example, the importance of the major doctrinal writings in favor of more pragmatically oriented works like the *Epistolae*, the *Sermones*, the *Quaestiones evangeliorum*.

This becomes evident when we look at the composition of his anthology, *Les Plus Belles Pages de saint Augustin*, published three years after the biography and made up of selections in translation from the *Confessions* and from the five categories of texts which Bertrand has listed as prime sources for "the authentic character" of Augustine. Now, although a nearly equal number of pages has been allotted to each of the six major divisions, the material has been weighed more toward Augustine the man and shepherd of a flock than toward the theologian and the philosopher; and, even when it came to selecting passages from the *De magistro* or the *De libro arbitrio*, from the *De Trinitate* or *De civitate Dei*, Bertrand consistently chose texts which emphasize the pastoral over the dogmatic, the practical over the speculative, the inspirational over the problematical. If the structure of the anthology is any guide to the orientation of the biography, then we should expect to meet in the pages of the *Saint Augustin* an eminently practical doctor and saint of the Church—a contemplative actively engaged, through his correspondence and polemical tracts, in the spiritual and temporal affairs of his day; an intellectual striving, through his sermons and scriptural commentaries, to put the subtleties of doctrine within the grasp of "des intelligences les plus incultes" (PBP, 19).

That Bertrand intended that there be a taut link between anthology and biography can be easily demonstrated. The statement we cited above is taken from the preface to *Les Plus Belles Pages* and was directed at those critics who had faulted him for not having cited more extensively his sources or for having failed to provide the scholarly apparatus that a study of Augustine would ordinarily be expected to contain. Implicit in their critique was the inference that he may not have had a thorough command of the Augustinian corpus. The anthology was meant to counter these objections by furnishing an impressive cross-section of texts on which the *Saint Augustin* had been based: "en publiant ces pages, je n'aurai fait en somme que 'sortir' quelques-uns des documents utilisés par moi dans mon précédent livre" (PBP, 9) was the way he described the interrelationship of these complementary works. Ideally, they should be read as companion volumes, with the documentary evidence set forth in the one serving to authenticate the image of Augustine projected in the other.

But a work is more than a sum total of its sources; and what gave to the *Saint Augustin* its originality, what made it such an effective vehicle of popularization, was ultimately Bertrand's ability to read these documents from a new point of view, to compose a portrait of his subject that was at once faithful to the evidence and in line with his conception of the saint as the quintessential embodiment of the Latin African character. Indeed, it was his contention that, in the person of the bishop of Hippo, that character had attained truly heroic stature and had, thereby, taken on, for twentieth-century man, exemplary value. For Bertrand, heroism meant ceaseless struggle against both the divisive instincts assailing the self and the destructive forces working for the dissolution of the social, political, and religious order. Augustine exemplified both aspects of that struggle, and the biography is so structured as to bring that fact into focus. Divided into six parts, the volume falls conveniently into two roughly equal halves, the first ending with his conversion, the second with his death at a crucial moment in the history of Christian North Africa, the moment when the Arian armies of the Vandal Genseric were about to overthrow Catholic and Roman authority in the region. But there should be no doubt as to where Bertrand's emphasis lies. In the dynamics of the *Saint Augustin*, the struggle to master self was but the prelude to the second and greater struggle, waged against the enemies of Church and Empire by a Latin African, "de tout coeur fidèle à Rome." [15] And, if we are to grasp the full import of this heroic biography, we must see Augustine, as did Louis Bertrand, as "l'Apôtre de la Paix et de l'Unité catholique," as "le dernier représentant de la culture latine en face des Barbares." [16]

It would be erroneous, however, to interpret that last phrase in a negative sense. For Bertrand, the great achievement of Augustine was precisely "qu'il a élargi nos âmes de Latins, en nous reconciliant avec le Barbare. . . . [qu'il] a fait entrer dans notre conscience les régions

15. Louis Bertrand, *Saint Augustin* (Paris: Arthème Fayard, 1913), 7. Subsequent references to this work will appear in the body of the article with the abbreviation SA and appropriate page number.

16. Part V of the *Saint Augustin* is entitled "L'Apôtre de la Paix et de L'Unité catholique," Part VI, "En Face des Barbares." The fuller citation is to be found in Bertrand's letter to Joachim Gasquet cited above (see note 12).

innomées, les pays vagues de l'âme qui plongeait dans les ténèbres";
that, "par lui s'est consommé l'union du génie sémitique et du génie
occidentale" (SA, 11). If the reader was to experience how successfully
Augustine had fused these multiple cross-cultural currents into a unique
and personal mode of thought, it would have to be through contact with
the texts, if not in the original, at least in translation. It is here that *Les
Plus Belles Pages* comes to the fore as a major work of popularization,
communicating, as no biography could hope to do, how profoundly
African was Augustine of Tagaste and how masterfully he had molded an
alien Latin idiom into the genial vehicle of a non-Roman sensibility.
Rarely had the standard French versions done this, Bertrand felt; and his
comments on the seventeenth-century Port Royal translation of the
Confessions go far in telling us about which sides of Augustine he had
himself sought to bring into focus: "Or, en bon janséniste, le traducteur
des *Confessions*, l'austère Arnaud d'Andilly, s'est évertué à éteindre et à
refroidir de son mieux les chaudes couleurs de ce style africain, à mor-
tifier cette sensibilité trop vive, à châtier la luxuriance des métaphores où
s'emporte cette imagination fougueuse, qui violente les signes conven-
tionnels du langage pour leur faire exprimer l'inexprimable" (PBP, 5). It
was ultimately this boundless verve of Augustine's spirit, one suspects,
that made him such an attractive figure for Louis Bertrand and, if we can
judge by the reception given the biography, for the French public of
1913 as well.

We suggested earlier that the composition of the *Saint Augustin* was to
prove a watershed in Bertrand's career; and there can be no doubt that the
publication of the biography, which both the secular and the religious
press recognized as the work of a professedly Catholic author, had a
marked effect on the future trajectory of his writing. That it fixed him
firmly in the orbit of the *renouveau catholique* and all that that implied
goes without saying.[17] But it also prompted him to rethink the role a
novelist could play in the writing of history, as well as how rich a vein
history could be for the writer of fiction. In 1921, after a decade of
reorientating his work in this direction, he would feel sufficiently confident to assert that, to restore a complete and living image of the past,
especially when the documents are few, the historian must resort to the

17. "Les Catholiques, qui peuvent déjà s'enorgueillir de Paul Claudel, de Francis Jam-
mes, de Charles Péguy, verront avec plaisir un écrivain de la valeur de M. Louis Bertrand
confesser sa foi en termes exprès," was the way the radical-socialist critic of *Le Temps*, Paul
Souday, described the impact of the *Saint Augustin*.

procedures and techniques of the novelist. [18] More importantly, however, the record sales it enjoyed both in its original version and in the edition for younger readers encouraged him to publish not only his translations of *Les Plus Belles Pages de saint Augustin* but a series of essays devoted to the man and his age. Six in number and covering a wide range of topics, they were written in the months following the appearance of the biography and during the early years of World War I. Originally composed for conservatively oriented periodicals with large readerships, they were subsequently collected and republished as part of *Autour de saint Augustin* and are best studied in the context of that volume.

Conceived as a sequel to the *Saint Augustin*, this miscellany explores in greater detail various historical and archaeological points alluded to therein (e.g., the actual site of Cassiciacum, Monica's role in her son's marriage plans) and proposes to relate Augustine to the concerns of a modern reader. [19] Contemporary events played as much a part as personal predilection in prompting Bertrand to develop certain topics. Thus, the dedication of a statue to the saint at Hippo, in April 1914, was the occasion for a journalistic piece emphasizing continuity between the Church of Augustine and the Church reimplanted in Africa under French auspices after 1830; and a Christmas letter from Cardinal Mercier to the Belgian Church during the war, the point of departure for an inspirational text on Augustine's instructions to the Numidian clergy at the time of the Vandal invasions. The latter piece, entitled "Les Devoirs du clergé en temps de guerre," was one of three essays based on Bertrand's study of Augustine's correspondence—the other two being concerned respectively with whether monks should perform manual labor and with an attempt by the faithful at Hippo to compel Pinian to accept ordination. [20] Taken together, they constitute the center of the volume and

18. See note 1, above, for reference.

19. The volume grouped together eight separate texts. Besides his response to certain criticism leveled against the *Saint Augustin*, it included a historical romance, "La Femme qui était retournée en Afrique," and six essays: "Au pays de saint Augustin"; "Sainte Monique et le projet de mariage de saint Augustin"; "Cassiciacum a-t-il disparu?"; "Le Travail manuel des moines et la question sociale à la veille des invasions barbares"; "Les Devoirs du clergé en temps de guerre"; and "Une Election sacerdotale dans la cathédrale d'Hippone."

20. "Le Travail manuel des moines et la question sociale à la veille des invasions barbares" was based on Augustine's *De opere monachorum*, a treatise written in the form of a lengthy letter to Aurelius, bishop of Carthage, circa 400; "Une Election sacerdotale dans la cathédrale d'hippone," on his correspondence, early in 411, with the principals in the affair, Pinian, Melania, her mother Albina, and Alypius, bishop of Tagaste (*epistulae* 124, 125, 126).

attest to his ability to popularize history by weaving together in closely knit strands past and present situations for the education and delectation of the reader. A brief glance at "Les Devoirs du clergé" will illustrate his approach.

Bertrand began his essay by noting that Cardinal Mercier's recent pastoral letter, "Patriotisme et Endurance" (December 25, 1914), had brought home to him the tragic relevance of a similar document, written fifteen centuries earlier by Augustine, in response to an inquiry from Honoratus of Thiave, on how the clergy should act at the approach of Genseric's pillaging armies. To put Augustine's reply (*epist.* 228) in a context familiar to the French public of 1915, Bertrand set out to establish a parallel between the situation that had long ago confronted the bishop of Hippo and the one currently testing the mettle of the Belgian primate in the wake of the German invasion and occupation of his country. To that end, he attempted to recreate something of the climate prevailing in North Africa circa 429–430, discussing briefly the background to the invasion of the Vandals, then describing their progress across Mauretania and Numidia, as reflected in the accounts of eyewitnesses or of their near contemporaries: Possidius of Guelma, Salvian of Marseille, Victor of Vita. If he insisted—frequently to excess—on overly facile analogies between the cruelty of the armies of William the Second and the ruthlessness of Genseric's forces, he did so to impress on readers acquainted with the horrors of modern warfare the heroic dimensions of Augustine's counsel to stand firm "vis-à-vis des Barbares, jusqu'au martyre." [21] Interestingly, Bertrand devoted less than a third of the essay to an exegesis of the text proper; and even there, he confined himself to summarizing the essentials of the argument, quoting liberally in order to convey the power and vigor of Augustine's message. His real goal was to project, once again, a heroic image of the bishop of Hippo, stressing that, by his counsel to resist persecution, Augustine had given to the North African Church the requisite spiritual sustenance to survive a hundred years of Vandal occupation. It is obviously an uplifting message that he wishes to communicate in his closing paragraphs, one in which a reader living through a world in turmoil can find hope: despite persecution, apostasies were few; and,

21. Louis Bertrand, *Autour de saint Augustin* (Paris: Arthème Fayard, 1921), 112. Subsequent references to this work will appear in the body of the article with the abbreviation ASA and appropriate page number.

when Belisarius restored Roman rule, Bertrand states, "le pays se retrouva, en majorité catholique, comme au temps d'Augustin. L'esprit et le coeur du grand évêque y vivaient toujours. . . . Grâce à lui l'Afrique resta romaine près d'un siècle encore" (ASA, 150–151).

The final text in *Autour de saint Augustin* belonged to a different genre of writing and was an application of the principle that, in certain cases, to fill in the lacunae of history, one must have recourse to the techniques of the novel. Bertrand found such a case in the veiled drama of the unnamed woman of the *Confessions*, of whom—though she was his mistress of many years—Augustine spoke but twice: once to mark the beginning of their liaison (*conf.* 6.2), then to recount the final break and separation years later in Milan (*conf.* 6.15). Having furnished the indispensable framing of a tale, the repentant doctor of the Church was content to leave to posterity its elaboration—along with any speculation a curious writer would care to make about the character and fate of its shadowy heroine. This was what Bertrand set out to do with *La Femme qui était retournée en Afrique*, the title of which he took from a poignant passage in Augustine's account of her departure: "Et illa in Africam redierat vovens tibi alium se virum nescituram relicto apud me naturali ex illa filio meo" (*conf.* 6.15).[22]

Its genesis can be traced to two distinct preoccupations on Bertrand's part. As a novelist, he saw the makings of a story in the way these painful events were likely to have affected not only the woman herself, but the gifted adolescent she had left behind; as a historian, and as a Christian troubled by the circumstances surrounding Augustine's break with his mistress, he was anxious to find some way of bringing into focus the genuine spiritual impulses behind the separation. Patristic scholars before and since Bertrand have found this a difficult task to accomplish,

22. *La Femme qui était retournée en Afrique* had originally been published in a limited edition in 1920 by the "Editions Le Livre" with illustrations by Clément Serveau; a review by Firmin Roz, entitled "Un Conte de Louis Bertrand," appeared in *La Revue Universelle* (mars 1921), 629–632. Bertrand is not the only twentieth-century writer, however, to have been intrigued by the person of Augustine's mistress. Mandouze observes that "Cet anonymat et la brièveté des passages où Augustin parle d'elle ont laissé d'autant plus de latitude à certains romanciers ou essayistes pour tracer d'elle un portrait et 'inventer' sa vie" (Mandouze, op. cit., 181, n. 6). In addition to Bertrand, Mandouze cites Léo Gaubert, *Prélude au calvaire* (the epigraph of which was *ad matrem Adeodati*), *Esprit*, T. I (1932–1933), 244–263; 417–440; 581–602; and *Confessions de Numida: L'Innomée de saint Augustin*, présentées et commentées par P. Villemain et précédées d'une lettre de Henri I. Marrou, L'Histoire au présent (Paris: Editions de Paris, 1957).

and with reason. Even if we admit that separation was a precondition for conversion, the actual break was dictated by a complex set of motives, some of which—his plan, for example, to marry into a comfortable and respectable family—did little honor either to Augustine or to his mother. In a brief essay written in 1914, Bertrand had already tried to disculpate Monica by arguing that it was out of concern for her son's salvation, and not from worldly considerations alone, that she had urged an end to the liaison.[23] Now, some six years later, he felt the need to carry the argument beyond the strictures of known fact; and with *La Femme qui était retournée en Afrique*, he has attempted to restate the separation motif in an artistically verisimilar, albeit unhistorical, context, one in which the decision to part would be seen as a mutually willed first step to perfection. He has imagined, consequently, a reunion several years after the original break, at Theveste in North Africa, where Augustine had gone to preach a Christmas vigil sermon to the catechumens; he was accompanied by a terminally ill Adeodatus hoping for one last visit with his mother, who had been living a cloistered life in the Numidian city. Around the bedside of their dying son, the estranged parents will meet in the spirit of reunion and reconciliation which must precede the ultimate separation in charity of Augustine and the unnamed woman, whom Bertrand has chosen to call Modesta.

In intention *La Femme* may be a symbolic text; in execution, however, it is an artistically plausible elaboration of the basic factual and psychological data given in Book 6, chapter 15, of the *Confessions*. That the separation had been a traumatic experience for Augustine we know from the language he employed to describe both the break and the imperfect healing process that followed—images of tearing, cutting, wounding, drawing blood.[24] Furthermore, the consciousness that he had lacked the moral fiber to live continently like Modesta—"at ego infelix nec feminae imitator"—had only added to his distress. It is an Augustine still smarting from the effects of the separation that we meet then on the way to Theveste, a man troubled by feelings of guilt and by the stirrings of old ties, as he relives in brief flashbacks his years with Modesta. In his

23. See Louis Bertrand, "Monique et le projet de mariage de saint Augustin," in *Autour de saint Augustin*, 23–33.

24. See *conf.* 6.15: "et avulsa a latere meo tamquam inpedimento conjugii cum qua cubare solitus eram, cor, ubi adhaerebat, concisum et vulneratum mihi erat et trahebat sanguinem. . . . Nec sanabatur vulnus illud meum . . . sed post fervorem doloremque acerrimum putrescebat."

anxiety about his son, he wonders whether he is now being punished for a sinful past in the illness that afflicts the fruit of that sin, Adeodatus. How to assuage Augustine's inner turmoil, how to heal the psychological and moral wounds left from the past, becomes then the focal point of *La Femme*. Indeed, the dominant theme of the entire romance is healing: from the vain efforts of the artful African woman to cure the physical malady of Adeodatus to the spiritual healing of the family brought about, paradoxically, through the boy's death.

Simple in structure and limited to a few essential episodes arranged in strictly linear sequence, the romance builds rapidly to its climax, as Augustine, increasingly conscious of his culpability, seeks to make amends. He accedes to Adeodatus' request to summon Modesta; goes, in the company of mother and son, to the midnight service, where the latter is to be a baptismal sponsor of one of the catechumens; and, with Modesta, brings back the mortally stricken youth from the basilica. The boy's death releases Augustine from the last vestiges of pride. Before all, he acknowledges his guilt, asks forgiveness of Modesta, and offers "à celle 'qui avait dormi avec lui' le baiser de reconciliation. . . . C'était le moment, où, dans la basilique, les catéchumènes, après leur première communion, ayant bu le breuvage de lait et de miel, échangeait le baiser de paix" (ASA, 283). The profound sense of Bertrand's tale lies precisely in this playing out of Augustine's personal drama against the backdrop of a liturgical action. That Adeodatus dies as the Christmas congregation intones the "puer natus est" is not an ironist's commentary on the pathetic turn of events, but a sensitive artistic intuition of the mystery of loss, for Augustine's posterity is destined to be not of the flesh, but of the spirit. As one of the witnesses of these happenings notes, "Si l'enfant de ta chair est mort, d'autres sont nés de ton esprit et de ton coeur. Augustin de Thagaste, réjouis-toi: tu sera le père d'une race innombrable!" (ASA, 284). If, in all this, the humble figure of Modesta assumes a self-effacing role, that is only in accord with Bertrand's decision to make of *La Femme* a symbolic tale of vocation, not a drama of an estranged couple.

She received her due some fifteen years later, however, when Bertrand contextualized his romance by composing, for the popular series "Les Grandes Repenties," a framing narrative of the history of the liaison under the title of *Celle qui fut aimée d'Augustin*.[25] Reading this work is

25. Published by Albin Michel, the volumes in the collections of "Les Grandes Repenties" and "Les Grandes Pécheresses" were popular works of erudition written by recognized authors on famous women converts and/or sinners.

analogous to looking at a familiar landscape through the narrow lense of a telescope: we recognize all the landmarks, only the perspective has changed. What Bertrand has done, of course, is to take material from the middle books of the *Confessions* and present it from the standpoint of a liaison with Modesta. He justified his approach on the grounds that there were two great dramas in the life of Augustine: his conversion, which is what the *Confessions* had stressed, and the necessary prelude thereto, the decision to separate from his mistress. It is the making and unmaking of their relationship, the essence of which was precisely that it had to be transcended, that constitutes Bertrand's subject. A glance at his chapter titles will show how he has restructured the data furnished by Augustine in order to drive home his point. After an introductory section on Augustine's "Education sentimentale," he takes us through the four acts of the drama: 1. "La liaison clandestine et l'enfant"; 2. "Augustine quitte sa maîtresse et son fils pour aller enseigner à Rome"; 3. "Le faux ménage installé à Milan"; 4. "Comment se fit la rupture."

Now, although his optic differs from that of the author of the *Confessions*, Bertrand was too scrupulous a historian to alter in any way the thrust of Augustine's original narrative. True, he had used his skills as a novelist to present the material as dramatically as possible, but at no time did he risk turning an essentially spiritual *agon* into the sentimental tale of the wronged woman. The workings of grace on fallen nature remain the central theme, only the focus has shifted so as to bring into relief the heroic virtue of the woman who had renounced, repented, and lived out chastely her remaining years, "having sworn to know henceforth no other man." Indeed, Bertrand has probed that laconic phrase to make it yield a whole psychology of spirituality, which may very well be latent in the *Confessions*, and which certainly allowed him to place Modesta, at least momentarily, on a par with Augustine: "On vénère et on célèbre la conversion d'Augustin, on admire le courage qu'il lui fallut pour rompre une liaison déjà si ancienne. Mais on ne parle peut-être pas assez du réel héroïsme de cette humble femme, qui brisa deux fois son coeur aimant, cette chrétienne qui renonça au fils de sa chair et qui s'immola pour qu'Augustin pût vivre selon la loi chrétienne de continence conjugale et—peut-être l'entrevoyait-elle déjà avec la divination de l'amour—pour qu'il fût un saint." [26]

26. Louis Bertrand, *Celle qui fut aimée d'Augustin* (Paris: Albin Michel, 1935), 135–136.

Only a writer of fiction, accustomed to shedding light on the unformulated motivations of his characters, could have done such justice to the unnamed woman of the *Confessions*; and it is to Bertrand the novelist that we owe this more rounded view of a figure left deliberately in the penumbra of history by the one author who would have been capable of telling her story. To appreciate fully, however, his application of the novelist's techniques to understanding the past, one must turn to an earlier and far more ambitious work, *Sanguis martyrum*, his first historical novel and the most elaborate articulation of his vision of Christian antiquity.

Set in North Africa during the age of Cyprian, it recounted how a moderate, somewhat tepid Christian aristocrat, hitherto enjoying the friendship of pagan humanists and the tolerance of civil authority, was brought to a crisis of faith, which led first to prison, and ultimately, death. Centered around the years 257–258, when Valerian renewed the persecutions begun nearly a decade earlier under Decius, *Sanguis martyrum* is solidly grounded in contemporary documents. Using four primary sources—the *Epistolae Cypriani*, the *Vita Cypriani* of Pontius, the *Acta proconsularia Cypriani*, and the *Passio ss. Jacobi, Mariani et aliorum plurimorum martyrum in Numidia*—Bertrand has structured his novel around two key events: the martyrdom by beheading of Cyprian at Carthage on September 14, 258, and the long agony of various lesser confessors to the faith at Cirta, Lambaesis, and the mines of Sigus, which reached its climax in the spring of the following year. Moreover, Bertrand has taken pains to re-create the religious and cultural climate of the age, using as his normative consciousness the figure of Cyprian himself. Indeed, the bishop of Carthage, the apostle of unity and reconciliation, is a major figure in the novel. We see him, for example, presiding over a council, defining points of doctrine, and settling disputes between rigorists and lapsists. In a society teetering on the edge of extremism, he remains a man of moderation, determined to resist the fanaticism both of the state and of "certains confesseurs, qui semblaient n'avoir donné leur sang que pour ébranler la foi, en propageant l'anarchie dans l'église."[27] In his resolution to stand firm, while avoiding any unnecessary provocation of civil authority, Cyprian defines at once the

---

27. Louis Bertrand, *Sanguis martyrum* (Tours: Maison Alfred Mame et fils, 1929), 18. All citations are from this edition. Subsequent references to this work will appear in the body of the article with the abbreviation SM and appropriate page number.

moral tone of the novel and the delicate line of conduct to be followed by the Christian citizen obliged to choose between two conflicting value systems.

The chief actor in this drama of conscience confronting the good man torn between his secular culture and the ethical imperatives of his faith is Cécilius Natalis, a name familiar to us from patristic literature and North African epigraphy. In creating his fictional, though historically plausible, protagonist, Bertrand has drawn on both sources. From the half-dozen inscriptions at Cirta, dating from 210–217, and referring to an important magistrate named Caecilius Natalis, he has reconstructed the socioeconomic background of his central character, making him the son of the individual mentioned in those inscriptions. Like that personage, his Cécilius is a great landed proprietor, on whom have devolved numerous hereditary civic honors and functions. In an effort to define the hero's religious and cultural antecedents, Bertrand has gone a step further and, following one line of speculation, identified the Caecilius of the inscriptions with the high-minded interlocutor of the same name in the *Octavius*; but, in a decision crucial to the subsequent development of the action, he presumes that the Caecilius of Minucius Felix, though disabused of his prejudices against Christianity, did not embrace the new faith. His putative son, of course, has become a convert in the Minucian mold, what the father supposedly would have become had he followed through on his state of mind at the end of the dialogue.

Although there are few direct references in the novel to the *Octavius*, the tie-in with the dialogue of Minucius Felix is crucial for a correct reading of *Sanguis martyrum*. The Cécilius Natalis whom we meet in its early chapters is an exponent of the accommodating humanism of the *Octavius*, whose conciliatory thesis he succinctly sums up as "unir l'enseignement de l'Evangile et ce que la pensée païenne a de plus pur et de plus élevé" (SM, 48). In dialogue with Cyprian, this man in his fifties, still living in the afterglow of the peace of the Church, states that he yearns to continue "cette tradition souriante et si doucement humaine" of his father's faithful friend Felix; to which Cyprian replies: "Sois sûr que si Minucius eût vecu davantage, il l'en eût blamé" (SM, 48). In this brief exchange we have encapsulated both the essence of the novel's ideational thrust and an implicit definition of the trajectory of its action. Not only does Cyprian argue that, with persecution, the time for accommodation has ceased, but he rejects Cécilius' assumption that one can continue, after conversion, living as any cultured and high-minded pagan would do, surrounding oneself with an art and literature grounded in the old religion's sacromythic tradition. How appealing that secular culture could be, the Louis Bertrand of *Le Jardin de la mort* knew all too well, and he has made Cécilius an articulate defender of its genuine values; not even Cyprian's forceful arguments can alter his basic convictions on this point. A character in a novel, not in a dialogue, Cécilius must experience directly the iniquities of the pagan value system if he is to be persuaded.

Now Bertrand has structured his action so as to lead Cécilius from awareness, through involvement, to commitment. For the awakening of moral consciousness in his protagonist, he has conceived an extraordinary scene: a visit, at Cyprian's behest, to the mines of Sigus, worked by prisoners and slaves, from whose output Cécilius profits, and where Christians, condemned under Decius, continue to languish. Using data gleaned from ancient texts, both Christian and pagan, and from his own descents into modern mines, Bertrand has depicted in minute detail the topographical and moral labyrinth in which Christian confessors suffer. Touched by their plight, Cécilius arranges the evasion of the aged exorcist Privatianus, shelters him until his death, and, from that point on, enters into the complex mechanism of official persecution, which inexorably links the fate of this wealthy senator to that of his most humble coreligionists. His witnessing of Cyprian's martyrdom completes the transformation, and at his trial he shuns all subterfuge, confessing his faith and accepting condemnation to the mines. His agony in the subterranean world of Sigus and his beheading at Lambaesis bring to a close this drama of the Christian hero in conflict with the social and legal mores of his day.

But there is another aspect of Cécilius' relationship to the action that we cannot ignore if we are to grasp the sweep of *Sanguis martyrum*. A frequent convention in the novels of Christian antiquity is the presence of a sentimental drama pitting the Christian against the pagan conscience, with the resolution of the conflict to be found generally in the conversion, sometimes even in the martyrdom, of the character embodying the pagan value system. Bertrand has dealt with the convention in a peculiar way. As the representative of the pagan conscience, he has created the headstrong young woman Birzil, who is the ward—actually the illegitimate daughter—of Cécilius Natalis. In the economy of *Sanguis martyrum*, she represents a resurgence of an indigenous pagan consciousness in a Romanized African, which manifests itself in a hostility toward both Latin culture in general and Christianity in particular. Until well into the latter half of the novel, there is considerable ambiguity about the actual relationship between Cécilius and Birzil, a structural flaw which suggests that Bertrand may have initially intended to create a standard love plot, then decided to circumvent the problem by giving it an unusual psychological twist. In the novel as we now have it, Birzil exerts a sexual hold on Cécilius because she is the image of her dead mother, still tugging at him, creating in him subliminal desires, from which he can free himself only by acknowledging his paternity. Although Bertrand built a major subplot around her—an abduction by Bedouins; a romantic rescue by a Christian legionnaire followed, presumably, by a change of heart toward his faith; finally a dramatic public recognition of Cécilius as her father, just as the latter is about to be beheaded—Birzil remains a symbolic rather than a fully rounded personality. Ultimately, she functions less as a character in her own right than as an embodiment of one of the many earthly ties which, in the early stages of the novel, had retarded Cécilius from a total commitment to his faith.

The shortcomings of the romantic subplot, however, are more than compensated for by Bertrand's ability to bring to life the drama inherent in the historical document and to make credible to another age the psychology of the martyr. An exponent of realism, he knew how to efface himself before the document and to integrate into the texture of his writings the spirit, tone, and style of the *Vitae*, *Acta*, and *Passiones* with which he was working. Indeed, the achievement of *Sanguis martyrum* lies less in Bertrand's ability to invent new material than in his skill at providing a modern reading and a credible contextualization of the historically given. A glance at certain critical episodes will confirm this. His narrative of Cyprian's death, for example, is a dramatic recasting of the accounts of Pontius and the *Acta Cypriani*; his relation of the arrest and trial of Cécilius, an imaginative use of data found in the *Passio ss. Jacobi et Mariani*. Moreover, without the material furnished by the latter text, it is difficult to conceive the two powerful climactic episodes of the denouement. For the first, Bertrand has discreetly adapted the naive accounts of visions recorded in the *Passio* to create an artistically verisimilar scene of a eucharistic banquet in the mines of Sigus, where Cécilius and his companions are visited by a Christlike figure bringing them the viaticum; for the second, he has skillfully amplified its succinct narrative of the executions at Lambaesis, on May 6, 259, to capture the awesome spectacle of rows of kneeling martyrs, Cécilius among them, being beheaded, each in his turn, by a colossal executioner, as sympathetic onlookers chant hymns of praise and hope. In the final analysis, it was Bertrand's dexterous use of his patristic sources that enabled him not only to impart an air of authenticity to the closing pages of *Sanguis martyrum* but to project for the modern reader something of the reality that was the Church of the martyrs. It is this heroic vision of early North African Christianity that we shall briefly consider in the last of Bertrand's works under discussion here: his *Martyrs africains* and his addresses to the Eucharistic Congresses of Carthage and Algiers.

Les Martyrs africains, as he readily admitted, was a derivative work, without any claim to originality or to serious scholarship, a popularization of more erudite vulgarizations by Henri Leclerq and Paul Monceaux.[28] At first glance, in fact, it seems to be no more than a digest of the African segments of the latter's *La Vraie Légende dorée*, published only two years earlier. It differs, however, in several ways from that volume, ways that mark it as a work of edification rather than of erudition, as a work intended for a pious as distinct from a scholarly public. Unlike Monceaux, who presented a complete translation of the *Acta* and *Passiones*, along with a historical introduction to each, Bertrand wove together into a single narrative prefatory material, text, and commentary. Rather than a translation, he provided a free paraphrase of the Latin text, omitting whatever might hinder the progress of the narrative, thereby allowing his volume to gain in reader impact whatever it may have lost in precision and thoroughness. As a result, *Les Martyrs africains* can be read at a single sitting, and from its pages emerges an impressive panorama of a community of heroic confessors spanning more than one hundred fifty years as well as several social strata. From the Scillitanian martyrs in 180 to Saint Salsa in the mid-fourth century, from Bishop Cyprian, humanist

28. *La Vraie Légende dorée: Relations de martyrs*, traduites avec introduction et notices par Paul Monceaux (Paris: Payot, 1928); and *Les Martyrs: Recueils de pièces authentiques sur les martyrs depuis les origines du christianisme jusqu'au XXe siècle*, traduites et publiées par le R. P. Dom Henri Leclerq, 20 vols. (Paris: H. Oudin, 1902–1924). It is from the first three volumes of the latter work that Bertrand would have drawn material. Bertrand's *Martyrs africains* was originally brought out by a Marseille firm, Publications Notre-Dame du Roc, or Publiroc, with an imprimatur dated May 10, 1930; it was subsequently republished in 1954 by the Editions du Vieux Colombier. Two other works by Bertrand popularizing the religious history of North Africa were also published in 1930 by Publiroc: a seventy-eight-page booklet entitled *Carthage* and, in the "Collection des petites hagiographies de Publiroc," a forty-eight-page volume on *Saint Augustin*. It is interesting to note that *Les Martyrs africains* was one of the rare books by Bertrand to have been published by a religious press and to carry an imprimatur.

and renowned rhetorician, to the slave girl Felicity and the obscure conscript Maximilian of Theveste, Bertrand has encapsulated for the reader unfamiliar with patrology a major segment of Church history.

Closely linked to *Les Martyrs africains*—though far more effective as works of popularization and propaganda—were his two addresses on "L'Eglise d'Afrique," in which he sought to demonstrate how profoundly Christian had been the Africa of antiquity and to argue that "c'est l'Eglise des martyrs et des docteurs qui explique et justifie l'Eglise d'aujourd'hui." [29] He had developed both points on various occasions in the past, and it was not so much the message as the context which gave, to the first of these discourses in particular, its significance. Delivered on May 10, 1930, before the International Eucharistic Congress assembled in the amphitheater at Carthage, it commemorated two crucial moments in the history of African Christianity: the fifteen hundredth anniversary of the death of Augustine and the centenary observance of the reimplantation of the Church in the region with the coming of French rule in 1830. The coincidence of the two events offered to Bertrand a made-to-order opportunity to orchestrate his fundamental theme of renewal, enabling him to retrace the history of the African Church from antiquity to the present, establishing, thereby, for his listeners, a sense of spiritual, if not physical, continuity, across the ages, between the Church of Cyprian and Augustine and that of Cardinal Lavigerie and his successors. [30] For the literary historian, however, the real significance of the discourses at Carthage and Algiers lies not so much in their themes—predictable, given the audiences before which they were delivered—as in their deep-seated roots in Bertrand's own work. Earlier, in discussing his novel *La Cina*, we referred to his failure to re-create, in a contemporary setting, the ethos of evangelical Christi-

29. Louis Bertrand, "L'Eglise d'Afrique," *Terre de résurrection*, 188. This citation is from the second of the two addresses, the one delivered before the Twelfth National Eucharistic Congress at Algiers, on May 3, 1939. The text has been reprinted in its entirety in *Terre de résurrection*, 188–215. The first address, "Au Congrès de Carthage: L'Eglise d'Afrique," appeared in *La Revue des Deux Mondes* 57 (15 mai, 1930), 402–415. The latter focuses more on the Church in the Africa of antiquity, the former with its tie-in to the nineteenth- and twentieth-century Church in the region. In fact, the 1939 address, which incorporates a significant portion of the earlier discourse into its middle pages, can be considered an amplification of Bertrand's original remarks.

30. There is, of course, a political dimension to these addresses which is quite outside the purview of this article. Very much a man of his age, Bertrand shared the imperial vision which had motivated French colonial expansion and French Catholic missionary zeal.

anity. What he had succeeded in projecting, nonetheless, in that complex work of utopian realism was a vision of militant Catholicism, emerging out of the turmoil of turn-of-the-century Algeria, to constitute a spiritual rallying point above the melee of partisan politics. And, in an extraordinary example of visionary realism, he had concluded *La Cina* with the description of a regional council of the contemporary North African Church, presided over by a politically astute archbishop, and held on the site of the ancient metropolitan see of Carthage! Surely, it must be accounted one of the ironies of literary history that, one day, Louis Bertrand would make what was probably his most widely disseminated statement about North Africa's Christian past in just such a setting.

In summary, then, this survey of Bertrand's treatment of the theme of early Christian North Africa, from its first appearance in his work before 1900 to its final articulation in texts of the late 1930s, has shown him to be a versatile popularizer of patrology. Drawing on his talents as historian, novelist, essayist, and lecturer, he has succeeded in conveying to the general and even the learned public a living image of the variegated world that was the patristic age in North Africa. If his interpretation was often colored by an essentially heroic vision of the period, he managed, nonetheless, to explore with finesse the psychology of both the saint and the martyr, and to demonstrate how fictional forms can enhance our comprehension of history.

JOSEPH F. T. KELLY

The Attitudes toward Paganism in
Early Christian Ireland

DR. ROBERT MEYER has devoted much of his professional career to the understanding of the ancient Celtic peoples. This essay hopes to aid in that understanding by investigating why in the early Middle Ages the attitude of the Irish Christians toward pagans and paganism changed from one of moderate acceptance to one of intolerant opposition.

Two preliminary points should be noted. Due to a variety of historical factors, most especially foreign invasions, little written material survives for the first two centuries of Irish Christianity. The fifth century in Irish history is largely unknown, and as scholars redate many texts previously thought to have been from the sixth century, that century is becoming almost as little known.[1] The extant literature is almost all Latin and is Christian literature aimed at Christian audiences—there are no *apologiae contra paganos*—and so the mention of paganism in the literature is often peripheral. But there is enough evidence to prove that a change occurred in the Christian attitude.

The second point is that there was no way the Irish Christians could ever have considered paganism to be something good or positive. It was always, at base, the veneration of false gods. The early Christian Irish, however, were not uncompromisingly harsh in their attitude toward it as were some of their Continental coreligionists.

---

1. Richard Sharpe, "St Patrick and the See of Armagh," *Cambridge Medieval Celtic Studies* 4 (1982), 34.

I

The oldest extant Christian writings from Ireland are the *opera* of Saint Patrick, who worked in the country during the middle third of the fifth century. These are his *Confessio*, a defense of his episcopate to some critics among the British clergy, and an *Epistola ad Milites Corotici*, Coroticus being a Christian British prince who had killed and kidnapped for purposes of sale as slaves some of Patrick's Irish converts. Patrick was not Irish but a British Celt who identified so completely with the people he evangelized that he could write "we Irish."[2] Although scholars have abandoned the older views that he evangelized the entire island, Patrick remains the major figure of the Irish Christian mission, and it is important to see what views about paganism he passed on to his converts.

Patrick does not use the word 'pagan' but prefers the less harsh *gens* or *gentes*, that is, the alien people(s). The term is routinely applied to the Irish, whether they have been converted (*conf*. 13, 15, 48) or not (*conf*. 18, 34, 61), so Patrick uses the word less religiously than culturally, that is, the Irish are barbarians, people to be contrasted with the Romans (*epist*. 1, 10). This is not to say that he sees no difference between the converted and the unconverted but rather that he sees the Irish first as a people. The unconverted are just that—unconverted, in need of Christ's word, but not necessarily evil.

Irish tradition has often portrayed fierce druidic opposition to the saint, but Patrick nowhere mentions druids, and his four references to persecution[3] hardly blacken the pagan image. He speaks of many persecutions (*persecutiones multas*) directed against him, but these resulted in temporary imprisonments, not death. These persecutions were apparently instigated by pagans.

His second reference is to persecutions endured by converted Irish women who wished to become virgins for Christ. The persecutors, however, are relatives who are not identified as pagans; indeed, it is not likely that young women would have been able to accept a new faith which their parents had rejected, and there is a good chance the "persecutors" were Christians. Whether or not this is so, the reason for the opposition was likely a concern for the maintenance of the family line, a concern also voiced by noble Roman Christians when celibate asceticism made inroads into their ranks.

2. *Epist*. 16; *opera Patricii*, ed. R. P. C. Hanson, *SC* 249 (Paris, 1978), 148.
3. In the order discussed in this text, *conf*. 37, 42, *epist*. 6, *conf*. 42.

Patrick's letter to the soldiers of Coroticus refers plaintively to all the persecutions he has endured, but in this passage he expresses his greatest concern, that is, that the devil has destroyed his work through the agency of Coroticus (*invidet inimicus per tyrranidem Corotici*), who is a Christian.

The fourth reference occurs in the *Confessio* where he claims that he took no advantage of his converts lest he "arouse persecution against them." That the pagan Irish would persecute the Christians if Patrick took advantage of them is difficult to imagine. Patrick's real concern is that complaints about his behavior should not jeopardize the acceptance of his converts by Christians in Britain, and that is the persecution he is afraid of stirring up.

Thus of his four references to persecutions, Patrick applies only one directly to pagans, one directly to Christians, one to relatives who may be Christians, and one in a passage which criticizes a Christian prince. In sum, Patrick's mission encountered more difficulties from Christians than pagans.

But what about that one reference? First, the persecutions did not result in Patrick's death. Second, they were directed only at him; the only evidence of an attack on his converts is by Coroticus, a Christian! Third, was the opposition to Patrick necessarily religiously motivated? Patrick was not only a Christian but also a Roman, something of which he was very proud at a time when Church and Empire were closely linked. The Roman Republic and the pagan emperors made it a policy to abolish druidism wherever it was found, and the possibility must be strongly considered that when a Roman bishop appeared in the last stronghold of Celtic druidism, the pagan religious leaders recognized and opposed an old enemy.

There is simply no evidence of intense pagan opposition to Patrick, who, after all, enjoyed considerable, if hard-earned, success.

Chronologically, the next Christian whose writings are extant is Columbanus, who went from Ireland to a turbulent and successful career in Gaul and Italy (ca. 590–614), where he founded the important monasteries of Luxeuil and Bobbio and did his best to raise the level of religious life in Gaul. He mentions pagans only once, in a letter to the Gallic bishops who had demanded that he appear before them in synod. He is defending his refusal to appear as well as his orthodoxy. He says that Christians should not dispute with one another lest their enemies (*inim-*

ici) rejoice, and these enemies are identified as "Iudaei . . . aut heretici sive pagani gentiles."[4] The reference is surely uncomplimentary, but the pagans are not singled out for censure, being instead linked with Jews and heretics. Furthermore, this is something of a rhetorical device and has a Continental setting—it is not likely that the recipients of the letter, the Gallic bishops, would think of Irish pagans, especially when their own church had its share of martyrs to pagan persecution. The reference cannot apply to the Irish scene.

The hymn "Audite omnes" was originally thought to have been written by Secundinus, a fifth-century disciple of Patrick, but scholarship has pushed it forward into the sixth and now the seventh century. It is an abecedarian hymn of praise to Patrick with several references to pagans. Patrick teaches the *barbaras nationes*, the *Hiberniae gentes*, whom he turns into a *plebs Dei* and *credentes*.[5] The author compares Patrick to Paul, the apostle of the gentiles. I quote the most telling passage in Ludwig Bieler's translation:[6]

> Christ chose him to be His vicar on earth.
> He frees captives from a twofold servitude:
> The great numbers whom he liberates from bondage to men,
> These countless ones he frees from the yoke of the devil.

"Secundinus" has followed his master faithfully. The pagans are not enemies but rather those in need of Christ's word.

Adamnan's *Vita Columbae* was written in Iona between 688 and 692. It shows the same pattern as the earlier literature—the pagans are the *populus gentilicus* who live without God's word. But Columba's biographer includes two remarkable references to pagans who had lived lives of natural goodness ("gentilis senex, naturale per totam bonum custodiens vitam")[7] whom Columba baptizes just before their deaths. Each goes to heaven, and although there is no formal statement that the baptism was a prerequisite, the implication is certainly there, especially in the second account, since the saint hastens to reach the man and Adamnan says that after baptism he (the baptized) faced death gladly and confidently, *laetus*

---

4. *Epist.* 2.7, ed. D. Meehan, *SLH* 2 (Dublin, 1970), 18.

5. Text edited by Ludwig Bieler, "The Hymn of St. Secundinus," *Proceedings of the Royal Irish Academy* 55C (1953), 117–127; references to lines 13–14, 23, 27, 65.

6. *ACW* 17 (New York, 1953), 64, lines 81–84.

7. *Vita Columbae* 1.33, in *Adomnan's [sic] Life of Columba*, ed. A. O. and M. O. Anderson (London, 1961), p. 274.

et securus.[8] Adamnan indicates the need for baptism, but the key element for this paper is the open acknowledgment of the naturally good pagan.

II

The foregoing section dealt with attitudes of the Christians toward the pagans. This next deals with actual contacts between Irish Christians and pagans. The so-called First Synod of Patrick, Auxilius, and Iserninus was once thought to be a fifth-century synod, but scholarship has pushed it and its decrees forward into the sixth[9] or seventh century.[10] The synod has reservations about pagan-Christian contacts but makes it clear that such contacts were routine and considerable. For example, it refers twice to the likelihood that a pagan will default on a debt (canons 8, 20),[11] thus acknowledging that the practice existed. Canon 13 says, "Alms offered by pagans are not to be accepted for the Church," a clear witness that this had occurred and that there were positive relations between Christians and pagans. The remarkable canon 14 refers to Christians who took oaths in the presence of druids, and the equally remarkable canon 8 acknowledges that clerics gave surety for pagans. On the practice of surety, Ludwig Bieler has written: "In ancient Ireland, as in all primitive communities, suretyship was an institution which involved those who undertook it in far-reaching obligations."[12] Pagan-Christian interaction was close and frequent.

But these same canons which testify to the positive contacts between the two groups also point to the changing attitude coming to prominence in the early seventh century, an attitude best evident in the *vitae Patricii* by Tírechán (ca. 680) and Muirchú (ca. 690).[13] (The *vita* of Saint Brigit by Cogitosus, the spiritual father of Muirchú, dates ca. 650 and has only one reference to a pagan—the word *paganus* is used—and it is a negative use.[14] Cogitosus did not influence the later hagiographers on this point.) Both of these *vitae Patricii* were composed at the time the see

8. Ibid., 3.14; p. 92.

9. Kathleen Hughes, *The Church in Early Irish Society* (London, 1966), pp. 45–46.

10. Sharpe, "St Patrick," p. 35.

11. Text edited by L. Bieler, *The Irish Penitentials*, SLH 5 (Dublin, 1963), 54–60.

12. Ibid., p. 240.

13. Edited by Ludwig Bieler, *The Patrician Texts in the Book of Armagh*, SLH 10 (Dublin, 1979).

14. *PL* 72:788B–C.

of Armagh was striving for the primacy of the Irish church. The work of Muirchú actively supported this effort; the relation of Tírechán's *vita* to Armagh's designs is uncertain, but it certainly helped them.

Tírechán deals mostly with the churches he wishes his readers to think Patrick had founded, but he also includes an important passage about the pagans. Two druids (*magi*) of King Loíguire oppose the saint in a deadly contest of miracles. One, Cruth, tries to set fire to Patrick's disciple, Benignus. The disciple's clothes are destroyed, but he is unharmed. Patrick then incinerates Cruth. He next turns to the second druid, Lochletheneus, lifts him into the air so high that he freezes to death, then brings him back down to earth where he remains as a stone (which Tírechán had seen). With reference to Cruth but applicable to both druids, Patrick ominously observes, "In hac hora consumpta est gentilitas Hiberniae tota." [15]

Muirchú works the same theme but at much greater length and far more dramatically. From his pen comes the famous account of Patrick's contest with the druids before King Loíguire on the hill of Slane, an account laced with biblical images, for example, the contest between Moses and Pharaoh's magicians (who were referred to as druids in vernacular Irish), or between Elijah and the prophets of Baal on Mount Carmel. This scene comprises 30 percent of Muirchú's total narrative, and it is rampantly antipagan.

The pagans are having a feast, replete with magic rites, idolatry, druids, and fortune-tellers, and it is held "at Tara, their Babylon" (*in Temoria istorum Babylone*). All the lights in the country are supposed to be extinguished, but Patrick is burning the Easter flame, so the king and his retainers and druids go charging over to Patrick to see who has violated this prohibition. A druid tries unsuccessfully to kill Patrick. He next resorts to a contest of miracles; his fellow druids join in. The druids, however, can only perform negative wonders, such as bringing darkness or snow upon the land, but they cannot undo them. Patrick can and does drive away the darkness and the snow. The contest continues, and Patrick again incinerates his main opponent, but this time the king decides to take revenge upon Patrick. Unafraid, the saint threatens death to the king, who sagely decides, "Melius est credere me quam mori"—"It is better for me to believe than to die." [16]

15. Tírechán, 8.4; *SLH* 10:130.
16. Muirchú, 1.10–21; *SLH* 10:74–98. Citation from 1.21; p. 96.

Less spectacular antipagan elements appear throughout the narrative. Before determining why the Irish changed their attitude toward paganism, it is necessary to determine why they were originally moderate in their approach to it.

Some scholars [17] think that up to the time of the canons of the "First Synod of Patrick" the Christians lived in a predominantly pagan society, and therefore they would have had to accommodate themselves to the politically more powerful majority. This suggestion has much merit, but it fails to explain the attitudes of Patrick and Adamnan, the former writing to Christians in Britain, the latter to monks in Iona, neither of whom had reason to moderate their views for a pagan audience.

A cultural rather than a political explanation makes more sense. At an early stage in their recorded history the Irish had a sense of 'Ireland.' By that I mean that the surviving texts, Latin and Old Irish, refer always to Ireland, not to the *tuatha* or petty states from which the authors came. Cultural unity long preexisted the political unity effected only in the opening of the eleventh century by Brian Boru. This sense of 'Ireland' saved the Irish from falling into a common pitfall associated with the conversion to Christianity in antiquity, that is, Latinization.

The Irish were the only Western people of antiquity to be converted in a non-Roman framework. They never identified Christianity with Roman culture, and they did not seek to understand themselves or their past in Roman terms, unlike, for example, the Ostrogothic king Theodoric, who had the Roman nobleman Cassiodorus write an appropriate *Historia Gothorum*. This Irish affection for the native traditions stands behind the many idiosyncrasies of Irish Christianity, such as the ecclesial prominence of monks, the composition of penitential books, the *peregrinatio pro Christo*, and blatantly barbarian Christian art. The Irish simply refused to renounce their past just because it was pagan. To quote the late Nora Chadwick, "The remarkable affection of the Celts in Ireland for their pre-Christian past allowed them, without compromising their newly won faith, to preserve something of their pagan tradition." [18]

This was a uniquely Irish attitude; even their Celtic neighbors, the Welsh, did not share it. [19] It was also a very persistent attitude. In the

17. Hughes, *Church in Early Irish Society*, pp. 45–46.
18. Nora Chadwick, *The Celts* (Baltimore, 1970), p. 168.
19. Ibid., p. 141.

story of Oisin and Patrick, written down extensively only in the eighteenth century but drawing upon earlier traditions, the pagan hero Oisin courageously prefers to forgo baptism and face the torments of hell rather than desert Finn MacCool and the other pagan heroes already there.[20] Since writing came to Ireland with Christianity, all the records of the pagan Irish were compiled by Christians, proof of their desire to preserve their past.

A second factor in the mildness toward paganism may be Pelagianism. Several years ago I studied the Irish use of Pelagius and demonstrated that there was neither a Pelagian party in Ireland nor adherence to radical Pelagian ideas.[21] But the Irish were very receptive to Pelagius' works, citing him constantly in their exegesis and, very importantly, citing him by name in spite of his unsavory reputation with Continental Christians. None of the moderate views toward paganism are Pelagian, not even those which speak of naturally good pagans, since even those good men receive baptism before death, but the Irish belief in a pre-Christian goodness may reflect Pelagian views. When Christianity was "available," natural goodness was no longer an acceptable alternative, but even practicing Christians could recognize that pagans could lead good lives and need not be rejected as hopeless sinners.

The less moderate attitude toward paganism appears in the seventh century. By that time the country had become largely Christian, and paganism had started an obvious and irreversible decline. To return to the political argument discussed earlier, one could say that as a majority of the Irish (and of the Irish rulers) became Christian, latent or repressed resentment against the pagans came into the open. This is certainly possible, but it encounters the same obstacle that the political argument for moderation toward pagans encountered, namely, the writings of Patrick and Adamnan, who had no reason to hide their resentment. Furthermore, one could reverse the argument and say that since paganism was fading as a force in Irish life, there was no need for resentment. Indeed, mercy would have been more Christian and more effective in winning over any recalcitrants. The political answer is again unconvincing.

I believe that the answer lies in the Romanization of the Irish church

20. The *Dialogues of Oisin and Patrick*, often retold; cf. Charles Squire, *Celtic Myth and Legend* (Los Angeles, 1975), p. 226.

21. J. F. T. Kelly, "Pelagius, Pelagianism, and the Early Christian Irish," *Mediaevalia* 4 (1978), 99–124.

in the seventh century, a topic still awaiting a full-scale study. The seventh century is best known for the Easter controversy, when the *Romani*, that is, Irish advocates of the Roman method for dating Easter, successfully turned the Irish away from the so-called (and badly called) Celtic Easter, a date determined by an older method in use at Iona and its daughter houses as well as among the Britons.[22] But the *Romani* introduced more than just the date of Easter, which was in many ways a point of entry for a larger Romanization.

In 640 a letter of Pope-elect John IV to the Irish bishops linked the erroneous dating of Easter to a "revival" of the Pelagian heresy.[23] Circa 632 an Irish Romanist named Cummianus cited *sanctus Patricius noster papa* in a letter advocating the Roman dating to a leader of the "Celtic" party, Segene, abbot of Iona.[24] By the end of the century, the bishops of Armagh, recipients *inter alios* of the pope-elect's letter in 640, had abandoned the "Celtic" Easter, adopted the Roman dating, and advanced their primatial claims via Saint Patrick, now proclaimed founder of the see and apostle of Ireland. There are unquestioned links between the *Romani*, the rise of Armagh, the glorification of Patrick, and the Romanization of the Irish church.

I wish to suggest that part of this Romanization was the importation of Roman ideas on several matters, including those on human nature, which is to say, Augustinian notions on nature and grace and certainly an opposition to Pelagianism, condemned by Rome in the first quarter of the fifth century, a censure subsequently repeated.[25] The pope-elect's letter of 640 linked and condemned Pelagianism and the "Celtic" dating of Easter. We know from Bede's account of the Synod of Whitby in 664, itself the product of the transferral of the Irish Easter controversy to Northumbria,[26] that the *Romani* sought papal support and constantly invoked papal authority. It is impossible to imagine that the *Romani* would have ignored the pope's attitude toward Pelagianism, since the valued support of Rome on the Easter question had included a censure of

22. The best account of the Irish church in this period is still Hughes, *Church in Early Irish Society*, pp. 39–120.

23. Bede, *Historia Ecclesiastica Gentis Anglorum* 2.19; in *Bede's Ecclesiastical History of the English People*, ed. B. Colgrave and R. A. B. Mynors (Oxford, 1969), pp. 198–200.

24. Cummianus, *De Controversia Paschali*, PL 87 : 969B–978C; citation from 975C.

25. For the Irish knowledge of Augustine, cf. J. F. T. Kelly, "Augustine in Hiberno-Latin Literature," *Augustinian Studies* 8 (1977), 139–149.

26. Bede, *h.e.* 3.25; pp. 294–308. Cf. also Henry Mayr-Harting, *The Coming of Christianity to England* (New York, 1972), pp. 103–113.

that heresy, and I suggest that the *Romani* would have been strong opponents of Pelagianism and of supposed Pelagian tendencies as well. Furthermore, if the see of Armagh were to align itself with Rome on the dating of Easter, which it did by the late seventh century, its bishops could hardly ignore Rome's attitude toward Pelagianism. Armagh's support for Roman and Romanist views is reflected in the anti-natural-goodness—and, therefore, anti-pagan—notions which appear in an episcopal synod now credited to Armagh's newly discovered patron saint (although the synod itself may not be an Armagh production and may antedate that see's change of heart) and in the two *vitae Patricii*.

Episcopal decisions and reformers' programs guaranteed a harsher official tone toward the pagans, but they did not eradicate popular ideas. The notion of a naturally good pagan survived the *Romani* and Armagh, and it was probably instrumental in the preservation by Irish Christians of so much material about the Irish pagans. Indeed, we moderns who value religious toleration should be glad that the early medieval Irish never said of their pre-Christian past: *anathema sit*.

ROBERT N. NICOLICH

Memorial Services and Funeral Orations for Louis XIV at Saint-Denis and in Paris: Jean-Baptiste Massillon and His Contemporaries

"DIEU SEUL EST grand, mes frères . . .": the drama of these words, which open in paradoxical fashion the *Oraison Funèbre de Louis le Grand* by Jean-Baptiste Massillon (1663–1743), Oratorian and, later, bishop of Clermont, has not gone unappreciated by either historians or literary scholars.[1] The phrase has remained impressed on the minds of many of the French who have received a traditional academic formation in their great classics. The circumstances under which these words were first pronounced, however, are considerably less well known. They are, indeed, even the source of considerable confusion, a confusion which seems generally to surround what is known of the events in honor of the remains of the late King Louis XIV, and subsequent commemorations of his passing on the morning of September 1, 1715.

It would seem that few historians are like John Wolf[2] in considering the funeral services for Louis XIV at Saint-Denis worthy of being in-

---

1. *Oeuvres de Massillon, évêque de Clermont*, ed. Lefèvre (Paris: Firmin Didot, 1853), I, 670. All further references to Massillon's texts will be to the first volume of this edition. For a collection of studies on Massillon, see J. Ehrard and A. Poitrineau, *Etudes sur Massillon* (Clermont-Ferrand: Institut du Massif Central, 13, 1975).

2. *Louis XIV* (New York: W. W. Norton, 1968), p. 619.

cluded as part of the dramatic "last act" of the reign.[3] The general
tendency, instead, influenced probably by prejudiced memorialists such
as Saint-Simon and Dangeau, and by antimonarchist historians of the
last century, has been to stress, as does Auguste Bailly,[4] a general popular
rejoicing at Louis' death, and a simple (even hasty), poorly attended
funeral service.[5] That this was not quite the case has been shown by
Daniel Meyer in an article entitled "Les obsèques de Louis XIV et de
Louis XV," based on the *Registre des Premiers Gentilshommes de la Chambre*
in the French National Archives.[6] Yet the question of the services held in
honor of the late king, and the identity of the preachers both at the
funeral service itself and at the subsequent memorial services, still
remains foggy, particularly for the literary historian who has read
Chateaubriand's *Génie du Christianisme*. Writing about the opening line
of Massillon's *Oraison Funèbre de Louis XIV*, Chateaubriand exclaimed,
"C'est un beau mot que celui-là, prononcé en regardant le cercueil de
Louis le Grand."[7] This remark, implying the presence of Massillon as
preacher at Saint-Denis on burial day, was often accepted at face value by
nineteenth- and early twentieth-century literary historians.[8] Others,
such as the rather thorough Massillon biographer Abbé Blampignon,[9]
seem to have been left puzzled, and even when they correct Chateau-

---

3. Among the other exceptions are Auguste de Caumont, duc de la Force, *Louis XIV et sa
cour* (Paris: Arthème Fayard, 1950), and Vincent Cronin, *Louis XIV* (Boston: Houghton
Mifflin, 1965), the latter with very erroneous datings.

4. *Le Règne de Louis XIV* (Paris: Flammarion, 1946), p. 499.

5. Among other historians taking the same approach are, for example: Amédée Gabourd,
Histoire de Louis XIV (Tours: A. Mame, 1861); Pierre Gaxotte, *The Age of Louis XIV*, trans.
Michael Shaw (New York: Macmillan, 1958); Alfred Apsler, *The Sun King, Louis XIV of
France* (New York: Julian Messner, 1965); and Philippe Erlanger, *Louis XIV* (Paris:
A. Fayard, 1965), who speaks of "une joie barbare . . . Jamais on ne vit rien de pareil."
(p. 676).

6. *Revue de l'Histoire de Versailles et de Seine-et-Oise* 58 (1970, publ. 1971), 67–86.
According to Meyer, "On voit donc que tous le rites, dont la tradition remontait au Moyen-
Age, avaient été observés et que le 'bâclage' et le désordre qu'évoque Saint-Simon ne
correspondent pas à la réalité historique" (p. 81).

7. (Paris: Garnier-Flammarion, 1966), Pt. 3, Bk. 4 ("Eloquence"), chap. 3 (Massillon),
p. 19.

8. Abbé Pauthe, for example, compares Massillon unfavorably to Bossuet, implying that
the circumstances were those of Louis' funeral: "Devant le cercueil de Louis XIV, Bossuet
. . . se fût trouvé plus à l'aise que Massillon" (*Massillon, sa prédication sous Louis XIV et sous
Louis XV: Les Maitres de la chaire en France* [Paris: Victor Lecoffre, J. Gabalda, 1908], p. 266).

9. Abbé Emile-Antoine Blampignon, *Massillon, d'après des documents inédits* (1879: repr.
Geneva: Slatkine Reprints, 1970), pp. 248–249.

briand, and accurately identify the Sainte-Chapelle as the place where Massillon delivered his oration, the date and other circumstances seem to have been almost deliberately omitted for lack of precise information. In 1872, Philippe Tamizey de Larroque particularly noted this absence in his review of contemporary Massillon scholarship by Blampignon, Godefroy, Abbé Bayle, and Mme de Marcey. [10] Thus it is perhaps not that surprising to find, in more recent times, a certain amount of misinformation persisting around the celebrated *Oraison funèbre* which Mme Saint-René Taillandier, for example, placed without evidence at Notre Dame on October 24, 1715, [11] whereas the actual Notre Dame service took place on November 28, and Jacques Maboul preached. It would seem, then, that a review and establishment of the dates and circumstances of the memorial services held in Paris to honor Louis XIV, and of the preachers who preached at them and at Saint-Denis, are very much in order. They are of both historical and literary interest. Evidence would seem to indicate, furthermore, that there was no widespread anti–Louis XIV sentiment, that the passing of the great king was commemorated appropriately, that everything that took place was normal. The subject is even more interesting in light of the considerable research in recent years on the history of death, and the focus it provides for understanding mental attitudes and the social and cultural history of the period studied. [12]

10. *Des récents travaux sur Massillon* (extrait de la *Revue des questions historiques* [Paris: V. Palmé, 1872]). Tamizey de Larroque reviews: Blampignon's *Oeuvres complètes de Massillon* (Paris: Guérin, 1865); Abbé A. Bayle, *Massillon, Étude historique et littéraire* (Paris: A. Bray, 1867); and Mme Louise de Marcey's series of twenty-two articles in *Le Contemporain*, February 28, 1867, to July 31, 1869.

11. *Le Grand Roi et sa cour* (Paris: Hachette, 1930), p. 252. Vincent Buranelli, *Louis XIV* (New York: Twayne Publishers, 1966), p. 186, actually dates Louis' funeral as September 9, 1715, whereas the funeral at Saint-Denis took place on October 23, 1715, over forty days after the September 9 procession to the Abbey.

12. See, for example, Philippe Ariès, *Essais sur l'histoire de la mort en occident du moyen âge à nos jours* (Paris: Seuil, 1975), and *L'Homme devant la mort* (Paris: Seuil, 1977); Pierre Chaunu, *La Mort à Paris: XVIe, XVIIe, et XVIIIe siècles* (Paris: Fayard, 1978); Robert Favre, *La Mort dans la littérature et la pensée françaises au siècle des lumières* (Lyon: Presses universitaires de Lyon, 1978); François Lebrun, *Les Hommes et la mort en Anjou aux XVIIe XVIIIe siècles* (Paris: Flammarion, 1975); John McManners, *Death and the Enlightenment* (Oxford: Clarendon Press, 1981); Jacqueline Thibaut-Payen, *Les Morts, l'église et l'état: Recherches d'histoire administrative sur la sépulture et les cimetières dans le ressort du parlement de Paris aux XVIIe et XVIIIe siècles* (Paris: Lanore, 1977); Michel Vovelle, *Mourir autrefois* (Paris: Gallimard/Julliard, 1974), and *Piété baroque et déchristianisation en Provence au XVIIIe siècle* (Paris: Plon, 1973). The funeral orations for Henry IV have been studied by Jacques Hennequin, *Henri IV dans ses*

Of the many formal commemorative events for the late king which were held not only in France but as far away as Jerusalem during the final months of 1715 and well into 1716,[13] the service which seems to have been the earliest of the memorial events formally organized as such to be held in Paris is that of the Assemblée Générale du Clergé, at the Church of the Grands Augustins, October 3, 1715, at which François Madot, bishop of Châlon-sur-Saone, preached.[14] Since Louis died while the Assembly was meeting,[15] its *Procez Verbal*[16] contains countless details of the Assembly's procedure for paying its respects to the remains of the late king, and to Louis XV and the regent, all of which was not just slightly fraught with procedural difficulty. Prayers and Masses had been offered for the repose of the monarch's soul, but on Monday, September 23, the president of the Assembly, Charles le Goux de la Berchère, archbishop and primate of Narbonne, received the Assembly's approval to begin arrangements for a special "Service solemnel," at which the bishop of Châlon would preach the *oraison funèbre*. On Wednesday, September 25, the October 3 date was agreed upon, as were the celebrants and assistants. Invitations were to be extended to all prelates present in Paris who were not Assembly members. The Assembly's agents were charged with the preparations for the decoration of the church. On Monday, September 30, the agents were sent to Cardinal de Noailles, archbishop

---

oraisons funèbres ou la naissance d'une légende (Paris: Klincksieck, 1977). The royal funeral in England has been studied for the commemorative ware trade it produced: Paul S. Fritz, "The Trade in Death: The Royal Funeral in England, 1685–1830," *Eighteenth Century Studies* 15 (1982), 291–316. Finally, for more art-historical detail concerning the funeral of Louis XIV and the Paris services, as well as the full texts of some of the archival documents cited here, see Robert N. Nicolich, "Les décors des pompes funèbres de Louis XIV à Saint-Denis et les services à Notre-Dame et à la Sainte-Chapelle," *Bulletin de la Société de l'Histoire de l'Art Français, 1975* (Paris: De Nobele, 1976), 171–190.

13. Many can be found listed in the *Gazette de France: Recueil de toutes les gazettes, nouvelles ordinaires et extraordinaires et autres relations,* for 1715–1716. The Jerusalem service is dated 16 May 1716. A detailed listing of various preachers and services is given by Abbé J.-P. Migne, ed., *Collection intégrale et universelle des orateurs sacrés, etc.* 46 (Paris: Ateliers Catholiques du Petit Montrouge, 1854), 1417–1420, in footnote.

14. *Gazette de France,* no. 40 (October 5, 1715).

15. "Réunie du 3 juin au 2 novembre, cette Assemblée se termine après la mort de Louis XIV: elle a eu à délibérer sur le don gratuit et sur un emprunt de douze millions de livres." Louis André, *Les Sources de l'histoire de France, XVIIe siècle (1610–1715)* VI, Histoire Religieuse (Paris: Picard, 1932), p. 169.

16. *Procez Verbal de l'Assemblée Général du Clergé de France, tenue à Paris au couvent des Grands Augustins, en l'année mil sept cents quinze . . . ,* A Paris, chez Pierre Simon, Imprimeur du Clergé de France . . . , 1723 (B.N. fol L'd 428).

of Paris, with the request for the necessary permission to hold the
Pontifical Mass in his archdiocese, and on the following day the permission was announced as having been received.

The *Procez Verbal* is rather detailed for Thursday, October 3. Approximately half of the account is an apparently precise description of the
church decorations, with painstaking indications of the measurements
according to width (*lê*) of the dark hangings everywhere, relieved by
lighted silver chandeliers, silver embroidery and fringes, escutcheons
and coats of arms. There was an especially constructed altar and a
representational catafalque for the rites of absolution. The entrance
procession between two rows of Augustinians holding candles is described, as is the seating of the Assembly and other movements of the
celebrants, strategic for the liturgy and *oraison funèbre*. On the following
day, the *Procez Verbal* records the expression of thanks by the archbishop of
Narbonne to Bishop Madot for his "vif, touchant & éloquent discours,"
delivered "d'une manière si digne du sujet, & qui fait tant d'honneur à
l'Assemblée" (p. 220). The company requested that the sermon be
printed and included in the *Procez Verbal*, but Bishop Madot declined,
maintaining that "son discours n'étant qu'une foible expression sans suite
& sans arrangement de ses sentimens suggerez, mais troublez par la
douleur & l'affliction, quelque respect qu'il eût pour les ordres de l'Assemblée, il la supplioit de le dispenser de faire paroître dans un plus
grand jour ce qu'il n'avoit accepté de prononcer que par soûmission & par
obéïssance" (p. 220).

Before proceeding to the actual funeral service for Louis at Saint-
Denis, it could be noted, in passing, that the *Gazette d'Amsterdam*
reports from Paris on Friday, October 18, of a "Service magnifique pour
le feu Roi" organized by the Hotel de Ville.[17] The only curious detail
recorded is that "On a remarqué dans cette Cérémonie, que tous les
Officiers avoient chacun une Sonnette, qu'ils sonnoient en allant à
l'Offrande."

The ceremonies of the Saint-Denis funeral on Wednesday, October 23,
which has often received such shoddy treatment at the hands of historians, need not be treated in detail here, thanks to the labors of Daniel
Meyer, to whom we have already referred. It suffices to cite again the
Gazette d'Amsterdam, which reports that the obsequies were carried out

17. *Amsterdam*, Avec privilege de nos. seig. les Etats de Hollande et de West-Frise, 1715,
no. 86.

"avec toute la pompe & la magnificence imaginable. Toute la Cour assista." [18] The ample decorations by Jean II Berain which heretofore have been unknown, even by the specialists of the Berains [19] and of their assistants, the Slodtz, [20] are, however, not described by Meyer's source, the *maître des cérémonies*, Desgranges, who was much more concerned with problems of precedence. Despite the absence of records for the Menus Plaisirs for 1715, a detailed description is nonetheless available in the *Registre Cérémonial de la Chambre de Comptes*. [21] Le Grand and de Beaufort, the Chambre's *conseillers maîtres* in charge of the *Cérémonial*, were apparently very observant as they accompanied the Chambre to Saint-Denis. Thanks to them, we know of the rich black velvet hangings, adorned with escutcheons carrying the arms of France and Navarre, on the facade of the church. Inside, a cornice around the nave bore obelisks with trophies and candelabra. Four white marble statues "représentant des personnes affligés" (p. 329) flanked the altars at the entrance to the choir, whose vault was hung in black. Eight tribunes on each side, above the stalls, were arranged in elaborately draped pavilions. Each tribune was separated by a large black-and-white pilaster supporting five silver candelabra and white, winged marble terms holding back the drapery from over the tribunes. Above these were large, abundantly illuminated gilded pediments. The high altar, supporting twenty-four silver chandeliers with large candles and a large silver cross, was topped by a black-and-silver canopy with valance embroidered in silver, bearing a large scalloped fringe. The *musique du Roy* was in the decorated *jubé* above the choir door. In the center of the choir, a large temple-shaped marble [22] mausoleum raised on five steps covered the coffin. A

18. No. 86 (Monday, October 28, 1715, "La Quintessence des Nouvelles"). This opinion would seem to be supported by the *Gazette de France*, but particularly by the special edition of the *Mercure de France*, October 1715: Sieur Le Febvre, *Journal Historique de tout ce qui s'est passé depuis les premiers jours de la Maladie de Louis XIV, jusqu'au jour de son Service à Saint-Denis avec une relation exacte de l'avénement de Louis XV à la Couronne de France* (Paris: D. Jollet et J. Lamesle, 1715).

19. Roger-Armand Weigert, *Jean I Berain, Dessinateur de la Chambre et du Cabinet du Roi (1640–1711)* (Paris: Université de Paris, Faculté des Lettres, thèse, 1936), p. 146. Weigert, however, gives October 25 as the funeral date.

20. François Souchal, *Les Slodtz, sculpteurs et décorateurs du Roi (1685–1764)* (Paris: Editions E. De Boccard, 1967), p. 386, footnote 3. Souchal, however, gives November 25 as the funeral date.

21. 1693–1717, Arch. Nat., P2608, pp. 327ff. For an age which, in literature at least, is not given to pictorial descriptions, this is a remarkable document.

22. According to practice, this may well have been just imitation marble, painted wood.

winged white marble *génie* was at each corner holding up an armorial-ornamented and illuminated cornice above which was a dome with four seated personified *renommées* holding a golden trumpet in one hand and, in the other, the large golden royal crown surmounting the edifice. The coffin was "un tombeau à l'antique" (p. 331), set on four gilded consoles faced with armorial cartouches. Above the coffin but beneath the dome was a rich black-and-silver canopy from which hung four pulled-back drapes of black sprinkled with gold fleurs-de-lys. The coffin was covered first with a black-and-silver pall of velvet and ermine, over which was the royal pall, "couleur de feu," topped by the crepe-covered crown itself. Ten gold-and-silver candelabra surrounded the whole, and above, hanging from the vault, was another enormous black drape canopy with gold-tassled fringe, gold fleurs-de-lys, and ermine, tied back into festoons falling from the vault. All this certainly does not suggest a carelessly organized service by uninterested parties!

Into such a decor, at the proper moment in the Mass, stepped Honoré Quiqueran de Beaujeu (1655–1756), bishop of Castres, to deliver the *oraison funèbre*. How he was selected for the task is puzzling since Migne's *Notice* implies some connection between this choice and the meeting of the Assemblée du Clergé.[23] Yet the Assembly's *Procez Verbal* contains no proof of the group's participation in such a selection. Born in Arles, Quiqueran de Beaujeu had become an Oratorian at seventeen, had studied theology at Arles, then Saumur, and had been sent on preaching missions to the Protestants at Poitou and Aunis which acquired for him such an excellent reputation that Fléchier, bishop of Nîmes, made him canon in his cathedral and diocesan vicar general. As *député de second ordre*, he particularly distinguished himself at the Assemblées du Clergé of 1693 and 1700. He was nominated by Louis XIV to the bishopric of Oléron in 1705, then Castres, and held the title of *associé* in the Académie des Inscriptions et Belles-Lettres. In the light of our present study, it is interesting to note with Blampignon that during Massillon's stay at the Oratorian house at Arles from September 23, 1682, to September 19, 1684, Père Quiqueran de Beaujeu's name is to be noted among the house directors (pp. 28–29). His *Oraison funèbre de Louis XIV* can be found in Migne's *Orateurs sacrés*. The *Mercure* notes that "ce Prelat fut applaudi" before Mass was resumed (October, p. 244).

23. Vol. 33 (1853), 1299–1300. The biographical information which follows is also based for the most part on Migne.

In view of Louis' favor for them during his lifetime it is not surprising that the Jesuits were among the first to commemorate with great dignity their royal protector's passing. If the *Mercure Galant* is to be believed,[24] it was a truly splendid event that occurred at the Collège de Louis-le-Grand, rue Saint-Jacques, on November 12, 1715. In fact, the November *Mercure* dedicates an extraordinary number of pages—approximately forty (pp. 25–64)—to describing the ceremony and its decorations, and to summarizing the *oraison funèbre* delivered in Latin by Père Charles Porée, S.J. (1676–1741), professor of rhetoric, who was later to be remembered as one of Voltaire's teachers. His life was the object of a full-length study in 1899 by J. de la Servière.[25] It thus suffices here to note that he had assumed his post as rhetoric teacher at Louis-le-Grand in 1708, and was to become known for a considerable period of time mostly as an author of school plays in Latin.

During the morning of Tuesday, November 12, there had been a Solemn High Mass in the Chapel of the College de Louis-le-Grand. Only one hundred *pensionnaires*, "d'une qualité distinguée . . . tous en grand deüil" (*Mercure*, p. 26), were able to sit in the nave because of the size of the representational catafalque. That evening Père Porée's *éloge funèbre* was greeted with "l'applaudissement general de la plus nombreuse & de la plus auguste assemblée qui se soit vûë depuis long-temps dans leur College" (p. 26). Present were two cardinals, one being Cardinal de Polignac, thirty archbishops and bishops, several abbés of distinction, and "des Consillers d'Etat, Messieurs les Avocats generaux, plusieurs Présidents, Conseillers du Parlement, & des autres Cours Superieurs" (p. 27). The *Mercure* talks of Père Porée in glowing terms: "Le nom de l'Orateur fait l'Eloge de la pièce, & sa réputation pouvait seule répondre du succés. . . . On . . . admira . . . ces rares talents pour l'Eloquence qui le font regarder comme un des premiers Orateurs de nostre siècle" (pp. 27–28).

The place where the *oraison funèbre* was delivered was "aussi superbement décoré que le peu d'espace que [le lieu] renferme, & la tristesse du

---

24. Also: *Gazette de France*, no. 46 ("De Paris le 16 novembre 1715"), p. 552; *Gazette de la Régence*, Janvier 1715–Juin 1719, publiée d'après le manuscrit inédit conservé à la Bibliothèque royale de La Haye, avec des annotations et un index, par le comte E. de Barthélemy (Paris: G. Charpentier, 1887), pp. 19–20 ("A Paris ce 15 novembre 1715").

25. *Un Professeur d'ancien régime: Le Père Charles Porée, S.J. (1676–1741)*, thèse, Poitiers (Paris: Oudin, 1899). Also, Carlos Sommervogel, S.J., ed., *Bibliothèque de la Compagnie de Jesus* (Paris: Picard, 1892; repr. Louvain: Editions de la Bibliothèque S.J., 1960), VI, 1021–1031.

sujet pouvoit permettre" (p. 61). The somberness of the dark hangings
was relieved by velvet scattered with gold fleurs-de-lys and silver teardrops, plus ermine festoons. A cornice held eight great "pyramids"
(perhaps obelisks) bearing shields and touching the ceiling. Among
them were magnificent cartouches with at least ten *devises* picturing the
sun, symbolizing stages of Louis' life, from rising to setting, dispelling
or surrounded by clouds, according to the events alluded to, each scene
with its appopriate motto, the whole generally paralleled in Père Porée's
sermon. The regent was symbolized, too, placed between a setting and a
rising sun. A special trophy in the rear of the hall, composed of all the
instruments of the Arts and Sciences, with an inscription, symbolized
the benefits the college had received from Louis. All was brilliantly
illuminated. At the end of the evening, a good number of Latin and
French verses praising the late king and the young Louis XV were
distributed. The *oraison funèbre* was eventually published in its own
bilingual Latin-French edition,[26] and in the two-volume *Recueil* of select
memorial sermons preached both in Paris and the provinces.[27] The
quarrel that broke out with the university over this sermon will be taken
up shortly.

Four days later, on Saturday, November 16, according to a report in
the *Gazette de France*, it was the turn of the Faculté de Droit to celebrate
its memorial service in the church of Saint Jean de Latran "où assisterent
plusieurs Docteurs, ayant à leur teste le sieur de Bechameil de Nointel,
Doyen d'honneur."[28] A 1715 *Brevis Oratio* in Latin for Louis XIV by the
dean of the Faculté de Medecine can be found listed in the Bibliothèque
Nationale catalogue.[29]

But it was on November 28 that all of Paris gathered at Notre Dame
for the Solemn High Mass for the repose of the soul of the late king, at
which Cardinal de Noailles, archbishop of Paris, officiated pontifically.
The *Gazette de France* (no. 48, November 30, p. 576) reports the presence of the duc d'Orleans, the duc de Bourbon, and the comte de
Charolais, "suivis d'un grand nombre de personnes des plus consider-

26. *Oraison funèbre de Louis le Grand, Roy de France et de Navarre* . . ., traduite en François
par M. M*** (probably L. Mannory), A Paris chez Joseph Monge, ruë S. Jacques, 1716
(B.N. Lb³⁷4484).
27. *Recueil de plusieurs oraisons funèbres de Louis XIV. Roy de France et de Navarre, surnommé Le
Grand*, Paris, 1716.
28. No. 48 ("De Paris, le 30 novembre 1715"), p. 576.
29. L³⁷b 4466.

ables de la Cour & de la Ville. Le Clergé, le Parlement, la Chambre des Comptes, la Cour des Aydes, l'Université, & le Corps de Ville y assisterent, ayant esté invitez par ordre du Roy. Les Ambassadeurs & Envoyez des Princes Estrangers y furent pareillement invitez." The *Gazette d'Amsterdam* ("Quintessence," no. 96, December 2) reports concerning the preparations that two thousand places had been prepared by order of the regent, "pour des Gentilhommes ou Cavaliers qui doivent assister à ce service, auquel les gens de la Maison du Roi ne sont point admis." It should be noted that Louis' entrails had been brought to Notre Dame for burial on September 4 (Meyer, p. 74).

As for the decorations, the *Cérémonial* of the Chambre des Comptes indicates that they were the same as at Saint-Denis, "d'ou l'on avoit raporté tous les ornements et le catafalque . . ." (p. 343). That this was just the usual practice, and was the case for the Notre Dame memorial services for the grand dauphin and for the duc and duchesse de Bourgogne, is proven by the evidence supplied by Weigert (pp. 144–145) and by the *Cérémonial* itself on these other occasions.

The *oraison funèbre* was delivered by Jacques Maboul (1650–1723), bishop of Alet, who seems to have had a more distinguished background than Quiqueran de Beaujeu for such endeavors. He had, after all, preached at the Saint-Denis funeral service for the duc and duchesse de Bourgogne on April 18, 1712,[30] and his published sermon for Louis XIV is much more readily available today.[31] Born into the nobility of the robe, and embracing the ecclesiastical state, he had been vicar general of Poitiers for quite a while before becoming bishop of Alet in 1708. His other funeral orations included one in 1680 for Michel Le Tellier and one for the grand dauphin (at Montpellier). He was to preach a funeral sermon for the archbishop of Narbonne in 1720.

At the close of the service, Cardinal de Noailles invited the regent to dine and, according to the *Gazette de France*, "le traita magnifiquement" (no. 48, November 30, p. 576). The *Gazette de la Régence* mischievously adds, "On n'a jamais vu tant de gaîté et une conversation plus enjouée

30. According to the Comptes *Cérémonial*. Migne indicates the wrong dauphin and a wrong date, 17 (1845), 9–10, by apparently following Abbé Antoine Albert, *Dictionnaire portatif des prédicateurs françois . . .* , A Lyon, chez Pierre Bruyset Ponthus, 1757, pp. 156–158.

31. *Oraison funèbre de tres-haut, tres-puissant et tres-excellent Prince Louis XIV. Roy de France et de Navarre . . .* , A Paris, chez François Fournier, rue Saint Jacques, 1715 (B.N. L³⁷b 4480). Migne indicates the existence of a 1748 *Recueil* of his *oraisons funèbres*.

parmi les convives" (December 2, 1715, p. 27). Much more generous
with detail, however questionable it may be, this *Gazette* even goes on to
relate certain indiscretions concerning "une fort belle fille," which occurred during the meal."[32]

December, it would seem, was the busiest month of all in Paris for
memorial services honoring the late king. There were no less than four
during a nine-day period in the middle of the month.

First, on December 11, the University of Paris paid its respects to
Louis XIV with a Solemn High Mass in the Sorbonne Chapel, celebrated
by Cardinal de Noailles, archbishop of Paris and *proviseur de Sorbonne*.
Both the *Gazette de France* and the *Mercure* carry announcements which
are exactly alike in wording, stating that "Le sieur de Montempuys
Recteur, les Procureurs des Nations, les Facultes, leurs Doyens à la teste,
y assisterent en habits de ceremonie, ainsi que le premier Président,
plusieurs Présidents & Conseillers du Parlement, les Gens du Roy, &
d'autres personnes de distinction."[33] Bénigne Grenan, professor of
rhetoric at the Collège de Harcourt, gave the *oraison funèbre* in Latin. It
was the start of a quarrel with the Jesuits, particularly with Père Porée,
which would be drawn out through the following year.

Both Charles Jourdain, in his *Histoire de l'Université de Paris au XVIIe et
au XVIIIe siècle*,[34] and Porée's biographer, J. de la Servière (pp. 12–16),
have described the battle of pamphlets waged by both sides, with de la
Servière supplying more details of the battle itself. Grenan's oration,
however, fits into a long history of academic politics and Louis' determination to impose acceptance of the bull *Unigenitus* on the university.
According to Jourdain (pp. 304–309), there had been a thirty-year-old
university tradition, established by the Paris *échevins*, of having an annual
panegyric for the king. In May 1714, the then rector, Michel Godeau,
had managed to turn his panegyric into praise for Cardinal de Noailles'
resistance against the bull. The following month, Louis forced the
election and subsequent continuation in office of a new rector, more
favorable to his point of view, Philippe Poirier, who, in his turn, in the
panegyric of June 1715, dared praise Louis' protection of the Jesuits

---

32. The duc de Noailles pointed her out to the regent who "parut sentir pour elle plus
que de l'honnêteté." Even the cardinal, perhaps somewhat out of character, "la trouva fort à
son gré."

33. *Mercure*, December 1715, p. 216; *Gazette*, no. 50 ("De Paris, le 14 Decembre"),
p. 599.

34. (Paris: Hachette, 1862–1866), p. 312.

("l'unique appui de l'Église et de la religion") as one of the benefits of the reign. This scandal from the university's point of view was repaired only when, in October 1715, with the support of Louis XIV gone, Poirier was replaced as rector by Demontempuys. Thus, for the university's funeral oration for Louis in December, Grenan was popularly chosen as one attached to the university's tradition, who, unlike Poirier, would not speak with praise of the Jesuits whom the king had favored above the university. Moreover, he would certainly not attack Jansenism as Porée had done in forceful terms: "une nouveauté étrangere, quoi que produite des cendres de hérésie de Calvin, vient de la Flandre répandre son venin dans la France; fille exécrable d'une exécrable mere . . ." (p. 109). Although Grenan's oration seems to be no longer available today, from the pamphlets which are available[35] it appears that while Grenan respectfully memorialized Louis, he passed over Jansenism in silence and did not praise the Jesuits. Moreover, according to Jourdain, "il dirigea contre [les Jésuites], sous le voile de l'allusion, plus d'un trait qui fut avidement saisi par la malignité de l'auditoire" (p. 312). Porée responded to Grenan in an open letter,[36] thus beginning a quarrel which became immersed in the Jesuit-Jansenist controversy, and the dispute over *Unigenitus*.

The tremendous debt the Jesuits owed to Louis' protection is attested to by the fact that they found it necessary a second time to commemorate his passing, this time in the chapel of their *maison professe*, today the church of Saint-Paul–Saint-Louis. It took place the day after the university's service, on Thursday, December 12. To this church Louis' heart had been brought by Cardinal de Rohan on September 6 (Meyer, p. 75), and it was to remain here in a special urn, as was the heart of Louis XIII, until the Revolution. The December 12 event seems to have been less grand than that of exactly one month before at the Collège de Louis-le-Grand. The publicity it received was certainly much reduced, limited to two similarly worded entries, one in the *Gazette de France* (no. 50, December 14, p. 599), the other in the *Mercure* (December, p. 217). The *oraison*

35. The items at the B.N. include: *Lettre à M. Grenan, Regent de seconde au College d'Harcourt, auteur de l'Oraison Funèbre prononcée en Sorbonne le 11. Decembre 1715* (1716; B.N. Ld³⁹265, probably by l'abbé Le Masson); *Réflexions critiques sur l'éloge funèbre du roi prononcé par le R.P. P***J.* (1716; B.N. Ld³⁹264, probably by Guérin); *L'Art Oratoire pretendu reformé ou Petit Catechisme a l'usage des disciples du Venerable Pejore* (1716; B.N. Ld³⁹263, probably by Du Hamel).

36. *Lettre du R.P. Porée à M. Grenan, au sujet de l'Oraison Funèbre du Roi qu'il a prononcée en Sorbonne le 11 Decembre 1715* (1716; B.N. Ld³⁹266).

funèbre (which seems not to have been published) was delivered by Père Louis Joseph de la Ferté, S.J. (1653–1732), a Parisian, who, according to the brief notation in the *Bibliothèque de la Compagnie de Jésus* (III, 702), had entered the Jesuit noviciate on July 13, 1676, and had dedicated himself to preaching. On August 25, 1706, he had delivered a *Panégyrique de saint Louis* for the saint's feast to the Académie des Inscriptions et des Sciences (*Bibliothèque*, Supplement, p. 334).

On Tuesday, December 17, the memorial service at which Massillon preached his famous *oraison funèbre* finally took place at the Sainte-Chapelle.[37] Contrary to Chateaubriand's implications, Louis' body was not present, having long since been deposited in the Bourbon crypt at Saint-Denis. The Sainte-Chapelle service was the result of a collaborative effort between the treasurer and canons of the Sainte-Chapelle, on the one hand, and the Chambre des Comptes, on the other, which was traditionally responsible for the Chapel's temporal administration, a relationship also traditionally fraught with tensions which were to surface even on this occasion.[38]

The Sainte-Chapelle *Registre*[39] and the Chambre's *Cérémonial* contain interesting background information. On Sunday, September 1, having just received news of Louis XIV's death, the Sainte-Chapelle Chapter, in extraordinary session, decided on the holding of a "Service solennel" for the repose of the soul of the late king, to be scheduled for the following Friday, and then planned the reception of the regent, who, on his way to the Parlement on the morrow, would be stopping at the chapel for Mass and the veneration of the relics (*Registre*, p. 150). On Friday, September 6, however, the chapel treasurer, Antoine Bochart de Champigny, without any further comments in the *Registre*, announced to the canons that he had had the honor of receiving orders from the duc d'Orleans for the service and the *oraison funèbre* and "en consequence il avoit prié le P. Massillon prestre de l'oratoire de faire l'oraison funèbre, ce qu'il avoit

37. *Gazette de France*, no. 51 ("De Paris, le 21 Decembre"), p. 612.

38. A. Vidier, *Le Trésor de la Sainte-Chapelle: Inventaire et Documents* (Paris: Extraits des Mémoires de la Société de l'Histoire de Paris et de l'Ile-de-France, 34–37, 1911): The authority of the Chambre in "la direction et l'administration du temporel de la Sainte Chapelle" is clearly stated in a letter dated September 5, 1694, by Premier Président Nicolay, holder of the reliquary keys, on the occasion of a controversy over the "cérémonial de l'ostension des reliques de la Sainte-Chapelle et des prétentions du trésorier et des chanoines touchant la garde de la châsse" (pp. 513–514).

39. *Registre des deliberations de Messieurs les Tresorier et chanoines de la Ste Chapelle Royalle du Palais a Paris commencé le premier jour de juillet mil sept cent neuf*, Arch. nat. LL611.

accepté" (p. 150v). The next mention we find made of all this is only on Wednesday, December 11, when the company scheduled the memorial service and sermon for the following Tuesday (p. 151v).

In the Chambre de Comptes, however, it was only on Saturday, December 14, that the *premier président*, Jean Aymard Nicolay, marquis de Goussainville,[40] actually reminded that body of its custom to collaborate with ("de concert avec") the Sainte-Chapelle for the celebration of memorial services upon the death of the great. He carefully cited precedents, particularly the more recent services for the late dauphins in 1711 and 1712, and said that "il avoit cru qu'on en devoit user de même au sujet du deceds du Roy Loüis quatorze" (p. 347), for which purpose "il auroit fait disposer ce qui estoit necessaire" in the Sainte-Chapelle to honor the late king "de glorieuse mémoire." Thus he, together with the treasurer and canons, had decided on a ten o'clock morning service on the seventeenth. Since Massillon would preach, the president "[l'] avoit fait prier par le controlleur de la sainte chapelle de vouloir s'en charger. . . ." The Chambre agreed. One wonders what, if anything, had transpired at this point among the regent, the treasurer, and the president. It seems to have been an obvious effort by the president to assert an active, if not superior, role in initiating the memorial service. Yet the record nonetheless reveals the Chambre's desire to show that, although not directly ordered this time by any royal agent to hold such a memorial service (as had been the case on the previously cited occasions according to the *Cérémonial* records), it independently felt the "rightness" of observing tradition, since it concerned the late Louis XIV.

The *Cérémonial* gives a detailed account of the event, so often referred to by historians, but in reality so unknown. It describes the Chambre's procession "en robes de deüil" to the Sainte-Chapelle staircase, where it was met by the Chapel's *contrôleur*. The seating is, as always, carefully recorded, the *premier président* occupying "la première stalle haute du costé de l'évangile." The decorations were magnificent. Outside, on two levels, there were black velvet hangings clasped together by a great cartouche with the arms of France and Navarre. Several hundred church officers (*suisses*) guarded the entrances. Inside, the entire structure was

---

40. *Table Chronologique de Messieurs les Officiers de la Chambre des Comptes suivant l'ordre de leurs réceptions*, Arch. nat. P2631. Forty-fourth *premier président*, born 1658, he became *avocat général* in the Chambre in 1680, and was successor to his late father in the presidency, from 1686 until 1734.

draped in black "et ornée superbement de décorations replies de devises et emblemes a la gloire du deffunct Roy" (p. 348). Woven among these was black velvet scattered with gold fleurs-de-lys and silver teardrops, with more escutcheons. One recognizes the Saint-Denis decorations (the white marble terms) in the Sainte-Chapelle's side pavilions whose draperies lined with ermine were held back in festoons by winged *génies* "qui en formaient les pilastres." Dazzling light was everywhere. Three rows of candelabra were on the main altar, from which hung embroidered black velvet fringed with silver. The representational mausoleum is familiar, too: raised, on five steps, topped with the four personified *renommées* holding up towards the vault the large royal crown from which (a variation?) hung four ermine-lined drapes pulled back in festoons to form a pavilion over the whole (p. 348v). It is the Sainte-Chapelle *Registre* which adds the precious heretofore-unknown detail that the decoration was "la mesme qu'a Notre Dame, de l'invention du Sieur Berrin [sic]" (p. 150v). Berain had once again, according to the usual practice, proven by the *Registre*[41] or *Cérémonial* on each previous occasion, shown his inventiveness in adapting the same decorations, first from Saint-Denis to Notre Dame, then also to the much smaller dimensions of the Sainte-Chapelle. Both records state that the choir screen had to be moved to make room, that extra tribunes were set up above the door "pour les gens de dehors et surtout pour les femmes" (*Registre*, p. 157v), and for the Chapel's musicians, who had been increased in number by a dozen "outsiders." This, then, was the scene that Chateaubriand confused with Louis' funeral itself, which became part of that Massillon legend perhaps invented by Cardinal Maury,[42] who pictured Massillon, eyes closed, holding his audience in suspense as he sweepingly gestured towards the vanity of all this earthly pomp (and Louis' absent coffin) before pronouncing the stunning opening words of his sermon.

Massillon, who was yet to become bishop, came to the Sainte-Chapelle with an already superb preaching reputation.[43] The *Registre* makes a point of referring to him as "un des plus celebres Prédicateurs

41. For example, on Tuesday, May 24, 1712, for the Sainte-Chapelle memorial service for the duc and duchesse de Bourgogne, the *Registre* clearly states that Berain's decorations were "de mesme qu'a St. Denis et à Notre Dame" (p. 70v).

42. Jean Siffrein Maury, *Essay sur l'éloquence de la chaire* (Paris: Firmin Didot, 1850), p. 278.

43. As described in Abbé Blampignon's biography.

de son temps" (p. 157v). Having been ordained in 1692, he soon came to the Oratorian house of Saint-Magloire in Paris, where he distinguished himself in preaching, particularly for his Advent sermons for Louis XIV at court in 1699, and for his series of Lenten sermons of 1701 and 1704, also at court. In 1718 he was even to be asked to preach a series of shorter Lenten sermons for the young Louis XV, his *Petit Carême*, which Voltaire was to keep always on his table along with Racine's *Athalie*. Massillon had already preached at the Sainte-Chapelle "avec beaucoup de pieté et d'eloquence" (*Cérémonial*, p. 240v) for the memorial service for the grand dauphin, July 13, 1711.

This time, however, he found himself involved in an incident, not unworthy of satire in Boileau's *Lutrin*, resulting from the Chapel-Chambre tensions. The tensions now surfaced over the addressing of the traditional "Monsieur" which opened all such funeral orations. The present chapel treasurer, it seems, unknown to the Chambre *président*, had been instructing preachers, including Massillon himself in 1711, to address the opening word to him as treasurer. The *président*, finally apprised of this "nouveauté," instructed Massillon that he would find himself interrupted should he dare address himself to the treasurer, to which Massillon agreed. Nonetheless, on the eve of the service Massillon informed the *président* that the treasurer had directed otherwise, claiming the regent's own support. Whereupon, at a hasty audience with the regent, the president obtained from him an order to Massillon that no opening word should be addressed to anyone. The Chambre *Cérémonial* which reports all this then adds that the treasurer refused to officiate at Mass: "il fit le malade" (p. 349v). The Chapel *Registre*, conveniently ignoring all, politely records that, "Monsieur le Tresorier s'estant exoneré indisposé," the Mass was said by Canon Paul Voullemy (p. 158). It was this quarrel, then, that made possible Massillon's striking and immortal opening address to "mes frères."

Before the year was out, there still remained one more commemoration for the late monarch which had to be held in Paris by those on whom he had bestowed his favor. It was the turn of the Académie Française on Thursday, December 19, in the Louvre Chapel.[44] That the Academy was last is not surprising considering that its deliberations on the subject had dragged on through the autumn, not without some turmoil which

---

44. *Gazette de France*, no. 51 ("De Paris, le 21 Decembre"), p. 612; *Gazette d'Amsterdam*, no. 104 (December 24, "Quintessence des Nouvelles").

nonetheless gives insight into the character of the persons involved, particularly the orators. On September 2, the Academy had resolved to make the expression of its regrets "aussy immortels at aussy publics que la gloire de son héros."[45] Two weeks later, on September 16, it resolved that a service would be held in the Louvre Chapel, at which the arch-bishop of Albi would officiate. Abbé Mongin volunteered to preach the *oraison funèbre* and was accepted "avec joye comme un homme très ca-pable de s'en bien acquitter" (p. 599). Abbé Caumartin was requested to prepare an *éloge funèbre* in prose and Houdard de la Motte one in verse, for a public assembly which would also be held. On November 4, however, Abbé Caumartin had to be asked when his *éloge* would be prepared so that a date could be set. When the secretary reported on November 9 that Abbé Caumartin was "mortified" at being unable to prepare it, a heated deliberation ensued over whether or not a formal convocation of the Academy was necessary to make the next decision. Houdard de la Motte temporarily solved matters by volunteering to undertake the prose *éloge* as well, but by November 12, having had second thoughts, he called for a convocation[46] which set off "de grandes disputes" (p. 604). They were resolved by his total refusal of the second task "par pure modestie," so that a formal convocation of the Academy could be sched-uled for November 21. The convocation forcefully debated the place where the service was to be held, some suggesting Saint Germain l'Aux-errois, for its space. In conclusion, it was determined that it was not a "service" that was being planned, but just a Mass for the Dead, accom-panied by an *oraison funèbre*. Two *commissaires* were appointed to look after the decorating, which would be done "proprement et décemment sans superfluité" (the last word had originally been "magnificence") (p. 605). And the prose *éloge* was put back into the "si bonnes mains" of Houdard de la Motte, who accepted it "avec toutes les marques de respect et de déférence" (p. 606).

Finally, on December 19, the Academy gathered in the black-draped Chapel of the Louvre. A *De Profundis*, ordered by Cardinal de Polignac, chapel master and academician, was sung by the *musique du Roy*. The *oraison funèbre* was delivered "aprés la messe" and with "beaucoup d'élo-quence" (p. 607), by Edme Mongin (1668–1746), abbé de Saint-

45. *Les Registres de l'Académie Françoise 1672–1793* (Paris: Firmin-Didot, 1895), 1 (1672–1715), 598.
46. In order that a better man than he be chosen, or, to be better protected from criticism, that he receive the entire body's consent or order to take on the prose *éloge* as well.

Martin d'Autun (1711) and future bishop of Bazas (1724), who had been received into the Academy in 1708,[47] and had been tutor in the Condé household to the duc de Bourbon and the comte de Charolais. In his *Dictionnaire portatif des prédicateurs françois*, Abbé Albert was to consider him a second Fléchier (p. 184).

A Public Assembly was held later in the day ("l'apres dinée"), at which time the prose *éloge funèbre*, "qui a esté receu avec beaucoup d'applaudissement" (p. 607), was delivered by Houdard de la Motte (1672–1731), who had been received into the Academy in 1710,[48] and would be known for his works of literary criticism. After the *éloge*, he recited an ode "sur le mesme sujet; qui a eu aussi beaucoup de succès" (p. 607). A poem on the new reign followed, recited by Danchet, and it was listened to "avec un très grand plaisir."

From all of the foregoing, then, which has been sorely in need of clarification, it is clear that, contrary to what has frequently been said or suggested, all the formalities to honor the late Louis XIV were more than observed. One by one, those who were expected to commemorate him did so, and not just reluctantly. Their responsibility was taken quite seriously and time and effort went into it. Despite Bénigne Grenan's reservations and allusions, Louis XIV was properly commemorated even by the university, as was to be expected, with Cardinal de Noailles there, as he had been at Notre Dame, notwithstanding past disagreements with the monarch. Everything was done normally. Even the bickering was normal: at the Sainte-Chapelle, at the Academy, and between the university and the Jesuits. The bickering at the Sainte-Chapelle even influenced the production of one of the immortal lines of French oratory.

The succession to the throne was assured. The reins of government had passed to the regent. Since a great man had died, the forms had to be observed; and they were, more than willingly, as the French gave themselves over to contemplating in admiration the brilliance of a spectacular sunset.

47. A 1709 Académie Française *Recueil* carries the *Discours* by Régnier-Desmarais on Mongin's reception on March 1, 1708.

48. A 1711 Académie Française *Recueil* has the *Discours* for his reception "à la place de Corneille."

ROBERT D. SIDER

Χάρις and Derivatives in the Biblical Scholarship of Erasmus

WHEN, DURING THE Reformation debates, Erasmus was finally in-
duced to declare his opposition to Luther, it was on the issue of "grace
and free will" that he invited the Reformer's consideration, by the
publication in 1524 of the *De libero arbitrio diatribe*.[1] This event in itself
must arouse a certain interest in Erasmus' theology of grace. In this
essay, however, it is not my intention to comment on that debate, nor
indeed to describe Erasmus' theology of grace.[2] I should like rather
to offer evidence, from an appropriate study of Erasmus' New Testament
scholarship,[3] which may contribute to continued efforts at a more
comprehensive understanding of the concept of grace as it appears in
Erasmus' work.

We still have much to learn about the methods Erasmus employed in
his biblical scholarship. It seems clear, however, that at least for his

1. For a succinct interpretation of the steps by which Erasmus was led to write the
Diatribe see Craig R. Thompson, ed., *Inquisitio de fide: A Colloquy by Desiderius Erasmus
Roterodamus 1524*, 2d ed. (Hamden, Conn., 1975), pp. 4–34. But Marjorie O. Boyle,
Rhetoric and Reform: Erasmus' Civil Dispute with Luther (Cambridge, Mass., 1983), esp.
pp. 33–38, qualifies the view that the treatise was written "against" Luther.

2. For a brief account of Erasmus' theology of grace see John Payne, *Erasmus: His Theology
of the Sacraments* (Richmond, Va., 1970), pp. 74–84.

3. For the purpose of this essay I shall define Erasmus' biblical scholarship as (1) translations of the Greek New Testament, (2) the *Annotations* (Notes) on the New Testament, and
(3) the *Paraphrases* on the New Testament. This material, along with Erasmus' Greek text,
and "prefatory" essays, fills two of the ten volumes—a very significant part, quite obviously—of the Erasmian corpus edited by Jean Leclerc in the Leiden edition (1703–1706)
known as LB.

Translation and *Annotations*, the Greek text was available, probably in manuscript, perhaps often in memory as well. The extent to which the Greek text was at hand when he composed the *Paraphrases* is open to question. It is evident that for the *Paraphrases*, he relied heavily on his own translation and the Vulgate;[4] at the same time the frequent correlation between his notes and paraphrases implies that the Greek text he so often cited in his notes was constantly present, in mind at least, when he wrote the *Paraphrases*.[5] The Greek text, therefore, plays an important role in Erasmus' biblical work and suggests an appropriate principle of limitation for our study: the biblical χάρις, and its derivatives χαρίζομαι, χαριτόω, and (from χαρίζομαι) χάρισμα, rather than the Latin *gratia* will define the field of our investigation. We shall follow Erasmus' interpretation of χάρις successively through his *Translation*, *Annotations*, and *Paraphrases*. The less frequent appearance of the derivatives in the New Testament will permit a much briefer study of them in the final section of this essay.

I

In his first edition of the New Testament,[6] Erasmus offered a fairly conservative translation, but in 1519 he departed more radically from the Vulgate readings.[7] In the case of the word χάρις, however, Erasmus generally preferred to retain the Vulgate's *gratia*: in 1516, with the exception of several occurrences in 2 Corinthians, he invariably translated χάρις by *gratia*, and he made virtually no changes in subsequent

4. A knowledge of Erasmus' methods is rendered more difficult by our uncertainty about the Vulgate text Erasmus used. In 1527 he himself, evidently taking a cue from the Complutensian Polyglot Bible (1514–1517, published ca. 1522), printed a Vulgate text along with the Greek text and his own translation. But the Vulgate text to which he refers in his notes does not always correspond to the text he printed. Nevertheless, when, in this essay, I refer to the Vulgate, it is to the text he printed in 1527.

5. This is not to deny the constant presence, at the same time, of the Vulgate. His translation seems to have the Vulgate as its point of departure—indeed his 1516 translation follows the Vulgate fairly closely; his notes are introduced by cue phrases from the Vulgate; and his *Paraphrases* appear generally to follow the Vulgate on text-critical issues—sometimes against both his translation and his notes.

6. Erasmus' New Testament, with the *Annotations* which accompanied it, appeared in five editions; the first edition, the *Novum Instrumentum*, was printed in 1516 by Johann Froben in Basle; subsequent editions (now, the *Novum Testamentum*) all printed by Froben in Basle appeared in 1519, 1522, 1527, 1535.

7. See Albert Rabil, Jr., *Erasmus and the New Testament* (San Antonio, Tex., 1972), p. 92.

editions. Some changes occur in his rendering of contextual prepositions in 1519, but very few thereafter. I shall consider the few instances where χάρις is rendered by a word other than *gratia*; then observe the translation of χάρις with some prepositions, and finally comment on several cases of special interest.

In 2 Corinthians 8–9 Erasmus translates χάρις by *gratia*, *beneficium*, and *beneficentia*. In these chapters Paul invites the Corinthians to contribute to the poor in Jerusalem. On the human level χάρις here implies an act of fairly tangible generosity, though the request for a money contribution is not without its appeal to the divine χάρις. If we exclude the use of χάρις = "thanks" (8:16; 9:15), we find that in the course of these two chapters Erasmus has retained the Vulgate *gratia* for the two instances where the χάρις is defined as τοῦ θεοῦ (8:1; 9:14), and has elsewhere chosen either *beneficium* or *beneficentia*. It is possible that the choice here among these three has been determined at least partly by stylistic considerations, for their arrangement effects a neat symmetry wherein the words translating χάρις (χάρις = "thanks" excluded) appear in the order: *gratia*, *beneficium*, *beneficentia* (four times), *beneficium*, *gratia*. And yet we must be cautious in drawing conclusions, for while in these chapters *beneficium* and *beneficentia* appear to refer to a specific act of human generosity, in 2 Corinthians 4:15 *beneficium* renders χάρις understood clearly as the divine grace. As it is the only instance outside 2 Corinthians 8 and 9 where χάρις is not rendered by *gratia*, it is difficult to assess the significance of the change.

In his *Annotations* Erasmus comments on these changes four times. These notes, however, are primarily philological, and with a single exception do not attempt to defend the particular word chosen for the translation. In 2 Corinthians 4:15 where χάρις appears for the first time as *beneficium*, the translation goes undefended. On the other hand, in 2 Corinthians 6:1 Erasmus retains the traditional *gratia* in his translation, but adds to his 1519 note, almost as an afterthought, that *gratia* here is used for *beneficium*. Three notes comment on the word in chapter 8 (verses 6, 7, 19). While from 1516 on Erasmus translates the word in these verses by *beneficentia*, his 1516 notes explain the word as *beneficium* and, in the note on 8:7, as "alms." In 1519, however, a brief defense of *beneficentia* does attempt to allay criticism: the word has the sanction of Cicero, both in the *De officiis* and elsewhere. The failure of the notes to clarify the purpose of the change in translation in these chapters adds to the difficulty in determining how far any of the three renderings was chosen to reflect subtle theological nuances.

In the biblical text, χάρις is often constructed with a preposition, either preceding or following. In many cases Erasmus retains the Vulgate rendering of χάρις with the preposition. Most of the changes from the Vulgate appear unremarkable, motivated by a desire for accuracy and elegance. But the translation of ἐν χάριτι warrants special consideration. First, where χάρις is constructed with other prepositions Erasmus never wavered from his 1516 renderings;[8] in the case of ἐν + χάρις a change is made in six of nine instances in 1519. Second, the nature of the changes might suggest, at first glance, a theological motivation. In four cases Erasmus replaces the Vulgate's *in gratia* with *per gratiam*, in two with *cum gratia*. The latter occur in Colossians 3 : 16 and 4 : 6. A note on Colossians 4 : 6 reveals that Erasmus understands the phrase there to mean "speaking 'gracefully,'" and it is reasonable to assume that Erasmus in 1519 understood the phrase in Colossians 3 : 16 analogously, as "singing gracefully," or possibly, as the paraphrase suggests, "singing joyfully." The change has the effect of neutralizing the theological color of the word: the language evokes a stronger image of human pleasure than of divine grace, though the latter sense is not necessarily eliminated. The change from *in gratia* to *per gratiam* may seem to suggest an even more decisive attempt to establish a subtle theological nuance by which Erasmus can stress the instrumentality of grace.

Again, however, caution is required. If one studies Erasmus' translations of the simple dative χάριτι without the preposition, where also Erasmus might have found opportunity to stress instrumentality, one discovers that no changes are made after 1516, and that he follows most frequently, though not always, the Vulgate translation. The case of Ephesians 2 : 5 and 8 is especially interesting. Here we have two similar expressions—χάριτί ἐστε σεσωμένοι ("By grace you are saved")— but 2 : 8 adds the words διὰ πίστεως. Erasmus changes the Vulgate's simple *gratia* in 2 : 5 to *per gratiam*, but follows the Vulgate's *gratia* without a preposition in 2 : 8, quite possibly for stylistic reasons: he might have felt that *per gratiam—gratia—per fidem* offered a more elegant sequence than *per* thrice repeated, and that the distinction between the action of grace and faith would be obscured if both phrases in 2 : 8 were

---

8. A single exception can be found—ἐπί + dat. in Lk. 4 : 22, 1519.

translated by *per* + acc. In Hebrews 2 : 9 he changes the Vulgate's *gratia* to *per gratiam*, but in 1 Corinthians 15 : 10 and Titus 3 : 7 retains the Vulgate's simple *gratia*.

The complexity of motivation behind changes in the translation of χάρις and contextual prepositions may, finally, be illustrated by two further examples. In 1 Corinthians 15 : 10 Erasmus replaces (1516) the Vulgate's *gratia in me* and *gratia mecum* (ἡ χάρις ἡ . . . εἰς ἔμε; ἡ χάρις . . . ἡ σὺν ἐμοί)[9] with clauses: *gratia quae profecta est in me*; *gratia quae mihi adest*. Stylistically, the clauses strive to retain the parallelism of the Greek and the Vulgate; at the same time they serve to define χάρις, and they do so in a theologically significant way. Though Erasmus has a brief note on both phrases in 1516, it is in 1527 especially that he draws out the theological implication of his change: the first of the two phrases stresses the goodwill of God towards (*erga*) Paul, the *favor* he has offered him; the second signifies the *auxilium* God brings to Paul, and supports the doctrine of "cooperating grace." Erasmus wished to capture the sense of benevolence towards another implied by χάρις + εἰς. Hence elsewhere, too, where the Vulgate had translated this phrase by "grace *in* you," Erasmus understood χάρις "*to* or *towards* you" (2 Cor. 8:6, 9:8, 1 Pt. 1 : 10). In these cases, a desire for accuracy and elegance appears to coalesce with a desire to bring theological clarity and interpretation into the text.[10]

The second example is a puzzling case. From 1516 to 1535 Erasmus printed in his Greek text of Acts 6:8 the words Στέφανος δὲ πλήρης πίστεως.[11] In spite of his reading he followed the Vulgate in rendering the words *plenus gratia* until the edition of 1535 when he changed his translation to *plenus fide* to accommodate his text. No note on the reading appears in any edition, while his 1535 *Paraphrase* still presupposes the *gratia* of the Vulgate and his earlier translations. This may well suggest that in spite of the availability of a Greek text, Erasmus sometimes based his translation on his memory rather than on

9. Erasmus' reading. The textual evidence is not uniform—see the note ad loc. in Kurt Aland et al., eds., *The Greek New Testament*, 3d ed. (United Bible Societies, 1975).

10. A survey of the patristic authors whose commentaries Erasmus followed closely—Origen (in Latin), Jerome, Ambrosiaster, Pelagius—does not suggest that the changes discussed in the section derive from the translation or commentary of the Fathers on these passages.

11. Aland et al., op. cit., read, Στέφανος δὲ πλήρης χάριτος. But the reading πλήρης πίστεως is attested, and can be found, for example, in Chrysostom (*PG* 60 : 119).

an immediate reading of the Greek. At the least, it points again to the need for caution in our efforts to explain the changes in Erasmus' *Translation*.

II

The *Annotations* were greatly expanded, and occasionally revised, in the editions from 1516 to 1535, and we can therefore take some measurement of the development of Erasmus' interests by following the discussions which arise from χάρις through the course of the five editions. In 1516 the comments are predominantly philological. In the first edition, Erasmus annotates our word at only three points throughout his discussion of the Gospels and Acts (Lk. 1:31, Jn. 1:14−17, Acts 18:27), and this in spite of its relatively frequent use in Luke-Acts. He offers a careful definition of the word when it first appears in Romans (1:5): it is used to signify a *beneficium gratuitum collatum*, or to designate *favor* (in the sense of the good will one person may have for another, and the delight in him), or to express thanks—the *obligatio beneficii*.

To a very great extent, Erasmus occupies himself in the remaining 1516 notes on χάρις with a fairly straightforward application, occasionally with some elaboration, of the three meanings, as appropriate. Little is said in 1516 about grace as *favor*, though the concept is implicit in several comments which, as we shall presently see, work out the meaning of χάρις as "joy." In the majority of cases Erasmus defines χάρις as *beneficium*; twice as *beneficentia* [12] (2 Cor. 9:8, 9:14); once as *eleemosyna* (2 Cor. 8:7); once as *dona* (1 Pt. 4:10)—a meaning he rejects for its use in Romans 5:20. In all of these cases the word implies a good deed, an act of kindness, and he occasionally notes its essential concomitant, that the kindness is freely bestowed (*gratuito* Rom. 1:5,

---

12. It would appear that, for Erasmus, the distinction between *beneficium* and *beneficentia* is rather slight. Both words are virtually interchangeable: for example, in 1516 though he translated χάρις as *beneficentia* in 2 Cor. 8:6, 7, and 19, he noted that the word meant *beneficium*, while in 2 Cor. 9:8 where he translated the word as *beneficium*, he noted that the word meant *beneficentia*. He uses both words to signify fundamentally a "good deed" which is done to another. Both words also imply an essential attitude of good will on the part of the doer exhibited especially in the fact that he acts "spontaneously"—often where kindness is not deserved. It is possible, however, that for Erasmus, *beneficium* cast in slightly higher relief the nature of the deed, while *beneficentia* carried a stronger reference to the persisting good will of the doer.

gratis 1 Cor. 16:3, *libenter* 2 Cor. 9:8). The 1516 notes also call attention at various points to the use of χάρις in expressions of thanks,
which Erasmus generally renders as *deo gratia* (χάρις τῷ θεῷ e.g.,
Rom. 6:17), *gratiam habere* (χάριν ἔχειν e.g., 2 Tim. 1:3). The
notes on these two idioms would be of little interest for us were it
not for two later additions. To his 1516 note on 2 Timothy 1:3 where
he justifies his translation by appealing to the authority of Valla and
Ambrose, he adds a comment in 1527 which expresses doubt about the
propriety of the expression with *deo*, a doubt grounded in his theology
of grace, for *habere gratiam*, he believes, reflects an intention to return
the favor, while *gratias agere* reveals simply the *animus gratus ac memor*.
In the 1535 addition to the note on Romans 6:17, he plays on the
meaning of χάρις as "that which delights" when he comments on the
difference between the expressions *deo gratias* and *deo gratia*: the former
is *gratissima deo*, the latter no less *grata* if each phrase is said with
devotion.

This sense of the root meaning of the word had already appeared in
his 1516 comment on 2 Corinthians 1:15 where he agrees with the
Greek scholia that χάρις here really stands for χαρά—*gratia pro
gaudio*—for in Latin, too, things which delight are said *gratiam habere*.
This sense appears to underlie Erasmus' interpretation of the word in
Luke 1:31. Following his interpretation of the preceding *gratia plena*,
he understands that the angel here informs Mary that she has found
grace with God, which is to say she is pleasing to him (*gratiosa apud
deum*). Similarly, in Colossians 4:6 Erasmus points out that our speech
will have "grace" if it has *iucunditas* and *modestia*—if it conveys pleasure, if it observes due restraint. Such speech contrasts with the harsh
maledictions cast upon ruthless rulers, and has its own redemptive
power, for it may lead magistrates *ad meliora*. It is perhaps the sense of
grace in its root meaning of that which gives joy and pleases which lies
at the heart of his reflection on the divine grace as a *beneficium*. Certainly
the contrast in Colossians 4:6 between the *iucunditas* of grace and the
acerbitas of *maledicentia* is picked up in a short note on Hebrews 4:16
where he suggests that the phrase "throne of grace" opposes "grace" to
the "severity" of the Law.

In his 1516 notes Erasmus elaborates the meaning of grace in two
further ways. First, he recognizes that χάρις is also used of ministry,
as though ministry were a *munus* conferred by God. Here, too, the
Erasmian emphasis on grace as "free gift" emerges, and with it hints of

his critique of the inflated importance of those who hold ecclesiastical office: in the case of Paul, it was *muneris divini* that he had been given a ministry (Acts 18:27), and Paul himself (in 1 Cor. 15:10) insists that his ministry was a matter of grace "so that we would understand that he credited everything to God." Second, in 1516 Erasmus' notes reflect, but only in an undeveloped way, the motif of salvation-history which is to provide in his *Paraphrases* and later annotations a framework for much of his thinking on grace. In the first edition grace is set rather simply in contrast to the Mosaic law (Gal. 2:21), to our trust in it (Gal. 2:21) and in its works (Ti. 3:5), or in contrast, as we have seen, to its severity (Heb. 4:16). Occasionally, as in Ephesians 2:3, Erasmus extends the contrast with grace to the law of nature, but we must wait for later editions to observe in his discussions how grace can be regarded as an image of the entire salvation-event.

The additions of 1519 continue to enunciate the themes of 1516, speaking of the contrast between grace on the one hand and nature and the Mosaic law on the other, as well as of the authority of office as a gift owed to the divine goodness; they define χάρις as *beneficium*, and, more frequently than in 1516, as *beneficentia* and even *munificentia*. What is new about the 1519 notes on χάρις is their interest in the christological implications of some biblical passages referring to grace. Erasmus' interest focuses upon two issues: the nature of the "grace" in Christ, the God-man, and the relation of the Persons of the Trinity to the grace conferred upon mankind. In a substantial note on Luke 2:52 Erasmus tries to solve the problem, long-standing among theologians, of how Christ the God-man could be said to "grow in grace," and he invites the reader, somewhat gingerly, to consider whether it would conflict with a "sincere faith" to think that while all the gifts with which Jesus as a man was endowed came from the divine beneficence, the Godhead imparted these in stages (*per gradus quosdam*) to the human nature he assumed. He concludes by pointing to the ambiguity of the word, which may refer either to the *dotes divinitus infusae* or to the fact that Jesus had become *gratiosior* through the virtues he displayed. Though in his notes on John 1:14–16 Erasmus describes Christ as the source—the *fons*—of grace, it is in his note on 2 Corinthians 1:2 that we see his reflection on the source of grace as a problem for Trinitarian theology—whether grace proceeds from the Father and the Son, or whether it proceeds from the Father who is common to Christ and to us.

In the discussions of χάρις there are very few additions in 1522 of any significance, but we can trace a continuing interest in the question of the divine source of grace. This is particularly clear in the note on Ephesians 1:2, where Erasmus points out on the authority of Jerome that while "grace and peace" may proceed from Father and Son alike, it is possible to understand the "grace" as from the Father, the "peace" as from the Son. We may recognize the grace of the Father in that he deigned to send his Son for our salvation, the peace of the Son in that we were reconciled to the Father through him. This definition attempts some clarification of the role of Father and Son in the economy of salvation and at the same time focuses on salvation-history at its central moment as the context from which the word χάρις receives its meaning.

Not only are the additions in 1527 to the notes on χάρις more numerous than those of any other edition; they are also more predominantly theological in character. In this edition, Erasmus repeatedly returns to three issues in his discussion of grace: (1) the significance of grace as salvation-history, (2) the source of grace in relation to the Persons of the Trinity, and (3) the relation between grace and works.

The note on Romans 1:5 provides a rather nice indication of a shift in emphasis from the 1516 edition. In 1516 Erasmus had prefaced the definition, of which the note was primarily comprised, with a brief statement contrasting grace with the Mosaic law. In 1527 he added as an epilogue to the definition a parallel statement which does not, however, return to the law-grace contrast, but marks a new emphasis on the personal significance of the salvation-event: "By grace, he means here that he was recalled from error, and not only recalled, but also chosen to call others to the grace of the Gospel." Erasmus returns to the theme of salvation in a 1527 addition to his note on Romans 1:7. The addition begins with a definition of grace familiar since 1516: grace is *gratuita munificentia* (*munificentia* preferred now to the 1516 *beneficium*), and the word indicates that our call has been undeserved. But Erasmus quickly passes on to the theme of grace as "redemption" characteristic of the 1527 notes: grace given brings forth remission of sins, which, in his customary way, Paul calls "peace." Sin puts enmity between God and man. He called us, we did not seek him; he loved us while we were enemies; to those deserving punishment he imparted the gift of the Spirit and through the Spirit forgiveness of sins and an abundance of *charismata*. We may note finally a brief but highly significant comment in a 1527 addition to the note on Ephesians 1:6 where Erasmus justifies the translation of δόξα as *maiestas*, a word which, though usually used of "power," can be appropriately applied to grace, "for God appeared more wonderful in redeeming man than in creating him." Here the complementary contrast between creation and redemption invites the reader to consider grace from the perspective of salvation-history.

In 1519 Erasmus had already noted on John 1:14 that Christ is the author and source (*fons*) of grace. He reiterates the theme in 1527 in a similar note on John 1:17. But he attempts to explain more decisively the relation of Father, Son, and Spirit in a note on 2 Corinthians 13:13, entirely new in 1527: Paul attributes *communio* to the Spirit, *gratia* to the Son, *charitas* to the Father. The redemption of the human race had its beginning with the Father who so loved the world that he gave his only begotten Son over to death; grace came through the Son who redeemed us by his death though we deserved nothing; the distribution of gifts was made through the Holy Spirit. Again, it is not until 1527 that Erasmus endeavors to clarify the relation of Father and Son, insofar as the question arises from the expression ἡ χάρις τοῦ θεοῦ σωτήριος in Titus 2:11. This, he says (referring to Jerome), may apply either to Father or Son—either because Christ is himself the living and subsisting grace of the Father, or because this is the grace of Christ our Saviour God, that we have been saved apart from any merits of our own.

Perhaps the most striking development of the 1527 notes on χάρις is a new emphasis on the relation between grace and works. We have seen that in 1516 the Mosaic law and (less frequently) the natural law provided the primary contrast with grace. In 1527 the contrast extended, in the note on Romans 7:25 for example, to *conscientia* and *opera*. So in Titus 3:5. In 1516 Erasmus had seen here a reference to the works of the Mosaic law; in 1527 he observes that the "orthodox" understand this concerning all the works of men. Some of his notes are especially interesting for the contemporary relevance he gives this theme. In the annotation on 2 Timothy 1:9 he excoriates those who "today" shrink from the message of Paul, which excludes trust in works, commends the grace of God. They boast of their own good works, honoring neither grace nor faith. But if most of his comments suggest an antithesis between grace and works, the note on Ephesians 1:6 appeals to the *via media*: the Apostle everywhere extols grace, minimizes trust in works. Some err on both sides, and the safest way is in the middle. But if we must turn to one side, it is safer to lean to the side of grace than to that of works. In light of this note, it is not surprising that where in 1516 he was prepared simply to quote Valla on 1 Corinthians 15:10, who saw no support in the verse for the doctrine of "cooperating" grace, in 1527 he takes up the case against Valla, for the divine *auxilium* does not exclude the work of the one who is helped.[13]

By 1535 Erasmus was ready, in his notes on χάρις, to contend for the necessity of works. In a 1535 comment on Titus 2:12 he says: "This passage should be observed by those who rely on grace and neglect good works, since grace delivers us from sin for this very purpose, that henceforth we should be free for pious deeds." Little else is remarkable in the 1535 additions, where Erasmus continues to comment on the characteristics of grace: he notes its *clementia* (Ti. 2:12) and its *magnitudo*[14] (Eph. 1:7), and follows Chrysostom in defining it (1 Cor. 10:30) as the *bonitas dei* by which the gifts of creation cannot, for the pure, be defiled by the wickedness of the ungodly.

III

In the dedicatory letter to Cardinal Grimini which accompanied his *Paraphrase on Romans*, Erasmus noted that in a paraphrase "one must say things differently without saying different things."[15] In this way, the paraphrase became, as Erasmus says elsewhere, a *textus explanatior*.[16] As such, the paraphrase offered an expansion of the text which drew out and laid open to view the meanings and implications of its language. One of Erasmus' characteristic methods of expanding the text was to offer alternative ways of formulating it, sometimes in sets of parallel affirmations (text = a + b), sometimes in contrasting positive and negative assertions (text = a, not c), sometimes in a combination of both (text =

13. Jerry H. Bentley, *Humanists and Holy Writ: New Testament Scholarship in the Renaissance* (Princeton, 1983), p. 179, sees a reflection here of the debate with Luther.

14. It is to be noted that both in his *Translation* and in his *Annotations* Erasmus characteristically expresses the richness and abundance of the divine grace by the verb *exuberare*, or by the expression *ubertim impartire*, rather than by *abundare*, preferred by the Vulgate.

15. R. A. B. Mynors and D. F. S. Thomson, *The Correspondence of Erasmus*, annotated by Peter G. Bietenholz, *Collected Works of Erasmus* 5 (Toronto, 1979), p. 196.

16. So in the *Divinationes ad notata per Beddam* (LB IX, 464C), and in the *Argumentum* to the *Paraphrase on Romans* (LB VI, 777–778). On the nature and form of the paraphrases see the chapter by John Payne, Albert Rabil, Jr., and Warren Smith, Jr., "The Paraphrases of Erasmus: Origin and Character," in R. D. Sider, ed., *The Paraphrases on Romans and Galatians*, *Collected Works of Erasmus* 42 (Toronto, 1984), pp. xiii–xxii.

a + b, and not c). [17] The method permitted Erasmus not only to unfold the implications of "grace," but to express alternative meanings when the word seemed ambiguous. The method also kept the paraphrase bound closely to the text, so that in most cases it is quite possible to distinguish the precise limits of Erasmus' expansion of, for example, the word "grace." There are occasions, however, where Erasmus' paraphrases convey the *idea* of a biblical sentence without attempting to represent in paraphrase the specific words and phrases of the text. In such cases no obvious formulation of our word will be found: the meaning of "grace" must emerge from the context. Elsewhere, too, the paraphrases reveal Erasmus' keen sense of the power of context to convey meaning. This can be seen perhaps most vividly in those places where Erasmus formulated a clearly identifiable expansion of the word "grace," but connected the formulation to the surrounding context by unmistakable verbal echoes which draw the context into the expression of the idea of grace, so that the context becomes part of the meaning of the word. This appears to be particularly true where Erasmus speaks of grace in terms of the central moments of salvation-history. In a field so broad, I can note here only a few of the more striking ways in which the paraphrases draw out the meaning of grace. [18]

In Luke-Acts, where the word χάρις appears with some frequency, Erasmus prefers in his paraphrases what we may call a "moral" interpretation of grace. In Luke 2 : 40 and again in 2 : 52 Erasmus presents the χάρις of Jesus as the intellectual, moral, and social virtues, which made him *amabilis* and so drew all who knew him to the love of virtue. The

17. The influence of rhetorical principles on Erasmus' methods of paraphrasing has been traced by Jacques Chomarat, *Grammaire et rhetorique chez Erasme* (Paris, 1981), I; see esp. pp. 587–588.

18. The analysis which follows is based on a collation of the collected editions published in Erasmus' lifetime—for the Gospels and Acts, the earliest (1524) and the latest (1535), for the Epistles, the earliest (1521), as well as those of 1524 and 1532. However, the paraphrases of scriptural passages providing context for the word "grace" offer only one example (Rom. 1 : 7) of any substantive change in the course of the editions. I make no attempt therefore to address the question of "development" in conception or expression in the *Paraphrases*. It is noteworthy that some of the conceptions we have seen associated predominantly with the later annotations appear already full-blown in the early paraphrases. The one exception of Rom. 1 : 7 is, undeniably, important, for the 1532 addition defines grace in terms of the personal significance of the salvation-event, a feature characteristic of the 1527 *Annotations*. Nevertheless, we may conclude that in general, the developments in the conception of grace which are registered in the *Annotations* seem to reflect a change in the interests or perspective of Erasmus rather than in his theology.

virtues he cites in 2 : 40 are: *sapientia, sanctitas, integritas, maturitas,* and further, *suavitas, comitas, modestia.* But he also makes clear that these are divine gifts—*rarae dotes*—hence the *gratia* of Jesus is not common popularity (which the word might imply) but something divine, which pleases, entices, and so redeems those who approach it. Here we can see how Erasmus works out the ambiguities of the word *gratia*: he denies its "popular" meaning, but affirms on the one hand the theological sense of "divine gift," on the other the "aesthetic" sense of "the pleasing," "the graceful," and combines the two in a statement implying the redemptive power of grace. Our word is paraphrased in much the same way in Luke 4 : 22, where Jesus' "words of grace" are interpreted as speech which is *placidus, mansuetus, amabilis, multa gratia conditus,* and *efficax ad salutem.* The same sense of grace as the devout and joyful life which secures the favor of God and man is apparent on some occasions where the word is applied, not to Christ, but to Christians, or to holy men of the Old Testament, as in the paraphrases on Acts 2 : 47, 6 : 8, 7 : 10, 7 : 46; and in Colossians 4 : 6 the "gracious" speech of Christians has, like that of Christ, redeeming power: *comis oratio citius flectit feroces animos.*

But the paraphrase on Colossians 4 : 6 is somewhat exceptional for the Epistles. Here, in the dominant interpretation, grace is the *benignitas* or the *beneficium* or the *beneficentia dei* elaborated in paraphrase as the central moment or moments of salvation-history: the forgiveness of the sins of our former life, freedom from the tyranny of the devil, and the innocence of the new life (so the paraphrase on Rom. 5 : 15–17). [19] At points, however, these central moments find an important extension. We may see in the paraphrase on 1 Corinthians 1 : 3 the tendency to extend the scope of reference the word enjoys. Here Erasmus expands the simple Pauline greeting χάρις καὶ εἰρήνη into a series of parallel statements which both distinguish and bind together the ideas inherent in the two words:

> grace will guard your innocence; of peace, concord is the companion.
>
> grace delivers you from sin and reconciles [*reconciliat*] you to God; peace unites [*conciliat*] you to your brother.
>
> through grace the benefit is experienced in such a way that the author is

---

19. Though the Gospels and Acts were paraphrased after the Epistles, there is no reason to assume that the predominantly "moral" conception of grace in the former represents a development in Erasmus' theological conceptualization. Erasmus' sensitivity to the context offers a sufficient explanation of the difference.

known; through peace it is revealed that you have indeed embraced Christianity.

through grace you have become sharers in the heavenly beneficence; through peace you share with one another what you have received from God.

In this passage Erasmus includes in the meaning of grace both the gift of knowing its author and our participation in the life of the world to come (the heavenly beneficence). At the same time, the parallels defining grace and those defining peace are not antithetical but coordinate, so that grace acquires overtones of meaning from the definition of peace: for example the coordinate *reconciliat-conciliat* invites us to see the unity of brethren as a concomitant of grace.

By developing verbal echoes of this sort, especially within a carefully structured sequence of ideas, Erasmus is able at times to provide for his paraphrase of "grace" a context through which the frame of reference for the word becomes the whole span of saving history. Perhaps the most obvious example of this can be seen in the paraphrase of 1 Peter 1 : 2, where we again have the greeting χάρις καὶ εἰρήνη. The expansion on these two nouns becomes the focal point of the paraphrase of the first two verses. A lengthy introduction, though ostensibly an expansion on all that precedes the grace-peace clause, in fact describes the crucial moments in saving history: our election in the eternal counsel of God, the Mosaic law and the ceremonies given for a time, the *gratuita dei bonitas* and the *evangelii munificentia* by which we have been adopted, the *lex evangelica* by which we have been cleansed from sin and through baptism restored to life. Erasmus is now ready for the paraphrase on grace and peace which he introduces as *ea bona* appropriate to those who through baptism have received the citizenship of heaven. The repetition of the word "baptism" ties all that has gone before closely to the "goods" for which he now prays, "that is, for grace, so that you place no trust in your own merits, or in the ceremonies of the law, but await true salvation *e sola gratuita dei munificentia, fiduciaque evangelii*; and for peace, so that, reconciled *gratis* through the blood of Christ, you have peace among yourselves, as well as with others, not rendering evil to anyone, but forgiving others, and responding to evil deeds with *beneficentia*." The word πληθυνθείη must still be paraphrased to complete the verse. This will be understood as the perseverance of the Christian until at the last day he achieves the reward of immortality. The allusion to the "last day" completes the account of salvation-history, begun with the paraphrase of verse 1, but this moment, too, is tied securely to the event of "grace," for it is introduced by the image repeated of the *bona* which we have received *gratis* from God: these "goods," as you have received freely from God, may you strive to complete by a zeal for piety and good works. Thus, both the structure of the paraphrase of these first two verses of 1 Peter and the rather subtle arrangement of verbal echoes assure that the meaning of "grace" will not be confined to the somewhat limited expansion on the word itself, but will be enriched by the entire context. Accordingly, "grace" here is to be understood not simply as the divine beneficence in contrast to law and merits, but as the entire event in which the divine goodness has begun and will complete its saving work.

To this understanding of grace as the salvation-event an important addition is made in the paraphrase on 2 Corinthians 8:9. χάρις is used five times in verses 1–9 of this chapter where Paul urges the Corinthians to give a contribution to the poor of Jerusalem. In verse 9 he holds up Christ as the true *exemplum*, who become poor for us that we might become rich. There are no obvious words in the paraphrase here to represent χάρις probably because Erasmus saw the word represented sufficiently in the narrative of Christ's self-giving—the χάρις of Christ *is* his act of assuming our poverty. If this is so, Erasmus' paraphrase of verse 9 acquires a special interest, for he offers an explanation of how the self-giving is redemptive: Christ, being rich, absorbed, as it were, our poverty, and imparted his richness to us. Grace appears as a transformation of the human condition through participation in Christ.

I must note briefly a few further images of grace in the paraphrases. The word appears to be represented by *laus* in 2 Corinthians 8:4, by *laus pietatis* in 2 Corinthians 8:6, while the ambiguity of ἐν χάριτι in Colossians 3:16 is expressed by both *hilares* and *laudes*: singing joyfully the praises. Again, in 2 Corinthians 1:15 the word appears as *gaudium*, joy. Quite frequently the word is elaborated in the sense of the divine aid available to Christians, as in Acts 14:26, 18:27, 20:32, 1 Corinthians 15:10, Galatians 6:8, Hebrews 4:16, James 4:6, and 1 Peter 5:12, where verbs (e.g., *adiuvare*, *opitulari*) are often used, no doubt to sharpen the impression of the divine grace as an active power. Further, in his paraphrases Erasmus is fond of the image of "the way," and he occasionally portrays χάρις as the gift of strength and wisdom or of faith to begin and to continue in "the way," certainly in 1 Peter 5:12, apparently in Hebrews 12:28, and perhaps in Acts 13:43.[20] One image is likely to

20. We have seen in the paraphrase of 1 Pt. 1:2 how the context imports into the meaning of grace the concept of the perseverance of the Christian.

surprise. In the paraphrase on Romans 11:5–6 Erasmus had carefully distinguished between *beneficium* and *praemium*: what is bestowed on those who merit nothing, this alone is a *beneficium*; if merits are calculated, we have no longer a *beneficium* but a *praemium*. In his paraphrase on 1 Peter 3:7 Erasmus represents the Apostle as urging husbands to share with their wives the "good works" of fasting, alms, and prayers, and to strive with a common zeal for the *commune praemium aeternae vitae* (χάριτος ζωῆς). Here grace is evidently understood as a reward for good works done! Significantly, *praemium* is used elsewhere by Erasmus to represent χάρις only in Luke 4:32–34.

IV

An examination of the words χαριτόω, χαρίζομαι, and χάρισμα confirms, but adds little new to, our understanding of Erasmus' theology of grace. In general, the interpretation of these words is brief, though occasionally the paraphrase of χάρισμα is drawn into a dynamic *explanatio* of χάρις. The notes, indeed, suggest that Erasmus found in χαρίζομαι and χάρισμα little to stimulate his thought subsequent to 1519, for to twenty-two notes on these words only two additions are made after that date—one to a note on χαρίζομαι in 1522, and one to a note on χάρισμα in 1535. This contrasts sharply with his continuing reflection on χάρις, to the notes on which the largest number of additions (eighteen) occur in 1527.

χαριτόω appears only twice in the New Testament—Luke 1:28 and Ephesians 1:6—and it therefore offered less opportunity for interpretation. Erasmus did, however, seize both occasions. In the 1519 edition, the *Translation* changed the Vulgate's *gratia plena* (Lk. 1:28) to *gratiosa* and, in Ephesians 1:6, the Vulgate's *gratificavit* to *charos reddidit*. The time-honored words of the address to Mary contained a potentially explosive issue. In 1516 Erasmus had suggested that the language is that of a lover addressing his beloved, but in 1519 and 1522 he discussed the theological implications of the word. He refuses to concede that the phrase is applicable only to Mary, for many people in Holy Scripture are said to be "filled with the Spirit." [21] The phrase finds it propriety rather in the fact that the angel's words signify the end of legal ceremonies, and the beginning of saving grace. If the phrase is used to address one

21. We should note here the implication of the argument that to be filled with the Spirit is to be filled with grace.

beloved it has a further nuance, that the affection has arisen not from any merit in the beloved arising from service rendered, but entirely uninvited, simply from the spontaneous will of the lover. We recognize here the familiar formula associated with χάρις. Indeed, the close relation to χάρις seems to be carefully represented in the paraphrase on χαριτόω in Ephesians, where Erasmus not only stresses the love by which God has transformed evil slaves into sons, but in rendering the word by the phrase *filios gratos et charos reddidit* also doubles the sense of delight in love.[22]

In a note on χάρισμα in Romans 1 : 11 Erasmus demonstrated the relation between χάρις, χαρίζομαι, and χάρισμα and there defined χαρίζομαι as *largior* (changed to *largior beneficium* in 1519), or *ad gratiam facio*. For Erasmus, χαρίζομαι was best expressed by a phrase which included the Latin word *gratia*. In various notes he explains the word as *in gratiam alicuius donare* (Acts 25 : 16) and *cuius rei gratiam facere* (2 Cor. 2 : 10), and in a 1519 note on 2 Corinthians 12 : 13 he writes that to the Vulgate's *donate* he would prefer *condonate*, or *huius iniuriae mihi gratiam facite*, for the latter better traces the contour of meaning in the Greek word. Yet in both his *Translation* and his *Paraphrases* he prefers other renderings. His 1516 translation followed with a few exceptions the Vulgate in translating the word by *donare*, while in 1519 he generally changed *donare* to *condonare* where the meaning is clearly "to forgive." Only one concession did he make to his sense of the "best translation" for the word: in 1522 and thereafter he added the words *ob gratiam* to the word *donare* in Acts 25 : 16. In the *Paraphrases* variations of the phrase occasionally appear (e.g., Acts 25 : 11, 16) but here too he prefers *condonare, ignoscere,* or *largiri*.

Though the word receives little theological exposition in either notes or paraphrases, three notes have an interest of their own. First, in the 1516 note on Galatians 3 : 18 he explains the word in terms of the familiar opposition between grace and the Mosaic law. Second, the note on 2 Corinthians 2 : 10 assumes a homiletical cast when Erasmus uses the word as a platform in 1519 and again in 1522 to contrast the *clementia* of Paul (1519) and of Christ (1522) with the harshness of Christians who thunder against their fellows over the smallest matters. Finally, his scholarship on the word in Ephesians 4 : 32 reveals an interesting growth in his reflection, and at the same time a disjunction between his notes

22. It is possible that with the spelling *charos* for *caros* Erasmus is attempting, through a play on the words, to represent both the Latin *gratia* and the Greek χάρις.

and his translation. In 1516 he argued that here the word "was preferably understood as 'to give liberally,' and so to do good to one another," but in 1519 he has changed his mind: the word means "to forgive." The new reading appears in the earliest extant edition of the *Paraphrase on Ephesians* (1520), but in all the editions of his *Translation* Erasmus never changed the rendering *largientes* of 1516.

In the note on χάρισμα (Rom. 1:11, 1516) to which I referred above, Erasmus is reluctant to distinguish between χάρισμα and χάρις. χάρισμα, he says, is derived from χάρις, and the latter is represented by the Latin *beneficium*. Either is appropriate when anything is given *gratis*, or as a benefit. He reiterates the point in a 1519 note on 1 Corinthians 12:4: "χάρισμα is a *donum gratuitum*, for the term comes from *gratia*." Elsewhere the notes do little more than insist on the Latin *donum* as the proper translation of the word, and repeatedly assail the translator of the Vulgate for "sporting his abundant variety." And, indeed, the Vulgate had not been consistent in its rendering. It had translated the word by *gratia* eleven times (two of them in the plural), *donum* thrice, and *donatio* (in the plural) twice, and transliterated it once as *charismata*. From 1516 in his own translation Erasmus never wavered from rendering the word on all occasions as *donum* (singular or plural), and his only note on the word after 1519 was a 1535 reply to critics who attacked him for continually observing the Vulgate's unnecessary *copia*. "I beg you, reader," he says, "what is the point of the [Vulgate's] change here?" Yet in spite of his insistence on *donum* in his *Translation*, he goes far beyond the variety of the Vulgate in his paraphrases. In them the word is represented by *beneficium, beneficentia, munus, gratis conferre, donum, dos, facultas, res, favor dei*, and *pignus immortalitatis*, and in 1 Corinthians 12 it appears as *vis medendi morbis* (verses 9 and 31) and is paraphrased (verse 28) in *qui valent tollendis morbis*. In the *Paraphrases*, as I have said, the word does not appear to be "theologically alive," for Erasmus, except where in the biblical text it is closely associated with χάρις. It is therefore, perhaps, important to note the special case of Romans 6:23, where the phrase τὸ δὲ χάρισμα τοῦ θεοῦ is rendered by *beneficium a propitio patre*. Here the meaning of χάρισμα colors the paraphrase on τοῦ θεοῦ, for Erasmus wishes to draw out the sense of divine clemency conveyed by the word—a characteristic, we have seen, of his understanding of χάρις.

V

In his New Testament scholarship, Erasmus' conception of grace appears to be fairly elastic. He understands the biblical χάρις in the sense of divine aid both in the ministry and in the perseverance of the saints; at times he sees it as the moral and social virtues by which Christ and his followers not only won the favor of God and man, but drew others to a better life; it can even be the reward God pays to his saints for their meritorious life. But the word elicits Erasmus' greatest interest in the sense of the divine goodness which is revealed in the entire scope of sacred history. The qualification is important, for in this sense grace is not merely "generosity" or "kindness," but the divine self-giving offered in the sequence of saving acts by which mankind is redeemed. This understanding of grace was evidently rooted firmly in Erasmus' thought from the early period of his New Testament publications: changing perspectives and interests bring forward new considerations in successive editions of the *Annotations*, but the *Paraphrases* reflect stability in his basic perception of the meaning of the word.

Erasmus' interest in the word goes beyond its mere definition. He recognizes in the concept of grace a problem for Trinitarian theology which he repeatedly undertakes to solve in his *Annotations*. He engages in contemporary debates on other issues, too, though in general his notes on grace show little taste for overt theological conflict,[23] and we may be surprised more by the absence than by the presence of explicit references to scholastic doctrine—in all the notes on χάρις there are only three such references. He seems to have enjoyed more the occasional application—somewhat homiletical in nature—of the significance of χάρις to the life of his contemporary society. It is perhaps this interest which led him in the *Paraphrases* to employ the rich resources of rhetoric available to him, in an effort to evoke for his readers an image of grace which might be effective in their lives.

23. It is not to be denied that in the *Paraphrases* in particular Erasmus *implicitly* addressed issues of contemporary theological debate, including the concept of grace. See John B. Payne, "The Significance of Lutheranizing Changes in Erasmus' Interpretation of Paul's Letters to the Romans and Galatians in his Annotations (1527) and Paraphrases (1532)," in Pierre Fraenkel and Olivier Fatio, eds., *Histoire de l'exégèse au XVIe siècle* (Geneva, 1978), pp. 312–330.

JOSEP M. SOLA-SOLÉ

Las versiones castellanas y catalanas de la "Epistola de gubernatione rei familiaris," atribuída a San Bernardo

A PESAR DE las contribuciones de los últimos años, la literatura didáctica medieval española todavía presenta aspectos y, sobre todo, ostenta textos prácticamente inexplorados. Quizás esto último se deba a que estos textos casi inéditos no son, en la mayoría de los casos, de la embergadura y magnitud de los más tradicionales y conocidos, aunque es harto posible que en su época no fueran menos trascendentes.

Entre los textos apenas abordados están los de las diversas versiones peninsulares (castellanas, catalanas y portuguesas) de la famosa carta latina atribuída a San Bernardo de Clairveaux, dirigida al caballero Raimundo, señor del castillo de San Anmbrosio. Esta famosa carta, publicada, por ejemplo, en la *Patrologia* de Migne, versa sobre "De cura et modo rei familiaris utilius gubernandae," por lo que es comúnmente conocida como "Epistola de gubernatione rei familiaris" o "Epistola de cura et modo rei familiaris" o, finalmente, "Epistola de gubernatione familiae."

Se trata de una epístola breve, llena de consejos eminentemente prácticos de economía doméstica y de cómo hay que comportarse con los amigos, criados, mujeres e hijos. Por su estructura, esta carta formaría parte de lo que se ha convenido en denominar "didáctica pura," es decir, sin fábulas ni "enxemplos," cosa esta última muy propia del enseñar deleitando. Su paralelo más cercano lo veríamos en obras como el *Secreta secretorum*, aunque las pretensiones de nuestra epístola son mucho más modestas y su didactismo de tono más general.

Por contener consejos tan prácticos y elementales y venir como vino respaldada muy pronto por su atribución (hoy ya desmentida) [1] al celebérrimo San Bernardo de Clairveaux, esta epístola gozó de una enorme popularidad en la Europa medieval, existiendo de ella, no solamente numerosas copias manuscritas y ediciones en latín, sino también una considerable cantidad de traducciones a las distintas lenguas vernáculas. Tanto es así que, por ejemplo, en el dominio lingüístico francés documentamos nada menos que seis versiones en prosa y una en verso, repartidas en un total de quince manuscritos. [2]

En catellano, dominio lingüístico menos productivo en la Edad Media, tendríamos, por lo menos, cuatro versiones distintas, aunque debieron de existir, de seguro, algunas más hoy perdidas. En catalán, por otra parte, se nos han conservado dos. Desconocemos, en cambio, si hubieron o no algunas traducciones portuguesas.

De las cuatro versiones castellanas que se nos han conservado, dos de ellas ya han sido publicadas. Una es la que, hacia mediados del siglo XVI, hizo el afamado canonista navarro, Martín de Azpilcueta (1493–1586/87), quien, además de canónigo de Sevilla (según se indica en el preámbulo de la versión), fue profesor de derecho eclesiástico en Tolosa, Cahors y Salamanca, y, a requerimiento de Carlos V, rector de la flamante Universidad de Coimbra. [3] Su renombre llegó a tal punto que se le conocía en su época simplemente por Navarrus o Doctor Navarrus. Su traducción de nuestra epístola, publicada por vez primera en la edición príncceps de la *Summa de doctrina Christiana* (Sevilla, 1545), del también canónigo de Sevilla y célebre heterodoxo Constantino Ponce de la Fuente, fue reeditada, juntamente con la *Summa*, por el cuáquero Luis de Usoz y Río en el volumen XIX de la serie de *Reformistas antiguos españoles* (Madrid, 1863). [4]

1. Véase, por ejemplo, Ferdinand Cavallera, en *Dictionnaire de Spiritualité Ascétique et Mystique* I (Paris, 1937), cols. 1499–1502.

2. Según comunicación por escrito de la Srta. Anna Fraçoise Labie, Secretaria de la "Section Romane," del Institut de Recherche et d'Histoire des Textes, del Centre National de la Recherche Scientifique.

3. Véase a propósito de este autor, J. Bund, *Catalogus auctorum qui scripserunt de theologia morali et practica* (Roma, 1900) y H. Hurter, *Nomenclator literarius theologiae catholicae* (Innsbruck, 1907), III, 934–948. La edición más completa de sus obras es la de Venecia de 1750, en tres volúmenes, sin que contenga, con todo, la traducción que comentamos.

4. Cp., en particular, M. Mz. y Pelayo, *Historia de los heterodoxos españoles*, n. ed., IV (Madrid, 1963), 82–104 y, en particular, 87–88.

Si bien en el preámbulo se atribuye la epístola latina a Silvestre de Bernardo, en el prólogo el Doctor Navarrus proclama que la compuso San Bernardo, quien, con su "prudencia y discreción," decidió escribir sobre "lo principal" que era menester para el regimiento de la casa, considerando con ello lícito nuestro Doctor que pueda incrementarla él mismo con "algunas adiciones y glosillas." Y, en realidad, esta versión representa una notable amplificación del original latino.

Aunque va siguiendo el texto básico, que a veces incluso traduce de una manera totalmente literal, muy a menudo se permite ampliar las frases y darles, como buen moralista que era, un giro mucho más grave y doctrinal: "Los testigos de la gula son pobres, bajos, de raez condición y deponen, no jurados ni llamados, salvo injeridos de su propia voluntad, los cuales son golosina epicúrea, vorazidad inhumana, sed artifiziosa, apetito desordenado." A veces Navarrus se permite incluso hacer gala de sus amplios conocimientos escriturarios: "Nunca vi más vana esperanza, que la del neglijente perezoso: espera que Dios hará sus negozios, estándose él durmiendo con oziosidad i no mira lo que dize la Scriptura: 'yo os mando que estéis aperzebidos, con vijilanzia'." Por otra parte, en ocasiones deja de traducir algunas frases del original, como las referentes a los hijos y su herencia conforme con su categoría: nobles, labradores y comerciantes. En cambio, como buen canónigo, aprovecha cualquier ocasión para censurar a la mujer, de la que, por ejemplo, y en gran parte de su propia cosecha, dice: "La mujer que tienes, si es virtuosa, hónrrala como discreto, que la tal es corona de su marido. Empero, si no es tal i supieres su traizión, este saber es herida incurable. Mitigarse ha tu dolor, cuando supieres que hai otra peor que la tuya, en fama y vida y condizión. E si la tuya es consuelo para otros, más te valiera no ser naszido que casado." No hay duda que el Doctor Navarrus llevó a cabo su versión con evidentes pretensiones literarias y de lucimiento personal. La epístola latina sólo le sirvió de marco. Justifica, por otra parte, su versión, que dedicó a los "mui reverendos señores deán i cabildo de la dicha Sancta Iglesia [de Sevilla]," con las siguientes extrañas razones: "I porque las personas eclesiásticas, espezialmente los que residen en iglesias catedrales i poco en sus casas, tienen más nezesidad d'esta orden i aviso de vivir, me paresziló cosa conveniente enderezarla a vuestras merzedes i a cada uno d'ellos; porque será dechado i enxemplo para las otras personas seglares; i los que quisieren usar d'ella en la parte que les tocare i a su propósito hiziere, bien soi zierto que sentirán descanso en sus personas i provecho en su hazienda."

Mucho más modestas serían, en cambio, las pretensiones literarias de las otra tres versiones castellanas que aún tenemos. Las tres siguen muchísimo más de cerca el texto latino, del que prácticamente no se apartan. Bastante aceptable es la que también ya ha sido publicada. Nos referimos a la contenida en el *Cancionero de Juan Fernández de Ixar*, cancionero que se custodia en la Biblioteca Nacional de Madrid (MS 2882, antiguo M-275) y que fue editado por José M. Azáceta.[5] Aunque la versión es completa, la introducción se limita a los siguientes términos: "Esta es la doctrina e regla, que San Bernaldo da aquellos que quieran tener la mas vtil manera en su beuir, para el sostenimiento de sus faziendas e gouernamiento de sus gentes, a lo qual breuemente respondemos." Le falta, por consiguiente, la mención del personaje al que va destinada la epístola, su relación con el castillo de San Ambrosio y la razón por la que el autor, es decir, el supuesto San Bernardo, la escribiera. Dada la naturaleza del *Cancionero de Ixar*, es casi seguro que nos hallamos ante una versión castellana de la segunda mitad del siglo XV, época en que se ubicaría la mayor parte del material contenido en este cancionero.

Algo superior a esta versión del *Cancionero de Ixar* sería, a nuestro parecer, la que se halla en otro cancionero: el de la Biblioteca Colombina de Sevilla (MS 83-6-10).[6] Por su tipo de letra gótica libraria o cuadrada, este cancionero debería datarse igualmente de la segunda mitad del siglo XV o, a lo sumo, de principios del XVI. Como se trata de un texto inédito y, además, de muy difícil acceso, lo insertamos aquí, tal y como lo copiara para nosotros don Pedro Rubio Merino, Canónigo Archivero de la Santa Iglesia Catedral de Sevilla:[7]

Epistola de Sant Bernaldo, la qual enbia a Reymundo Pardo [. . .] en [. . .]l grasçioso e bien aventurado cavallero Reymundo, señor del castillo Ambrosio.— Bernaldo, venido a grand vejez, salud.— Pedistenos que te enviasemos el modo e manera mas aprovechoso para saber todas las cosas que pertenesçen al regimiento de tu casa e de tu conpañia.— A lo qual te respondo:— Que maguer asy sea quel estado e la fin de todas las cosas

5. Véase José M. Azáceta, *Cancionero de Juan Fernández de Ixar*, 2 vols. (Madrid, 1956). La carta se halla en el vol. II, pp. 681–685.

6. Sobre este *cancionero*, cp. H. R. Lang, "Communications from Spanish Cancioneros," en *Transactions of the Connecticut Academy of Arts and Sciences* 15 (1909), 87–105.

7. Nos permitimos agradecer aquí a don Pedro Rubio Merino, el habernos procurado este texto. No estamos completamente seguros, sin embargo, que en algunos casos no tengamos que leer -z- en lugar de -s-. Según A. Paz y Melia, *Cancionero de Gómez Manrique* I (Madrid, 1885), p. xxxviii, parece que habría copia en la Biblioteca Nacional de Madrid, mandada hacer por el P. Burriel.

mundanales travajen e sean en ventura, nin por tanto el modo e la regla del vevir non deve ser dexado sin cura.— Et por ende ave (?) e para mientes, que sy en tu casa las recebtas e las despensas non fueren yguales, quando te non catares, caeras.— Et puedes destroyr el tu estado e non podras poner a ello remedio.— Et por ende tu renta syenpre sea mayor que tu gasto.— En el estado del ome negligente, que non para mientes por su fasienda, non es al, syno casa para caer.— ¿Que cosa es negligencia de governar una cosa?:— es fuego fuerte açendido, que non cesa de la destruyir.— Otra (?) e para bien mientes en la diligençia de aquellos que son tus servidores, como son diligentes.— Menos vergüença es aquel que va cayendo en pobresa faser abstinençia en despender, e de las sus cosas ser escaso, que caer de todo en todo en pobresa.— Grand prudençia e sabiduria es parar mientes a menudo e ver aquellas cosas que tuyas son, en que modo e en que manera estan.— Consydera de las tus animalias el su comer e beber, porque non lo pueden nin saber pedir.— Las bodas de grand costa traen danno syn honrra.— La despensa fecha por la cavallerria es cosa de grand honrra.— Honrra da e rrasonable cosa es entre los omes entendidos la despensa, que es fecha por ayuda de los amigos.— Segund nos ensenan los letrados e sabidores[8] perdida [es] la despensa que se fase en ayudar a los prodigos e desgastadores.— Sy quisyeres bien mantener tu casa e tu estado [sacaras tu compañia] de vianda gruesa.— Aquel q[ue] es goloso, puesto en tal costunbre qu[e] o no[n p]uede dexar synon por muerte aborresçible.— La golosyna [. . .] e [. . .]lig[. . .] su cuer[po].— La golosyna del ome deligente [. . .] o sus cosas a todas las gentes [. . .].— Los dias horrados de las fiestas da de comer a tu compañia [abondante]mente e non manjares delicados.— La garganta con la bolsa faras pelear e cuyda bien de qual dellas has de ser abogado, e qual e qual (sic) sentençia entre amas has de dar.— La garganta prueba por sus afecciones e malos deseos e testimonios non jurados e la bolsa prueva claramente porque ella e el arca muy toste son vasias.— Contra la garganta non puedes dar buena sentençia, quando el avariçia fase llegar a la bolsa mas de lo que cunple.— Por çierto, el avariçia entre la garganta y la bolsa deve judgar justamente.— ¿Que cosa es avaricia?: con vilesa ser omeçida de sy mesmo.— ¿Que cosa es avaricia?: tener riquesa biviendo syenpre en pobresa.— Derechamente bive el escaso avariento reteniendo en sy las riquesas, guardandolas non sabiendo para quien.— Mejor es las riquesas para los otros ser guardadas e escondidas, que por el [escaso] avariento ser del todo perdidas.— Sy tu has abundançia de trigo non ames carestia, porque aquel que carestia ama, cobdiçia ser omeçida de los pobres e de los menguados.— Vende el tu trigo quando valiere mucho, mas non quando por el pobre non puede ser conprado.— A los vesinos e a los amigos vende

8. Esta frase hasta aquí es un añadido del traductor.

mas rahes tu trigo, porque non syenbre por cuchillo, mas muchas veses con benefiçio se vençe el enemigo.— ¿Sabes que tienes enemigo?: non ayas conversaçion con ome que non conosçes.— Nunca çeses de pensar los caminos de tu enemigo, que sabes que te quiere mal.— La franquesa de tu enemigo non entiendas que es pas, mas tregua que se fas non sabes por quanto tienpo.— Sy te seguras, non catas de tu enemigo, tu te pones en peligro de muerte.— En los servidores de quien ovieres sospecha, demandales synplemente lo que fasen e non les declares que lo entiendes.— Despues que de la tu propia muger supieres que te fase pecado e maldad, jamas por ningund fisico puedes ser curado.— El rencor e dolor que ovieres de la tal muger, entonçes sera amansado quando oyeres que las mugeres de los otros son culpadas deste pecado.— La muger mala por mejor la castigaras con rriso, que non con vara.— La muger vieja e puta, sy la ley lo consyntiese, viva meresçe ser soterrada.— La vestidura presçiosa e rrica es señal de poco seso.— La vestidura muy aparente, muy ayna pare enojo.— Estudia por plaser en bondades e me[. . .] e non cures de plaser por vestiduras fermosas.— La mujer que vestiduras tiene y otras demanda, señal es que tiene poca firmesa en su coraçon.— De los amigos ten por mas fiel el que de lo suyo te da, que aquel que por palabra se te ofresce syn obra.— De amigos de palabras e de viento mucho es la copia sin tiento.— Por ende, te digo e consejo que non judgas por amigo al que te alaba en tu presençia.— Sy dieres consejo al tu amigo en fecho de su casa, consejandole, dile lo que te paresce, mas non le digas que ansy lo faga, porque de la fin del consejo nin lo es ome mas ayna reprehendido, que de la fin del tu buen consejo es presçiado e loado.— Para mientes que te non vesyten juglares, ca non biven synon por engannos e maliçias.— Ome que tiene juglares abra çedo muger cuyo nonbre es pobresa, mas quien seria su fijo escarnio escarnio (sic) e tristesa plasente.— Las palabras del burlador juglar finge que la non oyes e que otra cosa cuydas.— El que rihe e ha plaser de las palabras del juglar, ya le dio prenda e non se puede del escusar.— Los juglares que mal digan, vituperian a alguno en sus desires, meresçedores son de muerte.— El juglar que dise vituperios e mal de quien non esta presente, consigo trae alma de omeçida.— Los estormentos del juglar burlador nunca pluguieron a Dios.— El servidor del altivo coraçon, lançalo de ti como tu enemigo mortal.— Lança de ti otrosy el syrviente que con sus falagos te falaga suave e blandamente.— Sey çierto que el serviente que en tu presençia te loa, que en su coraçon piensa que te ha de engannar.— Al sirviente que ha vergüença de ligera cosa, amalo conmo a tu fijo, e tomaras por tu conpannero.— Sy quieres hedificar casa non te mueva voluntad, mas pura nescesidad, ca la cobdiçia de edidicar (?), edificando no se quita, mas antes se acresçienta.— La grande e desordenada cobdiçia de edificar acarrea que los edifiçios acabados se vendan en breve tienpo.— La torre conplida, el arca vaçia de su tesoro fase al ome artero e sabidor, mas avisose tarde.— Guardate que non vendas parte de tu heredad a ome mas poderoso que tu, antes la vende a menor por menos presçio.— El techo puedes bien vender aquel que mas te diere.— Mejor es padesçer hanbre, que vender el patrimonio que te quedo de tu padre; enpero, mejor es vender el techo que sojudgarte a usuras.— ¿Que cosa es usura?: ponçona del patrimonio con destruyçion, porque es ladron leal que furta syn temor.— Quando conprares alguna cosa por aver, compra de persona menos poderosa que tu.— Paçientemente sostiene el tu pequenno conpannero, e no te conpañes con el mas fuerte que tu, que sea despues tu heredero.— Aquel que en la bundancia de demasiados vinos es sabio e tenplado, tal ome conmo este es Dios eternal: entre todos deve ser honrrado.— La beudes no fase cosa mas derecha synon quando ome cae e se echa en el lodo.— Sy te sintieres del vino enbargado, fuye e demanda el sueño, e non fables con otros, mas echate a dormir; e aquel que beudo esta e por palabra se escusa, abiertamente acusa su beudes.— Non esta bien a ome mançebo conosçer de muchos vinos qual dellos es mejor.— Fuye del fysico, maguer sea sabidor, si tu sabes cierto que es beudo perdido.— Guardate del fysico que en ti quiere provar primeramente conmo los otros semejantes enfermedades ha de curar.— Blanchetes e xorginos dexalos para las rreyas e para los clerigos, mas los canes guardadores son mas provechosos.— Los canes de caçadores te faran mas honrra que provecho.— ¿Tienes fijo heredero de tus bienes?: non le fagas tu despensero.— Mas diras, si la fortuna te contraria, ¿que aprovecha la regla e la dotrina de bevir?— Para mientes que yo vi sandios que non curavan de las cosas continentes conmo ome de mal recabdo, mas desian e creyan que todo su estado era so poder de fortuna.— Pocas veses aconpannaras al ynfortunado con diligençia e buen cuydado; mas claramente separaras e partiras la peresa del tu fortuno mal aventurado.— El perezoso tiene esperança que Dios le ha de ayudar, el qual en este mundo nos mando que biviesemos por nuestro trabajo.— Vela e piensa con diligençia que lo mas humanamente que podieres espiendas tu aver.— La vejez se allega e non sabes quanto has de bevir: yo te consejo que tu mandes primeramente pagar a tus servidores.— Non encomiendes tu alma a aquellos que te aman, mas encomiendala a aquellos que aman sus almas.— Fas tu testamento antes que seas enfermo, ca muchas veçes es el ome fecho syervo de la enfermedad, e el syervo non puede faser testamento segund Dios e verdad.— Pues, fas tu testamento antes que seas fecho syervo de la enfermedad.— De los fijos: para mientes que sy su padre muere, cada uno levara su parte.— Los fijos, sy son pobres, mejor es su esparsimiento que partir la heredad e bevir en pobresa.— Sy trabajadores fueren, fagan lo que quysieren; sy mercadores, son mejores la partiçion que la heredad ser comun, porque la desaventura non venga en danno de todos.— ¿La madre, por ventura quiere ser casada otra vez con ome mançebo?: fas muy grand sandes, porque ella es ya vieja e el non casa con ella salvo por los sus dineros.— E el aver despen-dido, bevera el caliz de dolor e de amargura con aquel que deseo.

Aunque esta traducción también es bastante literal, en algunas ocasiones se aparta un tanto del texto latino, manifestando cierta tendencia a la amplificación. Tanto es así que, por ejemplo, una frase como: "Gran prudencia e sabiduria es parar mientes a menudo a ver aquellas cosas que tuyas son, en que modo e en que manera estan," corresponde a un original latino: "Saepius revidere quae tua sunt, quomodo sint, magna prudentia est." Además, por lo general, las frases exhiben una construc-ción más romance, invirtiendo a veces incluso sus distintas partes. Un ejemplo de ello lo tendríamos en una frase como: "Sy quieres hedificar casa, non te mueva voluntad, mas pura necesidat," que traduce: "Si vis aedificare, judicat te necessitas, non voluntas."

Con todo, muchísimo mas literal que las otras tres versiones que hemos considerado es la igualmente inédita que se halla en el MS 9428 de la Biblioteca Nacional de Madrid y que, por el tipo de letra, de-beríamos situar también en la misma época que los otros dos últimos textos considerados. Esta versión reza:

Carta de San Bernaldo enbiada a vn noble cauallero de cura e agora de cosa de familia de gouernar o regir.— Gracioso e bie[n] aue[n]turado cauallero Raymu[n]do sen[n]or del castillo de Ambrosio, Bernardo, de los viejos (?) dado, salud.— Ser ensen[n]ado dema[n]daste de nos de la cura[9] e agora de la cosa familiar mas p[ro]uechoso de gouernar.— En q[ue] man[er]a el padre de las co[n]pan[n]as se asi deua de au[er].— A lo q[ua]l a ti respo[n]demos q[ue] co[n]uiene de las cosas mu[n]danas estado e salimie[n]to (?)[10] de los negocios so la fortuna trabaje[n] no[n] en v[er]dat es de dexar la rregla del beuir.— Pues q[ue] assi es, oye e p[ar]a mie[n]tes q[ue] si en la tu casa el tomamie[n]to e el rretornami[ento] so[n] eguales acaesçimie[n]to en co[n]-trario podra destruir el estado della.— La casa q[ue] se q[ui]ere caer, estado es de onbre neglige[n]te.— ¿Que es la neglige[n]çia del gouerna[n]te la casa?: fuego en la casa muy valie[n]te e ace[n]dido.— Mucho para mie[n]tes dilige[n]teme[n]te la dilige[n]çia de aq[ue]llos q[ue] las tus cosas aministra[n].— Al trabaja[n]te e al deleznable o caydo de las rriq[ue]zas: menos cosa es v[er]go[n]çosa abstenerse q[ue] caer.— Muchas vezes reueer aq[ue]llas cosas q[ue] son suyas e com[m]o son, gra[n] sabidoria es.— Pie[n]sa en v[er]dat del ma[n]jar e del beuer de las animalias tuyas, por-

9. *De la cura* es un añadido supralinear de la misma mano.
10. No parece que podamos leer *saluamiento*.

q[ue] ha[n] fanbre e no[n] lo piden.— Las bodas mucho fartas da[n]pno sin honor trahen.— Abastado por caualleria mucho es ho[n]rrado.— Abastado p[ar]a ayudar a los amigos razonable cosa es.— Abastado p[ar]a los me[n]-guados desgastados desgastadis (sic) es.— A la co[n]pan[n]a, de gruesso e no[n] delicado ma[n]jar los fartaras.— Aquel q[ue] es goloso fecho, mala bez en ot[ra] man[er]a sino[n] la muerte las costu[n]bres mudara.— La golosina de la uil p[er]sona e neglige[n]te podedu[n]bre es.— La golosina del solicita[n]te e dilige[n]te solaz es.— En los dias de las pascuas abo[n]-dosame[n]te e no[n] delicada farta la co[n]pan[n]ia.— Faz a la gula litigar co[n] la bolsa et esq[ui]uate de aquel de q[ui]en estas abogado, o entre la gula e la bolsa q[ua]l sen[tenci]a (?) traheras.— En v[er]dat la gula p[ru]eua por afliçiones e testigos no[n] jurados.— La bolsa clarame[n]te p[ru]eua el arca e el çillero vazios o en breue t[ien]po vaziaderos.— Ento[n]çes mal juzgas co[n]tra la gula, q[ua]ndo la auariçia ata la bolsa.— Nu[n]qua (?), en ni[n]gu[n] t[ien]po, derechame[n]te entre la gula e la bolsa la auariçia juzgara.— ¿Que cosa es auariçia?: de si matadora.— ¿Que cosa es auaricia?: temer la probreza, sienp[re] en pobredat uiuiendo.— Derechame[n]te uiue el auarie[n]to no[n] p[er]diendo de sus rriq[ue]zas, mas a otros reguar-da[n]do.— Mejor cosa es en v[er]dat guardar a los otros q[ue] p[er]derse en sy.— Si q[ui]eres ser bla[n]do [11] no[n] ames la careza, porq[ue] el ama[n]te la careza cobdia (sic) ser de los pobres matador.— Vende bla[n]dame[n]te [12] dimientra q[ue] asaz vale, no[n] q[ua]ndo por el pobre mercar no[n] se puede.— A los vezinos por menor p[re]çio vende e avn a los enemigos, porq[ue] no[n] sie[n]p[re] por cochillo, mas muchas vezes por seruicio es vençido el enemigo.— Soberuia co[n]tra el vezino: (d)an[n]o [13] es es-pera[n]te co[n]trario co[n] la saeta.— ¿Has enemigo?: no[n] ayas co[n]uer-saçio[n] co[n] los q[ue] no[n] sabe[n].— Sienp[re] piensa las careras del enemigo.— El caymi[ento] del enemigo no[n] es lugar de paz o en lugar de paz, mas tregua al t[ien]po.— Si te seguras no pe[n]sar el enemigo q[ue] tu pie[n]sas, a peligro te expones.— De los tus fechos sospechosos, q[ue] cosa faga[n] ynora[n]cia e no sçie[n]çia busques.— Despues q[ue] sopieres el dan[n]o de la mala mujer de ni[n]gun fisico seras curado.— El dolor de la mala mujer, ento[n]çes seras ama[n]sado q[ua]ndo oyeres de las otras mu-jeres.— El coraço[n] alto e noble no busca de las obras de la mujer.— La mala mujer, mas co[n] rriso q[ue] co[n] palo la castigaras.— La fenbra uieja e mala mujer, si la ley lo p[er]mitiese, biua era de enterrar.— De las uestiduras: nota q[ue] la uestidura mucho abastada prouaçio[n] es de poco seso.— La vestidura mucho aparecie[n]te es enojo a los vezinos.— Studia

11. Traduce mal. En el texto latino hay BLADO, "trigo."
12. Tambien aquí, como en el caso de la nota anterior, traduce mal.
13. MS: *ban[n]o*.

por bondat a plazer, no[n] por uestidura.— La peticio[n] de la mujer
tenie[n]te vestiduras e de la q[ue]rie[n]te vestiduras no[n] demuestra her-
ma[n]dat.— De los amigos: ten a aq[ue]l q[ue] es mas amigo e despues
aq[ue]l q[ue] las sus cosas dio, mas al q[ue] a si mesmo ofresce.— De
palabras gra[n]des es [14] abasta[n]ça de amigos.— No[n] tengas por amigo a
aq[ue]l q[ue] tu p[re]sente te alaba.— Si aco[n]sejas al tu amigo, no[n]
q[ui]eras aplazer a el, mas a la rrazo[n].— Di al tu amigo en aco[n]seja[n]-
dole asi: a mi me p[ar]esçe, no entreta[n]jado (sic) assi es de fazer, porq[ue]
del mal co[n]sejo se sigue rredarguymi[ento], q[ue] del bie[n] alaba[n]ça.— Oy q[ue] te visita[n] los jublares: p[ar]a mie[n]tes q[ue] se sigue
del ente[n]dimie[n]to del jublar; ayn[a] la mujer avra al q[ua]l el no[n]bre
s[er]a pobreza; mas ¿q[ui]en s[er]a el fijo del?: el escarneçimie[n]to.—
¿Aplaze[n]te a ti las palabras del jublar?: faz q[ue] las oyes e pie[n]sa ot[ra]
cosa.— El rriye[n]te e el goza[n]te de las palabras del jublar ya p[re]nda a el
dio.— Los joglares ma[n]da[n]tes, dignos so[n] del colgami[ento].— ¿Que
cosa es jublar?: malma[n]dante, el anima traye[n]tese assi omicida-
me[n]te.— Los estrume[n]tos del jublar a Dios no[n] aplaziero[n].— Oye
de los s[er]uidores: el sieruo de altiuo coraço[n], esq[ui]uale assi com[m]o a
enemigo por venir.— Al sieruo en las sus costu[n]bres bla[n]do ala[n]-
çale.— Al seruidor vezino alaba[n]te a ti resistele; en algu[n] tie[n]po te
pie[n]sa auer engan[n]ado.— Al sieruo de ligero vergo[n]çoso amale assi
com[m]o a fijo.— Si q[ui]eres fazer casa, fazlo por neçessidat, mas no[n]
por volu[n]tad.— La cobdia (sic) de hedificar, hedifica[n]do no[n] se
q[ui]ta.— La muy gra[n]de e desordenada cobdicia de hedificar pare, e
espera de los hedificios vendimie[n]to.— La torre co[n]plida e el arca vazia
faze[n] al ho[n]bre ser mucho sabio.— ¿Quieres en algu[n] t[ien]po
uender?: guardate, no[n] ve[n]das parte de heredat al mas pote[n]te, mas
mas ayna por menor p[re]çio al menor q[ue] tu; mas en uerdat todo lo vende
al q[ue] mas te diere.— Mejor es padesçer g[ra]ue fanbre q[ue] vender lo
q[ue] ha heredado; mas mejor es venderlo q[ue] a l(o)s [15] vsureros some-
terse.— ¿Que cosa es vsura?: venino del pat[ri]monio, porq[ue] es legable
ladro[n] p[re]dica[n]te aq[ue]llo q[ue] entiende.— Ni[n]guna cosa no[n]
merques en co[n]pania del mas pote[n]te.— Al peq[ue]no co[n]pan[er]o
sufrele paçie[n]teme[n]te, porq[ue] no[n] te de otro mas fuerte.— ¿Bus-
caste del vso del vino?, el q[ua]l en la diu[er]sidat e en la habasta[n]ça
mesurado es el terrenal vino.— La enbriaguez ni[n]guna cosa derechame[n]te faze sino q[ua]ndo caye en el lodo.— ¿Sie[n]tes el vino?: fuye la
co[n]pan[n]ia; busca el sueno mas q[ue] la fabla.—Aquel q[ue] se excusa de
palabras esta[n]do enbriago, la su enbriaguez clarame[n]te la acusa.— Mal

14. MS: *grande es es*.
15. MS: *las* claramente.

se asie[n]ta en el ma[n]çebo conosçer el vino.— Fuye el fisigo enbriago.— Guardate del fisigo q[ue]rie[n]te en ti ser examinado o p[ro]uado en q[ue] man[er]a a los otros de semeja[n]te enfermedat curara.— Los perrillos chiq[ui]llos, dexalos a los cl[er]igos e a las rreynas.— Los perros q[ue] son guardas p[ro]uechosos so[n].— Los canes p[ar]a caçar mas cuesta[n] q[ue] trahe[n].— ¿Tienes fijo despe[n]sero de los tus bienes?: no[n] le establescas; si no tu diras: si l(a)[16] fortuna se trastorna, ¿q[ue] ap[ro]uecha la dotrina de beuir?— Oye q[ue] de aq[ue]sto ui locos dexa[n]tes las cosas co[n]tenie[n]tes e en v[er]dat escusantes se so la fortuna; mas guarda[n]te la dotrina pocas uezes acusara a la fortun[a].— En v[er]dat pocas vezes la dilige[n]çia co[n] el infortunado aconpanaras; mas pocas vezes el enfortunado de la p[er]eza le apartaras.— Spera el p[er]ezoso ser socorrido de Dios, el q[ua]l en este mu[n]do le ma[n]do velar.— Pues q[ue] assi es, uela e la ligereza de gastar co[n] la graueza de gastar de cabo lo pie[n]sa.—¿Allegase la uejez?: aco[n]sejote q[ue] a Dios mas q[ue] a tu fijo te acomiendes.— ¿Dispones las cosas allegadas?: aco[n]sejote q[ue] lo p[ri]m[er]o a los seruidores ma[n]des pagar.— A los q[ue] ama[n] la tu p[er]sona no[n] les acomie[n]des la tu a[n]i[m]a.— Encomie[n]da la tu anima a los q[ue] ama[n] la suya.— Disponer deues ant[e] de la enfermedat; muchas vezes aquel q[ue] fecho sieruo de la enfermedat, e el sieruo della testame[n]to no[n] puede fazer.— Pues q[ue] assi es, q[ua]ndo estas libre faz testame[n]to, ant[e] q[ue] seas fecho sieruo.— Abastate a ti lo q[ue] de ti es dicho.— Oye de los fijos: muerto el padre busca[n] diuisio[n].— Los fijos, si son nobles, mejor es muchas vezes dellos por el mu[n]do derramamie[n]to mas q[ue] diuisio[n] de la heredat.— Si son trabaja[n]tes faze[n] lo q[ue] q[ui]ere[n].— En uerdat, muchas vezes es de la generacio[n] dellos desatamie[n]to de aq[ue]]sta manera la diuisio[n] de la heredat.— Si son mercadores, de todo en todo es diuisio[n] dellos mas q[ue] comunicacio[n][17] ni[n] del vno enfortunado a los otros sea rreputado.— ¿La madre por aue[n]tura tornarse a casar q[ui]ere?: locamente lo faze, mas porq[ue] los sus pecados llore; por la volu[n]tad, ella vieja, ma[n]çebo le toma.

A pesar de terminar de una manera aparentemente abrupta, se trata de una versión íntegra. Resalta en ella su expresión arcaica y, sobre todo, su total y servil apego al latín del original, del que jamás se aparta, traduciendo incluso sus frecuentes construcciones participiales con sintagmas paralelos en castellano. Así, por ejemplo: "¿Que es la negligencia del gouernante la casa?," traduce: "Quid est negligentia gubernantis domum?"

16. MS: *lo* claramente.
17. MS: *cominicatio{n}* claramente.

De una rápida comparación de los tres textos castellanos del siglo XV, podría deducirse que hay cierta relación entre la versión del *Cancionero de Ixar* y la del MS 9428 de la Biblioteca Nacional. Esta relación, no obstante, proviene de que ambas traducciones están mucho más cerca del original, que, por ejemplo, la del Cancionero de la Colombina de Sevilla. Ello puede verse, en particular, en el manejo de la frase castellana, que, tanto en la versión de *Ixar* como en la de la BN 9428, tienden a poner, como en latín, el verbo al final, de manera que tenemos una ratio aproximada en los tres textos de 1.9/1.0/.2.1, ofreciendo el texto de la Biblioteca Colombina un coeficiente notablemente más bajo (1.0) que los otros dos, y el de la BN 82.18 el más elevado (2.1).

Como ya hemos señalado, no fueron estas cuatro versiones las únicas que se hicieran en castellano. Según R. Floranes, en el *Cancionero de Fernán Martínez de Burgos*, hoy perdido, se hubiera hallado una *Composición del bienaventurado S. Bernardo* sobre el "gobernamiento de la casa," dirigida al "gracioso e bienaventurado caballero Raymundo señor de Castro-Ambrosio," dividida en 22 capítulos y sin nombre del traductor, que, siguiendo a nuestro crítico, muy bien pudo haber sido el mismo Fernán Martínez de Burgos, colector del cancionero.[18]

Por demás interesante es lo que nos consigna el mismo R. Floranes en otra ocasión:

Entre nuestros españoles fue muy célebre esta carta desde que la tradujo en castellano cierto anónimo del reinado de Juan II, dividiéndola en capítulos hasta el número 22. El la tituló *Composición del Bienaventurado San Bernardo*. Tenémosla en un manuscrito de aquel tiempo. No sabemos si se ha impreso como están en la versión, pues se hallan alegadas sentencias en ella por Fernán Perez de Guzmán, en la crónica de aquel rey, año 1434, cap. 251, que es el 11 de la edición de Montfort, por nuestro Doctor Toledo en unas y otras glosas, como hemos dicho, y con mayor frecuencia por Mosén Diego de Valera en su tractado *De providencia contra fortuna*, dedicado a Juan Pacheco, marqués de Villena.

Por lo que este crítico nos señala de nuevo en cuanto a la división del texto en 22 capítulos, es casi seguro que continúa refiriéndose al ya mencionado texto del *Cancionero de Fernán Martínez*. Con todo, serían ya

18. Cp. también Marqués de Mondéjar y D. Francisco Cerda y Rico, *Memorias históricas de la vida y acciones del rey D. Alonso el Noble, octavo de su nombre* (Madrid, 1783), cxxxvii–cxxxviii.

cinco, por lo menos, las versiones que de nuestra popular epístola latina se llevarían a cabo en castellano en el transcurso de los siglos XV y XVI.

En cuanto al catalán, ya ha quedado consignado que documentamos, por lo menos, dos versiones distintas. Una de ellas sólo se nos ha conservado en una edición bastante tardía, que no conlleva ni fecha ni lugar de impresión, por lo que su datación se nos hace imposible de precisar.[19] Dice el preludio: "Del regiment e cura de la casa. Epistola de Sant Bernat, feta al cavaller Ramon de Castell-Ambros. Treta de un Ms. del quinzen segle." El texto de esta edición se halla dividido por temas, cada uno con su correspondiente epígrafe: "De la casa"; "De menjar e beure"; "De auaricia"; "De enemichs"; "De les fembres"; "De les vestidures"; "Dels amichs"; "Dels servidors"; "De edificar casa"; "De embriaguesa" y, finalmente, "De heretament."

Se trata de una versión extremadamente literal, con, además y de acuerdo con el texto original, gran cantidad de frases terminadas en verbo. Con todo, la traducción es bastante correcta, demostrando poseer el que la hizo un buen dominio del romance. Lo mismo podríamos decir, en términos generales, de la otra versión catalana, que, todavía inédita, se halla en el MS 921 (antiguo L. 2) de la Biblioteca Nacional de Madrid. Ahora bien, a pesar de que la lengua de esta segunda versión es bastante aceptable, se nos antoja menos fluida que en la anterior. Su texto completo es:

Translat de vna letra p[er] Monsenyer Sent B[er]n[a]t tramesa a'n Ramo[n] de Castell Ambros, caualler de Lombardia, sobre lo regiment de sa casa e d[e] la cosa familiar, la qual letra es estada trelladada de lati en romanç.—

Al gracios e benaue[n]turat cauall[e]r en Ramo[n], senyor de Castell Ambros.— Yo B[er]n[a]t deduit (?) en vellea, saluts.— Demanat-nos has d[e] la man[er]a e cura de regir la cosa[20] familiar; ço es, en qual manera hom deu o[r]dinar sa casa e ses co[n]panyes e ço d[e]l seu.— A la qual cosa te responch que jatsesia que'l stament de totes les coses mu[n]danals, lo come[n]came[n]t e la fi de totes les fahenes esta sots fortuna; empero la regla de viure no deu e[ss]er lexada.— Donchs ojes e enten que si en la tua casa les rendes que as e les mesions que fas son eguals, algun cas descuydat te pora

---

19. Se trata de una edición extremadamente rara. Hemos podido consultar el ejemplar que se guarda en la Biblioteca Universitaria de la Universidad de Wisconsin. En una adicion posterior se señala 1632. ¿Se trataría de la fecha? Es harto problemático.

20. Esta falsa lectura, que probablemente venía de un manuscrito más antiguo, queda asegurada por el hecho de que le seguía *publicha*, luego barrado.

esdeue[n]ir qui't destruira tot qua[n]t as e mi[n]uara ton stament.— Sapies
que'l stame[n]t d[e] l'hom negligent es axi co[m] casa mal ferma, la q[ua]l
leug[er]ame[n]t pot caure e perir; car la ignora[n]çia d[e] l'hom negligent,
lo q[ua]l deu gou[er]nar casa, no es sino foch ençes e poderos q[ue] crema la
casa.— Deycha diligentme[n]t e fes que aq[ue]lls qui ço d[e]l teu tene[n] e
administren haie[n] gran diligencia e vull[e]s en tot cas saber lur uolentat,
entenime[n]t e p[ro]posit q[ui]'n l'an.— Aquell qui p[er] masa despendre
comença a ami[n]uar sos bens, pero no'ls ha encara tots alienats ne despeses,
molt menor v[er]gonya e dan li es minuar e abstenir-se de tant despendre
que no d[e]l tot venir a pobrea.— Souen veure les tues coses com son ne com
estan, gran sauiea es.— Aies cura de regonexer soue[n] les besties e altres
animals que hom te en casa p[er] ço car com han fam e set non saben
demanar.— Gran messio fer en noces dan, sens honor porten.— Messio
p[er] fer caualleries honorable cosa es.— Messio fer p[er] ajudar a sos
pare[n]ts e amichs just e rahonable es.— Messio fer p[er] aydar a homens
deguastadors gran mal e p[er]dicio es.— Nodreny tes co[n]panyes, e ta casa
da a menjar viandes grosses e no delicades, car aquell qui es mal nodrit de
gola apenes mudara son mal costum tro a la mort.— Glotonia de hom de
poch estame[n]t, que sie negligent e mal curos, gran destruccio e p[er]di-
me[n]t es.— Glotonia de hom curos, diligent e solaçer confort e solaç es.—
En los dies d[e] les festes grans e d[e] les paschues qui vene[n] en l'a[n]y
dona a menjar a tes co[n]pa[n]yes abunda[n]tme[n]t e co[n]plida, mas no
delicada.— Guarda't que faces en manera que aja contrast e plet[21] entre la
gola e bossa, e guarda de qual seras aduocat ne q[ui]na sentencia daras.—
Car la gola proua son fet ab testimo[n]is no jurats, ço es, ab afleccio[n]s e ab
desigs; e la bossa p[ro]ua ab testimo[n]is ma[n]ifests, co es, ab los graners e
ab los cellers, que ja son buydats o fort poch hi roman p[er] buydar.—
Sapies que la donchs jutjaras mal contra la gola, com la auaricia liga la bossa
axi que null te[m]ps jutjara dretame[n]t auaricia ent[re] la boca e la gola.—
¿Quina cosa es auaricia?: auaricia es omeyer de si matex e aq[ue]ll qui es
auar.— Mes encara: auaricia es auer paor de pobrea.— E sapies que tots
te[m]ps l'om auar viu en pobrea, p[er] ço car no despen l[e]s riquees en si
matex, ne se'n s[er]uex, ans les res[er]ua e les estoja a obs d'altres.- Pero mes
ual estojar e seruar les riquees p[er] als altres que despendre-les follame[n]t,
ne en si matex deguastar aq[ue]lles.— Si has molt blat, no desigs carestia;
car aq[ue]ll qui desiga carestia cobeja e[ss]er omeyer d[e]ls pobres.— Ven ton
blat mentre que'n has couine[n]t for; no l'esperes a uendre en temps que valla
tans dines q[ue] lo pobre no'l puxa co[n]prar.— Ven ton blat a tos vehins p[er]
menor preu que als altres, hoc encara a tos enemichs, car los enemichs no
solame[n]t los venç hom ab armes, mas a ueguades ab s[er]uis.— Sup[er]bia

---

21. *o plet*, supralinear, pero de la misma mano.

auer cont[ra] ton vehi es axi com abayn qui esp[er]a tro ab sageta.— Si as
enemichs no vulles molt co[n]tinuar ne pe(r)seuerar ab pe(r)sones[22] que no
conegues.— Pensa e cogita en les vies de ton enemich; e si ton enemich es
flach, no't penses que la sua flaguea te sia pau, mas solame[n]t te pensa que
es treua a te[m]ps.— Si tu te asegures que no cogites en les fahenes de ton
enemich e en les sues vies, certes te dich que a gran perill te posses.— De les
fembres tues que tens p[er] sospitoses, vulles abans ignorar que saber ço que
fan, car depuys que auras sabut lo peccat de ta mala muler no sera metge al
mon que te'n pusca curar ne guarir en ne[n]guna manera.— De la dolor que
auras
de ta mull[e]r auras algun remey qua[n]t sabras sembla[n]t mal d[e] les
mullers d[e]ls altres, car cor noble ne alt no s'entramet d[e] les obres d[e] les
fembres.— Mala muller ans la castiguaras ab rialles que no ab ferides.—
Ffembra vella e auol de son cors, si la ley o soferia, viua la deuria hom
soterrar.— De uestidures te dich q[ue] vestidura de gran cost e de gran
despesa es p[ro]ua manifesta de poch seyn.— E uestidura massa aparent tost
engenra fastig e enug als vehins.— Estudia't de plaure a les gents p[er]
bonea e no p[er] vestidura.— Ffembra que ha uestidures e tots dies demana
uestidures, sapies p[er] cert que no ha fermetat de seyn.— Dels amichs rete
aq[ue]ll q[ue] major amor te portara, e majorme[n]t ama aq[ue]ll qui de ço
d[e]l seu t'ebandona, molt mes q[ue] aq[ue]ll qui's p[ro]fit a tu de p[ar]aula,
car sapies q[ue] de amichs de p[ar]aula molts (n)e[23] son.— E p[er] res no
tingues p[er] amich aq[ue]ll qui, tu p[re]sent, te loa.— Si conselles a ton
amich vull[e]s-li dir coses que ans placien a la raho que a ell, e q[ua]nt li
daras lo consell digues-li axi: mes sembla[n]t que dejats fer, e yo axi ho faria;
no pas dir-li: fets axi, mana[n]t-li-ho delliberadame[n]t.— Car sapies que
mes ueguades ha hom rep[re]nsio d[e]l consell que ha dat hom, qua[n]t ue
al cont[ra]ri, q[ue] no ha hom laor d[e]l consell que hom ha dat e hix a tot
be.— Hoyt he dir que juglas te vesiten: e dich-te que hom qui en juglas
enten, aura tost muller la qual aura nom pobre, d[e] la qual auras vn fill
q[ue] aura nom escarn.— E si les p[ar]aules d[e]ls juglas te plaen, fes
sembla[n]t que no les ojes e q[ue] penses en altra cosa, car, si tu te alegres de
l[e]s lurs p[ar]aules, pots te tenir p[er] dit que'ls has donada penyora.—
Sapies que juglas fan e cuyte[n] molts mals asp[er]eras, e acostan(t)-se[24] a
hom son dignes que sien penjats, car juglas no son res als sino anima
de omeyes, e a la final sapies que juglas ab estur[n]ines hanc a Deu no
plaguere[n].— Hom que stiga ab tu o hom q[ue] ajes a platicar ab ell p[er]
qualseuol man[er]a, si sera altiu de cor, foragita'l de tu mateix axi co[m] a

22. MS *peseuerar ab pesones*.
23. MS *me*.
24. MS *acostans se*.

aq[ue]ll que't pots tenir p[er] çert que sera ton enemich.— Si sera hom o missatge ab bell[e]s paraules e falaguer en tot[e]s ses man[er]es e costumes e dira a tos vehins be de tu, aquest aytal gita de ton s[er]uir e pots te tenir p[er] dit que't uol enguanar; e aço matex enten de aq[ue]ll vehi qui en ta p[re]sencia te loara.— Si aq[ue]ll que estara ab tu o sera en ta co[n]panya sera hom qui leugerame[n]t aura v[er]gonya, sapies que aq[ue]st aytal de[us] a tu retenir e amar co[m] a fill.— Si a tu coue[n]dra edificar o obrar casa o alberch, guarda que sia major la necessitat q[ue] la uolentat; car sapies q[ue] la cobejança e la gran uolentat de obrar ja no't sera tolta p[er] molt obrar ni p[er] molt edificar.— Massa gran e desmoderada cobejança de obrar: espera que'ls edificis se venen, car torre alta e be obrada e la caxa e la bossa buydada, fa l'om fort atart saui.— Si p[er] ue[n]tura p[er] algun cas co[n]ue[n]dra vendre p[ar]tida d[e] la tua eretat, guarda, no la venes a hom p[us] poderos que tu, ans p[er] menor preu ven aq[ue]lla a menor que tu, p[er]o si es cosa moble ven-la a aq[ue]ll qui mes te'n do.— Guarda't e enten be que mes ual soferir fretura e viurer estret en si mateix que vendre son pat[ri]moni.— Be't dich que mes val vendre de son pat[ri]moni que sotsmetre si mateix a vsures.— ¿Quina cosa es vsura?: vsura es veri de pat[ri]moni, e l'osurer es ladre leal, car ma[n]ifestame[n]t te diu ço que t'enten a f[er].— No vulles res co[n]prar en co[n]panya de hom que sia pus poderos q[ue] tu; mas si has co[n]panyo me[n]or que tu vull[e]s-lo soferir e co[n]portar graciosame[n]t e soste[n]ir.— Demanat m'as d[e]l vs d[e]l vi: p[er] que't dire que qui en habunda[n]cia e en diu[er]sitat de vins es amesurat e se'n sab guardar, que aq[ue]st aytal pot e[ss]er dit Deu te-rrenal.— Car²⁵ enbriaguea res als dretame[n]t no fa sino fer caure l'enbriach en lo fanch.— P[er]que si't sens q[ue] ajes massa begut, no vulles molt parlar, mas aparta't de tota co[n]panya e gita't a dormir.— Car verame[n]t sapies que qui ab paraules uol cobrir sa enbriaguea molt erra, car co[m] mes parla e mes respon a aq[ue]lls ab qui's rahona, mes acussa si mateix e[ss]er enbriach e fas escar[n]ir.— Malestar es a l'hom joue conex[er] los bons vins, car l'om joue, qui be es acostumat, tot vi li deu ve[n]ir en bon grat e no's deu delitar en bons vins.— Guarda't de metge enbriach e exi mateix de metge nouell qui vulla fer en tu alguna cura p[er] tal q[ue] p[ro]ue si p[er] sembla[n]t cura de aq[ue]lla que en tu aura feta, pora guarir a altres qui auran sembla[n]t malaltia d[e] la tua.— Si p[er] ue[n]tura a tu plaura tenir cans, sapies que cans petits se p[er]tanye[n] a clergues o a grans prelats e a regines e a grans senyors.— Cans de guaytar de mes p[ro]fitosos son.— Cans de caça mes costen q[ue] no donen de p[ro]fit.— Si as fills no'ls faces despenses de co d[e]l teu en ta vida, car sapies q[ue] lauores; sabras que uol dir doct[ri]na e regla de viure si la fortuna es cont[ra]ria.— Ultra hojes

25. MS sigue *en* tachado.

yo que't dire, sapies q[ue] yo he vists molts home[n]s q[ue] viue[n] de-
smesuradame[n]t e no uolen tenir regla segons que deuie[n] e co[m] ven-
ie[n] a pobrea dien que ço los era ue[n]gut p[er] fortuna.— E yo dich-te que
aq[ue]ll qui obs[er]uara regla, mesura e doct[ri]na en sa casa e en sos fets,
sies çert que aquest aytal fort atart se clamara de fortuna; enpero pus tart se
pora lunyar mala fortu[n]a de perea.— Sapies quel pereos espera q[ue]
De[us] li ajut e Deus ha manat en lo mo[n] que hom sia diligent e curos.—
Tu, donchs, uetla e co[n]pensa lo despendre que faras ab co q[ue] guan-
yaras.— Qua[n]t vendras a vellea, co[n]sell-te que comanes tu matex a
nostre senyor De[us], ans q[ue] a ton fill; e si en ton testament fas lexes,
consell-te que p[ri]merament manes satisfer a aq[ue]lls qui t'an seruit, e
apres als creadors ans que heretes fills ne filles ni pare[n]s.— Molt te consell
que no coma[ne]s la tua anima a aq[ue]lls que a amat molt la tua p[er]sona;
mas comana la tua a[n]i[m]a a aq[ue]lls que amen la lur a[n]i[m]a.— Fins
que sies malalt fes ton testame[n]t, car a ueguades lo malalt es catiu de la
malaltia, e catiu no pot fer testame[n]t; donchs, fes testame[n]t me[n]tre
q[ue] est fra[n]ch, ans que sies catiu fet.— Mort lo p[ar]e, los fills de-
mane[n] que los bens sien p[ar]tits; dich-te q[ue] si los fils son nobles o de
gran linatge, mes ual que se'n vajen p[er] lo mo[n] escampats que si partien
la eretat, car aytal p[ar]ticio de lur heretat es dissolucio de lur linatge.— Si
los fills son laurados o [26] home[n]s que visquen de lurs ma[n]s, consell-te que
façen ço que's vullen.— Si los fills son mercades, vull[e]s q[ue] la heretat sia
en [. . .] [27] vulles en dines.— Dich-te q[ue] p[us] p[ro]fitosa cosa es la
p[ar]ticio dels bens que la comunio, car la mala fortuna d[e] l'hu poria desfer
los altres.— ¿La mare d[e]ls fills volra pendre marit?: çert fara gran follia;
mas p[er] tal que sos peccats puscha plorar, ella vella pendra marit joue, lo
qual marit no pendra a ella p[er] mul[e]r, mas p[er] ço q[ue] ella aura, e
gitar-ho a a mal ho u despendra a son plaer.— E ella viura t[ri]sta e
malastruga e ab dolor, la qual dolor li durara tots te[m]ps p[er] om[n]ia
secula seculo[rum], amen.—

Ffinida es la letra tramessa p[er] Sent B[er]n[a]t sobre la manera de gouernar
la casa familiar.

Amen.

Esta versión que, por cierto, es bastante menos literal que la otra, se halla
en un manuscrito de varios, que contiene, además, el famoso *Libre de
doctrina*, del Rei Jaume d'Aragó,[28] el *Secret dels Secrets* y el *Libre de dits de*

26. *o* supralinear.
27. En el MS hay un término de cuatro letras, de difícil lectura.
28. Sobre este libro, véase actualmente Josep M. Sola-Solé, ed., Rei Jaume d'Aragó,
Libre de doctrina (Barcelona, 1977).

savis e filòsofs, de Jahuda Bonsenyor.[29] Todo el manuscrito es de una sola mano, con letra de fines del siglo XIV,[30] si bien nuestra traducción, por algunos errores de lectura que atestigua,[31] podría ser incluso un tanto anterior. Es posible, por consiguiente, que nos hallemos ante la versión más antigua de todas las peninsulares que nos han llegado.

Al final de este breve estudio, cabe preguntarse por el verdadero motivo de estas múltiples versiones de la epístola latina atribuída a San Bernardo. Si bien es cierto que, en gran medida, se debieron al carácter eminentemente práctico de sus consejos, es, al mismo tiempo, casi seguro que, como texto didáctico breve, sirvió de cartilla o catón de lectura[32] en algunas escuelas conventuales y, además, en su forma original latina, de texto de base para ejercicios de traducción de esta lengua a los distintos idiomas vulgares. Ello explicaría que, exceptuando la versión del Doctor Navarrus, las otras no demuestren demasiadas pretensiones literarias, presentándose más bien como producto final de unos ejercicios de traducción del latín al castellano o al catalán. Por otra parte, no nos cabe la menor duda de que ésta fue también una de las finalidades de la didáctica medieval. A veces, en efecto, esta didáctica no sólo hubiera sido una manifestación del "enseñar deleitando," sino también, y para usar un término de la época, de un más complejo "enseñar castigando," que consentía, sobre la base de unos textos doctrinales, prácticas de lectura, de escritura y de traducción de una lengua a otra.

29. En cuanto a este MS, véase J. Domínguez Bordona, *Catálogo de los manuscritos catalanes de la Biblioteca Nacional* (Madrid, 1931), 17–19.

30. Puede verse una muestra de la letra de este manuscrito en J. Domínguez Bordona, op. cit., lám. III, al final del libro.

31. Cp., por ejemplo, lo dicho en la nota 20.

32. Sobre la función de los catones, yéase M. Boas, "Het spaansche substantivum catón," *PhWochenschrift* 50 (1930), cols. 649–656. En cuanto a su relación con la didáctica en general, cp. J. M. Sola-Solé, "De nuevo sobre el *Libro de los gatos*," *Kentucky Romance Quarterly* 19 (1972), 471–483 y, en particular, pp. 480–82.

HAGIOGRAPHICA

ANTHONY J. CAVELL
(BROTHER LOUIS CAVELL, S.C.)

Le Livre du Saint Voult de Luques:
An Example of Medieval Imaginative
Literature and Christian Faith

THE PRESENT PAPER has been drawn from my doctoral dissertation, for which Professor Joseph P. Williman, of the Catholic University of America, was my mentor. He suggested to me a topic in which he was quite interested and which he knew had not been researched before. In his own doctoral dissertation,[1] he had come in contact with the *Livre du Saint Voult de Luques*, one of the several additions to the *Legenda Aurea* of Jacobus de Varagine. He urged me to make a critical edition of this fourteenth-century vernacular version of this addition.

Il Santo Volto di Lucca, the subject of the version, is mentioned by Dante in Canto XXI of his *Inferno*. He recounts his meeting with a citizen of Lucca, borne upon the shoulders of a demon and ultimately thrust by him into the black pitch of the Eighth Circle of Hell. The poet describes the taunt hurled by the demons at the newly damned in these words:

> Ma i demon che dal ponte avean coperchio,
> gridar: "Qui non ha luogo il Santo Volto:
> qui si nuota altrimenti che nel Serchio!"
> (ll. 47–49)

1. Joseph P. Williman, "*Le Racional des divins offices*: An Introduction and Partial Edition" (Ph.D. diss., University of North Carolina, Chapel Hill, 1967).

I have quoted from the very reputable edition *La Divina Commedia*, Testo critico della Società Dantesca Italiana col commento Scartazziniano, 9th ed. by Giuseppe Vandelli (Milan: Ulrico Hoepli, 1932), p. 170. Here I translate a comment by the great Dante scholar Scartazzini:

To understand the phrase, one must remember that in Lucca there was and still is venerated with great devotion an ancient Byzantine crucifix of black wood called the Holy Face because of the belief that the face was a miraculous work of celestial hand. The phrase of the devils is, then, in sarcastic and irreverent mood toward something sacred in life even to the old citizen of Lucca to warn him not to dare to show his black face as if he, being used to the display of the Holy Face of black wood, should presume to compare his face black with pitch.

The *Santo Volto* refers to two things: (1) the relic which bears this name and is preserved in the Cathedral of St. Martin in Lucca; and (2) the legend concerning this relic, a legend that grew from a small seed of historical data and was embellished by the fertile popular imagination and the simple faith of medieval populations.

1. The Relic

The Holy Face of Lucca is one of several representations of Christ to which is applied the term ἀχειροποίητος (i.e., not made by human hands). In this sense we may consider it a relic; in this sense alone do I refer to it here as a relic.

The crucifix known as the Holy Face is in the form of a *crux immissa*, or Latin cross. The vertical beam measures 4.34 meters; the crossbeam, 2.65 meters. The width of the beams is 27 centimeters, and their thickness is 7 centimeters.

Both cross and corpus are of walnut (*juglans regia*). The latter is carved in what might be termed Byzantine style and is vested in a tunic similar to that worn in the time of Christ. From head to foot, the corpus measures 2.25 meters, a height quite beyond normal. The head is bent forward and slightly inclined to the right. There is no crown of thorns. The feet are not crossed but hang side by side, so that four nails are used to affix the corpus to the cross. The color of the wood has certainly been darkened over the centuries by the smoke from innumerable lamps and candles.

The Volto Santo, the Cathedral of St. Martin, Lucca.
Reprinted by permission of the Parrocchia della Chiesa Metropolitana, Lucca.

The use of the word *history* in regard to the Holy Face must be in a qualified sense. The origins of the crucifix are lost in the deep mists of legend. The one date generally accepted is 742, that of the *translatio* from Luni to Lucca. The place of deposition in Lucca, however, is a matter of dispute. While Leobinus, the author of the legend, states that it was the Duomo di San Martino, the popular version holds for the Basilica di San Frediano. So, too, Blessed John could not have been the prelate; records show that he was bishop of Lucca from 780 to 810. In 742, the bishop was Walprand (732–754), the belligerent son of the duke of Tuscia, a man quite likely to have made "conquest" of the Santo Volto.

Father Pietro Lazzarini suggests a simple solution to this dilemma: the Holy Face was originally deposited in San Frediano and remained there until Blessed John I officiated at the solemn transfer to the Duomo (in 782, according to some writers).[2]

Thus apparently the date 742 given by Leobinus for the arrival of the Holy Face in Lucca is affirmed. Other suggested solutions have merely compounded the dilemma by discounting the one historical fact offered by Leobinus in support of his statement: the second year of the joint reign of Carloman and Pepin (741–746). Furthermore, this date is the only part of the legend to which we may ascribe the term *historical*.

2. The Legend

The literary legend of the Holy Face is basically that named *Legenda Leobiniana*. Of this there are two versions: *legenda minor*, the simple narrative of Leobinus; and *legenda maior*, which includes also a collection of miracles. This accretion is doubtlessly the result of popular additions to the original legend. In some places the *legenda maior* was used in the liturgy and was read, at least in part, in the *Lectiones* for the feast of the Exaltation of the Holy Cross, September 14. It is the *legenda maior* that served for the translation known as *Le Livre du Saint Voult de Luques*.

The *legenda minor* is truly the *Legenda Leobiniana*. Of Leobinus, who narrates the story, we know only what he himself tells us: he was a deacon, the least of the servants of Christ, eager to share his knowledge with his brothers in the faith lest he be deemed *malus et ingratus servus*. The sources of his knowledge, he tells us, are his personal observation and the information he received from religious persons.

The legend is as follows: Nicodemus, who had seen the Lord, decided to leave a memorial of the crucified Christ. Going into solitude, he began to carve a crucifix with corpus out of black walnut. Distrusting his memory, Nicodemus finished sculpturing "la figure de nostre Seigneur

Jhesucrist; c'est assavoir des epaules en bas seulement," leaving the Holy Face for later; then he fell asleep. When he awakened, he found the Holy Face had been sculptured by angelic hands.

The completed crucifix was placed on a boat without oars or oarsmen, but with sail alone, and shoved off to drift. By chance it landed on the shore of Luni in Italy. A contention arose between the citizens of Luni and those of nearby Lucca for possession of the Holy Face. The citizens of Lucca prevailed, and the relic was taken to their city, where it rests in the Cathedral of Saint Martin. Leobinus tells us that this took place in the second year of the reign of Carloman and Pepin, that is, in the year 742.

3. Latin Manuscripts

The Latin manuscripts of this legend can be divided into three groups: the French-Belgian group contains nine; the Lucca-Rome group contains ten; and the German group contains two.

4. Vernacular Versions: Translations

In the medieval climate of ready faith and relish for the miraculous, it is not surprising that such a narrative as that of the Holy Face should find its vernacular expression. Several versions in various vernaculars must have been made. Many of these were translations from the original Latin of the ninth or tenth century.

From the twelfth century on the translator became an important public instructor, so to say. His position was high in society and in the courts of nobles. His contribution to general learning can not be overlooked. He was very often a nameless benefactor of the community.

Certain translators acquired a veritable renown. Schools of translators gathered around these men. Many of these translators were Italian, and Italy was foremost in this literary effort. Jacques Monfrin mentions Guidotto da Bologna, Bartolomeo Siginulfo, and Filippo da Santa Croce among others. He goes on to say, "Il faut attendre le milieu du XIVᵉ siècle pour que commencent à apparaître en France, de façon suivie, de véritables traductions."[3] Here he obviously refers to translations into

---

3. In *L'Humanisme médiéval dans les littératures romanes du XIIᵉ au XIVᵉ siècle* (Paris, 1964), p. 227.

French made by French speakers. Among the most important that Monfrin mentions were Jean Corbechon, Raoul de Presles, Robert Godefroi, Jacques Bauchant, Jean Daudin, and Jean Golein.

The book of the Holy Face of Lucca is a fourteenth-century prose collection of *exempla* associated with the miraculous image of Christ preserved in the Cathedral of Saint Martin in Lucca, Italy. This Middle French version is a translation of the Latin *Legenda Leobiniana maior*. It is always appended to the fourteenth-century translation of the *Legenda Aurea* of Jacobus de Varagine; and it is the work of Jean Golein. As Joseph P. Williman states:

> There can now be little doubt as to the authorship of this appendix's translation. . . . The main evidence comes from a Geneva manuscript of the *Légende dorée*: . . . at the beginning of the manuscript:
>
> > Cy apres sont les intitulacions des festes nouvelles translatees de latin en françois par tres excellent docteur en theologie Maistre Jehan Golain de l'ordre de Nostre Dame du Carme. (Geneva *ms. fr.* 57)[4]

In contrast to this definitely established authorship is this veiled bit of information at the end of Brussels MS 3423:

> Ci fine l'istoire du St. Voult de Luques des festes nouvelles selon l'usage de Paris. Translates de latin en françois par .i. maistre en theologie de l'ordre de nostre Dame de Carme. L'an mil iiij.^{c} et ij.

As Williman suggests, the anonymity in Brussels MS 3423 could be the result of one of two causes: the personal modesty of Golein or the official disfavor in which he passed his last years. Golein died in 1403.

Le Livre du Saint Voult de Luques is antedated by a thirteenth-century vernacular version in Old French: *Le Saint Vou de Luques*. Wendelin Foerster edited this version as his contribution to the *Mélanges Chabaneau* in 1906. The composition consists of 509 verses in assonance.

5. Middle French Manuscripts

To my knowledge there are seven extant manuscripts of the Middle French prose version of *Le Livre du Saint Voult de Luques*. I have been able to obtain copies of all but one. The manuscript in question is located in

4. Williman, "*Le Racional des divins offices*: An Introduction and Partial Edition," p. 80.

the Bibliothèque de la Ville de Genève and belongs to the *fonds Ami Lullin*. Local restrictions prevent its being microfilmed or photocopied. The manuscript is listed as MS *fr.* 57 (Petau 174). I list it as MS G.

Here is my table of the manuscripts:

P^1 Bibl. Nat. MS *fr.* 242 (fols. 324v–336r)
P^2 Bibl. Nat. MS *fr.* 184 (fols. 415v–429v)
P^3 Bibl. Nat. MS *fr.* 416 (fols. 299v–316v)
P^4 Bibl. Nat. MS *fr.* 243 (fols. 404v–417r)
B^1 Bibl. Royale de Belgique MS *fr.* 3423
B^2 Bibl. Royale de Belgique MS *fr.* 3422
G   Geneva MS *fr.* 57 (Petau 174)

With the exception of MS B^1, which is in bastard script, the group are all in Gothic script of different times. In the catalogues they are simply listed as of the fifteenth century. Upon the authority of Dr. Aloysius Ziegler, professor of palaeography at the Catholic University of America, I suggest that MS P^1 is the oldest of the group and MS B^2 is the most recent. I chose P^1 as my base manuscript.

All these manuscripts are written two columns to a folio page, and ruling is evident in most. With the exception of P^3 and P^4, they all contain illustrations. MS P^2 has only one illustration, at the beginning; and B^1 has none in the text of *Le Saint Voult*, but it has an illustration for St. Yves, whose life immediately follows. P^1 and B^2 have illustrations throughout the text. In B^1 a list of chapter headings precedes the text. P^3 does not contain the whole text.

The manuscripts present some interesting similarities. The calligraphy in P^2 and P^4 would seem to be by the hand of the same scribe. The well-formed Gothic script of P^1 is similar to that of B^2, but different enough to indicate a separation in time. The latter is much more ornate both in script and illustrations. Though P^3 shows a similarity to P^2 and P^4, one can discern a difference much like that between P^1 and B^2. B^1 is *sui generis*.

In 1970 I traveled to Geneva to examine MS G. I was given every courtesy by the curator, M. M. Monnier, who permitted me to study the manuscript over a period of two weeks. By far the Geneva manuscript is the most beautiful, and I would place it on the same level in the tradition as my base manuscript P^1.

6. A Happy Experience

By way of conclusion, I should like to share with readers a very happy experience. On April 9, 1972, I received from Professor Mikhail Myrianov of the ERLE Academy in Leningrad a letter saying that he had noticed my work in the *Répertoire international des médiévistes* with the number 3044. He requested a copy in microfilm to help him in preparing an article on the Santo Volto for a Festschrift. He promised to send me a copy of the finished work with a notice where my own work was mentioned. He was true to his promise. The Festschrift is a beautiful volume, and Professor Myrianov includes in his article a full photo of the Santo Volto as it appears in the Cathedral of St. Martin in Lucca. This experience added much to the pleasure I had in doing the research and completing my dissertation. Both have left me with the feeling of being truly a *médiéviste*.

THOMAS F. COFFEY

The Homily of Alberic the Deacon
on Saint Scholastica

Introduction

THE FOLLOWING SERMON was delivered some time after the middle of
the eleventh century by Alberic the Deacon of Monte Cassino. Alberic
was one of the greatest rhetoricians of the Middle Ages and is considered
by some as the "father of the art of letter writing." His principal works
are the *Flores rhetorici* (*The Flowers of Rhetoric*), the *Breviarium de Dictamine*
(*The Compendium of Letter Writing*), and the *Liber de Barbarismo et
soloecismo, tropo et schemate* (*The Book of Barbarisms, Solecisms, Tropes, and
Schemes*). I will refer to these as the *Flores*, *Breviarium*, and *Liber*, respectively. The importance of the following piece is twofold: it is the only
significant example of Alberic's rhetoric to have survived, and it is one of
the most important works on St. Scholastica written in medieval times
apart from St. Gregory's *Dialogues*. The importance of this sermon is
underscored by its inclusion in the manuscript Vat. lat. 1202, which is
one of the most outstanding examples of the Beneventan period. In
translating, I have used the edition of Angelo Mai,[1] but have taken into
account the variant readings which Dom Anselmo Lentini found in
Cassinese manuscript 146.[2] The notes contain identification of many
biblical references and also point out rhetorical devices from Alberic's
own theory put to use in his sermon. These occurrences are indicated by

1. Mai, Angelo, "De Sancta Scholastica," *Spicilegium Romanum* 5 : 131–143.
2. Lentini, Anselmo, "L'Omelia e la vita di S. Scolastica di Alberico Cassinese," *Benedic-
tina* 3 (1949), 217–278. The variants are found on page 231.

work and chapter of a critical edition which I am preparing for publication. Special thanks are due to Fr. Roland J. Reichmuth, S.J., and Fr. Marion J. Sitzmann, O.S.B., both of Creighton University, for their help with this translation.

Text

At that time Jesus told His disciples this parable: The kingdom of heaven is like ten virgins who, having taken up their lamps, went forth to meet the bride and groom. However, five of them were foolish and five of them were wise, and so forth.[3]

You have heard, dearest brothers, the kingdom of heaven compared to ten virgins, who, having taken up their lamps, went forth to meet the bride and groom. You have heard that some of these virgins were lazy because of the vice of foolishness, and that others were diligent because of the virtue of prudence. You have heard that the foolish ones, although taking up their lamps, did not take any oil with them, while the wise ones had both lamps and oil in vessels. When the groom was delayed a rather long time, both the foolish and the wise virgins fell asleep. Then, in the middle of the night, when there was great noise because the groom was coming, all of them got up at once to prepare their lamps. The foolish virgins, whose lamps went out through lack of oil, were sent by the wise ones to vendors of oil, but while they were gone, those who were prepared went in along with the groom to the nuptial banquet. When the foolish ones came back to a closed door, they repeatedly cried with supplicant voices that the door should be opened for them. Then the voice of the groom came back with an answer in these words: "Amen I say to you, I do not know you." When the parable is finished an ending of admonition is injected when the Lord says: "And watch, since you do not know the day or the hour."[4] I wish to touch, my brothers, upon the profound mysteries of this parable[5] with as much brevity as I can without creating a cloud of obscurity, so that afterwards we may properly

---

3. Matthew 25 : 1-2.

4. Matthew 25 : 13. This entire paragraph is subordinated to the "You have heard [*Audistis*]" repeated three times. English usage does not permit the elegant expression of such extended indirect discourse.

5. For Alberic there is no difference between the concept of "parable" and that of "simile." Cf. *Liber*, chapter 4, where his examples of parable include "like lambs to the slaughter" and "the kingdom of heaven is like a mustard seed."

and appropriately pause upon the praises of the holy virgin Scholastica whose entry into heaven we celebrate this day.[6]

You know, dearest brothers, that it is the rule of the Catholic faith to consider the Father, the Son, and the Holy Spirit as three persons, and to hold each one of these persons to be God. The Church also teaches us to believe in heart for our salvation's sake and to confess in word for justice' sake that all three together are not three Gods but one God. Now, the unity of the Godhead, when added to the trinity of persons, makes the number four; and the number five is reached when we believe in the pouring out of the Word of God, as it is read that He emptied Himself, and accepting the form of a slave. He was made into the likeness of men, and He took on the condition of a man.[7] He humbled Himself, exhibiting obedience to the Father right up until death, even a death on the Cross. Because of this, God exalted Him and gave Him a name which is above every name; so that at the name of Jesus every knee would bend and every tongue confess that the Lord Jesus sits at the right hand of the majesty on high, from whence He will come to judge the living and the dead.[8] Since, therefore, the orthodox and apostolic faith believes that the unity of the Godhead exists in three persons, and that the Word made flesh has brought about the salvation of the human race through the flesh, it is right and fitting that all who hold this belief in

6. Alberic's theory on introductions, which he calls variously exordium, prologue, and proemium, shines through his words. He chooses concise expressions, tells what he intends to do with his usual expression "to promise," and picks those colors or figures which tend to capture the good will of his audience. The idea of brevity except when it might engender obscurity occurs throughout the *Flores*. His successful blend of anaphora and apostrophe in this initial paragraph are intended to capture the good will of the monks by a subtle implication that they are both cherished and knowledgeable. These two devices continue throughout the sermon to maintain this "captured good will." There are more than a dozen instances of both, although the anaphora is less apparent in the translation.

7. This paragraph presumes that the audience is aware of a particular symbolism for numbers. Many examples of this are found in the *Breviarium*, and we can establish the following general notions from this work. The number one stands for unity and for the first principle. Two stands, among other things, for the active and contemporary life and symbolizes those things which are naturally viewed as pairs or opposites. Three stands for the spiritual world and is especially important because of the Holy Trinity. Four stands for the material world. Five represents man, who is often depicted as touching five points on a wheel. Thus when Christ came into the world, he moved from the realm of three to that of four. One of Alberic's descriptions of death plays on the converse of this, as he says in chapter 14 of the *Breviarium*, "He has died . . . the fourfold embodiment is deserted for the threefold embodiment of virtue; the fourfold is left behind by the threefold; his share in the threefold virtue has forsaken its share in the fourfold matter."

8. Cf. Matthew 25 : 31 – 32 as well as the Nicene and Apostles' Creeds.

the count of five be symbolized by the number five. They are also most properly called virgins, as they could not be divided from the fullness of faith by any schism or harmed by any heretical infection. However, this faith, according to James,[9] has died in some from lack of works of love. In others, according to Paul, it does not cease to operate because of love.[10] In adding these two groups together, we arrive at the number ten. Therefore, those people are considered most fittingly to be like the five wise virgins, in whom the faith symbolized by the number five is always intent on works of justice through a motive of love. In other people this very faith produces things which perhaps seem to pertain to justice, but which really proceed more from a desire for temporal profit than from the prodding of a charitable disposition.[11] These are also called virgins, and they are five in number because unspotted faith is signified by a fivefold compunction, but they are called foolish because of the foolish and silly intentions behind their work. Because those lacking charity and love can perform many things which seem to be just but from which there follows no inward advantage for salvation, the vessel of choice[12] gives us a clear explanation when he writes: "And if I distribute all my goods as food for the poor, and if I hand over my body to be burnt, yet have no charity, it will profit me nothing."[13]

Charity is that oil which the foolish virgins do not have in the vases, that is, in the receptacles of the interior of man, and for lack of which they are called foolish. Charity is truly what is meant by this oil, since just as oil always rises above any liquids with which it is mixed, so charity is suspended above all other virtues.[14] For this reason the teacher of the Gentiles,[15] when about to speak of love, first says: "I will show you a more remarkable way," brothers.[16] After saying several things in praise

9. James 1:17.

10. Galatians 5:6.

11. This is just one example of Alberic's use of parallel construction in his writing. Though it is found throughout the sermon and is evident in his other works, he makes only one very short mention of it at the end of chapter 5 of the *Liber*, where he writes simply, "*Conpar* is the figure which occurs when a speech consists of equal or nearly equal components."

12. St. Paul.

13. 1 Corinthians 13:3.

14. This explanation demonstrates well Alberic's concept of *analogy*, which he deals with in chapter 5 of the *Liber*. He calls it "a reasoning which begins with those things which are apparent and leads one toward those things which are doubtful and not comprehensible to the senses, such as when an invisible Creator is discerned from the visible creatures."

15. St. Paul.

16. 1 Corinthians 13:1.

of charity, he adds this: "Now, however, there remain faith, hope, and charity, and of these three the greatest is charity." [17] So, most beloved brothers, this is the oil by which the lanterns, that is, the cherished and holy works of the wise virgins, emit a light of great intensity. Since the lamps, that is to say, the works, of these foolish virgins do not have the nutriment of this oil, even if they do not appear at all at the present to be extinguished, on close examination, [18] it is clear that they are ready to go out. All these virgins are prepared to meet the bride and groom, since the fivefold faith is grasped by all with this hope and is held by all with this hope: that after the course of life has been traversed, all, filled with thanksgiving, may be introduced into the presence of Christ and of His spouse which is Jerusalem. [19]

While the groom delays his coming, all the virgins fall asleep and dream, just as the judge delays his verdict while all start the course of this life and are given birth. To fall asleep is, in fact, to begin the course of life; to dream, truly, is, once the course life is started, to go through it. We are instructed, moreover, by the authority of the psalmist, that this sleep also means the course of life, when he says: "They slept their sleep and all men of riches found nothing in their hands." [20] All men sleep their sleep of riches while they still walk through the spaces of this life. Finally they do not sleep and it is said about them "they slept," when through death the course of their life comes to an end. Then they find nothing in their hands, since they have left behind here all the riches which they may have gathered together in vain. While this sleep is being enjoyed by both the foolish and the wise virgins, a call is heard in the middle of the night that all should hasten to meet the groom. The present world, my brothers, is said to be night in comparison with the future,

17. 1 Corinthians 13:13.

18. This probably also refers to the last judgment. The Latin is "in discursione districti examinis."

19. Though calling Jerusalem Christ's spouse might be considered personification or prosopopeia, Alberic would consider this example and others where no particular attribute of a person is described as a simple metaphor. It would, however, fall into one of the four classes of metaphor which he outlines in chapter 4 of the *Liber*, and which he probably borrowed from Bede's *De schematibus et tropis*. These classes are animate-to-animate, inanimate-to-inanimate, animate-to-inanimate, and inanimate-to-animate. This would be a case of animate-to-inanimate metaphor.

20. Psalm 75:6. The ambiguity of sleep/dream (*somnium, dormitare*, etc.) is lost in the English translation. I have used considerable license in this paragraph on the assumption that Alberic would have avoided above all an accurate but ill-sounding "They fall asleep and sleep . . . a sleep, etc."

since here, according to the apostle,[21] we see through a mirror and mysteriously. Then, however, we will see face to face. Here we know in part. Then, however, we will know just as we are known, when the Lord will come to light up the places hidden in darkness to make manifest the counsels of the heart, and when tribute will be given to everyone by God.

Therefore, in the middle of this night, in this night not yet over, not yet completed, a loud voice is heard saying that all the virgins must prepare themselves to meet the groom who is arriving. This is, dearest brothers, the cry which is brought to Isaiah by a precept of the Lord, who says to him: "Climb upon the high mountain, you who evangelize Sion. Raise your voice in strength, you who evangelize Jerusalem. Exalt, do not fear, say to the cities of Judah: 'Behold, the Lord God will come in strength and his arm shall rule.'"[22] He also cries to him: "Do not stop. Raise your voice like a trumpet and announce to my people their evils, and to the House of Jacob its sins."[23] You have heard, brothers, in the cry of the prophet, in other words, but not in another meaning: "Behold, the groom comes." "Behold," he says, "your God." "Behold," he says, "the Lord will come in strength." You have heard that the prophet is also ordered to use his voice and say: "Go out to meet him" when he is ordered by the voice of the Lord to announce to his people their evils and to the House of Jacob its sins, and the various other things which follow. In all of these things, it is really a question of nothing other than the warning which urges the virgins to go out to meet the arriving groom. This cry, brothers, while we sleep through the night of the world, comes to our ears through the law, it comes from the Psalms, it comes from the prophets, it comes from the Gospels, it comes from the apostolic letters and through the explanations and the admonitions of the orthodox fathers.[24] From all of these, this is the cry; this is the shout of all: "Behold, the groom comes. Go out to meet him. Behold, he comes. He

21. Paul, 1 Corinthians 13:12.
22. Isaiah 40:9–10.
23. Isaiah 58:1.
24. This is a good example of epistrophe. Oddly enough, Alberic never deals with this topic, although he mentions repetition in terms of anadiplosis, anaphora, epanaphora, epanalepsis, and epizeuxis. It is, nevertheless, used throughout this sermon and Alberic's other writings as is alliteration. Neither of these devices comes through well in a translation, and it is interesting to note that he classifies alliteration or paranomasia as a barbarism. It may be that he is inclined to consider a series of similar endings as homoioptoton or homoioteleuton, both of which are ascribed to barbarism. In spite of this belief, end repetition abounds in this sermon and there are over a hundred instances of alliteration.

is near. He will soon be here. Go out. Meet him. Hurry. It is already time to get up from sleep. Now, indeed, our salvation is closer at hand than we believed. Night has passed. Day has approached. Let us abandon the works of darkness. Let us put on the armor of light so that we may walk honorably in the day." At this cry, both the prudent and the foolish virgins get up. They adjust their lamps. They prepare themselves for their work. The foolish virgins have no oil. They have no disposition for love. They have no desire for love. They have no feeling of mercy, which, on close examination,[25] causes them to be worthy of mercy.

Oil takes its name from mercy, since *elaion* in Greek means "mercy" in Latin. Thus, mercy is symbolized fittingly by oil. Do not judge what I have said just now to be different, dearest brothers, from what you heard before from my own mouth.[26] For it can seem perhaps different to some that earlier I said love must be understood by oil, and now I say that mercy is signified by oil. Never, my brothers, will charity be lacking to a heart with mercy, and never will mercy be lacking to one moved by love. Therefore, oil will not be able to stand as a figure of love when it does not also stand equally well as a figure of mercy; and it will not be able to carry the image of mercy and not have an image of love as well. Therefore, when it is said that charity is symbolized by oil, it is also understood at the same time that mercy is symbolized by oil. When it is said that mercy is represented by oil, it is certainly necessary to be understood that love is also represented by oil. Thus, the foolish virgins do not have this oil, and they recognize, in general, that they do not have it. They are lacking a disposition for mercy. They are lacking a disposition for love. They also know that they are lacking this. For this reason they flee to the prudent virgins and beg them to give them some of their oil. Sinners sometimes understand that their works either are not good or else do not in any way proceed from a good intention. They understand and they are conscience-stricken,[27] but since they dally along the way and because they are creatures of time they believe for a time. Then in

25. Cf. note 18.

26. This paragraph begins the "argumentation." Alberic divides a work into four sections. There is the prologue, the narration, the argumentation, and the conclusion. (Cf. *Flores*, chapter 1.) Here he makes use of two devices: etymology, which he defines as "setting forth the cause and reason for something," a larger and more exaggerated application than is usual; and procatalepsis, which he calls "bringing up materials ourselves which might be brought up against us by others." Both of these are treated in chapter 5 of his *Liber*.

27. The Latin is "compunguntur." The Latin really means "to sting," but here it seems to have developed already into the idea of having an uneasy feeling in one's conscience because of guilt.

time of temptation they fail. The foolish virgins come to the wise virgins. They cry aloud that their lanterns are going out. They beg that they be given oil as sometimes sinners who are conscience-stricken flee to holy men and admit by their own testimony that the things which seemed to be good resulted from an intention that was not good. They commend themselves to their charity. They commend themselves to their love. They commend themselves to their prayers. They commend themselves to their merciful hearts. This is a request by them for oil. This is a desire to burn their lanterns with the others' fuel. You have heard what the wise virgins answered. "Lest, perhaps," they say, "there not be enough for us and for you, go instead to the merchants and buy for yourselves." [28]

Brothers, sometimes the fearful say this, and the humble of soul who are straining to commend themselves with their entreaties and with their prayers answer thus. "Hardly are our prayers, hardly are our entreaties, hardly are those things which we offer up to God sufficient for ourselves. Hardly do we find ourselves such as to be worthy to be heard for our own sake. Our prayers and the quality of our service are not such before God that through them others can win salvation. Do not put hope in our entreaties which are of no importance; instead strive to work for yourselves." You do not have oil, as you yourselves admit. You can find several vendors of oil. The vendors of oil, the vendors of mercy, are the poor, since when we extend mercy to them, we also deserve mercy from the Lord. These are those who, joined to us by the bond of friendship because of the mammon of iniquity, admit us into the eternal dwelling places. [29] In what measure we measure to them, in that very same measure will it be measured back to us. Go, therefore, to these people and make friends of them for yourselves, not out of a vain intention as you have up until now, but with the hope of oil, the hope of acquiring divine mercy. Give of your mammon of iniquity, certain and confident that they will give unto you a good measure, heaped up, pressed down, and overflowing. [30]

The foolish virgins listen to the counsels of the prudent ones. They go to buy oil but during their absence the groom comes, and he enters into the nuptials with those who are prepared. The gate is closed. What does it mean, "They go"? They make a decision. They decide on a course of

28. Matthew 25 : 10.
29. Cf. Luke 16 : 9.
30. Luke 6 : 38.

action. They determine something. To make a decision, to decide on a course of action, and to determine something in one's mind is "to go." They are said to have gone in order to buy oil. They are not said to have bought it. They go but they do not buy, since they make a decision but they do not act.[31] They pledge but they do not fulfill. They promise but they do not carry out. They put off. They procrastinate. They defer. While the foolish virgins go to buy the oil, and while the prudent ones prepare their lamps with the oil which they have in vases, the groom comes. Thus it is that while sinners are always putting off doing good things and while the elect are attending to them ceaselessly, the judge through death summons both the former and the latter to be judged. While the elect are taken up in glory through death, this glory is denied to the sinners through death, and the gate will never be opened for them at any time for all eternity. The time, in fact, is already here for them. Concerning this, Truth speaks, saying: "There will come a time when no one can work."[32] The appointed time has already gone by for them, as well as the day of salvation. The Lord speaks about this through the mouth of the prophet: "I heard you at the appointed time, and in the day of salvation I helped you."[33] For this reason, the crying voices are raised in vain. For them the time to be heard is finished, and they are told: "Amen I say to you, I do not know you."[34] He denies them in that life, who have denied Him in this life, if not by their words, then by their deeds. That the Lord can be denied by deeds while affirmed by words is obvious from the testimony of the extraordinary preacher[35] when, concerning those who teach virtue while not moving away from vice, he spoke in these words: "They confess that they know God; they deny it by

31. This is a case of paronomasia, which Alberic treats in all three of his works. He gives several examples of this, one of which comes from Psalm 21:6, "in te sunt confisi sed non sunt confusi." The Latin here reads "eunt sed non emunt." This seems to bring to rest the doubts lurking below the surface of Alberic's words. He is obviously troubled by the difficulty of exhorting his audience to practice mercy in the face of the five wise virgins who do not seem especially merciful. Having used a rhetorical question, etymology, and paronomasia to exonerate the wise virgins, he now soars into a quick series of statements common to his works and in harmony with his devotion to brevity. These are mentioned in both chapter 2 of the *Flores* and chapter 5 of the *Liber* under the headings of dialyton, brachylogia, collectio, conversio, asintheton, and chesis onomaton.

32. Cf. Mark 13:33.
33. Isaiah 49:8 and 2 Corinthians 6:2.
34. Matthew 25:12.
35. St. Paul.

their deeds." [36] To what end the course of this parable leads becomes immediately apparent from the following sentence of admonition where the Lord concludes and says: "Watch, therefore, because you do not know the day or the hour." [37]

Now that we have gone through a brief and concise explanation of the Gospel reading, as we promised already in our introduction, let this section of our sermon immediately turn to the praises of the virgin whose birthday is celebrated by us today. Let it be our first task to observe that Scholastica lacked none of those qualities at all which, we have learned from the Lord's narrative, the prudent virgins possessed. For she was in all ways renowned as a virgin who, in addition to the common purity of faith, and the modesty of the flesh, preserved unspotted the purity of her soul. She excelled in prudence by fixing her eyes on the purpose of creation, and she was tirelessly persistent in providing for herself truly good things. When she was about to meet the groom, she lit her lantern, and desiring eagerly the vision of Christ, she sent out the light of her holy actions in every direction and it was more brilliant in its rays than the sun. She took oil in vases, which she always carried in the receptacles of her soul as a source of holy charity. Through the deep power of this charity, Scholastica was able to display an astonishing miracle in which, by crying, she moistened the face of heaven with rain so that she might resist the will of her most holy brother, who was kept from going when he had arranged to return to his brothers. Prepared, therefore, with her lamps lighted, she went out on this very day to meet the coming spouse; and, awaiting the fullness of joy she entered into the nuptial banquet with him.

It became obvious to the world—through God's revelation—with what gentleness her soul watched over her bodily members when her soul was ordered to leave the prison of her body. To the brothers looking on, she was shown entering the recesses of heaven in the form of a bird

36. Titus 1 : 16.

37. Mark 13 : 32. The argumentation is ended with this protrope. This device is mentioned only briefly in chapter 5 of the *Liber* but occurs throughout this sermon as he exhorts his brothers to reject the ways of sin. At this point, he fulfills the promise made in the introduction, namely, to give fitting praise to one of the patrons of his order. Examples of this form are found in chapter 6 of the *Breviarium*. In all three works, however, he carefully balances the subject of praise with that of vituperation. In fact, in chapter 2 of the *Flores*, he gives only examples of praise, stating that "since praise and vituperation are approached in a similar manner, it suffices to speak of only one, since it will apply equally well to both."

without bile.[38] Dearest brothers, there are said to exist also other dovelike properties whose implications can most worthily and truly be applied to this very holy virgin. This bird is cited for freely and frequently building its nest in the openings of rocks. It is cited for eating nothing living. It is cited for defending itself not with its beak or its claws but with the motion of its wings. It is cited for loving company in flight. It is cited for having bleary eyes and for not being able to see an oncoming hawk with any clarity while flying toward the rays of the sun. For this reason, it is said that the dove is accustomed to sit on a tree planted along a stream of running water and to fix its eyes which it cannot direct toward the sun's rays down on the waters, and by means of the image reflected in the waters to avoid the traps and the attacks of the hawk which is hurrying to snatch it. Truly, my brothers, who does not know that the song of doves is nothing other than a sigh?

Dearest brothers, if we reflect on the implications of all these properties in Scholastica, several reasons will occur to us as to why it seemed good to divine wisdom to reveal to the brothers looking on the soul going out of the virgin's body in the form of a dove. Thus our dove built her nest in the openings of a rock. She clearly based all trust in her salvation and in her life on the passion and death of Christ. The vessel of election[39] taught you to call Christ a rock. This rock truly was opened at the time when it was fixed to the Cross with iron nails both in the feet and in the hands. An opening was also cut in this rock where the soldier pierced its side by thrusting in a lance. In these openings, therefore, Scholastica located her nest, since through them she established for herself the certain hope of an eternal mansion in the heavens. In these openings, she placed her nest, since she carried about the credulity of absolute faith that they were the basis of her salvation. In these openings, I say, she built her nest, in which she truly kept herself safe from that hawk of souls, the devil. Nothing living was food for our dove, who, hearing the apostle, strove to mortify her flesh along with its vices and desires. She did not defend herself with any claw or beak but only by the protection of her wings. Not knowing how to repay evil with evil, she alone protected herself from all adversaries with the love of God and neighbor. In her flight she chose to have company and took care to bring

38. This could be interpreted in the sense of "anger" or even "white."
39. St. Paul.

with her to heaven whomever she could. She had bleary[40] eyes and she saw in this life, like Paul, through a mirror and mysteriously. The tree, planted along the flowing water and on top of which this dove used to sit, is Christ the Lord, on whose head, which the apostle[41] testifies is God, she established for herself a more firm and fortified seat. This tree, according to the poet psalm-writer,[42] is planted along the stream of waters, since whatever the faithful believe of him is supported by the authority of the holy scriptures. In fact, the deep water, says the wisest of men,[43] is the words from the mouth of man, and the rushing flood is the fount of wisdom.[44] By fixing her gaze on these waters she detected the approaching hawk, because, attentive to the sacred writings, and recognizing the wiles of this crafty enemy, she avoided him. The song of our dove was a sigh, and she was the imitator of prophetic action. She toiled in her grief and each night she drenched her bed and flooded the covers with tears, and only from the sound of her grief did her bones clung to her skin.[45] In order, finally, to praise this sacred virgin with brief but adequate words, let us say that she was the sister of Benedict by both blood and holiness.[46]

Having finished our praise of the virgin with great brevity, let us proceed, most beloved brothers, to an exhortation to you, by bringing back to your ears and to your minds again and again that lesson of the evangelical reading: "Watch, therefore, since you do not know the day or the hour."[47] Watch, I exhort you, I urge you, I warn you. Watch, since you do not know the day of your dying, and you are unaware of the hour. Run while you have the light, lest the darkness of death overtake you.

40. This also can mean "misty" and could even have reference to the miracle of crying and causing rain as well as to the passage of Paul about seeing in this world darkly. Cf. 1 Corinthians 13:12. One of the elements lending harmony to this description of Scholastica is the extended use of wet imagery.

41. St. Paul. Cf. 1 Corinthians 11:3.

42. Psalm 1:3.

43. This example of antonomasia is another of the marks of Alberic's style. He almost never refers to St. Paul, but writes instead, "the vessel of choice, the teacher of the Gentiles, etc." In chapter 4 of the *Liber*, he uses this very example of "the wisest of men" for Solomon as his illustration of this device.

44. Proverbs 18:4.

45. Cf. Job 19:20.

46. Alberic concludes his praise of Scholastica with a play on words similar to one found in chapter 10 of the *Breviarium*, where he gives the following as an example of a salutation: *Benedicto nomine, Benedicto gracia, Benedicto et opere, A.*

47. Mark 13:32.

Work while there is time, while it is permitted, and while the judge delays his sentence. There will come, indeed, an hour in which no one will be able to work. We exhort you with the apostle so that you will not have received the grace of God in vain. For He says: "At an acceptable time I have listened to you, and in the day of salvation I have helped you." [48] Behold, now is the acceptable time. Behold the day of salvation. "Seek," therefore, my most beloved brothers, "the Lord while He can be found. Call on Him while He is near. Let the impious man forsake his way, and the evil man abandon his thoughts and return to God, and He will have mercy on him. Let him go back to our God, since He is generous in forgiving." [49] Is honor lost? It can be gained back. Is dignity lost? It can be gained back. Are riches lost? They can be gained back. Innumerable are the things which once lost can be gained back. The time for action, the time for repentance, the time for pleasing God, once lost, can never be gained back in all eternity. We know, dearest brothers, that it is still possible to return to God through repentance, but we do not know whether this freedom will remain for us until evening. Therefore, my beloved, knowing that the patience of God leads us to repentance, let us not, in our harshness and impenitent hearts, store up for ourselves wrath for the day of wrath and of God's revelation as the just Judge who will render to each one according to his works. Watch, therefore, dearest brothers, watch, since you know not either the day or the hour. "Blessed are those servants," says the truth, "whom the Lord when He comes will find watching." [50] Amen I say to you, that He will place them above all His goods. [51] May Christ our Lord make us participants in all these goods, who together with the Father and the vivifying Spirit retains eternal power, rule, and sovereignty for ever and ever.

Amen.

48. Cf. note 33.
49. Isaiah 55:6—7.
50. Luke 12:37. Cf. Matthew 24:46.
51. Cf. Matthew 24:47.

BENEDICT C. NJOKU

Vision of the Saint in Chaucer:
A Philological Approach

To HAVE A part in a Festschrift commemorating the work and spirit of
Professor Robert T. Meyer is a special pleasure to one who, having been a
graduate student of his in Comparative Philology, for both the master's
and the doctorate degrees in English at the Catholic University of America, owes him a particular depth of gratitude. But it requires no such
depth of indebtedness to respond positively to a call to participate in a
Festschrift to honor Professor Meyer.

At the same time one would gladly respond to a call to celebrate his
character and to appreciate the Christian achievement of his life. We
certainly honor Professor Meyer, for he realized early in his life that the
promise of America was in part intellectual, and in part ecclesial and
charismatic. He realized that the cultivation of the intellectual virtues is
a necessary concomitant of, and an indispensable element in, the health
and well-being of a mature and great society.

Some of the intellectual promise, religious sanity, Christian vision,
and pedagogical excellence that Professor Meyer saw in America have
been fulfilled, or, at least, have been partly fulfilled, in the dynamism of
Comparative Philology, literary scholarship, and literary criticism,
which have earned a fresh lease on life in Professor Meyer's lifetime. In
this little paper we are casting our lot with the movement described by
Matthew Arnold a century ago in these terms: "Of the intellect of
Europe in general the main effort, for now many years, has been a critical

effort . . . in all branches of knowledge, theology, philosophy, history, art, science." [1]

But Professor Robert T. Meyer is no Matthew Arnold. His quiet, mellow, and yet dynamic scholarship and effective philological pedagogy simply distinguish him as a Christian scholar. It is his Christian witness that led him to disregard contemporary lingering uncertainties, critical ambiguities, and linguistic vagueness in his philological approach to scholarship.

Nothing about this short work is definitive or complete. It does not pretend to be a fully examined critical study of Chaucer's vision of the saint. It only suggests a way to approach Chaucerian criticism, and yet some of its implications have serious critical signification.

The age of Chaucer was dominated by great religious, theological, and philosophical forces, such as Augustinian theology of emanation and Thomistic Scholasticism. As a result, even though Chaucer is not a religious poet in the sense of Dante, or John Langland, or John Bunyan, or Francis Thompson, or Gerard Hopkins, he must have been faced with a choice between drawing from the contemporary religious sensibility by focusing on "otherworldliness," and "this-worldliness." For sure he cast his lot on an art fully tinged with realism because it drew from the totality of contemporary sensibility and a philosophical matrix. [2]

Thus Chaucer's work is strewn with visions, references, and echoes of religious sensibilities. [3] Yet he does not pretend to be a mouthpiece for the religious orthodoxy of his age. [4] Writing in a culture which had a deep concern for man's earthly destiny, Chaucer's world was deeply Ptolemaic or geocentric and man was surely the king of creation. It was a world that

1. Matthew Arnold, "The Function of Criticism at the Present Time," in *Essays* ("Oxford Standard Authors," Oxford, 1925), p. 9; See also R. B. West, *Essays in Modern Literary Criticism* (New York and Toronto, 1952); J. T. Shipley, *Dictionary of World Literature* (New York, 1943 with subsequent editions); R. W. Stallman, *The Critic's Notebook* (University of Minnesota, 1950); and W. J. Rooney, *The Problem of "Poetry and Belief" in Contemporary Criticism* (Washington, D.C.: Catholic University of America Press, 1949).

2. Ester C. Quinn: "Religion in Chaucer's Canterbury Tales: A Study in Language and Structure," in *Geoffrey Chaucer: A Collection of Original Articles*, ed. George D. Eneonomou (New York, 1975), p. 55.

3. Ester C. Quinn, ibid., p. 55. Religion here means a belief in the "history of salvation."

4. Ibid., p. 55. For our purpose, "religion" stands for the quest for values of the ideal life; the recognition of the existence of a supernatural, superhuman Being who is entitled to our obedience, reverence, and worship.

saw the universe as a single whole, an ordered cosmos where all things assumed a proper place in prefect equilibrium. But religion in Chaucer is partly concerned with the story of God's dealing with man as well as with nonreligious frames of reference. This is a deviation that Ester C. Quinn calls an intrusion of the lot of fallen humanity in the progress of goodness and morality in Chaucer's age.[5]

To get at the root of the matter we shall examine cursorily some of the following words: *saint, caritas, virtue, conscience, noble, penitence, repentance,* and *perfection.* The word *saint* is derived from the Latin *sanctus,* meaning "holy," one who is sanctified. John P. O'Connell calls the saint "the choicest fruit of Christ's Redemption."[6]

Caritas, whose nearest English derivative is *charity* (love), means dearness, costliness, being highly priced. Charity is the virtue which inclines us to love God above all things, for his own sake, and our neighbor as ourselves for the sake of God. *Caritas* is dependent on the principle of immutable justice (*justitia*), a principle expressed in the saying: *Fiat justitia, pereat mundus.*[7]

Caritas is the fruit of Christian perfection, or mature sanctity, consisting of union with God, through Christ, by self-sacrifice, prayer, good works, and love. *Caritas,* on the part of man towards God, produces a counteracting love of God towards man.

Virtue (ME and OFr *vertu, vertue,* goodness, power, from L *virtus,* manliness, worth) has to do with general moral goodness, or simply right action and right thinking. Virtue is conformity of man's life and conduct with the principle of morality. In the same way we may derive the word *noble* (ME, OFr, L *nobilis, well-known,* famous, highborn). It may also come from *noble* (L *noscere, gnoscere,* to know). In this sense a noble man is a man of high moral qualities or ideals.

Conscience (L *conscientia*) is the practical judgment of reason on the morality of an act, or the judgment that something here and now is to be avoided because it is evil, or to be done because it is good; it is knowledge within oneself, an internal conviction of the rightness or wrongness of an act. *Penitence* (L *penitentia*) in ecclesiastical history means undergoing of some discipline or exercise either voluntarily or imposed by spiritual authority, an outward expression of repentance and expiation of an of-

5. Op. cit.
6. John P. O'Connell, *The Catholic Encyclopedia of the Bible.* In the New Testament a saint is one united to Christ by faith and Baptism.
7. "Let justice prevail, though the world perish."

fence. In this sense *penitence* and *repentance* are synonymous. Repentance is the state of being penitent or having sorrow or contrition for past action or conduct.

The big question remains: What is Chaucer's vision of the saint? Is Chaucer immoral?[8] Is the *Parson's Tale* the only work of Chaucer which shows deep religious emotions?[9] Using the words we have defined, we can say that Chaucer's saint is holy, charitable, conscientious, virtuous, and of noble disposition. He is one whose life on earth has qualified him for eternal happiness in heaven.

By examining the movement of the pilgrims, the themes of reward and punishment, of repentance and conversion, and by examining Chaucer's characterization, we will understand his vision of the saint as one of a simple but extraordinary life of virtue. To begin with, a pilgrimage is an act of religious worship, a journey to a holy place. Thus pilgrimage by its symbolism focuses our attention on the spiritual and celestial.[10] The main purpose of a pilgrimage is religious.[11]

A pilgrimage to Canterbury is a movement away from "worldliness" to the symbolic home which is "eternal" or "spiritual," as in Dante's *Divina Commedia*, where the movement is from *Inferno*, through *Purgatorio*, to *Paradiso*. This is a search for spirituality, for divinity and spiritual tranquility; it is a search for perfection.

Again, the world of the pilgrim is a realistic world of reward and punishment, of sin and conversion or repentance. Consequently there are numerous references to penitence, repentance, and conversion in Chaucer's work. The world of Chaucer's vision is partly that of fallen humanity where man is called to *metanoia*, to repentance.[12] Furthermore, Chaucer creates a gallery of characters of various description, characters who are of exemplary moral worth as well as those who are

8. Williams Witherly Lawrence, *Chaucer and the Canterbury Tales* (New York, 1969), p. 84.

9. Ibid., p. 17. Obviously the parson seems to have been endowed with a principle of action which enables him to perform supernatural actions.

10. Jeannette Richardson, *Blameth Not Me* (The Hague, 1970), p. 77, reminds us that Chaucer makes frequent reference to the Bible. Yet some of his characters often act in a manner verging on irreligion. See Richardson, ibid., pp. 78–79. Lawrence remarks that the *Parson's Tale* has some evidence of deep religious repentance. Lawrence, op. cit., p. 84. See also Ester C. Quinn, op. cit., pp. 56–57.

11. Ester C. Quinn, op. cit., p. 59.

12. Ester C. Quinn, op. cit., has remarked that the *Friar's Tale*, the *Pardoner's Tale*, and the *Parson's Tale* are replete with references to penitence and repentance. Salvation is a liberation from sin and evil runs through the *Man of Law's Tale* and the *Second Nun's Tale*.

scoundrels in a comic show. Thus the good Parson, Constance, and Griselda in the *Parson's Tale*, the *Man of Law's Tale*, and the *Clark's Tale* represent the former, and contrast with the rascals in the *Friar's Tale*, the *Summoner Tale*, and the *Pardoner's Tale*.

Unlike Dante, who conceives of man in his different relations with God, Chaucer focuses his attention on the human order, or at best, on the divine, from established natural order. The *Miller's Tale* can be understood in terms of antipodes: the "World," the "Flesh," and the "Devil"—diurnal reality (*Sein*)—and the "Power," the "Kingdom," and the "Glory" (*Schein*). This makes the tale a farce. On the other hand Griselda of the *Man of Law's Tale* is a martyr to the virtues of patience, perseverance, and calm endurance, which distinguish a saint from a sinner. These are born of Christian self-abnegation, forbearance as God's children, and of *caritas* and *charisma*.

Perhaps a brief comment on the Prioress of the *General Prologue* to the *Canterbury Tales* will further illustrate Chaucer's vision of the saint. In her, *caritas* and *charisma* assume deeper meanings, encompassing compassion, sympathy, and empathy. The Prioress sees God in His creatures. She preaches by example, for on her broad brooch is inscribed: *Amor vincit omnia*. By implication she calls for *Amor Dei* which filters to all, and not simply for *amor courtois*. [13]

The Prioress, however, blends the courtly elegance of *amor courtois* with the monastic ideal of holiness and personal sanctity. Chaucer speaks of "hir conscience," [14] or her sense of moral worth, which is not hindered by courtly elegance and social sophistication. Speirs has remarked that her conscience is "not a mere effusion of tender sympathies that are sentimental." [15]

To Chaucer, a saint is a religious man, one sanctified by a life of faith, hope, and charity. Religion is an individual's effort to bind himself to the Creator; it is relational and individualistic. Through it the saint, as an individual, seeks to discover who he is, in order to find deeper meaning in life, in relation to the Supreme Being. However, in the *Nun's Priest's*

13. G. G. Coulton has observed Chaucer's special tender feeling towards the Prioress. See his *Chaucer and His England* (London, 1968), pp. 138, 139–150.

14. Ester C. Quinn, op. cit., pp. 60–61.

15. John Speirs, *Chaucer the Maker* (London: Faber and Faber, 1951), p. 106. Conscience is the internal recognition of right and wrong as regards one's actions and motives. It is the ability to respond as a free, active human being capable of love. See also Speirs, pp. 106–116; also see Lawrence, op. cit., p. 83.

Tale of Chauntecleer and Pertelote, the goddess *Fortuna*—in English literature "wyrd," in classical literature "fate," "fatalism," "determinism"—plays a leading role. Here man is not supposed to be the master of his own success or failure. This means that man's stamina, self-control, success or failure, are determined by forces beyond his control.

But the saint's life is rooted in a belief that man has full control of his destiny. He believes that man can turn typical ills to his own advantage. Man's attitude, of course, determines his ability to surmount the obstacles and difficulties in his way to make his life saintly and worth living. Seneca of old held that a good conscience is the testimony of life as well as a reward of it. Thus he could say that the beginning of happiness is wisdom and virtue.[16]

In the medieval Christian synthesis, man's free will afforded him choices and options among alternatives. In short, man *in actio* helps to determine his own fortune. Man's universe is, therefore, in Christian religion, or in the saint's life, not painted with an incurable taint, or an irremediable stance, or an incorrigible flaw. His life is indubitably guided by Divine Providence.

In the *Franklin's Tale*, Chaucer almost states the Christian or saint's idea of marriage as a covenant, a covenantal relationship involving a commitment, mutuality of love, and sharing of responsibilities for the sake of the "Kingdom," the "Power," and the "Glory" of God through Christ.[17] Love as described here is an *agapē*, a self-sustaining give-and-take. The Christian saint's love is beyond *amicitia* ("companionship"); it is beyond superficial *amor* ("love"); it is rather a commitment, an *agapē*.

So we must get back to our honoree: Professor Robert T. Meyer. If "greatness" means something of general human relevance or values, he is great. His qualities are those of Chaucer's saint: virtuous, noble, penitent, charitable, loving, committed, dedicated and conscientious. I hope we can truly say *Sapiens dominabitur astris* or *Sapientia primi est stultitia caruisse*.

16. In the Middle Ages, "fickle-minded Fortune was portrayed by the goddess *Fortuna* and her Wheel of Fortune. She represented the possibilities of hazards unknown and unpredictable and catastrophes beyond man's foreknowledge." Walter Clyde Curry has observed determinism in *Troilus and Criseyde*. See his *Chaucer and Medieval Sciences* (New York, 1969), pp. 241–298.

17. When love is informed by charity, it becomes the Ignatian ideal of detachment.

BONIFACE RAMSEY, O.P.

Saint Lawrence and His Book in the Mausoleum of Galla Placidia

THE WELL-KNOWN MOSAIC in the north lunette of the mid-fifth-century mausoleum of Galla Placidia in Ravenna has been called one of the most puzzling representations in all Christian art.[1] It shows to the right a bearded and nimbed young man, clad in white and carrying a cross, which he grasps in his right hand, on his right shoulder, while in his left hand he holds an open book that displays to the viewer several lines of illegible writing. At the center of the mosaic stands a grill on wheels, under which burns a fire, and the young man appears to be hastening toward this grill. Finally, to the left there stands a bookcase whose two doors are open, revealing within the four gospels in codex form, recognizable as such because they are clearly labeled MARCVS, LVKAS, MATTEVS, and IOANNES. The whole is placed against a blue background. Inasmuch as this mosaic is opposite the entrance to the mausoleum and is thus the first thing to be seen upon going into the building, it occupies a position of prominence that even the so-called Good Shepherd mosaic above the entrance, which is equally well known, does not have.

It would seem beyond doubt that we have here a representation of St. Lawrence, carrying the book and cross that came to be attributed to him and hastening toward the grill that was associated with his martyrdom. In his study of the mosaic, however, Pierre Courcelle notes two other

---

1. Julius Kurth, *Die Mosaiken der christlichen Ära I: Die Wandmosaiken von Ravenna* (Leipzig-Berlin: Deutsche Bibelgesellschaft, 1905), 57.

FIG. 1. Mosaic of St. Lawrence in the Mausoleum of Galla Placidia, Ravenna.

significant interpretations that bear upon the personage in question.[2] The first, held by a few scholars, suggests that a saint, or perhaps even Christ himself, is bringing a heretical book to the grill to be burned. The bookcase with the four gospels stands in orthodox contrast to the hetero-dox book. The second, proposed by W. Seston in 1945, is slightly more elaborate. According to it, the person portrayed is the victorious Christ, appearing on the day of judgment and holding the book in which are written the merits and sins of the human race, and the grill is the altar of holocausts on which, according to an Eastern tradition, sinners will be immolated. As Courcelle points out, this second interpretation is, in addition to other difficulties, unable to give a good account of the bookcase with the four gospels[3] (although neither, for that matter, do most of the interpretations that see the mosaic as a depiction of St. Lawrence).[4] The first of the two, on the other hand, appears absurd in

2. Pierre Courcelle, "Le gril de Saint Laurent au Mausolée de Galla Placidia," *Cahiers archéologiques* 3 (1948), 30.

3. Ibid., 32.

4. Courcelle's argument, ibid., 39, that the gospels symbolize the testament given to Lawrence by Sixtus, is not sufficiently convincing to me. Equally unconvincing is Hartmann Grisar's that the bookcase symbolizes Lawrence's connection with the ancient papal library: "Zum ältesten Kultus des Martyrers Laurentius," *Zeitschr. für kath. Theol.* 27 (1903), 133–138.

that it requires a large grill for burning a single book, when a small fire by itself would have done just as well.[5]

Most scholarship favors the view that this is a representation of the deacon Lawrence, and Courcelle's own essay is significant in this regard.[6] If we accept this as a given, as we have every reason to do, we can then say with certainty of course that the person portrayed is Lawrence and that the grill is the instrument of his death—even though, as Pio Franchi de' Cavalieri wrote at the turn of the century, he was much more likely to have been decapitated than to have been burned alive.[7] What remains in dispute, however, is why Lawrence is carrying a book and what the meaning is of the bookcase with the four gospels.

That Lawrence—as opposed to an orthodox burner of heretical volumes—should be carrying a book at all is a fact that has been given hardly any attention. It is assumed that this book is an important one: it has a clasp and several ribbons hanging from it, all of which betoken an important volume in antiquity; consequently it must be a holy book.[8] Usually it is said to be a book of the gospels because by the time the mosaic was composed the liturgical reading of the gospel was entrusted to a deacon, at least in the Church in Italy.[9] But a book of the psalms has also been suggested inasmuch as the triumphal arch of the late sixth-century San Lorenzo fuori le mura in Rome shows Lawrence holding an open book with some words from Psalm 112:9: DISPERSIT DEDIT PAVPERIBVS—a phrase that sums up Lawrence's caritative activity as a deacon.[10]

What is overlooked here is that at this time, and for some time afterward, the deacon Lawrence seems to be the unique exception to a

5. Courcelle, 30.

6. Cf. also Hans Dütschke, *Ravennatische Studien* (Leipzig: Wilhelm Engelmann, 1909), 265–274; Sante Ghigi, *Il Mausoleo di Galla Placidia* (Bergamo: Istituto Italiano d'Arti Grafichi, 1910), 83–87; Giuseppi Bovini, *Il cosiddetto Mausoleo di Galla Placidia in Ravenna* (Vatican City: Pontificio Istituto di Archeologia Cristiana, 1950), 50–52; Lazar Mirković, *Die Mosaike des Galla Placidia Mausoleums in Ravenna* (Belgrade: Akademija, 1960), 10–15; Jean Gagé, "Le livre sacré et l'épreuve du feu," *Mullus: Festschrift Theodor Klauser* (Münster: Aschendorff, 1964), 130–142; Friedrich Gerke, *Das Christusmosaik in der Laurentius-Kapelle der Galla Placidia in Ravenna* (Stuttgart: Philipp Reclam Jun., 1965); Paolo Lino Zovatto, *Il Mausoleo di Galla Placidia* (Ravenna: A. Longo, 1968), 90–97.

7. "San Lorenzo e il supplizio della graticola," *Römische Quartalschrift* 14 (1900), 159–176.

8. Dütschke, 266.

9. Cf. ibid., 272.

10. Cf. Zovatto, 94.

rule in early Christian iconography as to who may be portrayed carrying a book. The book, particularly when it is open, is the symbol of teaching authority, and thus it is found held by Christ himself, by the Church (as on the mosaic in Santa Sabina in Rome, dating to the early fifth century, where two women symbolizing the *Ecclesia ex circumcisione* and the *Ecclesia ex gentibus* each hold an open book), and by prophets, apostles, evangelists, and bishops. A bishop is very often portrayed with a book, for it was in him that the teaching office in the ancient Church was clearly radicated.[11] Sometimes someone in his entourage carries it for him, as for example the deacon does in the mid-sixth-century presbyterium mosaic of San Vitale in Ravenna. While it is true that by the fourth century the deacon usually proclaimed the gospel, and in some places even preached, teaching authority as such was not his.[12] This was a right claimed so tenaciously by bishops that Jerome would accuse them of jealousy for not permitting priests to preach in their presence.[13]

That the book symbolizes the authority to teach is underlined by its use in a depiction of Christ that was coming into vogue toward the end of the fourth century. In this depiction Christ is shown seated and with his right hand raised in the oratorical gesture that would later become a gesture of blessing; in his left hand he holds a book or scroll, and often he is surrounded by his apostles. All of this in combination—the sitting, the hand gesture, the book or scroll, and the group of listeners— represents the teacher par excellence. Perhaps the most familiar example of the scene is the early fifth-century apse mosaic in Santa Pudenziana in Rome, which contains each of these elements, even though the simple teacher's *cathedra* has been transformed into a bejeweled throne for Christ and the book that he holds says on its open pages: DOMINVS CONSERVATOR ECCLESIAE PVDENTIANAE. Numerous examples of this motif could be given.

Inasmuch as the book is so closely associated with the teaching office during this period, it seems highly unlikely that it would become part of the iconographic accoutrement of a deacon except for very unusual

11. For the relevant information cf. Bernard Cook, *Ministry to Word and Sacraments* (Philadelphia: Fortress Press, 1976), 254–273.

12. On the deacon as proclaimer of the gospel cf. *Const. App.* 2.57.7 (Funk 161–163); Jerome, *epist.* 147.6 (*CSEL* 56:322); Sozomen, *h.e.* 7.19 (*PG* 67:1477). On the deacon as preacher cf. Canon 2 of the Synod of Ancyra (Hefele-Leclercq 1/1:303); Philostorgius, *h.e.* 3.17 (*PG* 65:508–509).

13. *Epist.* 52.7 (*CSEL* 54:428).

reasons. Otherwise the strong symbolism would be in danger of ambiguity and dilution. In fact Lawrence could just as well have been portrayed carrying a chalice as the identifying sign of his diaconate, since a liturgical relationship to the chalice and to the Blood of Christ therein contained was at least as much a characteristic of a deacon as the ministry of proclaiming the gospel. So closely linked to the chalice was the deacon that the early fifth-century treatise attributed to Jerome and entitled *De septem ordinibus ecclesiae*, for instance, forbids a bishop to take the chalice from the altar during the celebration of the Eucharist unless it has first been handed to him by the deacon.[14] The chalice could also very conveniently have doubled as a symbol of martyrdom, since it functioned in that role from gospel times.[15] Indeed, Augustine makes the connection between the chalice and Lawrence's martyrdom when he says in a sermon on the saint's *dies natalis*: "Ibi [at Rome] sacrum Christi sanguinem ministravit: ibi pro Christi nomine suum sanguinem fudit."[16] That the mosaicist chose to give Lawrence a book rather than a chalice, all things considered, must have some meaning.

If we are to understand why Lawrence is carrying a book, then, it seems that we must look to the saint himself as he was viewed by the fifth-century Christians who practiced his cult and who designed and built the mausoleum of Galla Placidia, rather than to his diaconal office. What we are aware of here is the quite remarkable popularity of this saint, who died in the persecution of Valerian in 258. It is striking but mysterious that of all those who suffered at Rome in that persecution, including several other deacons, it was Lawrence who should have emerged from obscurity to become a hero of legendary proportions. Even the bishop, Sixtus, who was also martyred, attracted less attention, and his cult was certainly less intense than that of his deacon.

The evidence of Lawrence's popularity is found in the numerous references to him in antiquity.[17] We look in vain in the written sources, however, for anything that might serve to explain our mosaic to complete satisfaction. We can simply tell from them that Lawrence enjoyed a

---

14. A. W. Kalff, "Ps.-Hieronymi, *De septem ordinibus ecclesiae*" (diss., Würzburg, 1935), 39. Cf. also *Chron. Palatinum* 19 (*PL* 94:1170); Isidore, *eccl. off.* 2.8.4 (*PL* 83:789).

15. Cf. Mt. 20:22; 26:39ff. par.; *Mart. Polycarpi* 14.2 (LCL Apost. Fathers 2:330); Origen, *mart.* 28–29 (*GCS* 1:24–26).

16. *Serm.* 304.1 (*PL* 38:1395).

17. Some of the classic references are noted in *LThK* 6:831.

reputation in Rome, and hence in the places influenced by Rome, second only to that of Peter and Paul. [18] With them he was seen as the preeminent martyr. This would appear to be the reason why he is often shown bearing a cross, which was the preeminent sign of martyrdom (an attribute that he shares in antiquity only with Christ and Peter and one or two other saints), [19] whereas the crown is by far the more usual attribute of the martyr in ancient iconography.

That martyrdom was an imitation of Christ and represented the perfection of evangelical living is a commonplace throughout patristic literature. It appears clearly already in *The Martyrdom of Polycarp* in the middle of the second century. [20] The same work introduces another idea which was also to become a commonplace—that Christ was the martyr's companion in a special way. [21] Sometimes this companionship is expressed in a manner that virtually identifies Christ and the martyr. [22] In the case at hand, although the written sources do not attest to this in any striking fashion, [23] we would not be wrong to assume that Lawrence, for reasons that are unknown to us, was particularly closely identified with Christ. One monument does in fact seem to bear witness to such an identification. It is a small gold glass fragment, presently in the Metropolitan Museum of Art in New York, dated to the fifth century, and broken diagonally in such a way that only half of the image remains. The image in question is that of Lawrence, and it is clearly labeled LAVREN-TIO. The saint, who is bearded, carries a cross exactly as in the manner of the Galla Placidia mosaic, but unfortunately we do not know whether he was carrying a book, since the part of the glass that might have shown

18. Cf. the evidence assembled in *DACL* 8/2 : 1929–1931. 1930 n. 8 should read Augustine, *serm.* 296.5.6 (*PL* 38 : 1355) instead of 226.5. Note also the gold glass reproduced at 1925, showing Lawrence seated between Peter and Paul and holding a scroll.

19. Cf. Kurth 61; *DACL* 8/2 : 1947. Kurth mentions only Lawrence and Peter as crossbearers but fails to note John the Baptist, who carries a cross in the cupola mosaic of the Baptistry of the Orthodox in Ravenna. For a patristic reference to Lawrence's cross cf. Ps.-Fulgentius, *serm.* 60 (*PL* 65 : 930).

20. *Mart. Polycarpi* 1.1–2 (LCL Apost. Fathers 2 : 312).

21. Ibid., 2.2–3 (ibid., 314). Cf. also, e.g., Eusebius, *h.e.* 5.1.56 (*GCS* 2/1 : 424); *Passio Perp.* 4.2 (van Beek 10–12).

22. Cf. Eusebius, *h.e.* 5.1.23, 29–30, 42 (*GCS* 2/1 : 410, 412–414, 418); Paulinus of Nola, *epist.* 38.3 (*CSEL* 29/1 : 326–327).

23. Augustine, *serm.* 303.2; 304.2.2 (*PL* 38 : 1394–1396), uses the feast of St. Lawrence as an occasion to discuss martyrdom as the following of Christ, but he does not single out Lawrence as a better imitator than anyone else.

FIG. 2. Fragment of gold glass showing St. Lawrence.
The Metropolitan Museum of Art, Rogers Fund, 1918. (18.145.3)

that has been broken off. The remarkable feature of this depiction is that Lawrence is endowed not with a nimbus but with a christogram. In addition to this there is an Omega to the right of the saint, and the implication is that there was an Alpha to the left of him, although that would have been on the broken-off part. The christogram and the Alpha and Omega, letters by which Christ refers to himself in Revelation 22:13, are only attributed to a saint with extreme rarity; one other example is known—a fresco of St. Januarius in a Neapolitan catacomb, which dates from the fourth century.[24] These symbols on the gold glass serve to link Christ and Lawrence in a very close way and even suggest that Lawrence is a type of Christ in a manner that most martyrs were not.

Is it possible to make the jump from these somewhat scattered data to the mosaic in the mausoleum of Galla Placidia? It seems at least plausible that our mosaic also seeks to portray Lawrence as a type of Christ—and that to a degree, once again, that most martyrs were not. To this end it depicts Lawrence not only with a cross, which is unusual enough, but also with a book. This book is the gospel, which is in turn symbolic of Christ, whom the martyr has imitated and identified with by his suffering and death. It is not simply held in liturgical fashion, as if it were being either read or carried in procession; rather it seems to be displayed by its bearer, and it is open to the viewer to indicate the clarity of the martyr's imitation and identification: all can see in the open book the archetype, Christ, of which Lawrence is the type. The bookcase with the gospels at the other end of the lunette is a counterbalance to the figure of Lawrence, and it serves to make still clearer the notion of the martyr in question as a type of Christ and of the gospel. That is to say, it suggests that Lawrence is the living out, the vivification, of the four gospels, which otherwise are mere words recorded in books and kept in storage.[25]

This iconography is not repeated a century later in the mosaic of the procession of the martyrs in Sant' Apollinare Nuovo in Ravenna. There Lawrence bears the conventional martyr's crown, as do the others in the mosaic, although he is distinguished from them by his gold tunic, while they wear only white. It does reappear, however, in the basilica of San Lorenzo fuori le mura, where, in addition to the book described earlier in this essay, Lawrence also carries a cross. His counterpart on the triumphal arch mosaic is the deacon St. Stephen, who bears no cross but who does carry an open book with some words from Psalm 63:9: ADESIT ANIMA MEA. Possibly in this case the books are merely vehicles for the two phrases from the psalms that attempt to characterize the two saints. Possibly Stephen was made to hold a book simply to balance the figure of Lawrence. Certainly it may be said that by this time—the end of the

24. For this information cf. Kurt Weitzmann, ed., *Age of Spirituality: Late Antique and Early Christian Art, Third to Seventh Century* (New York: Metropolitan Museum of Art, 1979), 572–573.

25. There is no need to make much of the precise way in which the bookcase doors are opened, as does Dütschke, 268: "die Türen des Bücherschrankes sind wie von Geisterhänden geöffnet." They are simply open to show the contents of the bookcase!

sixth century—the symbolism of the book has, in any event, begun to weaken. The seventh-century mosaic in the Oratory of St. Venantius in the Lateran Baptistry in Rome, for example, contains several depictions of nonepiscopal saints with books in hand, including the deacon St. Septimius.

The dilution of this symbol is undoubtedly tied to the fact that, by the beginning of the sixth century, both priests and deacons were being called to assist the bishops in their preaching ministry. Caesarius of Arles says that, while bishops should preach in the cities, priests and deacons should do so in the countryside, since this area was less accessible to the bishops. [26] The second canon of the Synod of Vaison in Gaul, held in 529, permitted priests to preach *in omnibus parrociis*. [27] At the end of the century we are even told by Gregory the Great of a monk named Equitius who, although unordained, exercised the preaching office with the approval of ecclesiastical authorities. [28] While it is true that priests and deacons had always preached to some extent, and while bishops continued theoretically to be the Church's preachers and teachers par excellence, nonetheless it is clear that the sixth century in the West saw a real fracturing of the consciousness of an episcopal exclusivity with regard to preaching. With the broadening of the preaching ministry the original meaning of the book in sacred art was lost or at least greatly expanded.

The book in Lawrence's hand, then, is the crucial aspect of the mosaic that we have been studying. That it should be there at all is remarkable. This essay ought to have demonstrated, if anything, that it is too facile to explain it unreflectively as the symbol of Lawrence's diaconate, given the restricted use of the book in fourth- and fifth-century iconography. The explanation can only be sought in the unusual and as yet unaccountable esteem with which the early Western Church regarded this saint, who, for reasons now lost to us, was felt to have imitated Christ and the gospel with particular clarity.

26. Cf. *Serm.* 1.12 (Morin 1:10–11).
27. *CCSL* 148A:78–79.
28. Cf. *dial.* 1.4 (*PL* 77:165ff.). It is interesting to note that this same Equitius was buried in a church dedicated to St. Lawrence: cf. ibid., 176.

RUTH STEINER

Matins Responsories and Cycles of
Illustrations of Saints' Lives

THE MUSIC OF the medieval Divine Office includes chants of three kinds: hymns, antiphons, and responsories. It is responsories that are to be discussed in this paper—the chants that follow the various lessons of a matins service. I wish to present to the reader one characteristic series of responsories for the feast of St. Benedict, and one for St. Martin, and to compare each with a cycle of illustrations of the saint's life.

In early times the observation of the Divine Office involved almost exclusively texts taken from the Bible, primarily from the book of Psalms. However, even the earliest source in which texts of individual chants of the Divine Office are written out, the antiphonal of the manuscript Paris, Bibl. nat., lat. 17436, dating from the years 860–880, includes several chant series on texts excerpted from or based on saints' lives.[1] To know how this source compares with others, we may consult a work by Dom René-Jean Hesbert, *Corpus Antiphonalium Officii*, in which the contents of six antiphonals of the Roman cursus and six of the monastic are set forth in parallel columns.[2] Even the most cursory glance

1. Concerning some of these, see Ritva Jonsson, *Historia: Études sur la genèse des offices versifiés* (Stockholm: Almqvist and Wiksell, 1968), pp. 30–76. Mme Jonsson takes account not only of matins responsories but of all of the chants for the Divine Office. For a survey of the early development of the Office, see Paul F. Bradshaw, *Daily Prayer in the Early Church* (London: Alcuin Club/SPCK, 1981).

2. 6 vols. (Rome: Herder, 1963–1979). In volume 5 of this work, the selection and ordering of matins responsories on the four Sundays of Advent is used as the basis for grouping hundreds of manuscripts of the Divine Office. As Dom Hesbert has pointed out (on p. vi of that volume), the antiphonal—the book containing chants—shows the least change

through this work is enough to establish the lack of uniformity in the organization of the services for one day after another; one cannot speak in general of, for example, "the matins service for the feast of St. Benedict"; one must always specify the source in which the service in question appears.

The matins service for a major feast, in the monastic form, consists of an introduction—made up of Psalm 3, the invitatory, and a hymn— and then three large sections, known as nocturns. The first two of these begin with six psalms and antiphons, the last with canticles and a single antiphon. All three nocturns continue with four lessons, each of which is followed by a responsory: thus there are twelve lessons and twelve responsories in all. The lessons are sometimes all from the same source; it may be a continuous text which they separate into sections. Or two texts may be involved, one in the first two nocturns, another in the third. There may be more than two texts. The dividing of the text into lessons may often have been a more or less mechanical process; but there are instances where it seems clearly to reflect thought and judgment.

To turn from lessons to responsories, the most obvious connection among the latter on a particular saint's day is that they all concern the saint; their texts are likely to be excerpts from his *vita*. A case in point is the series of responsories for the feast of St. Benedict in the St. Martial breviary Paris, Bibl. nat., lat. 743, of the eleventh century, which has been discussed in a recent article.[3] A different series of responsories for the same feast is found in a twelfth-century Monte Cassino antiphonal, MS 542 of the Archivio of that monastery. It is nearly identical with the series given in Benevento, Bibl. cap., V, 21, which is one of the sources

---

through time of any of those liturgical books of which the contents were combined to form the breviary. In a particular monastery or cathedral, the lessons of matins on a certain day were far more likely to be changed than were the chants. The notes by Peter Dinter for the new edition of the *Liber Tramitis* (*Corpus Consuetudinum Monasticarum* 10, ed. K. Hallinger [Siegburg: Schmitt, 1980]) show how often this happened in a relatively short period at Cluny, even without taking full account of the lessons in Paris, Bibl. nat., lat. 12601. Given the relative instability of the lessons of matins, and the fact that often within one manuscript a series of responsories may be sung on different days with different series of lessons, correspondence in theme between an individual responsory and the lesson that precedes it may be only the result of happy accident. There is thus a contrast here between the responsory of matins and that of the Mass (that is, the gradual)—a difference not always recognized by medieval commentators on the liturgy, whose writing on this subject was admirably surveyed by Daniel J. Sheerin in a paper delivered at Catholic University on 3 August 1982.

3. "The Music for a Cluny Office of St. Benedict," *Monasticism and the Arts*, ed. T. Verdon (Syracuse, N.Y.: Syracuse University Press, 1983).

surveyed by Dom Hesbert in *Corpus Antiphonalium Officii*, volume 2. The texts are given in Appendix I of this article as they appear in Hesbert's edition (in volume 4), modified only to reflect minor differences, in respect to the designating of verses and refrains, between the Monte Cassino antiphonal and the Beneventan manuscript followed by Hesbert.[4]

Every one of the responsories in the Monte Cassino series is closely connected to the *vita*, not only in content but in phraseology as well. For the first and second of them, the source is the Prologue; for the third and fourth (which are very similar in wording) it is the beginning of chapter 1. Responsories 5 and 6 tell of Benedict's flight to Subiaco and how he made his home there with the help of Romanus (chap. 1). Responsory 7 is a setting of words Benedict addressed to monks who attempted to poison him (chap. 3); Responsory 8 refers to the growing numbers of monks who sought his guidance (chap. 2; the verse is from the end of chap. 1). A story told in chapter 32, of how Benedict raised a child from the dead, is the subject of Responsories 9 and 10. Responsory 11 describes a vision of St. Benedict (chap. 35); Responsory 12 identifies him as the author of a Rule for monks (chap. 36).

What is conveyed through these responsories is thus primarily the broad outline of the saint's life and spiritual growth. There are no references to the miracles at Subiaco described in chapters 5–8, none to the miracles at Monte Cassino (chaps. 9–11), no accounts of how Benedict foretold the future (chaps. 12–22) or of events in daily life at Monte Cassino (chaps. 23–30). Just three miracles are highlighted by being included in this series. The first, which occurred before Benedict went to Subiaco, shows him already able to use miraculous powers to combat the influence of Satan over souls (R. 7). The second is that of raising the boy from the dead, the miracle in which Benedict's power is most evident (Rs. 9 and 10). The third, the vision of the whole world

---

4. Dom R. Andoyer called attention to these responsories in "L'ancienne Liturgie de Bénévent," *Revue du chant grégorien* 23 (1919), 42–44. The musical features that they have in common with other examples of Beneventan chant remain to be identified. (At the Eighteenth International Congress on Medieval Studies at the Medieval Institute of Western Michigan University, Kalamazoo, in May 1983, several papers concerning Beneventan liturgy and chant were presented; but the emphasis there was on tropes, sequences, and chants of the Mass.) An investigation of all of the responsories for St. Benedict in a representative sampling of medieval antiphonaries and breviaries is being carried out by Linus Ellis, a graduate student in the School of Music at Catholic University.

gathered up in a single ray of light, shows Benedict at a climactic moment in his spiritual development—absorbed in God (R. 11).[5]

Since there can be no more than twelve responsories in matins, deciding on the text for each of them requires a high degree of selectivity. The characteristics of the musical genre call for texts that are moderate in length, and consist of two principal parts—the respond and the verse.[6] In order for the musical setting to be successful, the texts must have good rhythm and balanced phrasing; and thus when the wording of responsories is compared with that of the section of the *vita* on which they are based, considerable reworking is often evident.[7]

How much selectivity is involved in the choice of lessons for a matins service? The answer to that question may vary a great deal, depending on how long the lessons are in proportion to the total length of the text from which they are excerpted. An eleventh-century Monte Cassino lectionary—Vatican Library, Vat. lat. 1202—contains the entire text of the life of St. Benedict by Gregory the Great divided into twelve lessons, as follows (references by page and line are to the edition by Umberto Moricca).[8]

Lesson 1: Prologue—end of chap. 2 (Moricca, 71–80,3)

Lesson 2: Chap. 3 nearly complete (Moricca, 80,4–84,6)

Lesson 3: End of chap. 3, chaps. 4–7 (Moricca, 84,7–90,25)

Lesson 4: First part of chap. 8 (Moricca, 90,26–94,8)

Lesson 5: End of chap. 8, chaps. 9, 10, and most of 11 (Moricca, 94,9–98,18)

Lesson 6: End of chap. 11, chaps. 12–14 and beginning of 15 (Moricca, 98,19–102,15)

Lesson 7: End of chap. 15, chap. 16 (Moricca, 102,15–106,20)

Lesson 8: Chaps. 17–21 (Moricca, 106,21–112,3)

Lesson 9: Chaps. 22–24 (Moricca, 112,4–117,3)

Lesson 10: Chaps. 25–29, beginning of chap. 30 (Moricca, 117, 4–121,9)

---

5. This outline of the *vita* follows that provided by Odo J. Zimmermann and Benedict R. Avery in the introduction to their translation of the *Life and Miracles of St. Benedict* (St. John's Abbey, Collegeville, Minn.: Liturgical Press, 1949), pp. viii–x.

6. See Helmut Hucke, "Das Responsorium," *Gattungen der Musik in Einzeldarstellungen*, ed. W. Arlt (Bern: Francke Verlag, 1973), 144–191, esp. 166–171 and 182–191.

7. For several examples, see the article referred to in n. 3.

8. *Gregorii Magni Dialogi Libri IV* (Roma: Tipografia del Senato, 1924).

Lesson 11: Continuation of chap. 30, chaps. 31–34 (Moricca, 121,10–128,7)

Lesson 12: Chap. 35–end (Moricca, 128,8–134,18)

If this is to be taken as a serious indication that the whole of this long text is going to be read at matins, and if the responsories of the Monte Cassino antiphonal are inserted after each of the lessons, then in the entire service there are only two responsories that in their texts recall material from the lesson that immediately preceded them. All the rest either return to material that was read somewhat earlier (Rs. 3–8) or anticipate a section of the *vita* that is still to come (Rs. 9–11).

This service can be compared with that of the manuscript Benevento, Bibl. cap., V, 19 (Benevento, twelfth century), which follows the Roman cursus—having only nine lessons and responsories—and in which only selections from the life of St. Benedict are read. The responsories are taken from the series of twelve referred to above; to bring the number down to nine, Responsories 9–11 are omitted. The content of the lessons is as follows:

Lesson 1: Prologue

Lesson 2: First part of chap. 1 (Moricca, 73,6–75,4)

Lesson 3: Continuation of chap. 1 (Moricca, 75,4–77,10)

Lesson 4: Continuation of chap. 1 (Moricca, 77,10–78,8)

Lesson 5: Conclusion of chap. 3 (Moricca, 84,7–86,3)

Lesson 6: Chap. 6 (Moricca, 89,1–19)

Lesson 7: Chap. 7 nearly complete (Moricca, 89,20–90,22)

Lesson 8: Chaps. 9 and 10 (Moricca, 96,21–97,19)

Lesson 9: Chap. 37 and the first part of chap. 38 (Moricca, 132, 4–133,18)

In this service, certain events are recalled only in the lessons: how at Subiaco Benedict recovered the blade of the brush hook from the bottom of the lake (Lesson 6), how Placidus was rescued from the lake (Lesson 7), and how, in the early days at Monte Cassino, Benedict through prayer made it possible for an immovable stone to be lifted and caused a fire in the monastery kitchen to be extinguished (Lesson 8). Through this choice of lessons, emphasis is placed on the power of Benedict as a protector of his monks, an emphasis that appears also in the *Dialogus Miraculorum* of Desiderius, written at Monte Cassino in the mid-eleventh century. Benedicta Ward has seen in this emphasis in the latter work a response to definite needs: "Desiderius . . . was abbot of the monastery of St. Benedict and responsible for many monks and wide possessions; the monks were not only spiritual sons but also tenants of St. Benedict, and for this reason his power was invoked more frequently than his holiness. The miracles recorded by Desiderius illustrate the power of St. Benedict as patron."[9] Another event is recalled only through a responsory—the attempted poisoning (R. 7). There is no reference in the lessons or responsories of this service to the raising of the dead child.

As in the lessons and responsories of matins, so also through series of pictures representing events in the life of a saint, certain emphases can be made. The more limited the number of pictures, the more critical the choice. For the life of St. Benedict, there is a celebrated series of illustrations in the Monte Cassino lectionary.[10] All of the pictures corresponding to events narrated in a single lesson are placed in the manuscript before the beginning of that lesson. Hence the pictures do not stand next to the narrative of the events they represent; they come in groups. Before the first lesson there are two full pages of pictures, showing a number of different episodes. They are accompanied by verses that serve as captions, helping to tell the stories. They are, to be sure, illustrations of the life of St. Benedict, but in this manuscript they are treated not as illustrations of the text they accompany but as a separate narrative—as a life of St. Benedict in pictures with verses that is presented in alternation, section by section, with a life of St. Benedict in words.

There is a direct correspondence between some of these illustrations and the texts of certain responsories. One of them, on fol. 26r, relates to the story of the attempted poisoning. Benedict is shown with hands raised, making the sign of the cross; the vessel of wine, elevated to receive the blessing, is shown at the very moment of its shattering—bits of it are falling through the air. Another group of pictures, on fol. 72r, shows the story of the boy restored to life. The body of the boy lies before the door of the monastery, on the right; on the left, the father meets Benedict returning from work in the fields, in the center, Benedict kneels in prayer. There are other examples; and the illustrations in this

---

9. Benedicta Ward, *Miracles and the Medieval Mind* (Philadelphia, Pa.: University of Pennsylvania Press, 1982), p. 44.

10. A facsimile edition of this manuscript is currently in press; it will include critical studies of the source, for which the general editor is Paul Meyvaert. The publisher is Johnson Reprints.

series are so abundant that it is difficult to be precise concerning what is stressed in the series and what is omitted from it—apart from the obvious point that there are certain kinds of psychological events, inner states, that are difficult to present in pictures. There is, however, on fol. 79v, a splendid representation of Benedict's vision of the whole world in a single ray of light.

The liturgy and the iconography for St. Benedict have counterparts in works for St. Martin of Tours, and it is with the latter that the remainder of this study will be concerned. For the series of illuminations in the Vatican manuscript there is a parallel in a series of embroidered medallions and panels showing events in the life of St. Martin that date from the first part of the fifteenth century (1430–1435). Their style is that of Franco-Netherlandish art works of the period; and they have been the subject of a distinguished study by Margaret Freeman.[11] Once again, the rather large number of pictures—here, thirty-two roundels, four arched panels, and one oval embroidery—makes it difficult to know what, if any, significance can be attached to the omission of certain events from the series. A further difficulty is that the series is now incomplete, and its original arrangement is unknown. A comparable work in which a more limited number of scenes from the life of St. Martin is shown is a thirteenth-century altar frontal from Iceland now in the Musée de Cluny in Paris.[12]

The work measures about 50 inches in width and $36\frac{1}{2}$ inches in height. There are twelve medallions, each of them about 10 inches across. The order in which they are to be read is that of lines of text on a page; there are four medallions in each horizontal row. Seven of them show events narrated by Sulpicius Severus in his *Life of St. Martin of Tours*, three are connected with stories told in the *Dialogues* (also by Sulpicius Severus), and two with the description of Martin's death given in his *Letter to Bassula*.[13]

In the medallions, Martin is shown first as a soldier, then, after

11. Margaret B. Freeman, *The St. Martin Embroideries* (New York: Metropolitan Museum of Art, 1968).

12. There is a black-and-white reproduction of it in Mrs. Freeman's book (fig. 72, p. 112). The reading of the scenes given here has followed hers, except for that of the first medallion in the lowest line. There are nearly full-size color reproductions of seven of the medallions in Walter Nigg, *Martin von Tours* (Freiburg: Herder, 1977); see plates 4, 12, 18, 19, 36, 39, and 40, and p. 114.

13. For the Latin text of the *Life* and the *Letters*, see Jacques Fontaine, *Sulpice Sévère: Vie de Saint Martin*, 3 vols. (SC 133–135; Paris: Editions du Cerf, 1968–1969). Fontaine's ex-

baptism, as a monk, and finally as a bishop. When the sacraments of baptism and consecration are shown (in the third and sixth of the medallions), the hand of God appears at the top of the picture, as it does also in the two scenes (four and five) that show two occasions where the monk Martin raised a man from the dead. For the two medallions at the beginning of the series, where the soldier Martin shares his cloak with a poor man, and then—in a dream—sees Christ holding the portion of his cloak that he has given away, there is a parallel in the medallions at the end of the second line. These tell a story from the *Dialogues* (2.1) about how Martin as bishop of Tours was asked by a poor man for some clothing, and later gave him his own tunic.

The first medallion in the lowest line shows Martin healing a paralyzed girl, an event that took place in the city of Trèves (*Vita*, chap. 16); the next two show him in the countryside. In one he casts out a demon from a cow (*Dialogues* 2.9); in the other, he puts a flock of birds to flight by speaking to them in a commanding voice. If in the first of these we are reminded of the section of Martin's *Vita* that describes his activity in the countryside of central Gaul (chaps. 12–15), in the second, it is clear that the end is at hand. For this episode is told in the *Letter to Bassula*, where it is immediately followed by a description of the death of Martin.

If this selection is compared with the outline of the whole of the *Vita* as Fontaine has sketched it out,[14] it is evident that the designer of the embroidery, wishing to present clearly the broad historical outline of Martin's life, has done so by limiting severely references to individual events in his later years. There is thus a parallel between what is shown in this series of medallions, and the handling of biography in the responsories for Benedict in the Monte Cassino antiphonal.

To what extent can similar procedures be detected in the choice of lessons and responsories for St. Martin in medieval sources? One manuscript that presents a matins service for St. Martin with fairly extended

---

tended commentary has been drawn on in a number of places in the present article. For the text of the *Dialogues*, the Latin is available only in Carolus Halm, *Sulpicii Severi Libri Qui Supersunt* (*CSEL* 1; Vienna: Apud C. Geroldi Filium Bibliopolam Academiae, 1866), 152–216. There is an English translation by Bernard M. Peebles, "Sulpicius Severus, Writings," in *FOTC* 7 (New York: Fathers of the Church, Inc., 1949), pp. 79–254. See also the translation by F. R. Hoare in *The Western Fathers* (New York: Sheed and Ward, 1954), 10–44.

14. Vol. 1, pp. 88–96.

lessons is a Cluny breviary dated ca. 1075—Paris, Bibl. nat., lat. 12601.[15] The lessons are as follows.

Lesson 1: *Vita* 2.1−5
Lesson 2: *Vita* 2.6−8
Lesson 3: *Vita* 3.1−4
Lesson 4: *Vita* 3.5−4.9
Lesson 5: *Vita* 5.1−6
Lesson 6: *Vita* 6.1−7.1
Lesson 7: *Letter to Bassula* 6−13
Lesson 8: *Letter to Bassula* 14−end
Lesson 9: Gregory of Tours, *History of the Franks* 1.9.48
Lesson 10: *Letter to Aurelius* (complete)
Lesson 11: Gregory of Tours, *Liber I de virtutibus S. Martini*, chap. 4 (complete)
Lesson 12: Gregory of Tours, *Liber I de virtutibus S. Martini*, chap. 5 (without last sentence)

In the lessons of the first nocturn, two events of profound significance are narrated: Martin shares his cloak with a beggar (and later has a vision of Christ); and he goes before the emperor to declare that he will no longer serve him, but only Christ. For Martin, the period of military service is transformed into a noviciate; and in the years covered by these lessons, he progresses from passive perfection in the Christian faith to active affirmation of it.[16]

In the lessons of the second nocturn, Martin places himself under the spiritual direction of Hilary of Poitiers. The manifold nature of his vocation becomes evident. Now he undertakes various forms of combat: against pagan error (represented by the brigands he meets in crossing the Alps), against heretics (the Arians), against Satan himself. He feels a call also to asceticism, and to the work of healing, a call to which Hilary gives formal recognition by ordaining Martin as an exorcist. At the very end of Lesson 6, Martin founds the monastery of Ligugé.

With that, the readings from the *Life of Martin* end; the next two

---

15. Concerning this manuscript, see J. Hourlier, "Le Bréviaire de Saint-Taurin: Un livre liturgique clunisien a l'usage de l'Échelle Saint-Aurin (Paris, Bibl. nat., lat. 12601)," *Études grégoriennes* 3 (1959), 163−173. In the length of the lessons in this breviary, Hourlier sees a reminder of "les grandes dévotions clunisiennes" (p. 165).

16. Fontaine, vol. 1, p. 89.

lessons, comprising most of the *Letter to Bassula*, describe his death. He had a premonition of it; though already ill, he undertook a trip to bring peace among the clergy in a nearby town, and there the end came. Sulpicius gives us the words Martin's disciples used in pleading with him not to die, and also his reply—addressed not to them but to God— "Lord, if I am still necessary to your people, I do not refuse the toil: Thy will be done." [17] The final scene is described in detail (detail faithfully reproduced in the last of the medallions in the Icelandic embroidery), and Martin's last words are reported: "Abrahae me sinus recipit." It is surely, as Bernard Peebles observed, "one of the most eloquent passages in all hagiographical literature." [18]

The lessons of the last nocturn are occupied with burial, with accounts of how news of Martin's death was conveyed to certain individuals, and with mourning. The first of them tells the story of how Martin's body reached its final resting place. The second is the whole of Sulpicius' *Letter to the Deacon Aurelius*. Sulpicius recounts how he learned of the death of Martin, and continues by alternating his laments with praise of the departed. Fontaine has pointed out an exact correspondence between the form of this letter and that proposed by the Greek rhetorician Menander (third century A.D.) for consolatory discourse. He observes that Sulpicius follows the form more strictly than does St. Jerome in his consolatory letters, but modifies the tone of the eulogy in such a way that in the praise of the departed there is more than a hint of cultic veneration. [19] The third and fourth lessons report how Martin's death was revealed to St. Severinus and St. Ambrose in separate visions.

Thus in half the lessons of this service, the central theme is the death of Martin. In the responsories (given here in Appendix II), there is an even greater preoccupation with this subject. No fewer than nine of them incorporate quotations from the *Letter to Bassula*; each of the three passages that follow is drawn on in three different responsories. "Domine, si adhuc populo tuo sum necessarius, non recuso laborem, fiat

---

17. Peebles writes, "The prayer of the dying Martin—and especially his expression of willingness to continue with his earthly work if God so willed, his *Non recuso laborem*— has often been repeated by other saints" (p. 87). Paul Antin cites several examples of this in his study "La Mort de Saint Martin," *Revue des Études Anciennes* 66 (1964), 108–120, pp. 110–111, n. 5.

18. Introduction to the writings of Sulpicius Severus, *FOTC* 7:87.

19. Fontaine, vol. 3, pp. 1180–1182. Concerning the development of the literature of consolation, see Martin R. P. McGuire, "The Early Christian Funeral Oration," in *FOTC* 22 (New York: Fathers of the Church, Inc., 1953), pp. vii–xxi.

voluntas tua," the beginning of the prayer in which Martin responded to his disciples' plea, shows him in inner conflict, his own will opposing that of God, and then yielding. (See Rs. 2, 3, and 9.) "O virum ineffabilem, nec labore victum nec morte vincendum, qui nec mori timuit, nec vivere recusavit," presents Martin as having reached a full monastic *apatheia*, the crowning touch in his sanctity. (See Rs. 3, 4, and 9.) "Oculis ac manibus in coelum semper intentus, invictum ab oratione spiritum non relaxabat," shows Martin steadfast in directing both body and soul heavenward. (See Rs. 2, 5, and 6.)

Still other phrases from the *Letter to Bassula* are found in Responsories 7, 8, 11, and 12. There is also a quotation (in R. 10) from the excerpt from Gregory of Tours that is read in Lesson 12. The only incident in Martin's earlier life referred to directly in these responsories is a vision described at the beginning of the second *Dialogue*: how Martin, having given his tunic to a poor man, entered the church to celebrate Mass, and a globe of fire was seen to spring from his head and rise through the air above him. The two responsories that refer to this event (5 and 6) juxtapose it with a description of Martin's attitude of prayer on his deathbed.

In being chosen to be set to music, these passages have been singled out as themes for meditation; for while they are being sung by some, others will listen. Transformed into the texts of Gregorian chants, they have become part of a cycle: they will be committed to memory, and performed in public year after year. In being incorporated into the liturgy they have had a place assured to them in a body of material that is widely, even popularly, known. The passages in the literature concerning St. Martin to which these chants correspond will become, for many, those that are most familiar.[20]

20. This is not the place for extended comparisons, but the two that follow may be of interest. A breviary from Marmoutier dating from the second half of the thirteenth century, Tours, Bibl. mun., 153, includes eleven of the Cluny responsories in its matins service, in the following order (the numbers here refer to the order in which the same chants occurred in the Cluny MS): 7, 8, 2, 9; 3, 4, 1, 11; 10, Hesbert 6621 *Ecclesia virtute roboratur*, 5, 12. (For several of these the verses are different from those of Cluny.) The lessons are all from a short passage (sections 6–12) of the *Letter to Bassula*; it seems likely that the responsories that accompanied the reading of the longer excerpt from the *Letter to Bassula* in the Cluny breviary appear here at the beginning of the service because of their connection with this text: for example, Cluny R. 7 begins with an echo of the opening of the excerpt, "Beatus Martinus obitum suam longe ante praescivit." An Amiens breviary of about the same date, Amiens, Bibl. mun., 112, which follows the Roman cursus, has the following series of responsories (again indicated by numbers derived from their position in the Cluny matins): 1, 7, 8;

Why are the responsories for this matins service for the feast day of St. Martin focused so much on his death? In the early centuries of Christianity, when persecution and martyrdom were facts of everyday life, the story of the Three Children in the Fiery Furnace was often evoked, in various ways, as a model for response to the threat of violent death. After the Peace of the Church, there was a need for models of other kinds; and Martin, as an aged man, rich in years and in achievements, free as only one can be who "neither fears to die nor refuses to live," meeting death with ineffable grace, meets the needs of a time when many Christians could reasonably expect to have a long life and a peaceful death.

It is thus evident that deciding upon texts for lessons and responsories in the medieval Divine Office was far from being a matter of routine. Different choices reveal different attitudes toward the material that was being drawn on, and they reflect the spiritual and even political needs of different times. There are thousands of manuscripts; at present, we can only guess at what a fuller examination of their contents will reveal.[21]

Appendix I

Responsories in Matina for the Feast of St. Benedict
in the antiphonal Monte Cassino, Archivio, 542 (twelfth century)

R. 1 (Hesbert 6751): Fuit vir vitae venerabilis, gratia Benedictus et nomine; ab ipso pueritiae suae tempore cor gerens senile, aetatem quippe moribus transiens, nulli animum voluptati dedit.

2, 5, 12; 3, 10, 11. The lessons in the first two nocturns are excerpted from the *Letter to Bassula*; those in the third nocturn are excerpted from the texts read as lessons 9, 11, and 12 in the Cluny service. It is remarkable that in all of these responsories there is no mention of the incident in Martin's life that has been presented most often through the visual arts—the dividing of his cloak with the poor man. In surveying responsories for the feast of St. Martin that appear in a number of different sources, Martha Fickett has found some that do refer to this event. Her doctoral dissertation, soon to be completed at Catholic University, is entitled "Chants for the Feast of St. Martin of Tours." It is primarily concerned with music, and includes transcriptions and analyses of a good sampling of the total musical repertory— antiphons as well as responsories, chants of the Mass as well as those of the Divine Office.

21. An earlier version of this paper was presented at the Seventeenth International Congress on Medieval Studies at Western Michigan University, Kalamazoo, in May 1982, and at the Conference on Medieval and Renaissance Music at the University of Manchester in August of that year. It was begun as a report for a seminar in Greek and Latin hagiography offered at Dumbarton Oaks under the joint direction of Giles Constable and Ihor Ševčenko in the spring of 1981.

V. Relicta domo rebusque patris, soli Deo placere desiderans, sanctae conversationis habitum quaesivit.—Ab.

V. (added later, over the preceding text) Recessit igitur, scienter nescius et sapienter indoctus.—Aetatem.

R. 2 (Hesbert 7252): Nursia provincia ortus, Romae liberalibus litterarum studiis traditus fuerat, sed cum in eis multos per abrupta vitiorum ire cerneret, eum quem quasi in ingressum mundi posuerat pedem retraxit.

V. Ne si de scientia ejus aliquid attingeret, ipse quoque postmodum immane praecipitium totus iret.—Eum.

R. 3 (Hesbert 6836): Hic itaque, cum jam relictis litterarum studiis petere deserta decrevisset, nutrix quae hunc artius amabat sola secuta est.

V. Relicta domo rebusque patris, soli Deo placere desiderans, sanctae conversationis habitum quaesivit.—Nutrix.

R. 4 (Hesbert 7448): Puer Domini Benedictus, cum jam relictis litterarum studiis petere deserta decrevisset, nutrix quae hunc artius amabat sola secuta est.

V. Recessit igitur, scienter nescius et sapienter indoctus.—Aetatem.

R. 5 (Hesbert 6248): Benedictus, Dei famulus, mala mundi plus appetens perpeti quam laudes, pro Deo laboribus fatigari quam vitae hujus favoribus extolli.

V. Nutricem suam occulte fugiens, deserti loci secessus petiit.—Pro.

R. 6 (Hesbert 7890): Vir Dei mundum fugiens, Romanus monachus hunc euntem reperit, quo tenderet requisivit. Cujus cum desiderium cognovisset, et secretum tenuit et adjutorium impendit, eique sanctae conversationis habitum tradidit, et in quantum licuit ministravit.

V. Tribusque annis, excepto Romano monacho, omnibus incognitus mansit.—Cujus.

R. 7 (Hesbert 7158): Misereatur vestri, fratres, omnipotens Deus! quare in me ista facere voluistis? Numquid non dixi vobis quia meis ac vestris moribus non conveniret? Ite, et secundum mores vestros patrem vobis quaerite, quia me post haec habere minime potestis.

V. Tunc ad locum dilectae solitudinis rediit, et solus in superni spectatoris oculis habitavit secum dicens.—Ite.

R. 8 (Hesbert 6298): Coeperunt postmodum multi mundum relinquere, et ad almi patris magisterium festinare: liber quippe tentationis vitio, jure jam factus est virtutum magister.

V. Nomen itaque ejus per vicina loca cunctis innotuit, factumque est ut ex illo jam tempore a multis frequentaretur.—Liber.

R. 9 (Hesbert 6532): Dum beatus Benedictus ab agri opere cum fratribus reverteretur, ecce quidam rusticus defuncti filii corpus ante januam monasterii luctu aestuans projecit.

V. Quem, mox ut orbatus rusticus aspexit, clamare coepit: Redde filium meum, redde filium meum.—Ante.

R. 10 (Hesbert 7223): Non aspicias, Domine, peccata, sed fidem hominis hujus qui resuscitari filium suum rogat, et redde in hoc corpusculo animam quam abstulisti.

V. Vix in oratione verba compleverat, coepit reviviscere qui erat mortuus, et jam viventem patri reddidit.—Et redde.

R. 11 (Hesbert 6974): Intempesta noctis hora, cuncta sub silentio, vidit beatus Benedictus fusam lucem desuper cunctas noctis tenebras effugasse.

V. Mira autem valde res in hac speculatione secuta est: nam omnis mundus velut sub uno solis radio collectus ante oculos ejus adductus est.—Vidit.

R. 12 (Hesbert 7894): Vir enim Domini, inter tot miracula quibus in mundo claruit, doctrinae verbo non mediocriter fulsit. Scripsit namque monachorum Regulam, discretione praecipuam, sermone luculentam.

V. Cujus si quis velit subtilius vitam moresque cognoscere, in ipsa institutione Regulae potest invenire.—Scripsit.

Appendix II

Responsories in Matins for the Feast of St. Martin of Tours
in the Cluny breviary Paris, Bibl. nat., lat. 12601 (ca. 1075)

R. 1 (Hesbert 6825): Hic est Martinus, electus Dei pontifex, cui Dominus post apostolos tantam gratiam conferre dignatus est, ut in virtute Trinitatis deificae mereretur fieri trium mortuorum suscitator magnificus.

V. Sanctae Trinitatis fidem Martinus confessus est.—Ut in virtute.

R. 2 (Hesbert 6513): Domine, si adhuc populo tuo sum necessarius, non recuso subire propter eos laborem: Fiat voluntas tua.

V. Oculis ac manibus in coelum semper intentus, invictum ab oratione spiritum non relaxabat.—Fiat.

V. Gravis quidem est, Domine, corporeae pugna miliciae; nec deficientem causabor aetatem: munia tua devotus implebo.—Non recuso.

R. 3 (Hesbert 7258): O beatum virum Martinum antistitem, qui nec mori timuit, nec vivere recusavit!

V. Domine, si adhuc populo tuo sum necessarius, non recuso laborem, fiat voluntas tua.

R. 4 (Hesbert 7301): O vere beatum, in cujus ore dolus non fuit, neminem judicans, neminem damnans; numquam in illius ore, nisi Christus, nisi pax, nisi misericordia inerat.

V. O virum ineffabilem, nec labore victum nec morte vincendum, qui nec mori timuit, nec vivere recusavit.—Numquam.

R. 5 (Hesbert 7310): Oculis ac manibus in coelum semper intentus, invictum ab oratione spiritum non relaxabat.

V. Dum sacramenta offerret beatus Martinus, globus igneus apparuit super caput ejus.

R. 6 (Hesbert 6558): Dum sacramenta offeret beatus Martinus, globus igneus apparuit super caput ejus.

V. Oculis ac manibus in coelum semper intentus, invictum ab oratione spiritum non relaxabat.—Globus.

R. 7 (Hesbert 6217): Beatus Martinus obitum suum longe ante praescivit, dixitque fratribus dissolutionem sui corporis imminere, quia indicavit se jam resolvi.

V. Viribus corporis coepit repente destitui. Convocatisque discipulis in unum, dixit.—Dissolutionem.

R. 8 (Hesbert 6463): Dixerunt discipuli ad beatum Martinum: Cur nos, pater, deseris? aut cui nos desolatos relinquis? Invadent enim gregem tuum lupi rapaces.

V. Scimus quidem desiderare te Christum, sed salva sunt tibi tua praemia, nostri potius miserere quos deseris.—Invadent.

R. 9 (Hesbert 6377): Cum videret beatus Martinus discipulos suos flentes, motus his fletibus, conversus ad Dominum dixit: Domine, si adhuc populo tuo sum necessarius, non recuso laborem.

V. O virum ineffabilem, nec labore victum nec morte vincendum, qui nec mori timuit nec vivere recusavit; sed conversus ad Dominum dixit.—Domine.

R. 10 (Hesbert 7257): O beatum virum, in cujus transitu sanctorum canit numerus, angelorum exsultat chorus, omniumque coelestium virtutum occurrit psallentium exercitus.

V. Ecclesia virtute roboratur, sacerdotes revelatione glorificantur, quem Michael assumpsit cum angelis.—Virtutum.

R. 11 (Hesbert 7295): O quantus erat luctus omnium, quanta praecipue moerentium lamenta monachorum! Quia et pium est gaudere Martino et pium est flere Martinum.

V. Beati viri corpus usque ad locum sepulcri hymnis canora coelestibus turba prosequitur.—Quia.

R. 12 (Hesbert 7132): Martinus Abrahae sinu laetus excipitur; Martinus, hic pauper et modicus, coelum dives ingreditur, hymnis coelestibus honoratur.

V. Martinus episcopus migravit a saeculo; vivit in Christo gemma sacerdotum.—Martinus.

JOSEPH P. WILLIMAN

Trauma and Healing in the
Vie de Saint Alexis

I

ONE OF THE earliest monuments of the French language, the *Vie de Saint Alexis* (ca. 1050, central Normandy), is also a work which has an astonishing degree of polish in its structure and its intellectual vocabulary. It is well known for its mathematically controlled outer structure, and somewhat less noted, undeservedly, for its dense and consistent inner motivic composition. There is every evidence that the 625-line work has survived in its integral and detailed form, although there have also survived with it, in its oldest and best manuscript, a curious "performance proeme," and a semiapologetic postlude about a doctrinal problem which may accompany the work, i.e., whether images are objects of worship, or teaching devices. This remarkable *Vie* almost defies comparison with earlier monuments of French dating back to 843, although many of these are also hagiographical: they are mostly in crude fragments and show a naive or ephemeral style which may in fact be one of the reasons for their not being better preserved. And perhaps most surprising are the sharp contrasts which the *Alexis* makes with its contemporary work of nearby coastal Normandy, or, at the most distant, Norman southern England: the *Chanson de Roland*. The *Roland* is male in orientation, Germanic in values and cultural references, spectacular, and fatalistic; the *Alexis* appeals to an audience of both sexes and a wide range of ages, is Latinate and introspective, and has a transcendent frame of reference and values.

But there are some ways in which the two works invite and even demand comparison. Each places a kind of hero or model on stage, who galvanizes the society within its narrative course, who seems to be presented as a kind of power from the spiritual past to awaken the society of the actual audience of the work to a new horizon of human achievement. In each work this action takes place through a self-sacrifice which specifically violates common sense. It is also true, though less obvious, that each of the two works has as a main source of energy or direction a history of interpersonal clefts or wounds, and the options or strategies for healing become the prospects of completeness or of aesthetic fullness. It is a cliché in presenting the *Roland* to students to say that Roland the brave and Oliver the wise, when together, are a salutary compound, and that when they are severed each is disabled to a large extent, and therefore Charlemagne is himself hampered in a specific way; that to sever the right arm (Roland) from Charlemagne would allow the defeat of the Franks; that to shear away Ganelon's pride is to unleash his dark, ruthless persona. Likewise in the *Alexis*, an ironic pattern of deprivations and disappointments in the values of this world becomes a kind of *gradus ad Parnassum* for the protagonist in his almost Manichaean agon with the material world. The society within each work is put in mortal danger through a series of traumatizing splits, and each is made whole again through the iconic death of the hero, an icon which is transferred to the imagination of the audience.

The terms *traumatic* and *iconic* are used deliberately in order to elucidate two powers of the *Vie de Saint Alexis* which have not been yet given adequate critical attention. The first, the potent use of a metaphor of healing to express spiritual reconciliation, may be anchored in the word *salus* (health and/or salvation), where the subject and its metaphor intersect. I will use the word *trauma* in both its medical and its psychiatric senses, and can do so because their common ground allows this: in both senses, trauma is a health-threatening shock which breaks into the flow of ordinary life; it causes the suspension or diversion of other life systems; it becomes the central fact of the whole organism whether psyche or soma. It is possible to obtain a very probing and integrated reading of the *Alexis* by establishing a sort of casebook or dossier of the sequence of traumas which make up the action of the whole work. This is especially true, and most artistically effective, because all external traumatic events refer to and have their ultimate meaning in the spiritual world.

It is less obvious to use the word *iconic* to release the second power of the *Alexis*, but there are several internal and external facts which encourage me to do so. Internally, the many echoes of the life and the very persona of Alexis with those of Christ in the Gospels and in Christian legend cause an inevitable scriptural aura to cling to the text. This is especially true of the suffering of the unnamed mother of Alexis, and her poignant grieving at the agony of childbirth, and again at the second agony of her son's immolation. The presence of Mary and her infant Son, and of the Crucifixion with grieving figures, in the iconic tradition could hardly have been more central; it becomes a kind of implicit text-of-reference on which improvisation and ornamentation are not only possible, they are unavoidable. To an Eastern audience—and the *Alexis* legend originated in Syrian and Greek versions—those iconic presences would form a dramatic backdrop to the text even in an oral performance which would be as crucial as the Romanesques and Gothic tympana to the early religious plays performed in front of them. It is also true that the *Alexis* text itself has not only a high rate of Latinisms, whether retarded or semilearned, but also a surprising number of Greek terms, which would have been exotic to say the least in eleventh-century Normandy. The text may well have been treated so much as a sacramental that changes even for the benefit of comprehension were resisted. In fact, the Hildesheim MS—widely accepted as the oldest and best complete text of the French *Vie*—is actually written in alternating lines of red and blue pigment, with a formal text-border and illustrations of very fine craftsmanship. It is a work of visual as well as verbal art.

The last major piece of evidence for the iconic status and content of the work is twofold. Within the work an *imagene* in the church at Alsis sends out a command to "call the Man of God" (l. 17)—who is shown to be Alexis the unknown, sitting outside the church as a beggar; he then returns to Rome for the last stage of his earthly vocation. This calls to mind almost automatically the indication of the *Agnus Dei* by St. John the Baptist (and the recognition of Christ by the voice from Heaven) and the beginning of the public ministry of Christ. And yet the author of the text of the Hildesheim MS apparently had some misgivings about the orthodoxy of images in churches, and he appends a text from St. Gregory which distinguishes between reverence for the meaning and referent of a sacred image on the one hand, and idolatry on the other.

But this twofold datum reveals an even deeper aesthetic problem:

what is the relationship between Alexis and the holy image in the church at Alsis, which seems almost to play the part of the *magister ludi* in getting the *Vie* back to life? It seems that the central meaning of the image is its power to call Alexis and to identify him when his very servants sent from home cannot do so; this calling, truly a vocation, is the point to which Alexis has been migrating for the length of the poem, especially since he put himself in the hands of God, the act of total submission which accompanies his flight from home and bride. The image and Alexis know each other in a curious way, as do Christ and John the Baptist, surrounded by well-intentioned followers who are not insiders to this secret. Late medieval and Renaissance paintings sometimes show this "twinning" of the two men, born at the same time and against great odds or circumstances; John is the last figure of the Old Testament and Christ the first of the New. There are medieval manuscripts of the Bible which end the Old Testament at this point within the Gospel, rather than at the start of the book of Matthew. Furthermore, Alexis is like the image himself, behaving and speaking in a wooden, formalized way; one could even say that he is himself a sacramental, and as such gives healing to the people of Rome at the end of the poem. It requires the intrusion of the narrator to tell us, none too convincingly, that he has feelings at all: the joy at not being recognized by his father's messengers (l. 125). Alexis is passive almost throughout the poem: he is sent to school, and he learns; sent to the emperor, he serves; placed in troth, he marries (almost); he sees the temptation of the flesh, and escapes; and so on. I hope to show that this iconic power which the physical text shares with the persona of Alexis is bound up closely with the patterns of trauma and healing in the total *Vie*.

II

. . . quin tu aliquid saltem potius, quorum indiget usus,
viminibus mollique paras detexere iunco?
invenies alium, si te hic fastidit, Alexim.
— Virgil, *Eclogue* 2.71–73

After nearly a millennium the *Vie de Saint Alexis* is an astonishing performance because of its internal and external principles of structure, the more so because a first reading, however sympathetic, usually shows that the poem has its *longueurs* and does not seem to be worked out on a high intellectual plane. But subsequent readings reveal that it was not written, and should not be read, as a simple linear narrative. There are simple patterns which individually may not be impressive, but in their interlocking and harmonious disposition make the poem, one of the earliest monuments of French literature, an achievement of a high order of craft.

The first structure, and the initial setting of the action, is the traumatic barrenness of the couple who will be Alexis' parents, which sets a biblical tone from the outset: Abraham and Sara, Zechariah and Elizabeth, are the implicit antecedents, and the implications for Alexis are obvious. After appropriate prayer and devotion, the woman is fruitful, and after the pain of childbirth comes the joy of Alexis. And this background is essential for their next traumatic situation, which lasts the length of the poem: Alexis departs without a word and deprives them of his presence and the chance of grandchildren. It is the best argument for the stately, liturgical pace of the poem, that the audience would be continually recalling the joy of Abraham and Sara at their progeny, an entire nation, and the wretched death of John the Baptist, and the grief and irony of Mary at the foot of the Cross. The poem should be read with all the meditative care and echoes back and forth in time that the Scripture itself calls for. It is also true that the audience is called upon to understand the deepest meaning of Alexis' saintly calling, yet at the same time to partake of the uncomprehending suffering of his parents. This too calls for a slower pace and a more complex kind of attention.

Then there is the spouse, whose betrothal and wedding stop short of consummation: she is suspended *in trutina* like the maiden in the *Carmina Burana*, although there is every evidence that she had no hesitation about the marriage. She goes on living with the parents, a family which is not a family, and all that she has of Alexis amounts to a ring, a sword, and a short, brutal sermon. In one of the poem's many ironies, the parents now have a child again, but not really; they once had joy, and it is now turned diametrically into grief, as their son is replaced by a daughter. She joins with the mother in what occasionally seems to be a contest in mourning. The mother's special suffering comes from having suffered through the carrying of Alexis, and the pain of his birth, and she had the joy of a son up to his young manhood; now it is as though the birth were reversed, and time reversed. This pattern of reversal is in harmony with the voyage of Alexis to the farthest lands, and then the return to the center, Rome; a diastolic/systolic movement as intimate and moving as the pumping of blood, or breathing in and out. In fact, a rereading of the poem in light of the physical references, images, and parallels reveals what is not obvious on the surface. Alexis represents life as surely as Isaac, and as Christ. But the choice made by Alexis early on is in direct relation to this imagery: life in heavenly terms is the only true life, and *iceste mortel vide* is contemptible in comparison, in fact it is another diametric reversal, life versus death.

But it is crucial at this point to emphasize that Alexis himself has no trauma in the strictest sense, that is, a disabling arrest of the whole being whether body or mind. The closest he comes to having one is when he, obeying his father, goes to the bridal chamber and sees the bed; far from being disabled, he swings into action immediately with his five lines of admonition and the legal details of the sword and ring to arrange for her protection, and he heads for the harbor, at a run one would imagine. From this point on he seems to be an automaton, programmed to the will of God, passing his years of wretched beggary and returning home to be unknowingly treated with contempt and abuse by his father's own servants. But he never wavers, doubts, or even, apparently, thinks for the length of the poem. Finally, after writing a brief account of his life, he dies and goes home to his real father, God. At this point one recalls with a start how carefully the poem has been written in a legal sense. The words his parents had used to get him from God in the first place had been "Enfant nos done qui seit a ton talent" (l. 25), in which the key word *talent* has two powers: "Give us a child to your pleasure, who will please you." In other words, even before conception Alexis was dedicated to God, a dedication which takes priority over all other loyalties and commitments, whatever other arrangements humans may try to make.

The personal fortunes of the characters are the first interest to a modern reader, to the point of obscuring other elements of structure that would have intensified the reading for an alert Christian of the eleventh century, and that heighten the status of the poem to an almost magical level, or rather the level of a thing which has extraordinary powers or charms of incantation. It has long been noted that the work is composed about the number five and its multiples: it is 625 lines long (5 × 5 × 5 × 5) and in five-line monorhymed stanzas, and there is no real doubt that we have it in its original and deliberate form (at least in the Hildesheim MS), even though later copies may not have always noted or attended to this structure. But what does the number five *mean*, if a number can mean anything independent of a content? In traditional numerical symbolism, it is a unification of four plenary units; for example, the four seasons form a plenum which is a fifth enclosing unity, a kind of quincunx. The Heraclitean elements, the points of the compass, one tradition of the ages of man, the bracing of the four sides of a square by the center which produces the stable triangle, all of these form the tradition and in fact become metaphors of each other. And this is also true of the four characters of the *Vie*: old and young, male and female, they represent the human race, with the hovering and invisible Father completing the plenum.

A second crucial element of construction is rhetorical, and so constant that eventually one feels battered by it: the patterns of reversal, conflict of opposites, antithesis in all of its forms, sometimes seem to be pulling the poem apart. But in their best use, they have a certain binary compactness, like yin and yang, and Alexis himself is the vehicle of most of them. He takes pleasure in a life of pain, he is an isolate in the midst of society, seen but not recognized, his health is in sickness, his true birth comes at his death, and so on. He represents a profoundly Manichaean world view, the dilemma of having body and soul, incompatible desires. The severity of this issue is well represented on this rhetorical level, and a modern reader will experience considerable discomfort when reading the poem seriously. Strangely enough, the *Chanson de Roland* of the same period and general region uses this device, but it remains as an amusing and often effective technical device, and has no radical relationship with the subject of the poem ("High are the mountains, deep are the valleys"). The maker of the *Alexis* is a master craftsman by comparison, but it may be more accurate to say that the intentions of the two works for the participation of the audience are quite different. The *Roland* is a thrilling, dramatic, almost cinematic entertainment, while the *Alexis* is a demanding, didactic exemplum crafted beyond anything else in the Legendary; curiously it is the *Roland* which shows a subtle knowledge of psychology, where the *Alexis* is rather leaden and juvenile.

Finally, there is a fundamental pattern of situations in which there is a confrontation followed by a solution; this is so steady that a reader comes to expect things to work out somehow, and it tempers the severity of the spirituality with a kind of comfort. The parents of Alexis are without children: the solution is prayer and dedication. Alexis is threatened with marriage and carnal pleasure: the solution is escape, which is shown to be foreordained when there is a ship waiting, apparently, just for him. The parents lose Alexis: a partial solution is for the bride to live with them and help them grieve. The last crisis threatens the entire city of Rome and its people, who are helpless, even to the pope and the emperors: the solution is to find the dead Alexis in the most unlikely place possible. This pattern may even be the basic one for the poem, since at the end it unifies and heals all of Rome, the center of the world, where the life of Alexis had begun; and the pattern of reversal is here too, since his death means health for Rome, and eternal life for him with God. His body is returned to its real mother, Earth, which is as appropriate as his soul going in the opposite direction to Heaven. Now things are where they belong, and the passage of Alexis through this work takes on a magical quality in the memory. In fact, the memory, and the poem as the sharp controlled holder of it, do have sacramental powers.

III

"Wie! sprach er, geschahen nicht von je die lächerlichsten Dinge bei uns alten Einsiedlern und Heiligen?"
—Nietzsche, "Der Schatten," from
Also Sprach Zarathustra IV

Trauma in the physical sense refers to a wound or shock to the body; the term is useful to distinguish sudden violence from disease or illness, which have a life, growth, and developments over a period of time. In the psychological sense *trauma* may borrow physical terms as metaphors for the expression or description of a severe and sudden emotional or mental crisis. These two senses have in common, however, the elements of shock and often paralysis before the injury, and so psychological trauma often involves a disabling conflict between elements which continue in an ordinary way, and elements which are arrested in their progress. *Trauma* is always used as a pejorative term, of course, a bad state of affairs whether psychological or physical; but a similar experience of sudden arrest may occur with a benign result, and in a medieval religious mentality this experience could often be referred to as a miracle. In the *Vie de Saint Alexis* the structures of diametrically opposed behaviors and values are deeply involved in this: one man's trauma may be another's salvation or release. This is developed with such care through the whole work that one may conclude that the poem has a sustained concern with this issue of inner options for health or disastrous illness.

From this viewpoint Alexis, from the moment of his halting his marriage—literally from the instant of the sight of the marriage bed—is psychologically arrested for the remainder of the poem. He behaves as though that apparition has put him under a spell, and as though he is hearing and obeying a voice unheard by others. On the other hand, it is physical trauma which provides the governing metaphor for his family and ultimately the city of Rome, starting at the same point. It is as though Alexis were dead to this world and its attractions and pleasures, even the pleasures of filial obedience and marital steadiness, ordinarily considered to be both virtues and forms of happiness.

It gives one special kind of reading of the poem to look for threats to vitality and examine how they are confronted and resolved, in other words, to look at the five threats which form the basis of the narrative, and see the gradually intensifying patterns of suffering and ascesis which heal them. First, the trauma of barrenness leaves the couple with no alternative but the one which was indicated from the first: complete submission to the will of God. Second, the threat of sin nearly is fatal to the soul of Alexis, and it is thwarted by his escape to his destined period of trial or purification in Alsis. Incidentally, this period of seventeen years is paralleled by the subsequent seventeen years at the home of his parents and intended wife, unknown and reviled. Alchemists, lapidaries, and later even poets often refer to a period of purification required before a liquid, a stone, or even a person can go through the period of taking on its particular character or function. If this is seen as the function of the journey to Alsis, then the true sainthood of Alexis takes place back in Rome, where he is transfigured in their eyes, sick and wretched in the eyes of the world. This second period of trial, that is, the time in Alsis, is simultaneous with the trial of the parents and intended bride enduring the trauma of losing Alexis, and it is healed or closed by the achievement of resignation, during the period when Alexis, unknown to them, has come back to work out his vocation. Finally, there is the trauma facing the people of Rome when they hear the voice from heaven threatening the city with destruction if they cannot find this holy man so favored by Heaven. The healing, of course, is the discovery of Alexis holding his life story in his dead hand, too late to be helped or honored or healed—in earthly terms. But the common people of Rome are the ones who find a special devotion to the body of Alexis, even to the point of being healed of greed for the money scattered by nobles who are trying to make a way through the throng: truly a miracle which would impress a Normandy audience even today. These commoners seem to have an intuitive and direct appreciation of Alexis which the nobles, the pope and the emperors, even Alexis' own family, all seem to lack. The message could well be one which is frequent in saints' lives: old remedies are always the best and simplest.

In conclusion, it may well be that this "trauma/healing" perspective gives a reading of the *Vie de Saint Alexis* which begins to explain why this obscure, unpleasant, and slightly ridiculous saint of the Eastern Church should have such an intensely crafted and textured legend written so early in the vernacular era in Normandy. Alexis is a sort of faceless, misty figure whose legend can be applied to any of the unending emergencies which we encounter in our inner and outer world, and the message is clear and twofold: always follow God's way over the world's; and God will always provide, no matter how difficult the problem. There are other messages which are not so simple or so pleasant, but they do not touch directly on the main theme of this paper. I have been examining the ways in which sacramental presences work in this poem, and how they make such good sense about the healing process that they bear up under modern modes of healing and reconciliation. There are many parts of the *Alexis* which require a substantial effort for a modern audience to take seriously, though it is obvious that the *Vie* expects them to be taken seriously. But the center of the poem is a sequence of episodes of trauma and healing, and they are both well observed and in harmony with the givens of the age of the poem and therefore of its anticipated audience. It is even moving as a dramatic work, though its content is not as subtly worked out as are the elements and methods of composition. After all, literature itself can be seen as exercises in problem solving, which is a form of healing, and at its most trivial when the problems are invented or fantastic. But when we see believable, simple people having terrible problems and somehow surviving, we can take part in the healing through literature, both in memory of crises of our own and anticipations of them. So in some way we take a vicarious part in the onrush of the simple people of Rome to the body of Alexis, simply for the healing in it now and for times to come.

Scripta

BOOKS

Athanasius, Life of St. Antony. Ancient Christian Writers, no. 10. Westminster, Md.: Newman Press, 1950. Reprinted 1979.

Merugud Uilix Maicc Leirtis. Mediaeval and Modern Irish Series, no. 17. Dublin: Institute for Advanced Studies, 1958. Reprinted 1976.

Palladius, Lausiac History. Ancient Christian Writers, no. 34. Westminster, Md.: Newman Press, 1965. Reprinted 1979.

Bernard of Clairvaux, The Life and Death of St. Malachy the Irishman. Cistercian Fathers Series, no. 10. Kalamazoo, Mich.: Cistercian Publications, 1978.

Palladius, Dialogue on the Life of St. John Chrysostom. Ancient Christian Writers, no. 45. New York, N.Y./Mahwah, N.J.: Newman Press, 1985.

Breuddwyd Maxen Wledig. With Brynley Roberts. *Mediaeval and Modern Welsh Series*. Dublin: Institute for Advanced Studies, in preparation.

Jonas, Vita Sancti Columbani. Kalamazoo, Mich.: Cistercian Publications, in preparation.

ARTICLES

Articles in the *New Catholic Encyclopedia*, *Collier's Encyclopedia*.

"The Sources of the Middle-Irish Alexander." *Modern Philology* 47 (1949), 1–7.

"The Middle-Irish *Odyssey*: Folktale, Fiction, or Saga?" *Modern Philology* 50 (1952), 72–78.

"Scraps from the Old Irish Law Tracts I." *Irisleabhar Ceilteach* 1 (1951), 22.

"The Scholiast and the Irish *Lucan*." *Irisleabhar Ceilteach* 1 (1951), 78.

"An Irish Version of the Cherry Tree Carol." *Irisleabhar Ceilteach* 1 (1951), 90–93.

"Scraps from the Old Irish Law Tracts II." *Irisleabhar Ceilteach* 2 (1953), 19.

"The Lonely Blackbird: Marginalia from *Leabhar Breac*." *Irisleabhar Ceilteach* 2 (1953), 46.

"'The High Wind': A Poem from O'Mulconry's Glossary." *Irisleabhar Ceilteach* 2 (1953), 71.

"Poem on Sliabh Cua from *Book of Ballymote*." *Irisleabhar Ceilteach* 2 (1953), 89.

"The Kunāla Story in Its *Avadānacataka* and *Divyādāna* Versions." In *Proceedings of the 23rd Congress of Orientalists*. Cambridge, England, 1954, p. 237. (Abstract of ten-page paper in 300 words.)

"Isidorian 'glossae collectae' in Aelfric's *Vocabulary*." *Traditio* 12 (1956), 398–405.

"Lexical Problems in Palladius' *Historia Lausiaca*." *Studia Patristica* 1 (1957), 45–52.

"West Kerry Interlude." *Carroll Quarterly* 11 (1958), no. 4 (summer), 31–40.

"The Middle-Irish Version of the *Pharsalia* of Lucan." *Papers of the Michigan Academy of Arts, Science and Letters* 44 (1959), 355–363.

"Early Irish Poetry." *Annuale Mediaevale* 2 (1961), 31–54.

"The Middle-Irish *Odyssey* and Celtic Folktale." *Papers of the Michigan Academy of Arts, Science and Letters* 46 (1961), 553–561.

"Vergilian Glosses in the Stonyhurst 'Medulla.'" *Transactions and Proceedings of the American Philological Association* 92 (1961), 340ff.

"The Middle-Irish Version of the *Thebaid* of Statius." *Papers of the Michigan Academy of Arts, Science and Letters* 47 (1962), 687–699.

"Glosses and Marginalia in Pembroke College, Cambridge MS No. 280 of the *Fasti* of Ovid." *Linguistic and Literary Studies in Honor of Helmut A. Hatzfeld*, pp. 255–262. Washington, D.C.: Catholic University of America Press, 1964.

"A Re-Reading of Rawl. MS 512 of *Scela Muicce MacDatho*." *Trivium* 1 (1965), 183–184.

"Adventures of a Celticist on the West Kerry Gaeltacht." *Mediaeval Studies in Honor of Urban T. Holmes*, pp. 129–141. Chapel Hill, N.C.: University of North Carolina Press, 1966.

"The Middle-Irish Version of the *Aeneid*." *Tennessee Studies in Literature* 11 (1966), 97–108.

"Proverbs and Puns in Palladius' *Historia Lausiaca*." *Studia Patristica* 8 (1966), 420–423.

"The T.C.D. Fragments of the *Togail na Tebe*." *Trivium* 2 (1967), 120–132.

"The Liturgical Background of Mediaeval Cornish Drama." *Trivium* 3 (1968), 48–58.

"The Middle-Cornish Play *Beunans Meriasek*." *Comparative Drama* 3 (1969/1970), 54–64.

"*Lectio divina* in Palladius." *Kyriakon: Festschrift Joannes Quasten*, vol. 2, pp. 580–584. Münster, 1970.

"Palladius and Early Christian Spirituality." *Studia Patristica* 10 (1970), 379–390.

"A Note on Wachter's *Glossarium Germanicum*." In *Studies in Honor of Tatiana Fotitch*, pp. 157–161. Washington, D.C.: Catholic University of America Press, 1972.

"Old Irish Rhetorical Terms in the Milan Glosses." *Celtic Linguistics: 1976*. Edited by Robert A. Fowkes. (This is a double issue of WORD 28 [1972].)

"The Relation of the *Medulla* to the Early English Glossaries." In *Papers in Lexicography in Honor of Warren N. Cordell*, pp. 141–150. Terre Haute, Ind., 1979.

"The Middle-Irish Version of the Story of Troy." *Etudes celtiques* 17 (1980), 205–218.

Index Nominum